Surfing the past

Sidestone Press

Surfing the past

digital learners in the history class

ACADEMISCH PROEFSCHRIFT
ter verkrijging van de graad van doctor
aan de Universiteit van Amsterdam
op gezag van de Rector Magnificus
prof. dr. D.C. van den Boom
ten overstaan van een door het college voor promoties ingestelde
commissie, in het openbaar te verdedigen in de Agnietenkapel
op dinsdag 10 januari 2012, te 10:00 uur

door

Olivier Nyirubugara
geboren te Byumba-Ville, Rwanda

Promotiecommissie

Promotores:	Prof. dr. F.P.I.M. van Vree Prof. dr. F.J.M. Huysmans
Overige leden:	Dr. P. Alkhoven Prof. dr. C.A.M. van Boxtel Prof. dr. J.F.T.M. van Dijck Prof. dr. F.C.J. Ketelaar Prof. dr. T.H.P.M. Thomassen

Faculteit der Geesteswetenschappen

To my father Charles and my brother François
who won't be able to hold and read this book.

Published by Sidestone Press, Leiden
www.sidestone.com

ISBN 978-90-8890-081-5

Illustration cover: Mikael Damkier / Dreamstime.com
Cover design: K. Wentink, Sidestone Press
Lay-out: P.C. van Woerdekom, Sidestone Press

The publication of this book was supported by the *NOT Fonds*, the *J.E. Jurriaanse Stichting*, and the *Stichting entoen.nu*

Contents

Acknowledgements

Thanking after more than three years of research conducted in many places with the help of many people and institutions is not an easy task, not because one wants to claim a single-handed achievement, but rather because of the risk of forgetting those who contributed in one way or another to the achieved work. For this reason, I would like first to thank all those I will forget or will not be able to mention in the lines below. Their support was highly appreciated.

Having said that, I would like to thank my promotors, prof. dr. Frank van Vree and prof. dr. Frank Huysmans, for their invaluable guidance during the completion of this research.

I am profoundly indebted to history teachers Antheun Janse at the Baarnsch Lyceum, David le Clercq and Lisanne Beekman at the Helen Parkhurst Dalton School, for opening wide the doors to their classrooms, thereby allowing me to see how new media work in the history class. I can't of course forget their respective pupils for warmly welcoming and integrating me into their environment and sharing their experience with digital media.

I owe much to Reinier van Deinum, Cor den Ridder and Huibert Crijns of *het Geheugen van Nederland*; Judith Moortgat and Toos Kruithof of the National Archives of the Netherlands; Hanneke Vroegindeweij and Irene Haan of the Eye Film Institute; Ineke Huysman of the Huygens Institute for the History of the Netherlands; Lammert Zwaagstra of the National Library's Databank of Digital Daily Newspapers project; Ynze Alkema of the Breda City Archives; and Paul Vermeulen of the LES 2.0 project. By openheartedly opening the doors into their institutions and offering their insights into their respective digitisation projects, I was able to have invaluable first-hand details crucial to the research presented in this book.

I am grateful to those who provided their critical comments for some of the chapters, namely dr. Arie Wilschut for Chapter 1, dr. Geert Lovink for Chapter 2, dr. Karel Dibbets and dr. Peter Horsman for Chapter 3. Their comments and suggestions were useful in refining some of the ideas presented in this book.

I want also to thank my office mates, dr. Tjeerd Schiphof, Trilce Navarrete, Nina Köll and Zeynep Gündüz for the many and fruitful discussions about our respective research.

I would like to express my profound gratitude to the Amsterdam University's Institute for Culture and History, the Amsterdam School for Cultural Analysis, the Media Studies Department and the Huizinga Institute, for offering an inspiring and motivating research environment that made the completion of this dissertation both enjoyable and possible.

I cannot forget my sister Marie-Généreuse, whose insight into child psychology was of great help; my brother Jean-Valéry and his wife Anita, with whom I have had frequent, informal talks about my research, and whose opinions on digital media and child psychology were illuminating; my brother Philippe, my sister Epiphanie and her husband Claude, my mother Madeleine, my aunt Françoise and her husband Juvénal, and my cousin André and his wife Thérèse for their constant moral encouragement.

Finally, special thanks to my wife Assumpta and my lovely daughters Fidelis and Regina, who, better than any other person, provided the affection and moral support that kept me working as hard as I could, even though my long hours of work sometimes meant sacrifice to them. It's over now. Their support and sacrifice have paid off.

Chapter 0

Introduction

-Canon clip[1] *narrator [showing William V in his office, reading a book and then walking around]*: Two hundred years ago, the Netherlands was a Republic. A country without a king. Instead, it had a State Holder [Governor]. He is the forefather of our Queen, thus a member of the Orange House. He was not, however, a king. Together with other important citizens he governed the Republic. William V was such a State Holder. He lived in a beautiful palace and acted as if he were a king. Actually he himself had the feeling that he was a king. Such was the extent of his power.

The Netherlands was not at peace under William V: it was at war with England. English warships were always lurking on the coast, which meant that Dutch commercial ships could not sail …

[Showing 3 men walking hastily] Many people started to complain. They blamed William V for all their problems. They thought that he was not governing the Republic well and that the power was in the hands of the same families. Moreover, the State Holder was acting as if he were a king …

-Braham [13 years], to himself: Guillotine!

-Canon clip goes on: It was time for a change. The unsatisfied citizens of the Netherlands wanted to take part in decision-making. Why couldn't they govern their own cities? These people were called 'the Patriots'. They were unsatisfied and they made it known …

-Canon clip narrator[Reading an excerpt from one Patriot's petition] '… The State Holder controls the army, that is why the citizens have no power. They cannot undertake anything against William V. He can do what he wants'.

-Braham, to himself: Echt niet! [No way!] Pff! *[His mouth mimicked a gun-shot with a fictive pistol – his hand – aimed at his temple].*

-Canon clip goes on: ...

---

1 The Historical Canon of the Netherlands, '*Schooltv Beeldbankclip: De Patriotten*'. http://entoen.nu/patriotten/beeld-en-geluid/schooltv-beeldbankclip-de-patriotten#beeld (Accessed 10 May 2011).

0.1 History Education as Communication

The vignette above is a real-life scene from a history class. Braham, 13 years old, was in the second year of secondary education at the *Baarnsch Lyceum* in the central Dutch city of Baarn. Together with his classmates, he was watching a Web-based clip from the Historical Canon of the Netherlands, as part of the history class. There are many ways and perspectives from which to analyse and understand the situation presented in this scene. One could look at it from the point of view of content and assert that the clip contributes to historical knowledge, as the narrative provides a number of details and a context for a historical event. With more focus on the motivation that led to selecting that particular event, on the pro-Patriots approach, one could maintain that the children were in fact involved in education relating to citizenship or Civics – the functioning of institutions at that time – via history. From another perspective, one could argue that the instantaneous interactions with digital media is a sign that history is better taught to the digitally-minded young generation with the use of digital media. Finally, a cognitive or adolescent psychological perspective could focus more on the verbal and gestural reactions as translating internal thinking processes.

The research presented in this book enquires into these and other similar and not-always-taken-for-granted interactions of young learners with digital media in history education. The history class is viewed as a communication process, involving a message, its representation in a medium or mediation, as well as its transmission, reception, internalisation or mental processing, and eventually the externalisation of that mental processing, in the form of verbal or gestural reactions. By stressing that the history education is first and foremost a communication process, I want to highlight the fact that each of the elements and actors in the process has a role to play, a role that can potentially have some impact on the other stages or elements of the process. To return to the vignette, it is clear that the message is the story of the Patriots; that the Historical Canon of the Netherlands [that is, the Commission that established it], via the teacher [who selected and played the clip, thereby conferring upon it some authority], is the sender of the message; that Braham and his classmates are the receivers; and that the Web and the video, or the Web-based video, are the channels through which the message is transmitted. It is worth wondering whether the reception would have been the same if, for instance, the audio narration had been replaced by subtitles, or if the audio had not been combined with images, or if the story had been read from a textbook, or if the story had emanated from an anonymous source.

There is no simple 'yes or no' answer to this, because one would need to observe all these scenarios before one could formulate a grounded answer. Hence the need to understand how the communication process is taking place, in particular how the World Wide Web is influencing that process. The central question in this research is thus: How does the Internet Generation use the Web and digital resources to learn about the past? I have explored this question theoretically on the one hand, through literature reviews, and empirically on the other hand, using qualitative and process-oriented approaches. The ultimate aim is to gain some understanding of what goes on in a history class where the Web is used. The starting point is that history education is much more than just the transmission of contents. It necessarily involves, among other things, the aims intended by the creator and the sender of the message, or by the system in which the communication process takes place, by the content selected or made available to achieve those aims, by the technologies used, and even by the aims of the audience for whom that communication is intended.

0.2 Why This Subject Now?

When I started this research in 2008, the Netherlands – and Western countries in general – had gone through almost two decades of identity crisis and cultural anxiety. An increasingly perceptible sense of cultural [and national] loss and disorientation prevailed in Western Europe during the late 1980s following globalisation and the political unification of Europe. That sense was subsequently exacerbated by some major events that served as catalysts, namely the fall of the Berlin Wall in 1989 and the subsequent collapse of the Soviet Union in 1991 and, ten years later, the 11 September 2001 terrorist attacks in the United States. In the Netherlands, other catalysts left their marks on the crisis, namely the assassination of far-right political leader Pim Fortuyn in May 2002, and the murder of film-maker Theo van Gogh in November 2004.

History education was increasingly perceived as one efficient channel that could help re-boost the 'threatened' national identity and the declining spirit of citizenship. At the same time, a particular generation, the Internet Generation, had just completed its maturation and had become the prime target of the entertainment industry, which, through the Web, exposed them increasingly to a global culture and drove them to global citizenship. It appeared then, that the same channel could be profitably used to infuse the contents of [history] education to boost the shaping of a national-identity and national-citizenship (Van der Ploeg, 2002b: 30 & 31; *Commissie*, 2006a: 27 & 40). Related to the latter, in some ways, the third, parallel development was the digitisation of cultural heritage collections on a very large scale, and the transformation of part of them into multimedia educational modules (WTR, 1998; *Raad voor Cultuur*, [2003] 2004: 13; De Haan *et al.*, 2006: 13).

Given the complexity, simultaneity and reciprocal influences of these developments, it would be interesting to try to understand how they function and intermingle in history education. For the first time in history, the pupils are described as more technology-literate than their teachers (*Onderwijsraad*, 2003: 37), and as multi-tasking, multiple-choice learners who have access to sources of historical information outside the classroom. In other words, alongside and in addition to the textbooks and the school's library, the pupils could potentially have access to sources located anywhere in the world, official or unofficial, conventional or unconventional. After about fifteen years of the existence of all sorts of Web contents and about ten years of cultural heritage digitisation, it is important to understand the interaction of digitally-minded young people with all these kinds of sources both in terms of digital sources as opposed to their analogue counterparts and, more importantly, in terms of conventional sources as opposed to, or complemented with, unconventional ones. This evaluation is needed both from the classroom perspective, that is, from the practices within the four walls of the classroom, and from the perspective of pupils, namely, through their independent choices of sources.

Moreover, as mentioned above, the Internet Generation is conceptualised as presenting new learning styles that largely integrate digital media. However, as far as I could find, no research has yet concretely mapped these styles with regard to history education. Assumptions do exist that digital media turn the history class into a livelier environment, foster pupils' historical thinking skills, and offer a greater variety of sources. The time is ripe to explore some of the *how* questions of those assumptions. In the chapters that follow, I intend to shed some light on the real-life history class, focusing on *how* the developments described above intersect, which, in the final analysis, will help detect the gaps, if any, between assumptions and practice, while raising new questions for further consideration and research. This will require a specific approach integrating both a theoretical part and an empirical one.

0.3 The Research Approach

The most suitable approach to this research would appear to be to first highlight the major issues and topics discussed in the last two decades with regard to history education, the Web and the digitisation of cultural heritage collections, and then to zoom in on case studies. The first aspect of this approach includes, thus, an extensive literature review including scholarly, expert and professional literature, as well as official and policy documents. While the former offer an insight into theoretical and practical aspects, the latter reflect official responses and strategies for addressing major issues discussed in this research. It also appears useful to use newspaper articles, which have documented and commented upon the developments that form the nucleus of this research. These articles are particularly interesting because on the one hand they captured and confronted the views of scholars, experts and professionals with those of officials and politicians, while on the other hand, they depicted the prevailing mood in society *vis-à-vis* those developments. The review part is also enriched and complemented by incorporating interviews with scholars, experts and professionals in the various areas at the heart of this research.

Some of the assumptions that emerge from the reviews are explored in an empirical, process-oriented way. At this stage, I must confess that when I started putting ideas together for this project, my approach was opposite to the one I finally adopted. I had initially intended to explore the uses of Web-based cultural heritage resources in history education based on existing digitisation projects with an avowed educational orientation. At the time, I wanted to identify classes that were using materials from: *het Geheugen van Nederland* [the Memory of the Netherlands], a large-scale digitisation project by the National Library; *Teleblik*, another digitisation project of public radio and TV channels' archives at the *Instituut voor Beeld en Geluid* [Netherlands Institute for Sound and Vision]; and the Historical Canon of the Netherlands. My reasoning was as follows: with the Memory of the Netherlands, I would have a perfect case of government-sponsored memory and heritage materials coming into the classroom via the Web; with *Teleblik*, I would have a perfect case of mainstream-media memory serving as pedagogical aids; finally, with the Canon of the Netherlands, I would have an excellent case of the officially and carefully crafted narrative of the history of the Netherlands, reaching pupils via the Web.

This approach proved both difficult and, retrospectively, inefficient. It was extremely difficult to identify teachers who were regularly using materials from these individual projects. Individual contacts with teachers even revealed that some of these projects were still unknown to many teachers. Instead of selecting case studies based on digitisation projects, the new approach consisted of selecting them from among end-users, regardless of the sources they used to teach or learn history. In other words the focus was not on the content-creation side, but rather on the side of content-consumption or users. The idea behind this case study-based approach is that pupils' interactions with media, online sources, new-media-driven behaviours and attitudes could be observed, recorded and interpreted as they unfolded. Subsequently, the eventual impact of the ways the contents are created and organised on the end-users' interaction with those contents could be analysed.

Later, after completing my two case studies, I realised that the initial approach would have been less productive, because the reality in the two classes I observed was that pupils used much more than one online source. The kinds of websites teachers and pupils would use were unknown to me. This seemed to me to be an exciting approach because it allowed me to observe matters unfolding without knowing in advance what they would be, or in which direction they were heading. Some of the projects on which I had initially intended to focus appeared either during the lessons or subsequently, in pupils' written assignments. The new approach became, thus: observing the use of online resources, whatever their source, and mapping them, together with the different attitudes they apparently provoked.

0.4 The Structure of the Book

The two approaches discussed in the previous section correspond to the two parts of this book: the theoretical, historical part, which also includes the institutional and official perspectives on various subjects, and the process-oriented, empirical part. The first part aims to map the major themes discussed in the last two decades with regard to history education, the Web, the Internet Generation [that received such momentum from the Web] and the digitisation of cultural heritage collections. In Chapter 1, I start by identifying the aims of history education as they were conceptualised, various suggestions regarding teaching approaches and methods as well as the orientation that history education should take between the national and global study of history.

While understanding the present world has been presented as the main aim of history education, diverging views appear as to whether that understanding should be reached first and foremost by imparting a specific package of knowledge or by opening learners' eyes and minds to the functioning of history as a discipline. While neither excludes the other, this chapter shows that the difference between the two lies in the stress put either on historical knowledge or on an awareness of the process leading to that historical knowledge. Questions also arise about whether the Netherlands should be the focus or whether it should be studied as part of larger structures – Europe or the world. This chapter also shows that mostly politicians advocate teaching 'our history', reflecting 'our values' and 'our culture', while most scholars and experts tend to advocate teaching Dutch history from an international, world perspective.

Chapter 2 takes up the second important theme of this research – the World Wide Web – its gradual but steady spread into the wider society, its late appearance in [history] education, its decisive fostering of the Internet Generation, and the early embrace it received from pioneering history teachers. Despite the fact that, from the late 1990s, the government started investing heavily in Information and Communications Technologies [ICT] in general, and in the Web in particular, some history teachers had been experimenting with the Web as early as the mid-1990s. While most other sectors were enthusiastically and excitedly embracing the new medium, the educational sector lagged behind. Despite this lateness, the school-going generation was already showing it had a special appetite for digital media. The Internet Generation – the cohort of people who were born around or after 1980 and who grew up with digital technologies (Van Steensel, 2000; Huysmans & De Haan, 2003: 177-178; Palfrey & Gasser, 2008: 239) – seemed to be attracted by the media that offered more choices, increased interactivity and freedom. They also appeared to be much more inclined towards images, either moving or still. At the time when the Web was becoming a more or less stable and reliable medium, the Internet Generation was also emerging as an inescapable population to be reckoned with. Hence the huge amounts of money pumped into education in the late 1990s and early 2000s, in order to get all schools connected to the Internet (Van Egmond *et al.*, 2005).

At the same time, as Chapter 3 will show, digital contents are needed alongside the infrastructure. Though education is not the sole reason behind the digitisation of cultural heritage collections, it does occupy an important place in digitisation plans. The selection policies of most digitisation projects include the need to rescue fragile and decaying objects, starting with those deemed unique and of educative or historical value [preservation], and to make them accessible to the widest audience possible. Many of these projects pay special attention to the educative value of these new, digital collections and develop modules intended for teachers and pupils. I must also stress that many cultural heritage institutions have misunderstood digitisation as consisting of, and being restricted to, the conversion of analogue objects into digital objects. I will show that pedagogic-value-enhancing functionalities like hyperlinking – which is meant to connect related objects and thus create a context for those objects, and to increase the visibility of objects on the Web – have been largely neglected either for reasons related to corporate identity and other interests, to the still prevailing vision that heritage professionals are not concerned with content organisation, and to government-imposed restrictions regarding subsidised projects. As time passes, however, more and more institutions are gradually embracing social networking platforms, and encouraging teachers and other education professionals to create collection-based educative modules and share them online.

Some assumptions emerge from Chapters 2 and 3, which, as I explained earlier, need to be explored in real-life classes. Chapter 4 opens the second part of this book and sketches briefly the methodological approach I used to collect data while conducting my field research. In addition to defining the research question and the three assumptions I explore – all relating to the attractiveness of the Web, its fostering of historical thinking and the fact that it offers a variety of sources – it also explains the ethnographic techniques I used for two case studies, namely participant observation, interviews and content analysis, as well as the recording techniques. In Chapters 5 and 6, I present the findings of the first and the second case studies, respectively, in which each of the three assumptions is descriptively discussed. The two case studies are about history classes at the more or less traditional *Baarnsch Lyceum* and at the more or less digital-media-dominated *Helen Parkhurst Dalton School* in Almere. Pupils in both classes were aged 13-14 at the time of the field research [2010].

While Chapters 5 and 6 present findings in a descriptive way, Chapter 7 discusses them more analytically, establishing patterns, and attempts to position these patterns in current debates. Based on the findings of the two case studies, the attractiveness of the Web, its fostering of historical thinking, and the variety of sources it offers are presented not in isolation, but in a way that highlights their interconnections. In addition, the convergence that results from the mixture of conventional and unconventional sources is presented as a new phenomenon brought about and encouraged by the Web. This phenomenon is discussed not only with regard to pupils' class assignments but also with regard to heritage institutions, a few of which have attempted to join that trend. This analytical chapter ends with a discussion of some of the issues currently being debated, especially, the digital divide in education and the concepts of 'New Learning' and 'New Heritage', and the ways in which the two intersect in history education.

Concluding this book and drawing from the research findings, Chapter 8 makes some observations about what digitally-minded young history learners appear to be doing with the Web, that is, the ways in which, and the extent to which, they interact with Web-based contents and digital media in general; about their perception and uses of digitised cultural heritage contents; and about some of the ways in which the Web-driven learning styles discussed in this research appear to contribute to the key targets of history education in the lower cycle of secondary school. Some recommendations are formulated and perspectives for further research proposed.

Chapter 1

Acquaintance With the Past: Which Past and Why?

Whatever its contents and aims might be, history education has always been an organised encounter of individuals and representations of events or actions that are held to have taken place in the past. The majority of scholars, theorists and thinkers who have discussed the teaching and learning of history agree that, like museums, libraries, courtrooms and monuments, history education is another channel society uses to inculcate the values, skills and knowledge deemed necessary for its members.[2] Since the late 1960s, debates have been going on in the Netherlands – the country on which this research focuses – regarding the goals at which history education should be aiming.[3] These debates took place within different frameworks and from different perspectives – scholarly, political, didactical and practical [involving teachers]. In this chapter, I want to introduce some of the most frequently recurring topics from the early 1990s to 2010 with regard to the goals assigned to history education, and the contents and approaches deemed suitable to achieve those goals. The early 1990s serve as point of departure because history education started undergoing unprecedented changes, both in terms of contents and learning/teaching approaches, following on the one hand the fall of the Berlin Wall in 1989 and other related developments, and, on the other hand the birth of the World Wide Web.[4]

---

2 The following authors, among others, consider the preparation of individuals for valuable participation in social life as the primary goal of any educational system: Wells, 1938: 86; Cunningham 1986: 6; Mayes & De Freitas, 2007: 19; Beetham & Sharpe, 2007: 2.

3 In 1968, the Dutch Government completed major educational reforms commonly referred to as the Mammoth Act [*Mammoetwet*]. From that time on, history became compulsory only for the lower cycle [12–15 years] and became optional in the higher one. The time allotted to history was also reduced, and Civics was introduced as a new subject. Social studies were introduced as a new compulsory subject (Van Boxtel & Grever, in press; Wilschut, 2010: 702).

4 In his recent comparative study of history education in Germany, England, and the Netherlands, history didactics expert Arie Wilschut (2010: 711) described the 1990s and the first decade of the 21st century [the two decades I am interested in] as a period of 'Renewed interest in history teaching in politics and society'. The reason, he wrote, was, among others, the fact that the nation-state was becoming less recognisable as a consequence of: [1] the communication revolution [the Web] that made national boundaries less important for economic developments; [2] migration on a massive scale; and [3] the intensified integration of the European Union [following the fall of the Berlin Wall and the collapse of the Soviet Union] (see also Stuurman & Grever, 2007: 2 & 7)

This chapter is, therefore, not intended as a critical review but rather as an attempt to map the ways in which scholars, education theorists and experts, politicians and other interested stakeholders perceive history education, its function and its goals. This mapping effort will provide one with a broad picture of history education during the last two decades, which is essential for any research enquiring into the uses of digital media and resources in that same history education. I will start by mapping out the discussions around the final goal of history education, which, despite its varying conceptualisations, is almost always considered to be 'understanding of the [present] world'. I will then consider a second major discussion, *i.e.*, the one about whether history education is a method – an approach – to attain understanding of the present world, or rather an end in itself, that is, *the* understanding of the world. I will finally focus on contents, and how the various stakeholders have argued about their scope. While some have advocated an internationally, globally oriented approach, others have called for a more local, national orientation. Alongside the Dutch literature, I will also make reference, as and when relevant, to the writings of non-Dutch and non-history-education scholars.

1.1 Understanding the World

> ... history is 'for' human self-knowledge. It is generally thought to be of importance to man that he should know himself: where knowing himself means knowing not his merely personal peculiarities, the things that distinguish him from other men, but his nature as man ... Knowing yourself means knowing what you can do; and since nobody knows what he can do until he tries, the only clue to what man can do is what man has done. The value of history, then, is that it teaches us what man has done and thus what man is (Collingwood, [1946] 1994: 9-10).

Why is knowledge of the past considered essential if any one is to make sense of the present? This is the main question on which I want to focus on in this section, to try and discover the various explanations provided by scholars, didactics experts, and politicians. Three major answers emerge from these discussions: the present, to a great extent, makes sense in the light of some knowledge of the past; learning about the past is essential because it allows individuals to locate themselves historically, socially, and psychologically – in other terms, individual or community identity takes shape in the light of what the past is held to have been; finally, learning about the past is essential because the past is a reservoir containing values and norms considered inspirational for present-day citizens. In this section, these three approaches are subjected to separate discussions.

In order to gather thoughts on this subject – the value and final goal of history [education] – the Dutch government-appointed History Education Advisory Commission, commonly known as the De Wit Commission, spoke in 1997-1998 with various social stakeholders who were not directly involved in the teaching of history. Regarding the aims of history education, all stakeholders 'pointed in the same direction':

> General comments on the function or aim of history education referred to the cultivation of 'historical awareness' and, if possible, the stimulation of 'interest for history' ... In addition, references were made to the importance of knowledge of the past as a required condition for a valuable citizen to be able to work in a democratic environment. It appears further that history is considered as a key discipline for the transmission of society's values and norms ('democratic spirit', 'tolerance', 'relativism'). Finally, the stakeholders placed a high value on the insight that history can give about the roots of national identity ...[5]

History education, as social stakeholders had expected, fulfils one major function: helping pupils, or citizens-in-making, to understand present social and political phenomena, concepts and structures. These expectations also include the various perspectives encompassed by the notion of 'understanding of the world': the cultivation of 'historical awareness', which implies, among other things, understanding present happenings in their broad historical contexts (discussed in length in Section 1.2), the training of valuable citizens and the insight into the roots of national identity.

In 1984, Alaric Dickinson and colleagues co-edited a book with the title *Learning History*, in which history education scholars P.J. Lee and P.J. Rogers addressed the following questions: 'Why Learn History?' and 'Why Teach History?' respectively, maintaining that learning history is essential and necessary because it provides one with a better understanding of present issues. People acquire a sound knowledge of their background and developments and can easily place them in their historical context (Lee, 1984: 13; Rogers, 1984: 21; see also Thompson, 1984: 171; Den Boer, 1998a: 99). In this

5 *Adviescommissie Geschiedenisonderwijs, Het verleden in de toekomst: Advies van de commissie geschiedenisonderwijs* (The Hague, 1998). Psychologist Jean Piaget (1969: 137) criticised such an approach which ignores 'the growing subject' – the pupil – while paying solely attention to 'initiating that individual' from the adult point of view. In this respect, [history] education is conceived of as 'a mere transmission of collective social values from generation to generation'.

perspective, contemporary gender roles and debates – for example: equal salary for equal work, women's representation in institutions, *etc.* – are better understood when approached equipped with knowledge of their roles in domestic labour in the 19th and 20th centuries and the periods that followed (Barton & Levstik, 2004: 70-71). Although concerned with the past, not explicitly with the future, such knowledge 'gives us a purchase (however slight) on the future' like a 'seaman [who] may know what weather is likely, without being able to explain how he knows' (Lee, 1984: 11 & 12; see also Barton & Levstik, 2004: 80). For historian Pim den Boer (1998a: 99; see also Barton & Levstik, 2004: 71), the necessity and the importance of the knowledge of the past lay not only in its role in predicting the future, but also in what he termed 'conscious functioning in the present':

> Only with the help of history is it possible to explain the dramatic events that took place in Yugoslavia. Only with the help of history is it possible to explain why Germany, though an economic giant, is still a political dwarf, and even to predict that the situation will not remain so for centuries.

According to former Dutch Socialist Party leader Jan Marijnissen [now retired] (2005: 3), this future-predicting/shaping role of history education is in fact inescapable, because 'just and wise decisions about the future are unthinkable without knowledge of the developments that led to where we are now'. Addressing history teachers gathered at a congress in 2005, Marijnissen held that one can never know where one is going if one ignores the point of departure.

In addition, history education has been described as an identity-shaping framework. European history scholar Siep Stuurman (2006: 59) perceives history education as fulfilling two major tasks: the cognitive task, which refers primarily to the above-described task of enabling one to cope with the present world and to some extent predict the future, and the ideological or moralising task. The two tasks are not mutually exclusive. On the contrary, 'in history education both perspectives go mostly and smoothly hand in hand'. The cognitive part focuses on historical insight, while the ideological part is about identity-shaping. Identity, according to history theorist Ed Jonker (2006: 26), is boosted by history education through its provision of a 'collective history that comprises elements of pride and shame'. However, history education expert Joke van der Leeuw-Rood (2001: 72) maintained that history education in Europe is inevitably 'a selective representation of the past' that refrains from highlighting those elements of shame. Instead, she noted, '[M]ost school history presents national mirrors of pride and pain, in which pupils are made aware firstly of sufferings and secondly of credits to national pride'. In the process, 'The damage done to others [elements of shame] and the mere fact that others can even have been victims of one's own country are issues which hardly feature in any history curriculum or syllabus in Europe' [text in brackets added]. Discussing the same subject in his attempt to answer the question 'Why Study History?', historical cognition scholar Samuel Wineburg (2001: 5-6) contended that history is a 'basic human need', as it

> entices us with the promise that we can locate our own place in the stream of time and solidify our identity in the present. By tying our own stories to those who have come before us, the past becomes a useful resource in our everyday life, an endless storehouse of raw materials to be shaped or bent to meet our present needs. Situating ourselves in time is a basic human need. Indeed, it is impossible to conceptualize life on the planet without doing so.

In this respect, then, identity and knowledge of the past are presented as non-dissociable and largely coinciding (Iggers, 1999: 49). This coincidence appears in the assignment letter, dated 26 May 2005, to the chairman of the Historical Canon Development Commission [the Canon Commission], in which Maria van der Hoeven, then Minister of Education, Culture and Science, set the goal of the Historical Canon:

> The social developments in recent years once again push us to reflect upon the identity of the Netherlands and how it can be emphasised in education. The beginning of the twenty-first century seems to have speedily spoiled this identity-shaping process. Clearly a new 'story of the Netherlands' is needed.[6]

The minister was most likely referring to the rise and assassination of far-right political leader Pim Fortuyn in May 2002, followed by the murder of film-maker Theo van Gogh in November 2004 after he had made a controversial film that criticised Islam.[7] Both events provoked a shock response within Dutch society. Cultural historian Wijnand Mijnhardt (2005: 12) called these two events 'our own September 11' that prompted the government to redefine the norms and values of the national identity that everyone, especially immigrants, should acquire. The two murders made both

---

6 Education minister Maria van der Hoeven's letter: '*Taakopdracht voor de commissie Ontwikkeling Nederlandse Canon*' in *Commissie, Entoen.nu: de Canon van Nederland Deel A* (The Hague, 2006a), p. 95.

7 The film, *Submission* (2004), is based on a script by Ayan Hirsi Ali, then a member of the House of Representatives.

society and politics nervous, to use the words of Dutch writer and journalist Lucas Ligtenberg (2005: 238). These events caused everyone, including the government, to wonder which approach people – especially pupils – should adopt *vis-à-vis* the Netherlands. The Dutch Scientific Council for Government Policy [WRR] observed that in recent years, efforts to ease the cultural malaise had focused on strengthening the national identity, which is regarded as a vehicle for national harmony and an example that migrants should follow and interiorise (WRR, 2007: 29-30).

Former Minister Van der Hoeven cited the problem of the Dutch identity in crisis on the one hand, and, on the other hand, proposed a solution to work on, namely establishing of a new 'story of the Netherlands' to be taught to children aged 6-7 and 7-14 years. This suggests that at the time when the Canon Commission was set up in 2005, a [hi]story was being taught that did not sufficiently, satisfactorily and explicitly highlight the Dutch identity. However, in one of its reports, the Canon Commission declared that it was an impossible mission to reflect a nation's identity through a historical canon: 'The Canon can reflect a nation's collective memory, but never its identity' (*Commissie*, 2006a: 23). For history theory and methodology scholar Maria Grever (2005: 27), the use of history education for the transmission of the 'true Dutch identity' is a 'risky exploitation of history as a discipline'. She contended that the suggestion that there was a need to know one's true identity was motivated much more by anguish [caused by 'the social developments of recent years'] and by a neo-nationalist agenda [that originated from those developments] and would not be viable in the long run (Grever, 2006: 51).

Identity is also described as a paradoxical concept, as it is simultaneously uniting and disuniting. History education scholars Keith Barton and Linda Levstik (2004: 60) maintained that while national identity anchored in history is likely to be durable, it nonetheless has a dark side, since '[E]stablishing who we are also means establishing who we aren't'.[8] For Grever (2006: 34), identity is better conceived of as a multiplicity, since many frameworks exist, including the national one, in which it is manifested.

For their part, political stakeholders regard history education as the ideal framework for fostering human rights, anti-racism, collaboration, discipline, democratic spirit and tolerance (*Adviescommissie*,

8 A similar argument has been used with regard to historical canons. While they present the advantage of offering a workable and tangible framework for teachers (Grever, 2007: 41), they nonetheless have considerable drawbacks, namely contributing to stereotyping and ethnic categorisation. In this respect, Grever (2007: 42) argued that 'Where there is a canonized nation, there will also be non-canonized "others"'.

1998; *Onderwijsraad*, 2003: 39). According to Marijnissen (2005: 3), those values and norms 'have crystallised themselves in people's struggle for a better way of life', and 'we inherit them from our forefathers'. The duty of political actors and society at large, he maintained, is then 'to actualise and maintain those norms and values, and in doing so, maintain the bridge of civilisation'. That bridge often takes the form of canonisation of those among the 'forefathers' whose deeds are deemed outstanding. In the political discourse, they have been referred to as being 'important figures' in Dutch history (Plasterk, 2007b: 1-2). Barton and Levstik (2004: 105-106) called for caution when teaching about heroic figures, arguing that since each hero has both positive and negative character qualities, the focus should be not on the person but on his or her heroic actions.

The last form in which 'understanding of the world' has been discussed is with regard to citizenship education. The official and political view is that history education is the main support for 'our democratic state' and it is there in order to foster 'civic, democratic values' among the Dutch.[9] For this, and in addition to the Canon project, the government disbursed 1 million euros in June 2006 to start up a two-year project known as the Centre for History and Democracy. Explaining and advocating the use of the Historical Canon, Van der Hoeven's successor, Ronald Plasterk (2007b: 2) contended that the Canon encourages 'the democratic spirit and active citizenship', as many of its windows offer 'an overview of the basic values of our democracy'. For this reason, the Canon should be introduced into schools, precisely into history education, because, 'knowledge of history and democracy begins at school'.

Throughout their book, *Teaching History for the Common Good*, Barton and Levstik (2004: 12) used a different concept of citizenship education. In the view of these two authors, democracy is better served in history education when the pupils are told about, and exposed to, diverse standpoints, competing perspectives among which none reigns as supreme [sacralised or canonised]. Pupils learn more about democratic values when they deliberate about those standpoints, which not only triggers reflection and mutual understanding, but also invites them to '[take] action toward a mutually satisfying future' (*Ibid.*: 34-35). This approach to citizenship education as embedded in history education is the opposite of the 'our democratic values/spirit' approach, as it emphasises democratic ex-

9 Maria van der Hoeven and Alexander Pechtold [Ministers of Education, Culture and Science and of Administrative Reform and Institutional Relations, respectively], Letter to the National Assembly Speaker. Object: Centre for history and democracy, (The Hague, 22 June 2006), p. 1. http://www.minocw.nl/documenten/1438.pdf (Accessed 8 June 2009).

perience – *e.g.*, participation, pluralism, deliberation – rather than selected narratives about democratic values.

The inclination towards ideologically tainted citizenship education has prompted scholars' suspicion *vis-à-vis* politicians who claim to be enthusiastic about history education. Politicians, they maintain, want a one-sided, feel-good history, which neglects history as a cognitive subject (Stuurman & Grever, 2007: 12; see also Voss & Carretero, 1994: 6). Historian Hermann von der Dunk (2005: 215), for instance, considers that the political plea for more history in the curriculum is simply a call for a *chronologised* nationalism. This remark is made plausible by the repeated and emphatic use of 'our' and 'own' by the various officials: 'their [pupils'] own culture and that of others' (State Secretary for education Tineke Netelenbos in 1998), 'our democratic state' (Ministers Maria van der Hoeven and Alexander Pechtold in 2006), and 'our democracy' (Minister Ronald Plasterk in 2007). Many scholarly and expert voices have been raised to suggest that history education should not be subjected to that kind of citizenship education (Van Vree, 1998a: 51; Wilschut, 2005: 32).

This section has attempted to capture and map some of the major debates about history education in the Netherlands between the 1990s and 2010. I have identified an understanding of the present world as the ultimate, all-inclusive aim of history education, while pointing out the various, often conflicting ways in which that understanding is perceived. In one sense, understanding the present world means being able to decipher present phenomena and situations with the help of historical knowledge; in another sense, it means regarding one's peculiarities as emanating from, and being rooted in, the past; in yet another sense, it means acquiring the knowledge or experience of democratic values deemed necessary if one is to function as a valuable citizen in society. The prime goal of this section was to pave the way not only for the subsequent sections in this chapter, but also for the next two chapters, where the same themes of coping with the present based on knowledge of the past, identity-shaping, and the two approaches to citizenship education [as narrative or as experience] keep coming back in different perspectives.

1.2 Historical Knowledge and Historical Awareness

> Another ridiculous mistake is that they make them study history: they think that history is within their reach, because it is but a compilation of facts. But what does the word 'facts' mean? Do they think that the connections underlying historical facts are so easy to grasp, that the ideas about them effortlessly form themselves in the children's mind? Do they think that the true knowledge of events is separable from the knowledge of their causes, of their effects, and that the historical account is less based on the principle that you can know one without the other? If you see only external and strictly physical movements in men's actions, then what do you learn in history? Absolutely nothing … (Rousseau, [1768]1966: 136).

Unlike the first section, which focused on the aims of history education, this one concentrates on how history education fosters one's understanding of the world [in the various meanings it bears], based on the scholarly and expert literature, as well as policy documents and politicians' writings and views. This section aims to bring together the various main approaches to teaching history – not as practiced in history education, but rather as perceived by the various stakeholders – and group them into two broad categories. In the first place, I will deal with the approach that advocates a history education centred on identity-shaping and citizenship education in the ideologically motivated sense referred to in the previous section. This category comprises an approach to history education that consists of conveying a body of historical knowledge, deemed necessary to strengthen identity and citizenship. In the second place, I will discuss the other broad category that includes two approaches: the 'historical awareness' approach, which is not centred on any fixed body of knowledge but rather on history as a discipline; and the one that lies in between the 'historical knowledge' approach and the 'historical awareness' counterpart. One must suppose that this in-between approach will contain a short-list of core, must-know, historical facts and events.

The category described as 'history as identity-shaping and citizenship education' is best reflected in the reports of the Canon Commission, which proposed fifty windows containing a body of knowledge – people, events, and processes deemed the most significant in Dutch history and culture (*Commissie*, 2006a; *Commissie*, 2006b) –primarily designed for educational purposes. The stress is clearly on knowledge of selected people, events, and processes with a perceived ideological, political aim to foster citizenship and national identity. As shown by the assignment letter to the Canon

Commission cited in the previous section, the aim of the Canon would be to tell the 'new story of the Netherlands' by defining the 'core' historical knowledge that makes up that story. The must-know list of the new story includes William of Orange [1533-1584], the 'rebel nobleman' who became the 'father of the country' after a long battle against Spanish troops;[10] and King William I [1772–1843], the first 'king of a unified state' who, in 1830, sent troops to Brussels to oppose Belgium's independence, though to no avail.[11] It also includes 'The Patriots' [1780–1795], the '[C]itizens who up until then had had almost no say in the administration of the towns and the country itself', and who organised volunteer corps and rebelled against State Holder William V, whom they regarded as a dictator;[12] and 'The Dutch East India Company' [1602–1799], whose first sailing expedition opened a trade route to the East, and which later 'developed into a power to be feared'.[13]

This approach to history as aiming at achieving citizenship education and fostering identity is mostly advocated and supported by politicians. The view of former Socialist Party leader Marijnissen (2005: 3), that values and norms [constituting the Dutch identity] 'have crystallised themselves in people's struggle for a better way of life', implies that pupils should be taught about those people and their struggle in order to perpetuate those values and norms. This approach emerged in the 1990s after about three decades of history education that focused on enquiry skills, to the detriment of a historical overview (Van Boxtel & Grever, in press; Wilschut 2010: 711). At that time, the national identity crisis that was already perceptible in the late 1980s following the political integration of Europe and globalisation, was reaching its paroxysm: the fall of the Berlin Wall in 1989 and that of the Soviet Union in 1991, and the subsequent acceleration of the European integration, were all perceived as threats to the national identity.

The second category could be called the 'history education as historical awareness' category, as it places much more stress on the way history functions as an academic discipline, rather than on the absorption of historical accounts. Within this broad category two approaches can be distinguished: one that needs no particular key

---

10 The Canon of the Netherlands, 'William of Orange [1533–1584]. From rebel nobleman to "father of the country"'. http://entoen.nu/venster.aspx?ID=4&lan=e (Accessed 16 June 2009).

11 The Canon of the Netherlands, 'King William I [1772–1843]. The kingdom of the Netherlands and Belgium'. http://entoen.nu/venster.aspx?ID=28&lan=e (Accessed 16 June 2009).

12 The Canon of the Netherlands, 'The patriots 1780–1795'. http://entoen.nu/patriotten/en (Accessed 6 July 2011).

13 The Canon of the Netherlands, 'The Dutch East India Company (VOC) 1602–1799'. http://entoen.nu/voc/en (Accessed 6 July 2011).

or core historical events or figures as starting point, and one that works with a few key, core historical events and figures alongside which others can be added *ad libitum* during the learning process. To be able to distinguish between these two in the paragraphs below, I will dub the first one the 'no-must-know and historical awareness' approach, and the second the 'must-know and historical awareness' approach.

The 'no-must-know and historical awareness' approach is best embodied by the 2001 report by the Commission for Historical and Social Education, commonly known as the De Rooy Commission. This report was a follow-up of the 1998 De Wit Commission report, upon which to some extent it continued to build. It shows that unambiguous stress was placed on historical awareness and the skills and methods that contribute to this awareness. It provided a reference framework of ten eras and left room and freedom to teachers to fill in the contents. Reacting to the criticism that some eras were given inappropriate names, Arie Wilschut, one of the architects of the De Rooy Commission's report, argued that the naming of eras had no scientific pretention whatsoever, as the main goal was merely to find names with a such strong significance that they immediately bring to mind an image of the past. When pupils ultimately realise that the naming is just a way to help them learn history, that history cannot actually be divided into eras, they will have acquired the necessary historical awareness, including *relativisation* (Wilschut, 2009: 33).

In this light, then, the choices made by teachers only serve as illustrations because pupils are able, and trained, to make their own choices. One pupil might choose to consider the Reformation movement from Luther's or Calvin's perspective, while another might prefer to handle it from Zwingli's or Erasmus' perspective.[14] Proponents of this way of making sense of historical processes want to make pupils understand that history is a multiple-perspective discipline, where '[T]here is no one true story about the past, but a multiplicity of complementary, competing, or clashing stories' (Lee, 2004: 129; see also Grever, 2007: 42). For that reason, the De Rooy Commission avoided the term and concept of 'canon' and preferred 'historical awareness', in order to prevent any fixedness and arbitrariness of the curricular contents (De Rooy, 2001: 2-3).

Similar views were expressed in a book published in 2000 with the title *New Learning*, by education scholar Robert-Jan Simons and his colleagues. For them '[F]inding one's way in the growing body of knowledge becomes more important than having many factual

14 *Commissie historische en maatschappelijke vorming, Verleden, heden en toekomst* (Enschede: SLO, 2001), p. 23.

details in memory' (Simons *et al.*, 2000: 2). Aligning themselves behind this approach, history education scholars Carla van Boxtel and Jannet van Drie (2004: 8) pleaded for 'historical reasoning', which consists of training pupils on how to provide grounded interpretations of historical sources and facts. They consider this argument-supported interpretation of the past to be one important goal of history education.

Peter Fisher (2002: 2 & 5) and his 'Thinking Through History' team at the Newcastle University Department of Education also perceive history education as a framework in which 'pupils should be challenged to think', and in which teachers should be 'teaching thinking'. They defined 'teaching thinking' as creating challenging learning experiences that call for high level thinking, including information processing, reasoning, enquiry, creative thinking, and evaluation. Inspired by the findings at Newcastle University, since 2002, a group of Dutch didactics experts and history teachers associated with the University of Nijmegen have been exploring a similar teaching approach, the 'Active historical thinking' approach (Havekes *et al.* 2005; Havekes *et al.* 2009; Havekes *et al.* 2010). The essence of this approach is to have pupils realise that a historical reality is not self-evident and ready-made for assimilation, but rather subject to judgment from a given historical perspective (Havekes *et al.* 2009: 49). Pupils are therefore stimulated and motivated to think not only about their own answers but also about those of their classmates in order to ultimately come to a better argumentation regarding a particular question. For this to succeed, teachers are expected to ask relevant questions, and stimulate and guide discussions.

Harry Havekes and his colleagues have provided many learning activities and models, including, among others, the 'Living Graph' [*Levende Grafiek*] model, whereby pupils are requested to choose statements and position them in the right place in the graph and justify their choice (Havekes *et al.*, 2005: 18-26); the 'Mystery' model, whereby pupils list a number of causes and consequences of one particular historical event (*ibid*: 27-38); and the 'Odd One Out' [*Welk Woord Weg*] model. In the latter, pupils are presented with a list of names – for instance, Stalin, Mussolini, Hirohito, Hitler – and are asked to proceed to eliminate them, with arguments, by answering the following question: 'who should be removed from the list?' Some would remove Hirohito arguing that he is the only Asian on the list. Others would remove Hitler as the only one who conceived and executed a genocide, yet others would remove Mussolini as the only one without a moustache, and so on (Havekes *et al.* 2010: 52). In this case, as in the Thinking-Through-History approach, 'there is no one single correct answer, and the teacher does not necessarily offer a best solution' (Fisher, 2002: 5).

The 'must-know and historical awareness' approach is best embodied in the 1998 De Wit Commission report, which attempted to ensure a degree of balance in the knowledge – awareness relationship. Asked 'specifically to give its judgment about such aspects as facts and skills, thematic approach or chronological overview, and the underlying relationships between them' (*Adviescommissie*, 1998), the Commission stated that 'people, events, and processes are only understood when placed in their historical context' (*Ibid.*). This implies a balance between a certain body of knowledge [people, events, and processes] and enquiry skills [placing people, events, and processes in a historical context]. Regarding citizenship education, the Commission stressed the exceptional importance of history education in shaping 'fully-fledged citizens' able to function in the Dutch democracy, in perpetuating values and norms based on events of the past, and in contributing to social cohesion (*Ibid.*). The Commission was prudent on the facts–chronology versus skills–thematic issue and 'abstained from opting for one approach rather than another', as history education offers enough space for both and their combination (*Ibid.*).

I should mention here that I have discussed the two categories separately only to give some structure to this review. In reality – that is, in the history class – things happen differently, as the various approaches are intermingled depending upon, among other things, the subjects and teachers' own perceptions. It appears to be a matter of emphasis rather than of clear-cut differentiating aspects. In other words, a teacher who is inclined toward citizenship education and identity shaping together with the corresponding fixed body of knowledge, will also convey some enquiry and awareness-creating skills, though as a secondary aim. The same goes for a teacher inclined toward the 'no-must-know and historical awareness' approach, who chooses examples while discussing a given concept and, thus, will inevitably introduce a certain body of knowledge [however small and flexible]. At his stage, it is important that I clarify this in order to avoid any misconception of the two categories as two separate and mutually exclusive blocks.

Another important element in the discussion has been the notion of the relevance of historical knowledge taught in schools. In their study of the developments in history education during the last four decades [1968-2008], Van Boxtel and Grever (in press) showed how the relevance of historical knowledge has shifted over time. For instance, from the late 19th century until the 1960s, only historical knowledge that nourished patriotism and national feelings was deemed relevant, with a strong emphasis on the 'great-man'-view (see also Wilschut, 2010: 700); from the late 1960s until the 1990s, contemporary history gained relevance, as the aim was 'to provide students with more insight into contemporary society by explaining its historical development'; from the 1990s, as shown above, historical awareness gained greater prominence. History textbook author Herald Buskop and colleagues (1998: 12) added another dimension to the discussion:

> The pupils live, hopefully, another half-century after their school time. Is there any list of facts that could remain relevant all their lives without needing any expansion? No one can think of such a list. In that case, who is to teach the [former] pupils how to collect new facts once they have left school? Anyway what sense does knowledge of facts make if one is not taught how to handle it?

The authors are clearly pleading for more historical awareness than for 'any list of facts' that would only be relevant for a given period of time and irrelevant or out of date for another. This suggests one important thing, namely that historical knowledge is one side of the coin, the other side being the indispensable skills that would enable former pupils to make sense of new historical facts deemed relevant at a later moment, or old facts that were not handled during their school time. For Buskop and colleagues, a former pupil should be able to study the subject himself, to 'look at so-called facts with a new eye' (*Ibid.*: 8).

The suggestion is that pupils, while trying to understand historical events, should acquire historical literacy (Lee, 2007: 51), simultaneously [or even in advance]. Historical literacy is the ability to understand how historical accounts of events come into being, that those accounts are not copies of the past, that they may conflict with one another, that the agents' beliefs and intentions play a role in the shaping of those accounts,[15] that some accounts may be simplifications of complex events, and that some may be claimed to have greater importance than others (see Perfetti *et al.*, 1994: 258; Barton & Levstik, 2004: 84; Lee, 2004: 139; Lee, 2007: 51). In other words, pupils need to acquire contents or knowledge while learning about enquiry skills in order to be able to properly understand those contents. 'When understanding is needed', as claimed

15 In this respect, historian of war Michael Howard (1991: 2) maintained in his book – *The Lessons of History* – not only that historians' agenda 'is set by current controversies, whether we wish it or not', but also that 'Historians are as prone as anyone else unconsciously to formulate conclusions on the basis of temperament, prejudice and habit, and then collect evidence to justify them' (see also De Certeau, 1974: 8-9; Lowenthal, 1985: XXII-XXIII; Howard, 1991: 11).

by Barton and Levstik (2004: 189), 'enquiry appears to be one of the best ways to get there'. Historian of war Michael Howard (1991: 13-14) extended the metaphor used by colleague David Lowenthal (1985) – that the past is a foreign country – to conceptualise those enquiry skills as the language spoken in that country, and without which very little would be understood about that country's beliefs and assumptions.

This section opened by drawing a distinction between two ways in which approaches to history education have been conceptualised. On the one hand, I referred to certain views as being part of the 'history as citizenship education' approach. These views stress the transmission of a body of knowledge reflecting the values and norms considered indispensable for citizens. On the other hand, under the 'history as historical awareness' category I placed those views that stress history as a discipline rather than as the mere assimilation of a given body of knowledge. I have signalled that, in practice, these approaches are not separated by some invisible wall but are often intermingled either consciously or unconsciously. The main point that emerges from this section is that history education is not merely an overview of historical facts, nor is it the provision of skills and reflexes for handling historical knowledge, but a combination of both, with more emphasis being placed on one or the other, depending on one's own pedagogical approach (see Van Vree, 1998a: 52; Haydn, 2003: 32; Van Drie, 2005: 8). The next section takes up a closely related discussion about which contents are suitable for history education.

1.3 World History and Local History

> In the United States to-day history is taught far too generally from the national point of view. Frequently pupils are given an unconscious impression that the world began in the American year 1776! This may be patriotic, but the narrowing influence of such teaching upon the pupil is evident. Only by learning history as world history and all subjects on the basis of the universe, can the child grow into a complete man or woman as well as a good citizen (Parkhurst, [1922] 1924: 58).

The contents of history education are meant to facilitate one's understanding of the world [as discussed in Section 1.1] and to serve as materials with which to convey a certain body of knowledge or exercise one's enquiry skills (Section 1.2). Discussions about contents are thus closely linked to discussion about the aims of, and approach to, history education, because contents are designed according to, and based on, the aims to be achieved and the approaches to be implemented. This section distinguishes two trends in these discussions, namely the world history trend, which puts forward an international approach to history education, and the local, national history trend, which focuses on specific localities, regions or nations. In what follows, I will review the scholarly and expert literature, mostly Dutch but also international, as well as policy documents and politicians' opinions. While considering the world history trend and its local counterpart, I will highlight the points at which the two intersect.

The notion of world history or the international approach to history teaching in Western Europe received unprecedented momentum after World War I, when it was realised that history teaching had contributed to war and could contribute to its prevention. In 1921, scholars from ten countries met at a conference in Geneva to discuss *the teaching of history and the international spirit*. One major conclusion was that 'teachers should have in mind this idea that universal history is a reality, the sole historical reality ... to which national history is contingent' (Claparède, 1931: 15-16). Writing about the United States, where history education is dominated by national history, Barton and Levstik (2004: 37-38) advocated the teaching of world or humanistic history, arguing that it would promote 'an expanded view of humanity'. Their main argument is that studying people, cultures, and social institutions different from those in one's own country would enable pupils to 'understand the multiple ways of being human', thereby making them 'really Competent Receiver[s] for world affairs' (Wells, 1938, xiv). In doing so, as suggested by Howard (1991: 18), pupils learn how to 'step out of their cultural skins and enter the minds of others', including their own forebears but also their contemporaries with a different heritage.

Stuurman is among the pro-world history advocates in the Netherlands, as he maintained that the 'Dutch Nation' refers to the Dutch people rather than to the small territory at the deltas of the Rhine and the Meuse. His suggestion is, therefore, that since the Dutch were present in other parts of the world in past centuries, and since people from other parts of the world found themselves in the Netherlands [in the past], the teaching of history should place that tiny European territory in its global network and context (Stuurman, 2006: 60). Advocates of world history suggest that world history should be like an inverted pyramid, starting with the nation [or the locality, or the region], and establishing 'global connections' (Stuurman, 2006: 68; also see Mijnhardt, 2005: 17), because 21st century citizens are both national and global citizens (Stuurman & Grever, 2007: 3). For instance, the Batavian Revolution, which is part of local, national history, should be taught in a comparative way, even from a 'non-domestic perspective', which would constitute another way of mapping the evolution of the Netherlands (Stuurman, 2006: 75-76; see also Stuurman & Grever, 2007: 8).

As it appears here, the world history approach to history education contents includes both the domestic and the international perspectives of historical events and processes. While attempting to establish a new balance between knowledge of 'core' events from the past and their contextualisation (see Section 1.2), the De Wit Commission attempted at the same time to introduce a similar balance between the domestic and international perspectives of historical events and processes (*Adviescommissie*, 1998). Its report confirmed the need for enough national history, but indicated that the local, national approach was only suitable for primary education, while the European [thus international] approach was recommended for the lower cycle of secondary education. One of the major recommendations was to establish a historical canon, a concept the Commission used in a very broad sense. That canon would be taught differently but in a complementary way in the primary school and in the lower cycle of secondary school. In primary school, subjects like pre-history, the Romans, the Middle Ages, the Republic in the 17th century, *etc.*, would be handled with a particular focus on the Netherlands. The aim at this level would be 'to foster the communal awareness of all school-going children for *their own past* and *their own culture*, and cultivate a critical attitude toward them' [italicisation is mine]. In the lower cycle of secondary school, the same topics would return but now they would be placed in a 'broader European perspective', coupled with a limited number of diachronic key concepts and skills (*Ibid.*).

Although this approach employs expressions such as 'their own past and their own culture', it could not be called purely national or local history, nor can it be fully considered as world or international history. Rather, it is an in-between approach that provides room for contents that make pupils aware of 'their own past and their own culture', while [at a later stage] making them aware that other perspectives and other cultures exist elsewhere. In other words, it is meant to 'help students achieve a better appreciation of not only one's own country but also how one's own country is a player in the increasingly broader global perspective' (Voss & Carretero, 1994: 6).

Advocates of local history have suggested other ways of conceptualising the contents of history education. Rural and economic historian Pim Kooij (1996: 5-6), for instance, proposed the 'local environment as a laboratory' model, arguing that the local small details contain aspects that could be observed globally, such as the banal 'neighbourhood disputes that bore World War germs'. Kooij was implying that local history is global history in miniature. For him, the house where a pupil lives, the street where it is built, the area and the region in which it is located have morphological, demographic, social, economic, political, cultural, and religious aspects that are able to present a bigger picture than just that of the small localities whose history is being studied. In this respect, what is observable on a local level can be generalised to an extent or offer the possibility of understanding similar situations in other parts of the world. Hans van der Linde (1997: 2-3) of the Brabant Regional History Foundation [*Stichting Brabantse Regionale Geschiedbeoefening*], explained that the strength of this model resided in the fact that 'one's own local environment offers a familiar and trusted field ... [with] concrete links to the past ... [and] images of the past and the present side by side. Here, knowledge and emotion play an important role'.

A 1997 enquiry in 26 European countries and Israel, into the interest of young people in history, showed that this was the approach most valued by pupils. They wanted to learn about 'family history' and – specifically for the Netherlands – 'the history of ordinary people's everyday history'. Joke van der Leeuw-Rood and Marjon Kuiper (1997: 13-14), who conducted the Dutch part of the study in 21 classes in 14 different schools, with a total of 596 pupils and 21 teachers responding, noted that the Dutch demonstrated the most interest in their own national history. National history as used in this context is not necessarily opposed to world or international history, because, as the laboratory model discussed above shows, the family, ordinary local people, the nation, *etc.*, can serve as laboratories, from which some transnational generalisations may be made.

Despite the De Wit Commission's call for a canon, whose implementation would be Netherlands-oriented for primary school and Europe-oriented for the lower cycle of secondary school, no concrete steps were taken in that direction. The De Rooy Commission was appointed in 1999 to 'translate the main recommendations [of the De Wit Commission] into new history education targets and examination programmes' (Netelenbos, 1998), but did not suggest making a canon (De Rooy, 2001: 2-3). Instead, it proposed ten historical eras, which constitute a reference framework that allows teachers to start their lessons somewhere, without actually imposing restrictions as to where they should begin or end (*Commissie*, 2001: 20). Such a framework could accommodate both local and world history approaches.

The Netherlands-focused, national history inspired Canon – thus different from the partly Europe-oriented one proposed by the De Wit Commission – did not appear until October 2006, when another commission – the Canon Commission – handed over its first report containing fifty windows – www.entoen.nu – which it regarded as most representative of the Dutch history and culture, and therefore intended for all Dutch citizens (*Commissie*, 2006a: 27). Political actors warmly welcomed the Canon, which, according to Plasterk (2007b: 1), then Minister of Education, Culture and Science, corresponded with the motto of the government then in place: 'Living together, working together'. Plasterk made it clear that the Canon, with its selected events and figures drawn from the country's past, fulfilled a political task by making the encounter between the Dutch – either native or naturalised – and that past easier (*Ibid.*: 1-2).

Five months prior to publication of the first report of the Canon Commission, Jan Marijnissen, then opposition Socialist Party leader and Maxime Verhagen, then leader of the Christian Democratic Party fraction in the House of Representatives, co-authored an article in *Trouw* – a Dutch daily newspaper – and confirmed this explicit unanimity of viewpoint in the matter of national history and identity. Their opinion reflects the motivations behind the national history [and culture] contents of the Canon: 'With the Internet and globalisation, but also the individualisation of society and the arrival of more people with different cultural backgrounds, it seemed as if we had no longer had a collective identity' (Marijnissen & Verhagen, 2006). This approach to national history could be interpreted as a limitation of the laboratory model discussed above. Local figures, events, and processes deemed significant were included in the Canon with the purpose of strengthening a threatened 'collective identity', rather than the one of facilitating global understanding based upon them. It is also the reverse of world history, as discussed above, which integrates non-domestic approaches to domestic historical events and processes [globalisation].

Satisfied with the ten-era framework, which, as mentioned above, imposes neither national, nor world history contents, many history education scholars and didactics experts resisted the imposition of the Canon as a compulsory component of history education in the lower cycle of secondary school.[16] The Advisory Council of the

16 According to Hubert Slings, one of the architects of the Canon, acceptance was almost total in primary schools (Author interview with Hubert Slings, director of *Stichting Entoen.nu*, the Canon of the Netherlands Foundation, The Hague, 16 April 2009).

Netherlands Institute for Teaching and Learning History [IVGD][17] admitted that the Canon is a 'source of inspiration', but rejected the idea of making it a 'compulsory prescription'. For that Council, the Canon contains 'extremely detailed' facts, which prevents it from fitting in with the prevailing policy of 'deregulated and globalising education' (IVGD, 2007: 1; see also Grever, 2006: 44; Grever *et al.*, 2006: 116-117). The use of *globalising* here suggests that the Council perceived the Canon as rather *nationalising*. The ultimate effort to oppose the Canon as a compulsory component of the key targets [*kerndoelen*] of history education in the lower cycle of secondary school resulted in a petition sent to the House of Representatives on 30 October 2008.[18]

A similar joint action had taken place in 2006, just after the first report of the Canon Commission, when prominent historians from Rotterdam Erasmus University and the University of Utrecht published their *Controversies Surrounding the Canon* [*Controverses rond de Canon*] (Grever *et al.*, 2006). In these *Controversies*, they mainly criticised the Canon as a visible sign of the prevailing political anguish that had led to some forms of neo-nationalism (Grever, 2006: 51; Stuurman, 2006: 59), as lacking a global perspective (Stuurman, 2006: 68), as being too *monoculturalist* (Grever, 2006: 53), as lacking the culture-shaping aspects of religions (Jonker, 2006: 25), or simply as undermining the study of history through sacralising some parts of the past (Ribbens, 2006: 83). In the end, following a recommendation of the State Council [*Raad van State*] in 2009, the Canon was not proclaimed compulsory in the lower cycle of secondary school. Arguments of the State Council included the fact that given the depth of the details, the specificity and the [large] number of windows [50], the Canon could not fit in the Key Targets of history education, but, rather, it could serve as a source of inspiration (*Raad van State*, 2009: 2).

---

17 Founded in 2003, the IVGD is a collaborative organ involving among others, the University of Amsterdam, the Amsterdam University of Applied Sciences, the VU University Amsterdam, and primary school training colleges [PABO]. It mainly conducts research, offers refresher courses to history teachers and develops teaching aids.

18 The 30 October 2008 letter addressed to Members of the House of Representatives on the subject: '*Verplichte invoering van de "Canon van Nederland"*', was signed, among others, by its initiator Arie Wilschut of the Amsterdam University of Applied Sciences, Carla van Boxtel of the University of Amsterdam's Graduate School of Teaching and Learning, T.F. van der Heugten of the Tilburg Fontys Institute, Harry Havekes of the Nijmegen Radboud University, Paul Holthuis of Groningen University, Stephen Klein of the University of Leiden's Graduate School of Education. The 23 signatories, all historians or history didactics experts, warned the House that the Canon, as a compulsory component of the history education in the lower cycle, would hamper the freedom of choice that Dutch schools had long enjoyed.

The aim of this section was to briefly map the major discussions regarding the contents of history education. I have distinguished two main approaches in the ways those contents have been conceptualised. On the one hand the international approach to history education contents has been discussed as allowing the consideration of local events, phenomena, or processes not only from local, national point of views, but also from international perspectives. On the other hand, the local, national approach has been described as presenting two faces: one consisting of studying local history as a sample or case study that leads to understanding of much broader, global mechanisms; and one that avoids understanding of the local within, and in relation to, the global.

1.4 Summary

The foregoing has presented some of the ways in which scholars, history education experts, and politicians have conceptualised 'understanding of the world' as the main goal of history education. I have mentioned how history education has been presented as preparing pupils so they can make sense of situations, phenomena and events in the present, while enabling them to predict what the future could be like. History education has also been considered as a pipeline linking pupils to 'their roots' and, thereby making them aware of their identity. I have pointed out that while politicians are keen on this way of 'understanding the world', scholars and history didactics experts are opposed to its being part of history education. Closely related to this is an understanding of the world through the lenses of citizenship education. Education officials and politicians find it a key aim of history education, as it tells the story of 'our democratic values' and 'our culture'. Opposing this view, history education scholars feel that the best way to prepare democratically-minded citizens is to let them practice democratic values during history education.

Two broad categories of approaches to history education have been distinguished. On the one hand there are politicians – the ones mostly interested in history education as an identity-fostering and citizenship education framework – who place a specific body of knowledge, with a set of 'must-know' figures and events, at the heart of history education. On the other hand, there are others, mostly scholars and history didactics experts, who consider the aim of history education as making pupils alert to, and aware of, how history functions as a discipline by, for instance, acknowledging the multiple perspective character of historical accounts, and questioning the taken-for-grantedness of accounts. However, one trend within this approach presents a limited body of key historical knowledge as *sine qua non*. A related topic in this discussion is the relevance of any given body of knowledge at any given time. Some history education scholars propose a balance, allowing pupils to know subjects relevant to their era, while understanding how history works in order to be able to interpret for themselves historical events and processes that are relevant at later dates.

Finally, this chapter discussed the contents that the various stakeholders have presented as suitable for history education. The scholarly literature presents world history, or the international approach to history, as the most suitable form in which history education contents should be delivered. As such, though, world history does accommodate local, regional and national histories, it goes beyond local boundaries to integrate non-national perspectives and contexts. Some advocates of local history have also conceptualised local historical figures, events and processes as laboratory materials capable of making the study of history more direct whilst also leading to a much broader, transnational, understanding. On the politicians' side, national history, protected from the influence of globalisation and the effects of immigration, and aimed at preserving and perpetuating the national identity, appears to be the most suitable form that history contents should take. Whereas this chapter has focused on the aims, approaches to, and contents of history education, the next will discuss two other major themes of this research, namely the World Wide Web, which is the medium upon which my research focuses, and the Internet Generation, who are the population at the heart of this research.

Chapter 2

A New Medium, a New Generation

The early 1990s witnessed the birth of the World Wide Web [the Web], a medium that has considerably affected the traditional ways in which history was taught and learnt. By making contents of all kinds accessible, the new medium challenged the traditional, top-down relationship with sources of knowledge. As it had steadily developed into an inescapable medium by the mid-1990s, persistent sociological, behavioural, and epistemological signs indicated the emergence of a new generation of users. Both the new medium – the Web – and that new generation – the Internet Generation – are the subject of this chapter. In order to understand how the Web entered and transformed Dutch society, it is essential to have a broad picture of official policies relating to it, and to grasp the main media-related features of the subjects in which I am interested, before properly considering how these subjects use digital media in real-life history classes. All these elements are interlinked and an understanding of each facilitates one's understanding of the others. Thus, based on scholarly and expert literature as well as policy documents, the first section of this chapter briefly traces the history of the Web in the Netherlands, and maps out various government plans to introduce the medium into [history] education. The second section explores the different features and attitudes the Internet Generation is thought to display in their relationship with the Web in particular and digital media in general. The last section highlights the early efforts of history teachers to integrate the new medium into their teaching activities.

2.1 The Early Days of the Web

> And for me at any rate this is no utopian dream. It is a forecast, however inaccurate and insufficient, of an absolutely essential part of that world community to which I believe we are driving now (Wells, 1938: 56).

At the dawn of the second decade of the 21st century, the Web is already being taken for granted, both in society at large and in education. The Web has entered into people's everyday routines, as all schools, all official services, and almost all households have access to the Web. However, this status of being taken for granted was not reached suddenly – at least in the Western world – but rather after a process that began with the public breakthrough of the medium during the early 1990s. In order to provide a background for later discussions in this research about how the Internet Generation uses this medium, I want to briefly highlight the major moments in the evolution of the Web in the Netherlands, and in its gradual integration into society at large.

The history of the Web begins in the 1960s with the birth of the Internet in the United States. I would like to distinguish between the Internet and the Web at this stage, because the Internet is very often wrongly used to mean the Web. The Internet consists of computers connected and able to communicate with one another, while the Web is an application created in the early 1990s that runs on the Internet and uses protocols and coding systems to transfer and display text, image, and audio files. In the early 1990s other applications, such as e-mail, Usenet, and bulletin board had been running on the Internet for years.[19] The Web was invented by scientist Tim Berners-Lee and a few of his colleagues at the Geneva-based European Organisation for Nuclear Research [CERN]. In his book, *Weaving the Web: The original design and ultimate destiny of the World Wide Web by its inventor*, Berners-Lee (1999: 6) held that 'there was no "Eureka!" moment' for the Web, as it was, on the contrary, the culmination of a process.

This process had started much earlier, firstly with thinkers in the 1930s [*e.g.*: George Wells] and 1940s [Vannevar Bush, among others], and then with computer scientists in the 1960s [Joseph Carl Licklider, Ted Nelson and Douglas Engelbart, to name a few]. According to Berners-Lee (1999: 28-30), the Web was ready by Christmas 1990, when his computer and those of his colleagues could communicate with the info.cern.ch server, the first Web server. Traffic on the info.cern.ch website grew considerably, as the Web quickly gained more popularity: 10-100 page views a day were recorded in the summer of 1991; 1,000 in the summer of 1992; 10,000 in the summer of 1993 (*Ibid.*: 75). In the meantime, the number of known Web servers had also grown from 50 in early 1993 to 100 later that same year (*Ibid.*: 67 & 79), and in the next three years, the Web would grow from 130 to 600,000 sites (Batelle, 2005: 40). In that same year of 1993, Mosaic, the most popular browser at that time, grew by 11 percent per week and by the mid-1990s, the population of the Web was increasing by 10 percent per month (Negroponte, 1995: 5-6).

19 A recent *Wired* article indicated that other applications such as peer-to-peer transfer, email, Virtual Private Networks, Skype, games, *etc.*, account for three-quarters of the traffic on the Internet (Anderson & Wolff, 2010).

In the Netherlands, the Web owes much to activist and hacker Rop Gonggrijp, an early user of the computer. Everything started in 1992 when he and his friends – Paul Jongsma and Felipe Rodriguez – connected their computers to the Internet system of the University of Amsterdam thanks to its system manager at the time. In 1993, the University administration ordered them to terminate that connection, prompting Gonggrijp and Rordiguez to start their own XS4ALL project, which aimed at providing Internet access to all. As early as May 1993, the XS4ALL Foundation was already providing access to the Internet for very little money (Doppert, 2002: 46-48 & 60). This kind of publicised intrusion on big Internet systems had the great merit of getting access to electronic communications for the masses onto the political agenda (Lovink, 2002: 43). At that time, activists used *Hack-Tic* – a 4-year-old magazine intended for hackers but which was also 'interesting for any person who wants to take a critical look at the information society'[20] – to disseminate information about the latest technological developments. The same activists organised an international hackers' festival, which they dubbed *Hacking at the End of the Universe*. 700 hackers from 15 different countries attended the festival which was held near Lelystad, spending three nights in tents. During that unprecedented event 'People travelled day and night from Flevopolder around the world via the Internet'.[21]

While the initial steps had been taken in mid-1993, concrete progress was being observed by early 1994. Not only were news media being inundated with stories about the 'Electronic Highway' (Overdijk, 1997: 13), but also two significant developments took place: firstly, the first [at least, it is regarded as such] Dutch Web page –www.mediamatic.nl – was put online by two designers, Kristi van Riet and Chris Remie (Doppert, 2003: 60). Secondly, in January 1994, the Amsterdam-based *Balie*, a cultural and political debating centre, in partnership with the municipality of Amsterdam as funder, and XS4ALL as technical partner, launched a Web-based, free-access project, named *De Digitale Stad* [The Digital City, DDS] (Limburg, 1994: 2; Lovink, 2002: 47). The DDS was a major and significant step in at least two respects: in the first place, it brought the Web to thousands of people, thereby serving both as an eye-opener and also as a reception test.

20 Hack-Tic, '*Hackers beginnen Nederlands eerste kritische computerblad*', *Hack-Tic*, no 1, 1989, p. 3.

21 Hack-Tic, '*Hacking at the End of the Universe: Belevenissen van de organisatie*', *Hack-Tic* no 22-23, 1993, pp. 3-8.

Launched on 15 January 1994, and accessible from various public places such as museums and libraries, the DDS quickly became jammed. In two days, more than 3,000 people from all over the country had sought connection to the DDS server and, as one user said, 'it was so jammed that one could not [easily] get through' (Limburg, 1994: 2). The DDS was an experiment in 'electronic democracy' (Lovink, 2002: 47), the main intention of which was to mobilise the residents of Amsterdam in anticipation of the municipal elections that were to be held on 3 March 1994. It was supposed to last six weeks, but due to the unprecedented enthusiasm with which it was received [12,000 regular users in the first ten weeks], the experiment was extended for another ten weeks and then later still for an even longer period,[22] until in 2001 it was 'forced into the market' mainly, though not exclusively, due to lack of subsidies (*Ibid.*: 56-57).[23]

In the second place, by using metaphors as it did, the DDS brought the emerging *cyberworld* a step closer to the real-life world. The project itself was referred to as a Digital City, headed by a mayor, and it had residents, streets, squares, service-providers, houses, rooms, *etc.*[24] This way of using real-life language to name new phenomena guaranteed a smooth arrival for the Web, as users perceived the new medium as a new way of looking at the world and conducting everyday activities, rather than a new world or a new way of living. In 1995, six more digital cities were 'built', for Eindhoven, The Hague, Twente and Utrecht, among others. That year also saw the emergence of digital villages [*de digitale dorpen*, DDD], beginning with Lopik in February,[25] a phenomenon that proliferated through-

22 Doppert (2003), p.61; and *NRC Handelsblad*, '*Opnieuw subsidie voor digitale stad*', *NRC Handelsblad*, 1 July 1994, p. 3. http://archief.nrc.nl/index.php/1994/Juli/1/Binnenland/3/Opnieuw+subsidie+voor+digitale+stad (Access 12 November 2009).

23 The *Digitale Stad Maassluis* emerged when the other DDS were going commercial in the early 2000s. Although initiated by the *Digitale Stad Maassluis* Foundation with a dozen volunteers, the website was commercially oriented, with many advertisements, and tourism and shopping information in the Maassluis municipality. http://www.digitalestadmaassluis.nl/ (Accessed 23 April 2010).

24 *NRC Handelsblad*, '*De Digitale Stad verbouwd: meer beeld en interactie*', *NRC Handelsblad*, 12 June 1995b, p. 3. http://archief.nrc.nl/index.php/1995/Juni/12/Binnenland/3/De+Digitale+Stad+verbouwd%3A+meer+beeld+en+interactie (Access 12 November 2009); and Theo Stielstra, '*Digitale Stad is eerste succesvolle telematica-project in Nederland*', *De Volkskrant*, 30 January 1995. http://www.volkskrant.nl/archief_gratis/article628227.ece/Digitale_Stad_is_eerste_succesvolle_telematica-project_in_Nederland (Access 19 November 2009); and Limburg (1993b: 3).

25 *De Volkskrant*, '*Gemeente Lopik opent als eerste digitaal dorp*', *De Volkskrant*, 26 January 1995. http://www.volkskrant.nl/archief_gratis/article627748.ece/Gemeente_Lopik_opent_als_eerste_digitaal_dorp (Accessed 8 January 2010).

out the late-1990s.[26] Writing back in 1995, Bill Gates, as Microsoft's Chief Executive Officer, a key player in disseminating information on the new medium, described that period as one marked by 'a lot of excitement about the Information Highways', as 'people suddenly seemed to notice the Internet ... started to look much more carefully at the "World Wide Web"' (Gates, [1995] 2008: 30).

The political and administrative response to the emergence of the Web in the early 1990s was nothing short of timid, as the government seemed to confine itself to the margins, only granting subsidies to universities, the natural and original home of the Internet (Doppert, 2002: 134). What happened in the early 1990s is clearly a repetition of the situation in the 1920s-1930s and that in the 1940s-1950s, when the government allowed almost all radio and television initiatives to remain in the hands of individuals and private organisations (Overdijk, 1997: 92). Under the title 'The government shows little action on the infoband', dated 27 December 1994, Dick van Eijk, writer for the *NRC Handelsblad* [Dutch national daily newspaper], accused the government of indifference: 'The government regards the electronic highway mainly as the responsibility of the market', he wrote, regretting that the Netherlands had missed the pioneering phase, even though it had the necessary infrastructure.[27]

In this section I briefly traced back the arrival of the Web in Dutch society, within which the educational system in which I am interested operates. It seems that by the mid-1990s there was a growing general awareness of the Web among the Dutch public as it became increasingly accessible to them, mostly thanks to a number of hackers and activists. The role played by the Digital City and other similar projects throughout the country in the second half of the decade was crucial in familiarising the public with the cyberworld, different aspects of which were named after real-world objects. However, despite the excitement in the mid-1990s, the government still did not get involved in developments relating to the new medium. The next section discusses official policies aimed at connecting education to the Web, starting from the late 1990s, at which time nationwide plans were laid down to that effect.

26 See for instance *Het Digitale Dorp Uithuizermeeden*, which was launched in 1997, and which is still in the air to bring out news about local developments: http://www.uithuizermeeden.nl/ (Accessed 5 May 2010).

27 Dick van Eijk , *'Overheid laat te weinig zien op infobaan'*, *NRC Handelsblad,* 27 December 1994, p. 9. http://archief.nrc.nl/index.php/1994/December/27/Overig/9/Overheid+laat+te+weinig+zien+op+infobaan (Accessed 24 November 2009). In another article dated 5 May 1995, Van Eijk (1995: 2) indicated that the Netherlands had 6.1 million cable connections in 6.5 million households in 1995, which was the densest network in the world.

2.2 Getting Education Connected: Official Policies

> Considered at any given time in its development, each society has an educational system which imposes itself upon individuals generally with an irresistible force. It is thus vain to think that we can educate our children the way we please. There are customs with which we have to conform, and if we refrain to a large extent from doing so, they will avenge themselves upon our children. Once they become adults, they will be unable to find their way among their contemporaries and will not live in harmony with them (Durkheim, [1922] 1966: 6).

In the late 1990s, almost all sectors of Dutch society were connected to the Web, with one notable exception of education. In its first report about new media technologies and their place in education, the Education Council pointed out the widening gap between education and the rest of society: 'in comparison with the rest of society, education should not lag behind in the use of ICT … this is not an artificial issue but an urgent one …'[28] This gap was mostly blamed on the lack of government policy for education, which new media theorist and critic Geert Lovink (2002: 43) described as the 'Zeitgeist of the "absent state" and the triumph of market liberalism'. By the time the first plans were being laid down [around 1997], as history teacher and *Kleio* editor Oattes (1997b: 40) very significantly wrote, 'everybody [society] is "online", "surfs" and sends "e-mails"' out into the world, thereby implying that teachers and pupils were excluded. This section, then, is tasked with reviewing the official policies aimed not only at creating the right ICT infrastructure, but also at fulfilling all the other related requirements for a fully connected and networked educational sector. The review is largely based on official reports, policy documents, press releases, and newspaper articles, and is limited to 1997-2005, a period in which unprecedented investments were made, and also during which the Web-driven history education I am researching took – more or less – its current shape.

It was only in April 1997 that the Ministry of Education, Culture and Science started thinking about renewing education to take recent technological developments into account. The newly created ICT Directorate within that Ministry wondered: 'Wasn't this somewhat late?'[29] In March, Minister Jo Ritzen said that the govern-

28 Onderwijsraad, *Informatie- en communicatietechnologie en onderwijs* (The Hague: Onderwijsraad, 18 March, 1998), p. 23.

29 Annelou van Egmond *et al.*, *Pionieren met Passie; directie ICT 1997-2005* (The Hague: Ministry of Education, Culture and Science, August 2005), p. 15.

ment's reaction was definitely late, as the computer–pupil ratio was 1/40, while in Sweden it was 1/10 and in Finland it was close to 1/5.[30] Referring to that same period, the last ICT Director Rob van Wuijtswinkel (2005: 9) noted that the Ministry of Education was finally realising that the Internet Generation had arrived, with its totally different learning style: 'Youngsters choose en masse for ICT .... Without ICT, education is a world outside of reality'. In all probability the last part of this quotation refers to the Web-related reality, which is that almost all other sectors had gone digital or were currently doing so.[31]

Thus, it was in 1997 that the government finally woke up and admitted that, unlike other sectors which were already part of the network[ed] society, education had not benefitted from the arrival of the Web and related technologies. From about late 1996, attention for the Web and education became vaguely perceptible in political discourse. In September of that year, Minister Ritzen proclaimed: 'Schools must be connected with other institutions'.[32] This announced change was only marginally reflected in the 1997 budget for education. Though it was increased to 37.2 billion guldens [±16.7 billion euros], that is, in excess of 1 billion guldens [±450 million euros] more than in 1996, the extra money was dedicated not to the Web and related ICT-infrastructure, but to salaries and 'policy impulses'.[33]

During 1997, it became increasingly clear that, as of January 1998, the government would be set to catch up at full-speed. I shall refer to the 1997-2005 efforts as the 'Big Project period'. In November 1997, the House of Representatives granted the status of 'Big Project' to the plan initiated by Ritzen in April of that year, because of its 'social significance and the amount of public funds' it would involve (Van Egmond *et al.*, 2005: 19). The same House of Representatives withdrew the 'Big Project' status in May 2005 (*Ibid.*: 55), hence the 1997-2005 delimitation. Despite numerous

30 *NRC Handelsblad*, '*Europese Ministers: leraren aan computer*', *NRC Handelsblad,* 4 March 1997a, p. 8. http://archief.nrc.nl/index.php/1997/Maart/4/Binnenland/8/Europese%20Ministers:%20leraren%20aan%20computer (Accessed 26 November 2009).

31 See: *NRC Handelsblad*, *'De digitale nomade pakt de uitdaging van IT op'*, *NRC Handelsblad,* 11 July 1995e, p. 10. http://archief.nrc.nl/index.php/1995/Juli/11/Economie/10/%27De+digitale+nomade+pakt+de+uitdaging+van+IT+op%27 (Accessed 26 November 2009). See also Van Eijk (1995: 17) and Doppert (2002: 124-125).

32 Minister Jo Ritzen quoted in *NRC Handelsblad*, '*Onderwijs, cultuur en wetenschappen: Meer aandacht voor het leren leren*', *NRC Handelsblad,* 17 September 1996, p. 32. http://archief.nrc.nl/index.php/1996/September/17/Binnenland/32/ONDERWIJS,%20CULTUUR%20EN%20WETENSCHAPPEN;%20Meer%20aandacht%20voor%20het%20leren%20leren (Accessed 13 December 2009).

33 *Ibid.*

modifications, changes, and contradictions, the Big Project period can be divided into three main sub-periods: the catch-up investment sub-period [November 1997–August 1998], the Education Online sub-period [September 1998–August 2002], and the Learn-with-ICT sub-period [September 2002–May 2005].

The initial catch-up action plan was dubbed *Investeren in voorsprong* [Investing for a forward-leap] and was expected to cost about 1.3 billion guldens [±582 million euros].[34] Ritzen, its initiator, wanted to achieve a 1/10 computer–pupil ratio in four years. His deputy, State-Secretary Netelenbos specified that in 1998, 78,000 computers would be distributed in 700 secondary schools and 146,000 in 8,000 primary schools. Vocational schools would receive 35,000, while teacher education schools would receive 15,500.[35] The 1997 budget for education had taken into account refresher courses for teachers, though the latter thought it would be better to equip each of them with a computer at home. A representative of the Association of School Leaderships [VVO] argued: 'Half of all refresher efforts consist of [home-based] self-instruction, as teachers have no personal offices at school' [text between brackets added].[36] Even though everything seemed – in theory – to be ready, the plan did not get implemented in January 1998 as had previously been announced. On 1 January that year, 220 selected schools [101 primary schools and 119 secondary schools] were supposed to receive computers that would be connected to the Internet. However, as the government was implementing a strong austerity plan, Ritzen had only been able to secure 116 million guldens [±52 million euros] right from the beginning, which was of course an insignificant sum (Van Egmond *et al.*, 2005: 19). In June, journalist and journalism scholar Wubby Luyendijk (1998: 2) wondered whether the announced 'digital revolution' would ever take place in education.

The plan prompted a great deal of criticism: for example, the House of Representatives claimed that the project 'lacked clarity' and that more information about it was needed.[37] For their part, the Education Council denounced not only the exaggerated focus

34 *NRC Handelsblad, 'Ritzen "tevreden" over computerplan', NRC Handelsblad,* 24 June 1998b, p. 2. http://archief.nrc.nl/index.php/1998/Juni/24/Overig/2/Ritzen+%27tevreden%27+over+computerplan (Accessed 15 December 2009).

35 *NRC Handelsblad, 'Bijscholing voor leraren: Extra geld voor computers op scholen', NRC Handelsblad,* 28 April 1997c, p. 3. http://archief.nrc.nl/index.php/1997/April/28/Binnenland/3/Bijscholing+voor+leraren%3B+Extra+geld+voor+computers+op+scholen (Accessed 18 December 2009).

36 R. van der Horst quoted by *NRC Handelsblad, 'Leraar heeft thuis PC nodig voor bijscholing', NRC Handelsblad,* 24 April1998a, p. 6. http://archief.nrc.nl/index.php/1998/April/24/Overig/6/%27Leraar+heeft+thuis+PC+nodig+voor+bijscholing%27 (Accessed 1 December 2009).

37 *NRC Handelsblad, 'Ritzen "tevreden" …'* (1998b), p. 2.

on hardware, software, infrastructure, and teacher refresher courses, but also the lack of attention being paid to educational contents for which the ICT is supposed to be used, and the lack of new didactic norms that teachers should follow (*Onderwijsraad*, 1998: 32). In this respect, communication media sociologist Manuel Castells (2006: 16) criticised ICT and education policies in Western Europe in the early 2000s for having provided the technology – the hardware and software – without ensuring productivity, innovation and human development. The result was that the 'infrastructure improved considerably' while the 'effects on productivity, on learning, on creativity, and on entrepreneurialism were very limited'. Ritzen's plan was never implemented in full, as the above-mentioned criticisms and funding-related delays were followed in the summer by the arrival of a new government, and thus of a new Minister of Education, Culture and Science, Loek Hermans of the Liberal Party [VVD].

The arrival of Hermans meant a drastic modification in his predecessor's plan, including a new target of a 1/15 computer–pupil ratio and more freedom for schools with regard to the purchase of computers and teacher ICT courses.[38] With 1.4 billion euros – 80 percent of which was going directly to schools – for the 1998–2002 period, Hermans wanted to fully concentrate his efforts on getting education online, by focusing more and solely on the school network, which, in the meantime, had been given the name of *Kennisnet* (Van Egmond *et al.*, 2005: 27 & 29). The orientation of the Big Project had shifted from the *Investing in a forward-leap* approach to the *Education online* approach. In November 1999, the Ministry of Education signed a contract with Nl.tree, an Internet Service Provider which should have connected all 11,000 [primary, secondary and vocational] school locations to the Web by June 2002. The Ministry would pay an annual sum of 91 million euros (*Ibid.*: 29, 31, 33 & 35). *Kennisnet*, the knowledge network intended as 'a countrywide electronic educational network',[39] remained the direct responsibility of the ICT Directorate until 2001, when educational organisations set up the *Kennisnet Foundation*, with guaranteed government subsidies (*Ibid.*: 41).

38 *NRC Handelsblad, 'Plan: school beslist zelf over computers'*, *NRC Handelsblad*, 20 February 1999b, p. 2. http://archief.nrc.nl/index.php/1999/Februari/20/Binnenland/2/Plan%3A+school+beslist+zelf+over+computers (Accessed 19 December 2009).

39 Ministry of Education, Culture and Science, *Kennisnet krijgt centrale rol bij ICT in het onderwijs: Ministerraad stemt in met hoofdlijnen nieuwe aanpak* (The Hague, 19 February 1999). Press release. http://www.minocw.nl/persberichten/11609 (Accessed 15 September 2009).

In the meantime, in order to hasten realisation of the 1/15 computer–pupil ratio, in January 1999 the government introduced a fiscal incentive for companies and other organisations to donate second-hand computers to schools. This one-year incentive came after private companies had donated more than 60,000 second-hand computers during the two previous years.[40] Similar efforts and initiatives took place throughout the 1990s, and a Foundation – *de Stichting Computerbemiddeling* – had been set up to coordinate computer donations and their distribution.[41] While these efforts did undoubtedly bring the computer–pupil ratio closer to the target, they raised another crucial issue: the system requirements. These second-hand computers were not compatible with the most recent software, which was perhaps the reason why companies, ministries, municipalities and other organisations had replaced them with up-to-date devices. The Education Council remarked that hardware in schools did not permit making optimal didactic use of ICT, in particular because the text-editing, spreadsheet and Web-surfing software that could be installed was old. The continuous installation of updates was the most worrying issue, because of increasingly higher system requirements (*Onderwijsraad*, 1998: 25 & 30).

Considering the timing of Hermans' new approach to introducing ICT into education – that is, late 1990s–early 2000s – one might even suggest a role was played by an increasingly palpable dot-com disenchantment, followed by the ICT-related stock market crash in 2000. In other words, Ritzen's plan had probably been inspired and influenced by the dot-com hype of the mid-1990s, which had created 'a metaphysical realm' and made everyone believe that 'the future resided in cyberspace' (Nevaer, 2002: 12-13). The trend at that time was to defy age-long principles, to consider the online world as independent from offline realities (*Ibid.*: xii). The result was the so-called 'Dot-com debacle' in 2000, which saw most dot-com companies go out of business and hundreds of thousands of jobs lost worldwide (*Ibid.*). Hermans' new approach most likely drew lessons from the economic debacle and implemented the introduction of ICT – the metaphysical world – while maximising the involvement of schools in determining approaches and priorities – offline realities.

---

40 *NRC Handelsblad, 'Fiscus beloont geven computer', NRC Handelsblad,* 16 January 1999a, p. 3. http://archief.nrc.nl/index.php/1999/Januari/16/binnenland/3/Fiscus+beloont+geven+computer (Accessed 22 December 2009).

41 *NRC Handelsblad, 'Netelenbos: een computer per tien leerlingen', NRC Handelsblad,* 11 March 1997b, p. 10. http://archief.nrc.nl/index.php/1997/Maart/11/Binnenland/10/Netelenbos%3A+een+computer+per+tien+leerlingen (Accessed 22 December 2009).

The first change in the plan was to end the approach based on selected pilot schools (Van Egmond *et al.*, 2005: 27). All schools would receive the same budget and decide for themselves how it would be used. This was quite the opposite of Ritzen's top-down plan. The Ministry announced not only that *Kennisnet* was responsible for encouraging refresher courses for teachers and for the implementation of ICT, but also that 'no [further] school will be selected for pilot projects'.[42] Situated right at the heart of education, *Kennisnet* emerged as the most important portal for educational websites. In the same vein, in 2001 the Ministry of Education initiated another body, the *Stichting ICT op School* [ICT in Schools Foundation, SICTS] (*Ibid.*: 43). This Foundation aimed to support and foster the efficient and effective use of ICT in primary and secondary education. The SICTS's approach subsequently revolved around four aspects: vision [on the use of ICT in education]; knowledge and expertise [in ICT-based didactics]; educational applications and software; and hardware. In the eyes of the Foundation, the efficient and effective use of ICT depends on how these four aspects are kept in balance (SICTS, 2004: 5 & 6), hence the name of its yearly report: *Vier in Balans* [Four in Balance].

The *Education online* sub-period and its liberal approach to ICT implementation did deliver some results: by the school year of 2000-2001, schools were already beyond the 1/15 ratio target, as there was 1 computer for 8.5 pupils in primary schools and 1 for 12.6 in secondary schools (Steyaert & De Haan, 2001: 68). Moreover, the percentage of secondary school teachers who used ICT had increased from 29 percent in 1999-2000 to 47 percent in 2000-2001. In 2001, pupils in 88 percent of schools had access to the Web, while teachers had access in 96 percent of schools.[43]

While the Web and other ICT were making steady progress in education, the issue of contents was becoming acute. The tasks had been shared, but none of the actors involved had been entrusted with the didactic generation, organisation, and distribution of digital contents. Educational publishers – the conventional brokers and providers of educational contents – saw no market in digital contents, as the Ministry had clearly not provided schools with enough money for those contents. It became an impasse, a sort of vicious circle, with on the one hand publishers waiting for budgets from schools before starting to produce digital contents and on the one

42 Ministry of Education, Culture and Science, *Kennisnet krijgt centrale rol ...* (1999).

43 Statistics from the Ministry of Education, Culture and Science (2001), in Jan Steyaert and Jos de Haan, *Geleidelijk digitaal: Een nuchtere kijk op de sociale gevolgen van ICT* (The Hague: SCP & Fontys Hoogeschool sociaal werk, December 2001), pp. 68-69.

hand, schools waiting for ready-to-use contents before applying for money to purchase them (*Onderwijsraad*, 1998: 29). In December 1998, leading publishers Thieme, Malmberg, and Wolters announced that an 'absolute minimum' of 150 million guldens [±67 million euros] was needed to stimulate the educative software market, because 'developing a one-hour digital lesson costs three times as much as producing a one-hour book-based lesson'.[44] The sole digital content generators were individual teachers, but the production was too low.

For the 2000-2002 period, the Ministry of Education disbursed 'a small amount of 23 million euros' to subsidise and stimulate digital content-generating projects (Van Egmond *et al.*, 2005: 43 & 45). Within this framework, cultural heritage institutions took on part of the role previously played by publishers, namely becoming educational content brokers. In 2001, the National Library of the Netherlands, with obvious educational ambitions, launched *het Geheugen van Nederland* [the Memory of the Netherlands]. Digitisation is discussed in more details in the next chapter, but I should already mention that, since then, digitisation and other Web-based educational projects have continued to multiply.

The Learn-with-ICT sub-period, which kicked off in September 2002, focused on two major issues that had arisen in the previous sub-periods: the digital content impasse and teachers' ICT-didactic skills (*Ibid.*: 51 & 53). In relation to the matter of the generation of digital contents, in 2002 the SICTS received 22 million euros in order to start working on a joint venture which would bring together schools, educational organisations, educational publishers, and software developers and suppliers. In April 2005, these efforts culminated in the launch of *Kennisrotonde*, a virtual roundabout where all the above-mentioned actors could place their contents, as well as find those created by others. The idea was that 'the demands of schools would lead to more knowledge and information being generated' (*Ibid.*: 61-63).

The foregoing aimed to review official policies on the integration of Information and Communication Technologies [ICT] in education and the latter's connection to the Web between 1997 and 2005. Initially geared towards getting as many connected computers as possible at the disposal of teachers and pupils, the top-down, multi-million plan subsequently changed focus and adopted instead a more bottom-up approach. Under the former plan, the Ministry

---

44 S. de Valk of Wolters quoted by *NRC Handelsblad, 'Meer investeren in computer op school', NRC Handelsblad*, 3 December 1998c, p. 3. http://archief.nrc.nl/index.php/1998/December/3/Overig/3/%60Meer+investeren+in+computer+op+school%27 (Accessed 12 December 2009).

of Education, Culture and Science managed almost the entire process and focused on pilot schools, while the latter plan meant abandoning the pilot approach and allowing schools to manage most of the budget according to their own vision. What one can be sure of is that, by the time the Big Project ended in 2005, all schools had access to the Web, and that the medium had become a common didactic tool. Having explored the introduction of the medium in which I am interested – the Web – into society (Section 2.1) and into education (Section 2.2), I would like now to turn to the subjects I am researching, namely the 13- to 14-year-olds who, due to their peculiar way of interacting with digital media, belong to the generation known as the Internet Generation.

2.3 The Internet Generation

> … a generation finds itself confronted with *one* essential question, which is really a meta question, namely: 'What is the essential problem facing us?' In other words, at what point must we rethink our traditions in as innovative and radical a manner as possible? (Lévy, 2010: 108)

Recent reports and research about the use of ICT are unanimous about the fact that the current school-going generation interacts with information and knowledge in new ways strongly marked by the use of the World Wide Web.[45] For instance, in 2009 it was reported that 64 percent of Dutch pupils were able, in their first two years of secondary education, to make their own homepage or profile site, while 45 percent could make their own weblog (Kennisnet, 2009: 57). The last two decades have produced a considerable body of literature about this new generation, commonly referred to as the Internet Generation or the Digital Generation, or Digital Natives (Palfrey & Gasser, 2008), to give them some of their names. From this literature, a number of features and attitudes towards digital media keep appearing among the characteristics of this generation.

Given that the subjects of this research –13- to 14-year olds, are all members of the generation – and that their interaction with Web-based historical contents constitutes the heart of my enquiry, it is indispensable to first describe the generation. In this section, therefore, I will go through existing scholarly and expert literature to identify and then describe the most important media-related characteristics of the Internet Generation. I first want to discuss the location of that generation in time and its inclination towards digital

45 Examples: Hermes and Skylla (2006); Ten Brummelhuis (2006); De Haan & Van 't Hof (2006); Palfrey & Gasser (2008).

media, before focusing on its enthusiasm *vis-à-vis* interactive media, its desire to control media contents, its tendency to multitask and its image-mindedness. At some point, some illustrations will be provided using examples of Internet Generation-oriented websites.

In their 2003 study, media sociologists Frank Huysmans and Jos de Haan (2003: 177-178) referred to the cohort then aged between 12 and 19 years [born in 1984 and after] as being more attracted to, and comfortable with, the computer than to, or with, other technologies (see also Palfrey & Gasser, 2008: 239). Other theorists and researchers largely agree that a particular learning style has emerged that demonstrates connections with the age of a certain cohort of media technology users. Dutch author K.M. van Steensel (2000; see also Palfrey & Gasser, 2008: 1), for instance, has established a direct link between the Internet Generation and the cohort of people born in or after 1980. She argued that these people were confronted right from the beginning with the existence of new digital technologies that later culminated in the Web.[46] Don Tapscott, who has published on the application of technology in business and society, cited almost the same period, 1977, as the birth date of the first 'technologically fluent' children (Tapscott, 1998: 3 & 37). Other scholars have stressed not merely the birth of a particular cohort of people, but rather its causation by another birth – 'the birth of the affordable personal computer in 1981' (Harwood & Asal, 2007: 2):[47]

> The launch of the IBM5150 in August 1981 not only created a benchmark for personal computing but also marked the birth of a new generation, a generation that would grow up and socialize in a digital environment ... While computers had been around for decades, Americans' usage of the technology took off with the arrival of affordable, personalized microcomputers (*Ibid.*: 1).

From the 1980s onwards, computer manufacturers and providers of computer-related products and services have been directing their strategies towards that new generation. Writing about the booming of Web-stimulated business in 2003, Dutch ICT journalist Monique

46 In their book, *Born Digital: Understanding the First Generation of Digital Natives*, John Palfrey & Urs Gasser (2008: 40-43) maintained that the digital life of Digital Natives begins well before they are born, with the 'digital dossier' including the first sonogram stored in various databases [at home, obstetrician's office, at the hospital and at the paediatrician's office]. Other entries are added to the digital dossier before, during and after birth.

47 Other birthdays in or around 1980 are also worth noting, namely the ones of the era-marking Cable News Network [CNN] and Music Television [MTV], which reflected the unprecedented expansion of global media that made 'the preceding thirty-five years appear almost like mounds of dirt against the backdrop of a mountain range' (Herman & McChesney, 1997: 38-39).

Doppert (2003: 65; see also Buckingham, 2007: 76; Castells *et al.*, 2007: 245) observed that the most successful products and services from the entertainment industry were those designed for, and targeting 'mostly the generation younger than *thirty years* who cannot do without the Internet' [Italicisation is mine]. Calculation takes one to somewhere in the mid-1970s,[48] which is not far from the periods suggested by Tapscott [±1977], Van Steensel [±1980], Harwood and Asal [±1981], and Huysmans and De Haan [±1984].

From these authors' writings, it could be generally said that the Internet Generation was born around 1980 and after, and that its members, having grown up with digital media, have gone – or are going – through what education and technology scholar David Buckingham (2007: 75) has termed 'Digital Childhoods'. According to him:

> ... childhood is now permeated, even in some respects defined, by the modern media – by television, video, computer games, the Internet, mobile phones and popular music, and by the enormous range of media-related commodities that make up contemporary consumer culture (see also, Ito *et al.*: 2010: 30, 32 & 65; Ito, 2007; Deuze, 2007: viii; Hutchby & Moran-Ellis, 2001: 1; Negroponte, 1995: 5).

It is important here to briefly discuss the expressions and concepts 'Internet Generation' and 'Digital Generation', which have been used interchangeably to refer to the cohort of people with whom I am concerned in this chapter. From the literature on the subject, the stress in the concept 'Digital Generation' lies on the hardware or devices that make it possible to conduct certain digital activities such as gaming, computing, playing music, *etc.* This concept received considerable momentum in the early 1980s with the popularisation of the personal computer (Harwood & Asal, 2007: 2). The concept of the 'Internet Generation' appears to stress one kind of activity, namely networking or connecting to the Internet or the Web, which is made possible by digital devices. Since most digital devices now generally connect to the Web, the concepts of Digital Generation and Internet Generation end up referring to the same cohort of people.

---

48 Journalism and mass communications scholar Mitchell Stephens takes the year 1975 as the starting point for an astounding technological development. Between that year and 1995, the entertainment products referred to by Monique Doppert (2003: 65) first saw the light of day: personal computers, home video games, CDs, home videotape systems, the World Wide Web, the Walkman, CD-ROMs (Stephens, 1998: 88).

Another equally important point is the distinction between the Internet or Digital Generation and the older generation, which is not always clear-cut. Many members of the older generation are intensive users of connected digital devices and, in that respect, belong in some ways to the Digital Generation (Buckingham, 2006: 1-13). The difference is then expressed in terms of digital nativeness [born after the arrival of, and surrounded by, digital media] and digital immigration, which generally determine the intensity [as well as the extent and the type] of interactions likely to take place between digital media and members of that generation (see Huysmans & De Haan, 2003: 177-178; Van Driel, 2003: 144; Palfrey & Gasser, 2008: 115).

Thus, constant interaction with a variety of digital media and objects is presented as a decisive factor in the shaping of the Net Generation, as Tapscott calls it. As he sees it, children assimilate and soak up new technologies, which they subsequently use in a more or less comfortable manner (Tapscott, 1998: 40-41; see also Ling, 2004: 83-121; Castells *et al.*, 2007: 127 & 248-249; Livingstone, 2007: 105; Palfrey & Gasser, 2008: 1). This conceptualisation of the Internet Generation brings together the notions of knowledge acquisition [assimilation, soaking] and feeling comfortable using media technologies. Digital culture scholar Hans van Driel also stresses the assimilation and soaking-up aspects with regard to the way children interact with technological novelties. While an adult first reads the manual and related instructions before inserting a CD-based game into the computer, a child immediately pushes the CD in the CD-player and starts his or her discovery process. For both players, the aim is the same, but the style is different (Van Driel, 2003: 144). It is important to note here that both players are dealing with digital devices and digital objects, which then raises the following question: why do they belong to two different generations? Based on Van Driel's argument, a distinction should be made between the digital generation and the digital culture in which both players are evolving at different levels of intensity and at a different speed.

Apart from the general assumption that the Internet Generation is inclined towards digital media rather than towards their analogue counterparts (Palfrey & Gasser, 2008: 239), more specific features have been identified as characterising that generation. Interactivity is one such characteristic feature (Tapscott, 1998: 56; Pachler, 2001: 20; Van Dijck 2007: 65 & 70). Discussing the use of this concept from the digital culture perspective, Van Driel (1999: 27-30) called for more caution, because commercial companies have picked up on it as their 'selling point', without actually producing interactive products or services. Interactivity should not merely refer to interaction [action-reaction] between the user and the system, but instead, and particularly, to 'the explicit possibility' for the user to make choices and make changes in the contents.

On the subject of media-audience relationships, philosopher Jacques Derrida considered the use of the concept of interactivity to be 'slightly ridiculous' and claimed that 'we will never achieve it completely' (Derrida & Stiegler, [1993] 2002: 58). For complete interactivity to take place, the consumer has to be able to intervene to 'ask questions, reorient the discourse, propose new rules', *etc.*, and 'this is done to such a feeble degree!' (*Ibid.*). Considering the concept from the perspective of virtual reality and education, virtual reality scholar Maria Roussou (2010: 248; see also Economou & Pujol Tost, 2008: 243) commented that there is no consensus on what interactivity means, what its goal is, or even whether there are many different types of interactivity: 'the word has become confusing'.

Computer theorist Lev Manovich (2001: 55-56) also felt that the concept of interactivity was 'too broad' and tautological when applied to computer-based media. He preferred to divide it into two broad categories – 'closed' interactivity and 'open' interactivity – and then into smaller sub-concepts such as 'menu-based interactivity', 'scalability', 'simulation', *etc.* For other media scholars, interactivity is better understood within the specific context of each medium (King & Krzywinska, 2002: 22-23; Jenkins, [2006] 2008: 137). In this respect, interactivity in computer games or video games is not to be understood in the same light as interactivity in a DVD-based film or in digital television, as different communication technologies enable differing degrees of interactivity. Without entering too deeply into details, one could say along with Tapscott (1998: 78), that interactivity, regardless of its degree or sophistication, its openness or closedness, is at the heart of the N-Gen culture, as 'N-Geners are refusing to be reduced to spectator status'. Instead, the Web has turned many of them into active creators of contents who use their own or existing materials to create new works, either through remixing, mash-ups or sampling,[49] or through other forms of manipulation (Palfrey & Gasser, 2008: 112-117; Burgess & Green, 2009: 58; Jenkins *et al.*, 2009: 3).

This refusal to be passive spectators also manifests itself through the multiple-choice mindedness of the Internet Generation. Observing 'the generation that is now growing up in the Netherlands' back in 1994, journalists Birgit Donker and Sjoerd de Jong (1994:

49 Remixing and mash-ups are described as a 'type of digital collage' (Palfrey & Gasser, 2008: 115) and are close to 'sampling' which applies to songs and means to 'take a portion of one song and reuse it as an element in a new recording' (*Ibid.*: 116).

3-4) pointed out that those 'young 1990ers' wanted to choose for themselves, whatever the circumstances [job, studies, *etc.*]. The two journalists concluded that this was a case of a 'multiple-choice generation'. New media writer Chris Anderson (2006: 166) maintained that the many possibilities of choice offered by new media have forced the Digital Generation to migrate from broadcast media to the Web. Empirical research shows, however, that the younger generation has not wholly abandoned old media. Instead, their use of the Web takes place mostly at the expense of, for example, watching TV (Huysmans & De Haan, 2003: 177-178 & 181). Because of the amount of information from which they have to choose while online, the Dutch Education Council referred to the new generation as the MTV Generation,[50] 'a generation that is used to the availability and handling of large quantities of information sources' (*Onderwijsraad*, 1998: 8-9; see also Palfrey & Gasser, 2008: 244). The Council advocated an appropriate alteration in the role of teachers, who should become coaches and help the new generation to manage the growing amount of audiovisual information with which they are faced (see also Van Dijk, 2005: 155-156; Anderson, 2006: 98).

Another observation is that the Internet Generation's style of watching TV is no different from the way they read hypertext, as the remote control has made it possible to continually switch from programme to programme (Van Driel, 2004b: 33; see also Rushkoff, [1996] 2006]: 32, 39 & 127; Buckingham, 2007: 76). This non-linear style of watching TV has a great deal in common with reading hypertext, the form that uses hyperlinks to enable the reader to be *telepresent*, that is, to be 'simultaneously here and there' (Lévy, 1998: 37; see also Manovich, 2001: 164-165). With regard to the desire to control media contents through personal choices, one might be tempted to suggest that the Internet Generation, through the hypertexts and hyperlinks that make up the Web, are being offered a chance to be where they want to be – rather than where the older generation expects them to be – in the cyberworld.

It has also been stressed that in their multiple-choice mindedness, members of the Internet Generation often choose and carry out many activities at the same time, a phenomenon referred to as *multitasking* (Van Driel, 2003: 144; Rushkoff, [1996] 2006: 39-40; Jenkins *et al.*, 2009: 61-62). This kind of distributed attention or

50 Media theorist Douglas Rushkoff ([1996] 2006: 35-36) held that the Music TV channel resulted from the dissatisfaction caused by the linearity of television programming. MTV came as 'a celebration of the gaps', whose music contents were quick segments of rock videos that required comprehension on an individual basis: 'MTV juxtaposes its images so quickly and so disjointedly that it creates another level of imagery. This style of rough, disjointed media was precisely the landscape preferred by the channel surfers [the other name for screenagers]'.

'multiple threads of thought running simultaneously' (Salvucci & Taatgen, 2011: 7) is said to be have gained prominence thanks to the Web (Somekh, 2004: 57). Unlike other media, the Web makes many sources of information simultaneously reachable and, in doing so, makes it possible to process these multiple-source pieces of information simultaneously. This processing implies a capacity to 'shift[ing] rapidly among tasks' (Jenkins, [2006] 2008: 16), without losing track of any of them. It should be mentioned that multitasking as opposed to focusing on one single activity, has often been decried and is frequently equated with distraction. Digital culture scholars dismissed this criticism, arguing that multitasking should not be considered from the older generation's point of view, but rather within the digital culture, where it involves on the one hand 'a method of monitoring and responding to the sea of information around us', and on the other hand, the need 'to know when and how to pay close attention to a specific input as well as when and how to scan the environment to search for meaningful data' (Jenkins *et al.*, 2009: 63-64). Multitasking can be *concurrent*, if tasks progress either simultaneously or with very short interruptions (Salvucci & Taatgen, 2011: 8-9); or *sequential*, if one switches tasks after a lengthy period spent executing only one of the tasks (*Ibid.*: 9). In their book, *The Multitasking Mind*, cognitive scientists Dario Salvucci and Niels Taatgen (2011: 26) indicated that in some cases, certain conflicts do emerge among tasks that require the same resource at the same time.

Finally, the Internet Generation has been described as being image-oriented, rather that word-minded. This characteristic is itself embedded in the Web, which, since the integration of multimedia functionalities in 1997 (Berners-Lee, 1999: 116), has altered the relationship between the written word and images. Journalist and author Peter Giesen (2003: 98) wondered whether the Web is an image-based medium or a written-word-based one. According to him, on the Web, words are read from a *beeldscherm* [literally: an *image* screen] and are generally not read in the literary, attention-demanding fashion. For him, therefore, the Web is much more image-based, as it encapsulates all existing forms of media and brings them to the computer's *beeldscherm* (*Ibid.*: 106). For this reason, as claimed by communications and social computing scholar Alexander Halavais (2008: 42), reading has become 'browsing' or 'surfing'. It has been suggested that most of the onscreen written texts are meant to be read in a non-linear way, which is a break from the traditional left-to-right, top-to-bottom way of reading. This non-linearity involves the use of hyperlinks, the coding system that connects various documents, objects or fragments thereof, to others. Generally distinguishable by their blue colour and underlining, hyperlinks have somehow turned words into images, as they are scanned, or zapped through rather than read (Steyaert & De Haan, 2001: 70; Van Driel, 2003: 144; Giesen, 2003: 98). This reading style, popular as it is among the Internet Generation, has earned them another nickname, that of *Zap Generation* (Steyaert & De Haan, 2001: 70).

The homepage of *Kennisnet*'s website, www.kennisnet.nl, the most frequently visited educational Web portal, offers an excellent illustration of the new image-centred and hyperlink-driven reading style. A large percentage of words and all images, with the exception of the main site banner, are hyperlinked. The few non-hyperlinked words tell the reader what to expect on the page behind the link. This page is definitely not meant to be read from left-to-right and from top-to-bottom, but rather to be scanned in search of the most relevant hyperlinks. The suggestion remains, therefore, that written text does still play an important role even on the Web, where it has ceased to be mere text and has become *hyper*text (Oosterbaan, 2002: 16). Similarly, as shown by Figure 2.1, the homepage of the Historical Canon of the Netherlands, www.entoen.nu, is almost an all-image, all-linked page: there is not a single written word, with the

Figure 2.1: Homepage of the Historical Canon of the Netherlands (Photo: O.N., 1 June 2011).

exception of the navigational bar and the years marking the broad periods or eras symbolised by iconic representations. Additional text [more precisely: years and window titles] appears when the users position the cursor above an icon, or once they click on one of the icons to reach the back-pages. On those back-pages, almost two-thirds of the page contains a linear text, while about one-third – the right column and the top bar – contains hyperlinked pictures.

Explaining the logic behind the fifty-window website, the Canon Commission stated that 'after each icon and title follows the story behind the window' (*Commissie*, 2006a: 38). This is to say that the image is the beginning point, the doorway that leads to the text. The written word has become an option, but not the first option.[51] The Memory of the Netherlands,[52] another Web-based project managed by the National Library and which targets secondary-school pupils, presents a homepage similar to the one of the Canon, and one that was initially designed as a digital image website that had been intentionally made text-unfriendly (Schouten, 2009a: 11).

In short, the population of school-going children I am currently researching belongs to a cohort of people born around 1980 and after, whose lives are marked by digital media. Beside their general eagerness to interact with digital media, the Digital Generation has been described as seeking much more than mere interaction. They want more control over the contents and the freedom not only to choose but also to carry out multiple tasks simultaneously. In addition, that generation is said to be exceedingly image-minded, mostly because of the multimediality of digital media in general and of the Web in particular. Many major educational projects targeting the Digital Generation have responded to this by integrating enormous quantities of images and hyperlinks in their website design. The last point discussed in this chapter relates to the early attempts of history teachers to appropriate the Web.

51 This new relationship between the written word and images, and their new roles, fall under what visual media and culture scholar José van Dijck (2002: 39-41 & 45-46) has called a self-adjusting mechanism, whereby media and their forms and properties adapt to each new situation, renew themselves, temporarily lose or gain their hegemony, but never [threaten to] disappear.

52 *Het Geheugen van Nederland*: http://geheugenvannederland.nl/ (Accessed 30 May 2011).

2.4 History Teachers and Their Embracing of the Web

> Every thinker expresses only that which has been consciously perceived by his epoch, consequently the education of the younger generation in the sense of this consciousness is quite superfluous: this consciousness is already inherent in the living generation (Tolstoy, [1862] 1967: 9).

The previous section discussed one of the two types of actors involved in the history class – the learners – who could be called digital learners, since they belong to the Digital Generation. This section focuses on the other actors, namely the teachers, attempting to trace – from their own writings and those of history education didactics experts and scholars – how they have gradually embraced the Web as a didactic tool. A discussion of the teachers' embracing of the Web and their thoughts about the importance of the medium is important for this research in the sense that its central subject – the uses of digital media and resources in the history class – involves both learners and teachers. Without this background, the empirical findings presented later in this book would appear to exist in a vacuum. In this section, then, attention is first paid to the pioneering period of the mid-1990s, when early adopters started – on their own or their schools' initiatives – to integrate the Web into their teaching activities. Secondly, I discuss how teachers and history didactics experts and scholars have managed to share information namely via the magazine of the History and Civics Teachers' Association [VGN], *Kleio*.

In 1996, history teacher and early adopter of digital media Reinard Maarleveld (1996: 26-27) published in *Kleio* an article entitled 'Internet in the history class'. He began that pioneering article by expressing a regret: 'You are reading this article from paper and that is unfortunate, because you could have accessed the sources used to create it with the help of a computer connected to the Internet'. As an enthusiastic user, he had discovered the basics of the Internet, especially its *hypertextuality*, and the advantage it offered to history teachers:

> When I write about Thomas Jefferson for instance, the American flag and the American national anthem ... you can immediately search for more information in the United States about these subjects. How is it done? Very simply: you see in the text ... that the words 'Thomas Jefferson', 'American flag' and 'American national anthem' are underlined. Put the cursor on the underlined words, click with the mouse and a few moments later you have the information you have requested. This

> is what is called 'hypertext'. If you don't know what hypertext or the Internet is, it is urgent that you go and take a refresher course. If you don't know what a cursor or a mouse is, then it's extremely urgent that you take a refresher course. If you don't know what a computer is, then it's too late (*Ibid.*: 26).

A number of points are important in Maarleveld's article: to begin with, it was the first ever to appear in *Kleio* on the subject of Internet in the history class.[53] Secondly, its intimidating, frightening, apocalyptic tone, a sort of 'it's now or never', is on the one hand a translation of the expectations of early adopters and, on the other hand, an indication of the prevailing anguish among teachers. As seen in Section 2.2, the general idea was that teachers were not part of the network society. This implied that history teachers had to make extraordinary efforts to survive or otherwise they should renounce their careers. Maarleveld emphasised the *hypertextuality* of the Internet as the most important aspect he had enjoyed from his experience with the Web, especially because it allows one not only to contextualise historical events, experiences, and figures, but also to expand pieces of knowledge to related, relevant sources.

Around the same period, other history teachers were experimenting with the Web in their classes. For instance, with a 16-computer media room, three history teachers at Cals College in Nieuwegein turned their classes into digital classes (Van Boxtel & Oattes, 1997: 27-29). They divided the class into groups of four and gave assignments that were to be conducted using online resources. The pupils had to report back to the teachers for group evaluations as well as individual evaluations. The teachers were satisfied about the results of this experience. Furthermore, the three teachers also noted certain challenges posed by the new medium: there was too much information, and most of it was in English; it was not always an easy task knowing whether a source was trustworthy. Despite that, their conclusion was unambiguous: it was very profitable and possible to teach history this way, in particular because pupils enjoyed and appreciated the freedom of choice offered by the new medium. Speaking about this unique experience, the teachers remarked that 'there are fewer low marks, but also fewer high marks. There is now more balance', despite the fact that 'the challenge is bigger'. What they found most positive is the fact that the Web made it possible to discover a different side to pupils – a side they would otherwise not have discovered 'Pupils whom one hardly noticed in the traditional

53 The Internet should be understood as the World Wide Web, two different concepts that are often used as synonyms (see the beginning of Section 2.1).

class environment suddenly emerge as the motor for the group. The reverse is also observed' (*Ibid.*: 28).

This experiment provides one with some understanding of the perceived influence of the Web on the learning process during the late 1990s. It also brings to light three essential points: first, teachers perceived the Web as fostering collaborative work, as certain pupils developed to become the motors of their groups; second, they perceived it as allowing pupils to show their previously hidden sides, that is, their strengths and/or weaknesses, on the basis of which teachers could develop personalised approaches and solutions; third, they perceived the Web as increasing pupils' engagement with the subject matter.

For his part, Albert van der Kaap, who was teaching history at Jacobus College in Enschede at the time, was experimenting with the Web as a pedagogic, didactic tool from a different perspective. He had turned himself into a webmaster as early as 2001. Van der Kaap was running his own history class website hosted by his school. He understood that 'pupils have new expectations based on ICT' and, for that reason, highly valued the Web, as 'they want to work in a fast, speedy way'.[54] Not only did he become a webmaster, but his pupils became Web-authors and self-publishers. Learning from this experiment, Van der Kaap spoke of the new challenges facing the history teacher:

> Pupils can publish the results of their research in the form of a website. In that respect, teachers must ask themselves a number of questions: as a teacher, what technical knowledge do I need? You must ask youserlf what you are going to judge: only the content? Or the design as well? The Web is a communication medium: are you going to check how efficient a pupil is at communicating with the visitors to his site?[55]

The above-mentioned experiments were not part of a larger, coordinated endeavour, but rather the isolated initiatives of individual teachers who were enthusiastic about ICT. However, as early as the mid-1990s, *Kleio* started publishing not only articles about those pioneer initiatives, but also about the basics of digital media in general and the Web in particular. Oattes, who emerged as *Kleio*'s new media didactics editor in 1997, authored several articles. For example, he wrote articles on 'Film, Sound and New Media' (1997); on the 'Internet: The First Time' (1997); on 'The Media Room as an Impulse to Innovation' [co-authored with Van Boxtel] (1997); and on 'The Net in the Class' (1998); and many other related subjects.

---

54 Albert van der Kaap interviewed by Huub Oattes (2001: 20).

55 *Ibid.*, p. 23.

He was instructing history teachers on the basics of both the computer and the Web because 'In many schools, pupils and teachers are discussing the advantages of the Internet' (Oattes, 1997b: 40). This sort of eye-opening articles for a wider public started appearing in mainstream newspapers starting in 1994 and with growing intensity in 1995.

Kleio intensified eye-opening articles in the late 1990s, culminating in September-October 2002 in a special issue dedicated entirely to ICT.[56] The articles compiled in that special issue reflected the metamorphosis that the history class had gone through in the previous years. One might say that the Big Project (Section 2.2), which had just completed its *Education Online* phase [September 1998–August 2002], had started to bear fruit. One article demonstrated how history was currently being taught and learnt in 'Electronic Learning Environments'; another discussed 'The virtual world in practice: collaborating in Active Worlds', thereby suggesting that *virtuality* and factuality or materiality were no longer mutually exclusive; yet another suggested ways of learning about 'The Middle Ages in [digital] Images'. Others were about the National Library's Memory of the Netherlands project, '*Het Geheugen van Nederland*'; and 'Virtual exhibitions on the Internet'. The issue also briefly introduced cultural memory websites and digital projects. I should remind the reader that digital contents did not exist in 2002, which explains why history teachers were being provided with an overview of the few existing digital projects relevant to their discipline.

The 2004 *History didactics: Handbook for teachers* (Wilschut *et al.*, 2004), in particular the chapter on ICT, could be regarded as an assessment of the experiments and findings of the previous ten years or so. The authors, all prominent history didactics experts – Arie Wilschut, Dick van Straaten and Marcel van Riessen – identified, among other things, the potential of new technologies *vis-à-vis* the teaching process, and formulated recommendations for teachers. The assessment focused on the five main functions of ICT in the history class, and remarked that [1] ICT offers and facilitates access to an unlimited number of sources, which is 'unthinkable with traditional means'; [2] it makes the presentation of the resources found more attractive and helps teachers to structure their presentations in a logical way; [3] it has simplified the editing of resources; [4] it has speeded up communication between teachers and pupils via e-mail and other learning environments; [5] finally it offers good testing and evaluation options for history teachers (Wilschut *et al.*, 2004: 200-212; see also Kanselaar & Andriessen, 2000: 96). Wilschut *et al.* (2004: 199) stressed that 'working with a computer

56 *Kleio*, 6, September/October 2002.

motivates pupils', and 'surely makes history education more attractive'. Therefore, they concluded, departing from the previous print-dominated era, each course should be supported with digital illustrations, because only then would pupils be able to 'follow the lesson easily' (Wilschut *et al.*, 2004: 204).

Despite this praise of the Web and the new didactic possibilities it offered, other voices have called for caution. For instance, in its 2006 report entitled *Naar meer evidence based onderwijs* [Towards More Evidence-Based Education], the Education Council observed that teachers tended to adopt new approaches and methods without having any evidence of their efficiency and superiority over existing ones (*Onderwijsraad*, 2006: 12; see also Haydn, 2003: 11 & 13; see also Buckingham, 2007: 177). In an earlier report – *www.webleren.nl* (2003) – about Web-based learning, the Council recognised the existence of tested or evidence-based methods and to-be-tested Web-based methods. It suggested that teachers would have to find a balance between these two categories (*Onderwijsraad*, 2003: 34).

I started this section with one aim in mind: to map the early integration of the Web into the history class. This mapping has shown that integration began with the pioneering initiatives of individual teachers, who, as they discovered the new medium's potential, used *Kleio* to exchange experiences and views with colleagues. Early experiments showed that the Web had many advantages as a pedagogic tool for the history teacher: it made contextualisation easy through hyperlinking, it increased the efficiency of collaborative learning while bringing to light previously hidden strengths and weaknesses of pupils, and it introduced new communication skills among pupils through online self-publishing, to name a few. It is also clear that the History and Civics Teachers' magazine *Kleio* played an eye-opening role from the mid-1990s onwards. The above-mentioned experiments and the ground-breaking work by *Kleio* showed that, although the Web was a useful tool for history education, it should be approached with some caution.

2.5 Summary

This chapter provided a short but comprehensive background of four main aspects relevant to my research, namely, the Web, official policies leading to its integration in education, the Internet Generation, and the early attempts of history teachers to appropriate the Web. With regard to the Web, as I pointed out, just after its birth in the early 1990s, activists and hackers succeeded in making it available to a wider Dutch public and even managed to associate themselves with official institutions in order to create the freely accessible Digital City. I also mentioned the fact that, unlike the involvement of local official institutions in digital cities and villages, government officials remained in the margins. The main loser in this situation was the educational sector, which is generally forced to rely on government investment rather than private investment.

On the subject of government policies on connecting education to the Web, I reviewed the various steps taken by the Ministry of Education, Culture and Science in order to bridge the gap between education and the rest of society. I discussed the Big Project, the multi-million investment plan that ran from 1997 until 2005, highlighting the successive stages it went through. Although the plan's implementation witnessed many shifts in focus, it ultimately managed to fill the gap. All schools have been equipped with computers that are connected to the Web since 2005.

The Internet Generation, the subject of my research, has been presented as referring to the cohort of people born around 1980 who grew up – or are growing up –with digital technologies. Interactivity was identified as one major feature about which members of the Internet Generation are enthusiastic. They are exceptionally interested in media objects that offer them the possibility of bi-directional engagement. Control over media contents is another major feature that characterises this generation. In one sense, control refers to the freedom to choose which route to follow when using media objects and contents. In another sense, it implies the possibility of engagement with many of those contents and objects simultaneously, without losing track of any of them. Image-mindedness, too, was identified as an important characteristic, which has been amplified due to the visual nature of the Web itself.

Finally, this chapter briefly traced the early appropriation of the Web by history teachers. A number of pioneering initiatives of individual teachers show how history teachers were being seduced by the Web. Some welcomed the new ways in which it easily provided historical contexts; others discovered that it created a favourable environment for collaborative learning that brought to the surface previously invisible strengths and weaknesses of pupils; yet others found that it was an empowering tool, as it provided pupils with an opportunity to publish their own historical accounts. By now, I have discussed the medium and the subjects at the heart of this research. The medium is digital, and the Internet Generation is described as being digitally minded. The missing piece in the puzzle is the digital contents intended specifically for that medium and designed with the Internet Generation in mind. The next chapter focuses on the digitisation of cultural heritage collections for educational purposes.

Chapter 3

DIGITISING THE CULTURAL HERITAGE FOR HISTORY EDUCATION

The Netherlands is said to be among the top digitisers of cultural heritage collections in the world, as almost all Dutch cultural heritage institutions had websites by the year 2006 (De Haan *et al.*, 2006: 5; see also *Museumvereniging* & DEN, 2008). My own survey, conducted in April–May 2010, showed that 97.1 percent [553] of the country's 569 museums had a website, while 2.9 percent [16] did not.[57] However, this digitisation fever did not reach the archival sector, where only 103 archives [38.8 percent] had a website, while the remaining 162 – mainly municipal archives – did not.[58] In 2006, the public had access to 10 percent of all museum objects and there were digital surrogates for 15-35 percent of those museum objects. The biggest of all the Dutch museums, the *Rijksmuseum*, had digital surrogates for 400,000 of the one million objects in its collection, 50,000 of which could be accessed by the public (De Haan *et al.*, 2006: 5, 13 & 44; see also SNK, 2009: 7). The efforts aimed at digitising cultural heritage collections started in the early 2000s and involved many fields of interest, including political, ideological, educational, commercial, *etc.* The aim of this chapter is to discuss some of the most important aspects of the digitisation process, in order to understand which objects make it to the Web and why,

57 These figures are based on data provided via the *Stichting de Museumserver*'s website. This offers an overview of Dutch museums and indicates which ones have websites. http://www.museumserver.nl (Accessed 8 April 2010). It should be stressed that it is not an easy task to determine the exact number of museums. Statistics Netherlands [CBS], a government organisation that provides official statistics, indicated that in 2007 there were 773 museums in the country [67% of which were open all year round]. This was 169 less than ten years before [1997]. (http://statline.cbs.nl/StatWeb/publication/?VW=T&DM=SLNL&PA=7089MUS2&LA=NL [Accessed 27 September 2010]). For 1995, The CBS cited two diverging figures: 744 on the above-mentioned Web page, and 758 on another page, http://www.cbs.nl/nl-NL/menu/methoden/dataverzameling/vergelijking-musea-1995-en-1997.htm (Accessed 27 September 2010). Following a redefinition of the concept of museum by the International Council of Museums from 1998 onward, with the latest [2007] updated version [http://icom.museum/who-we-are/the-vision/museum-definition.html (Accessed 10 July 2011)], the number of museums fell again, though no exact figures are currently available.

58 These figures are based on an April–May 2010 survey I conducted using the details provided by *Archieven WO2*, an initiative of the National Archives and the Dutch Institute for War Documentation. A list of archives' websites is provided with respective URLs: http://www.archievenwo2.nl/ (Accessed 8 May 2010).

and where students of history can expect to come across them and hopefully use them in their learning activities. My focus is on museums and archives and does not include libraries, nor their 'special collection' departments, which also preserve a large amount of this country's cultural heritage. This choice to leave libraries out was due mostly to time constraints.

In what follows, I first review the motives behind digitisation itself, focusing on its preservation and access-providing side, on its ideological and educational functions, and the commercial potential that hovers over each of these aspects. I then go on to review the most recurrent selection criteria that digitisers take into account when determining which objects to prioritise. I must remind readers that in some cases selection never takes place or it is defined in very broad terms. After this, I discuss hyperlinking as one important way of enhancing the pedagogical value of objects, not only by facilitating contextualisation, but also by optimising the findability of objects. Finally, this chapter takes a look at the latest Web 2.0-driven trends among cultural heritage institutions, including the use of Social Media and the gradual involvement of users as content creators.

3.1 Why Digitise? Motives and Policies

> Every day the urge grows stronger to get hold of an object at close range in an image [*Bild*], or, better, in a facsimile [*Abbild*], a reproduction. And the reproduction [*Reproduktion*], as offered by illustrated magazines and newsreels, differs unmistakably from the image (Benjamin, [1936] 2008: 23).

The question I would like to explore in this section is: Why have huge numbers of cultural heritage objects been digitised and why have institutions gone online? Exploring the various answers to this question, either from scholarly or professional perspectives or from the standpoint of official policies, is important for this research, because cultural heritage collections have traditionally served as sources of information for history education. In this respect, understanding the ways that the different stakeholders have conceived for converting analogue objects to their digital surrogates is crucial for my enquiry into the use of digitised material in history education. In the next few paragraphs, I first consider 'preservation' and 'access' as the main reasons for digitisation, though they are often presented as two sides to the same coin. I then identify and review the motives behind digitisation, including education, ideology and the [re-]unification of objects, all potentially underlain by corporate and commercial interests. I provide examples of Dutch digitisation projects, and, at certain points, make use of the international literature on digitisation or other related fields.

In almost all cases, the digitisation of [parts of] cultural heritage collections aims either to preserve objects, or to make them accessible (Lazinger, 2001: 111), or both. Information studies and digital preservation scholar Paul Conway suggested that preserving 'is equivalent to maintaining access' and *vice versa*, as '[P]roviding electronic access to information sources reduces wear and tear on paper or film originals' (Conway, 1994: 44-45 ; see also Smith, 1999: 6). This equation between preservation and access is a very recent development, as both concepts were initially mutually exclusive (Conway, 2010: 375). Conway distinguished three preservation-versus-access paradigms in the cultural heritage sector: the *Preservation OR Access* paradigm of the pre-World War II period, in which preservation precluded access; the *Preservation AND Access* paradigm underlying modern preservation plans and which posits that 'preservation and access are mutually reinforcing ideas'; and the *Preservation IS Access* paradigm of the digital world, where 'preservation is the action and access the thing – the act of preserving access' (*Ibid.*).

The *Comité des Sages* – a reflection group appointed in April 2010 by the European Commissioner for the Digital Agenda and the Commissioner in charge of Education, Culture, Multilingualism and Youth to make recommendations on the digitisation of cultural heritage – is advocate of the Preservation IS Access view. On the one hand, the three scholars stressed that 'If one word should encompass and summarise the vision of the Comité des Sages, it would be "access"', as 'there is no more urgent question than to secure the access of current and future generations to this heritage' (Lévy *et al.*, 2011: 9). On the other hand, the *Comité des Sages* stipulated a condition in relation to that access: 'It must be understood that if access is the final objective, a tall order, *it can only be achieved through preservation*' (*Ibid.* Italicisation is mine).

The *Beelden voor de toekomst* [Images for the Future] project is one illustration of that view. This project strives to digitise 137,200 hours of video material, 123,000 of audio recordings, and 2.9 million pictures (SNK, 2009: 11) and calls itself 'an unprecedented rescue and digitisation operation' (*Ibid.*: 17). While 'rescue' here refers to preservation and restoration, 'digitisation', according to the six project partners,[59] 'makes sense only when the digital material can be used – now and in the future' (*Ibid.*: 20). From this point of view, digitisation is not meant solely for either preservation or ac-

59 The six partners are the Netherlands Institute for Sound and Vision, the Eye Film Institute, the National Archives, the Union of Public Libraries, the Rotterdam Central Music Library, and the *Stichting Nederland Kennisland* (SNK, 2009: 9).

cess. Instead, as digital preservation scholar Susan Lazinger (2001: 260) noted, it is 'both an access tool and a viable preservation technology for those important materials that are at the end of their analogue life-span'.

In the late 1990s, an important and ambitious project was launched in the Netherlands to preserve paper-based cultural heritage objects, especially those dating between 1840 and 1950, said to be most threatened by decay (Schouten, 2009a: 10-11). Known as *Metamorfoze* [Metamorphosis], the joint National Library–National Archives project initially aimed to restore books and other paper-based documents produced during the above-mentioned period and preserved in various heritage institutions. This was purely a preservation endeavour – including conservation and restoration – with the access issue solved through microfilming and within the limits of that analogue medium. Later, after realising that '[M]icrofilms are actually less suitable as access-medium', it was decided that 'from 2009 onwards no microfilming will take place' (Schouten, 2008: 24). From then on, '[M]ost of the conservation projects will be conducted by digitising the originals' (*Ibid.*). It was only in 2008 that *Metamorfoze*, with a yearly budget of 7 million euros, started using digitisation as a 'mass conservation method' (*Ibid.*: 13). The directors of the two institutions behind the project referred to this inevitable shift from preservation-only to a preservation-and-access approach as follows:

> In recent years, one of the ways in which hundreds of thousands of books, newspapers, magazines, collections, and archives have been preserved was by transferring information to another medium [microfilm], in order to limit using the originals as far as possible. Although preservation is the most important function of *Metamorfoze*, a new development has been underway in the last years, whereby *increasing emphasis is being placed on permanent access to the preserved material.* Digitisation and Internet make this possible (Bossenbroek & Berendse, 2009: 7. Italicisation is mine).

Thus far, preservation and access appear to be two sides of the same digitisation coin and therefore as non-dissociable. However, other motives have been cited to justify why objects should be preserved and made accessible online. Scholars, heritage professionals, and politicians have all pointed out that education is a major target for digitisation projects. Digitisation presents an undreamed-of opportunity to make previously inaccessible materials available to teachers and students (Hazen *et al.*, 1998; Smith, 1999: 8; Bryant *et al.*, 2004; Hughes, 2004). While still in office as State-Secretary for Culture, Heritage and Media, Rick van der Ploeg announced that Dutch cultural heritage institutions had 'receive[d] new ways of reaching out to their public' by making their collections accessible to the general public, to pupils and teachers as well as to researchers (Van der Ploeg, 2002b: 23). The public to which Van der Ploeg was mainly referring was 6- to 18-year-olds – the Digital Natives (see Chapter 2, Section 2.3) – who are known to be ICT-enthusiasts. This is also the school-going generation, whose curriculum contains many disciplines with considerable cultural contents, including, among others, history, civics, mankind and society [*Mens en Maatschappij*]. Van der Ploeg was convinced that 'the use of multimedia can make the contents livelier' (Van der Ploeg, 2002b: 30), an assumption that is explored on the basis of case studies in Chapters 5, 6 and 7.

Cognitively speaking, digitisation has 'tremendous benefits for education' and this explains why many institutions present educational modules on their websites, presenting packages of educational material based around their collections' (Hughes, 2004: 15; also see Beetham, 2007: 31; Mayes & De Freitas, 2007: 22). For information sciences scholar Abby Smith (1999: 8 & 10), institutions undertaking digitisation could consider resources from the classroom perspective and digitise primary materials, offering teachers and students at all levels previously unheard-of opportunities and new raw materials from history. Table 3.1[60] shows figures of educational activities – either on-spot or online in the form of modules – as presented on the websites of Dutch museums and archives.

First of all, it is worth noting the considerable difference in the 'Have website' columns for both museums and archives: while 97.1 percent of museums had websites, only 38.8 percent of archives did. This difference could be interpreted as reflecting the differences be-

Table 3.1: Figures of educational programmes on museums' and archives' websites in May 2010.

MUSEUMS				ARCHIVES			
Have website	Have educ. progr.		No educ. progr.	Have website	Have educ. progr.		No educ. progr.
553 (out of 569) 97.1%	278		275	103 (out of 265) 38.8%	52		51
	On-spot	Online			On-spot	Online	
	230	48			39	13	
	41.5 %	8.6 %	49.7 %		37.8 %	12.6 %	49.5 %

60 These figures are based on surveys I conducted in April–May 2010 on the websites of museums and archives listed by, respectively, *Stichting de Museumserver* [http://www.museumserver.nl] and *ArchievenWO2* [http://www.archievenwo2.nl/].

tween the two types of heritage institution in terms of being public-oriented. Museums appear to target a wide audience, while most archives seem to be niche-oriented [academics, genealogists, *etc.*]. In other words, an object at a natural science museum or an art history museum will probably, though not definitely, have a wider appeal than a baptism card in a parochial archive or a birth certificate in a municipal archive. Having said that, Table 3.1 shows that a great number of websites belonging to heritage institutions have special pages dedicated to education. However, only a few – 8.6 percent for museums and 12.6 percent for archives – offer online educational packages (see Table 3.1). Many of those offering educational modules do so in a non-interactive way, generally by offering a Portable Document Format [PDF][61] containing some text and a few pictures from their collections. Others have more sophisticated, interactive modules, including audiovisual materials.[62]

In addition to, and often in combination with, educational motives, ideological motives such as identity-shaping and citizenship education appear, explicitly or implicitly, as a major justification for digitisation. Similar to history education (see Chapter 1), cultural collections also provide identity-shaping, citizenship-training opportunities, especially for the Digital Generation. The same fears of multiculturalism, globalisation, the Web, and their implications in relation to collective identity could be seen in the policies surrounding digitisation. In its seminal report – *Alles uit de kast* [Pulling out all the stops] – in 1998, the Dutch Scientific Technical Council [WTR] noted that ICT in a multicultural and globalising world bring *youths* into contact with *their culture*, which, in its turn, plays a crucial role in determining *their identity* (WTR, 1998: 17). Pulling out all the stops, primarily so that young people know their culture, thereby influencing their identity, is what museum studies scholar Fiona Cameron (2008: 171) has called 'the polarization of culture and the mobilization of cultural forms for ideological ends'.

Identity [and citizenship]-driven digitisation took a very explicit shape when the State-Secretary at the time, Van der Ploeg – who had placed digitisation at the top of his agenda (Van der Ploeg, 2002a: 1) – defended before the House of Representatives, the project known as *Boulevard van het actuele verleden* [Boulevard of the Current Past].

---

61 See for instance the education page of *Deltapark Neeltje Jans*: http://www.neeltjejans.nl/index.php/nl/scholen/lesmateriaal (Accessed 3 May 2010).

62 *Het Geheugen van Nederland* – the Memory of the Netherlands – has 33 educational modules mostly for history. http://geheugenvannederland.nl/?/onderwijs/lessen/overzicht (Accessed 3 May 2010).

Jointly set up by the Ministry of Education, Culture and Science and various national heritage institutions,

> The Boulevard project provides an answer to questions about the changing Dutch identity in an integration-driven Europe; it is *the* venue [*dé plaats*] to acquire knowledge about *Dutch history*; it offers new [naturalised] Dutch citizens an opportunity to get to know *our country* better; and it provides insight into the significance of democracy for *Dutch society* (Van der Ploeg, 2002a: 11-12. Italicisation and parentheses are mine).

The tone and the content of this letter to the House of Representatives bear a marked resemblance, almost *verbatim*, to official communications surrounding the Canon of the Netherlands four years later (see Chapter 1). The 'Dutch identity', 'know our country' and 'our scientific and cultural riches'[63] approaches can also be seen with regard to the role political actors assign to history education.

The same 'our' approach reappears in the policies and politics underlying *Metamorfoze,* which later emerged as the biggest producer of digital cultural heritage contents in the Netherlands (Schouten, 2009a: 13). According to the directors of the National Library and National Archives, 'the preservation of paper heritage is of great importance to *our history and identity*' (Bossenbroek & Berendse, 2009: 7. Italicisation is mine). Cameron (2008: 174) noted that a similar policy is observed in Australia, where 'digital heritage is central to building a national identity'. She further held that this 'commodification of the past' has turned out to be an attempt 'to salvage *a* future from the ruins of the past' [Italicisation is mine]. The use of *a* instead of *the* in front of *future* suggests that some other possible futures exist and could be salvaged as well.

Discussing the same subject – the commodification of the past – literary critic Andreas Huyssens (2003: 18-20) noted that 'media do not transport public memory innocently'. He postulated that '[T]hey shape it in their very structure and form'. As the late 1990s and the early 2000s formed a period of political and cultural anxiety, marked by profound identity crises exacerbated in the West especially in the aftermath of the 9/11 attacks in the United

63 Rick van der Ploeg [then State-Secretary at the Ministry of Education, Culture and Science], Letter to the Speaker of the House of Representatives. Object: Digitisation of cultural heritage (Zoetermeer, 27 May 2002). www.minocw.nl/documenten/brief2k-2002-doc-18765.pdf (Accessed 5 April 2010).

States,[64] it was quite likely that political actors would favour *a* certain digital structure and form of the past to project *a* certain *future*. Hence the 'our' approach being repeatedly stressed in official communications surrounding digitisation and policies relating thereto. Philosopher Jacques Derrida suggested that the presence of the state in the digitisation process presupposes the existence of a 'politics of memory' which mainly influences the choice of the materials to be preserved:

> Isn't it a state agency that is ultimately going to decide, when it increasingly represents this or that power in civil society, what the nation-state will have to preserve, always privileging, moreover, the national and the public? Why have we preserved what is French rather than what is German or Japanese? And what part of national history are we going to preserve? (Derrida & Stiegler, [1993] 2002: 62-63; see also Bowker, 2007: 34).

Another important motive cited, when justifying digitisation has been the [re-] unification of collections. In this respect, theoretically, heritage institutions strive to bring together all objects that were once preserved in the same place, or which cover the same subject. For instance, the National Archives has digitised maps that came from the *Verenigde Oost-Indische Compagnie,* the Dutch East India Company [VOC], explaining that

> This programme provides information on the archival records to which the visual material originally belonged. This version of the Atlas of Mutual Heritage lists the archival records held in different archives of the *Nationaal Archief* from which the illustrations were removed in the 19th century.[65]

In this Atlas of Mutual Heritage, the map showing 'The foremost cities of the besieged Colombo in 1656', physically located in Colombo, Sri-Lanka,[66] is shown side-by-side with the 'Map of the coast near Bantam' (1598–1600), physically located in Bantam, in

---

64 This anxiety should be placed in a much broader context that includes the fall of the Berlin Wall in 1989 and the European Integration that allowed the free movement of people [immigration] and goods, including those from former communist countries. According to some political discourses, these events constitute a threat to national identities and turn the nation-state into a relative concept.

65 *Nationaal Archief*, 'Archive'. http://www.nationaalarchief.nl/amh/help.aspx?lang=en&page=verant-arch (Accessed 15 June 2010).

66 *Nationaal Archief*, 'The foremost cities of the besieged Colombo in 1656'. http://www.nationaalarchief.nl/amh/detail.aspx?page=dafb&lang=en&id=209#tab4 (Accessed 15 June 2010).

Indonesia.[67] Similarly, in its mass-digitisation of Dutch daily newspapers published between 1618 and 1995, the National Library digitised papers not only from its own collection, but also from over twenty local archives and libraries, as well as from institutions in the Vatican, Russia, Switzerland, Sweden, Belgium, Suriname, to name a few. The Library announced that the effort had made the especially hard-to-access 17th-century newspapers accessible online, primarily for researchers and scientists.[68] By doing so, all issues of the same outlet were brought together in a single database – and were thus united –, as were all other outlets of that period.

Considered from an institutional point of view, certain corporate interests are often cited in justification of digitisation efforts. In this respect, the assumption that digitisation increases the prestige and image or visibility of institutions and contributes to their growth, with new staff being employed and new departments opened to manage the new digital collections. The Netherlands National Library is a good illustration of this, with its policies oriented towards enhancing its international position. In its 2009 Annual Report, the Library reported under the heading 'Enhancing the international position' that it 'strives to maintain its leading position in the area of digital preservation' (KB, 2009: 18).

Commercial interests could perhaps be added to these institutional interests. Preservation, access, education, ideology, and item [re-]unification often represent sources of income for institutions. In other words, institutions may be hoping to generate income and increase their prestige by making collections accessible, with or without some ideological agenda, for educational purposes, or with the aim of bringing [related] objects [back] together. The Van Gogh Letters project undertaken by the Van Gogh Museum is a good illustration of the commercial side of digitisation combined with some of the other motives.[69] This project resulted in a six-volume edition in Dutch, English, and French, containing 902 letters [819 written by Van Gogh and 83 written to him] and 4,300 reproductions of drawings and paintings. The ISBNed edition costs 395

67 *Nationaal Archief*, 'Map of the coast near Bantam'. http://www.nationaalarchief.nl/amh/detail.aspx?page=dafb&lang=en&id=3632#tab4 (Accessed 15 June 2010).

68 The National Library, '*KB presenteert 400 jaar kranten online*'. http://www.kb.nl/nieuws/2010/historische_kranten.html (Accessed 15 June 2010) & Author interview with Lammert Zwaagstra, project manager in charge of selection and copyright clearance at the National Library's Historical Newspaper Project (The Hague, 24 June 2010).

69 Vincent van Gogh, '*Vincent van Gogh - De brieven*'. http://www.vangoghmuseum.nl/vgm/index.jsp?page=200942&lang=nl (Accessed 31 May 2011).

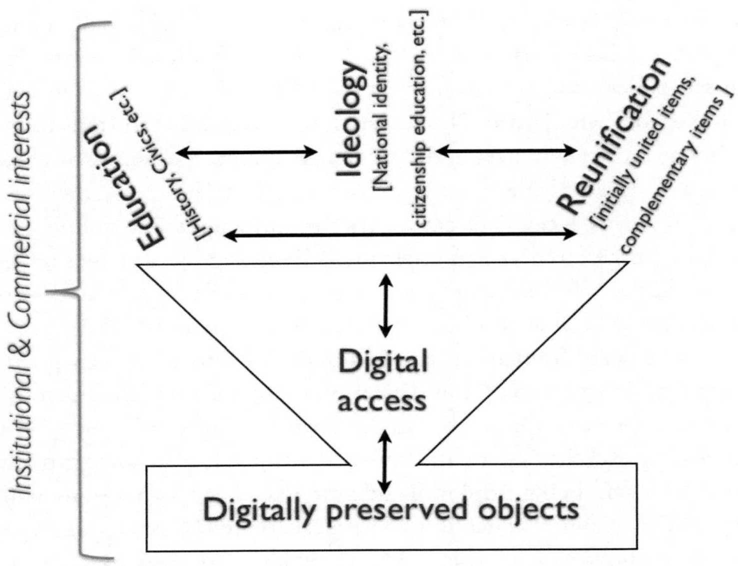

Figure 3.1: Access, preservation, and derived functions.

euros and offers a free 18-page online preview.[70] Not only have the letters been preserved and made accessible [partly free, partly at a fee], but they have also been unified to a certain extent [for example, replies were brought closer to the letters to which they responded], which makes them of a greater interest to, for example, history education, as they 'contain indications about Van Gogh's place in the artistic and intellectual context of his time both in the Netherlands and in France'.[71]

As can been seen from Figure 3.1, the five motives mentioned above – preservation, access, education, ideology, and item [re-]unification – form a chain, with institutional, commercial, and economic motives potentially underlying each individual motive: they are both interconnected and interdependent. Access is provided to that which has been preserved, and preserving digitally often makes digital access easier; education implies access to preserved materials. Similarly, identity-shaping and citizenship education can only take place when and where there is access to the preserved material. Also, the reunification of items first requires them to go through the process of preservation and of being made accessible. Moreover, there

70 *Vincent van Gogh – De brieven.* Preview: http://www.vangoghmuseum.nl/download/VanGogh_boekeditie_preview_NL.pdf (Accessed 31 May 2011).

71 *Ibid.*, p. 2.

are many ways in which it is extremely good at fostering education and shaping identity. On the other hand, decisions may be made to reunite collections for educational or ideological purposes. The last three processes – education, ideology, and reunification – can therefore be said to depend on the first two – preservation and access, as the former processes begin when the latter are in place.[72]

This section has identified preservation and access as the main reasons for digitising cultural heritage collections. Connected with one another in the digital era, these two concepts have turned around the idea that rescuing threatened and valuable objects would be of little significance if no access were provided to the digital surrogates. Apart from these two general reasons, other specific motives have also been pointed out. These include education, as digitisation is also meant to make previously hard-to-access, primary sources available to teachers and pupils. They also include ideological motives, such as identity-shaping and citizenship education, which are often placed at the heart of digitisation efforts, mostly by politicians and government institutions. The [re-] unification of collections or objects, which can also be cited as a motive, consists in digitally gathering related objects or previously united objects together in a single collection. Finally, corporate and commercial interests seem to underlie the entire digitisation process, as many of its stages and aspects could potentially contribute to the prestige and growth of institutions and help to generate income. The next section shows how, once one gets involved in the details in order to understand the various selection criteria, many of the above-mentioned motives actually benefit history education in one way or another.

3.2 Selection Criteria

> ... we can and in fact do record almost anything: the volume is enormous. But because it is not possible to preserve everything, choices, and therefore interpretations, structurations, become necessary (Derrida & Stiegler, [1993] 2002: 62).

From the previous section, digitisation has emerged as aiming primarily at preserving cultural heritage objects and, by doing so, making them accessible online. This section goes a step further and reviews the main – and recurrent – criteria that heritage institutions implement when selecting collections or parts of them or in-

72 Paul Harwood and Victor Asal (2007: 54) stressed that teachers must have access to digital technologies and, by extension, to digital contents: 'Without access', they maintained, 'there is simply no device or conduit for teachers to apply for administrative or instructional purposes. Without access, obviously no change can occur'.

dividual objects to undergo digitisation. Apart from reviewing these criteria in the light of the scholarly literature, both national and international, and policy documents as well as interviews and correspondence with heritage professionals, this section also strives to identify the implications of those criteria for history education. It is important at this stage to understand how heritage contents are filtered on their way to the Web, because, after all, the resulting digital collections are the ones that will hopefully make it onto the computer screens of history learners and into the history class that is the subject of this research. I should start by mentioning the fact that in some cases selection is either excluded or defined in broader terms, based on periods or on themes. I subsequently discuss the selection criteria that recur most frequently, namely the physical condition of objects, patron use, user demand, and the potential for theft. At the end, I consider the historical or intellectual value of objects as an umbrella criterion for weighing objects that are deemed unique, rare, or otherwise significant.

Despite the general digitisation principle that not everything can be digitised (see epigraph; Smith, 1999: 13), some digitising institutions decided not to become engaged in the selection process, either because their collections are relatively small, or because selection would be too expensive and time-consuming. Generally, it is the other way around. Selection is carried out in order 'to stretch limited resources in as wise a fashion as possible' (Conway, 2010: 372). While The Hague-based *Mauritshuis* has completely digitised its 800 paintings, 50 miniatures, 20 sculptures as well as a few drawings and prints,[73] *het Geheugen van Nederland* [the Memory of the Netherlands] made selections at collection-level rather than at an individual level, and 'conform[ed] with the [concerned] institution's priorities'.[74]

The National Archives followed a similar policy when re-digitising its collection of 550,000 photographs within the framework of the 2007–2014 *Beelden voor de toekomst* project. These photographs were first digitised in 1995 but did no longer meet current quality standards. Another 1.2 million photographs, which originated from a private press photo company that went out of business in 2008, have also been digitised.[75] Selection took place, but not the type of

73 E-mail correspondence with Lea van der Vinde, Conservator/Curator at *Mauritshuis* (09 November 2009. See also *Mauritshuis*, 'Hele collectie'. http://www.mauritshuis.nl/index.aspx?ChapterID=1163 [Accessed 08 April 2010]).

74 Author interview with *het Geheugen van Nederland*'s project coordinator, Reinier van Deinum (The Hague, 11 November 2009).

75 *Beelden voor de Toekomst* project: http://www.beeldenvoordetoekomst.nl/nl (Accessed 29 April 2010).

selection to which reference is usually made: only redundant objects were discarded and it was estimated that the final collection would comprise 650,000 photographs. The intention was to digitise the *entire* collection, avoiding double digitisation. In the end, no picture was lost, though selection had taken place.[76]

In some cases, only parts of a collection are sampled out based on time or period, and no further selection takes place within the sample taken. For instance, in 1999 the Amsterdam-based Film Museum [recently renamed the Eye Film Institute Netherlands] digitised all films, without making any distinction whatsoever, produced *between 1899 and 1940*. The 1,000 hours of physically restored, digitally-preserved, and digitally-accessible [*i.e.*, within the Institute and using the Institute's devices] films were obtained thanks to a 2-million-euro donation from Floris Kolvenbach, a culture-loving Dutch businessman involved in the digital film industry. The sole selection criterion in this case, was the date of production.[77] The *Kolvenbach Collection*, as it is called, is almost entirely copyright-free and has been integrated into a larger Web-based, cross-institutional, education-oriented project [LES 2.0] that will be discussed in Section 3.4. Similarly to the Eye Film Institute, the Breda City Archives systematically digitised all its Civil Status documents – baptism cards; birth, death, and marriage certificates – from the oldest [14th century] *until 1909* for birth certificates, *1915* for baptism cards, *1935* for marriage certificates, and *1960* for death certificates. In this case, selection took place at two levels: the sub-collection level – documents with a civil and religious status – and within the sub-collection. In the latter case, selection was imposed by the legal restrictions relating to privacy.[78]

Similar projects were carried out both by local heritage institutions with regard to local newspapers[79] and by the National Library, which undertook to digitise the most important daily newspapers

76 Author interview with Judith Moortgat, *Beelden voor de Toekomst* project leader at the National Archives (The Hague, 11 November 2009).

77 Author interview with Hanneke Vroegindeweij, project manager at the Eye Film Institute (Amsterdam, 2 November 2009).

78 Author interview with Ynze Alkema, Head Back Office at Breda City Archives, together with digitisation consultant Erika Hokke (Breda, 26 April 2010).

79 *E.g.*, the Rotterdam Municipal Archives has digitised 'all the issues of *Het Rotterdamsch Nieuwsblad* published between 1929 and 1946'. http://rjb.x-cago.com/kranten/index.do (Accessed 6 May 2010). Similarly, the Rijnstreek and Lopikerwaard Regional Historical Centre announced [on 7 May 2010] that 'Our newspaper [*Nieuwe Woerdensche Courant*] has been digitised from 1925 until 1985. It is integrally and fully searchable'.
http://woerden.courant.nu/?&mod=krantresultaat&sort=datum+asc%2Ckrant+asc%2Cpagina+asc&pagina=1&datering=%3E%3D07-05-1927 (Accessed 7 May 2010).

from 1618 to 1995.[80] In this project, selection took place at three levels. First, based on the time of publication: 1618–1995 was identified as the period to be considered. Second, within that period, *all* newspapers published between 1618 and 1800 were systematically digitised. Third, those published between 1800 and 1995 underwent a much stricter selection process, taking into account the criteria that I discuss later in this section.[81]

In addition to selection based on time or period, some digitisation projects employed a theme-based selection policy (De Haan *et al.*, 2006: 14). For instance, prior to the [September 2009] 400-year jubilee of the foundation by Dutch merchants of New Amsterdam, later [1664] re-named New York, the Breda City Archives, in partnership with *Metamorfoze* – which provided half of the funding –, systematically digitised *all* its documents on the *Vrede van Breda,* the 1667 Dutch-British-French-Danish Peace Treaty signed in that southern Netherlands city to end the Second Anglo-Dutch War. Among other things, the Treaty stipulated that the Dutch would exchange New Amsterdam for Suriname.[82] Although the official documents are in the respective national archives,[83] the 'small details' remained in Breda: restaurant bills, contracts with house-owners who rented out homes to accommodate delegations, butchers' receipts, *etc.* The same occurred with documents relating to the 1624–1625 Breda Siege by Spanish troops during the 80-Year War.[84]

The *William of Orange Correspondence* project carried out by the Huygens Institute of Netherlands History is another example of a theme-based selection approach.[85] The project 'aims to present a complete survey of *all* the surviving correspondence associated with William of Orange (1533-1584)' [italicisation is mine].[86] What is more, the project's policy is to digitise even the copies – including

---

80 The National Library, '*De belangrijkste Nederlandse kranten van 1618 tot 1995*'. http://kranten.kb.nl/ (Accessed 15 June 2010).

81 Author interview with Lammert Zwaagstra, project manager in charge of selection and copyright clearance at the National Library's Historical Newspaper Project (The Hague 24 June 2010).

82 *Stadsarchief Breda*, '*De Vrede van Breda*'. http://www.stadsarchief.breda.nl/index.php?option=com_content&view=article&id=87&Itemid=91 (Accessed 28 April 2010).

83 See for instance on the British National Archives' website: http://www.nationalarchives.gov.uk/catalogue/displaycataloguedetails.asp?CATLN=6&CATID=5509734&j=1 (Accessed 28 April 2010).

84 Author interview with Ynze Alkema, Head Back Office at Breda City Archives, together with his colleague Erika Hokke (Breda, 26 April 2010).

85 The project was initiated by the Institute of Netherlands History which merged on 1 January 2011 with the Huygens Institute to become the Huygens Institute of Netherlands History.

86 Huygens Institute of Netherlands History, 'The Correspondence of William of Orange 1549-1584'. http://www.inghist.nl/Onderzoek/Projecten/WVO/en (Accessed 28 April 2010).

born-copy or original-copy letters [William of Orange used to write one letter many times] and those that were written much later.[87] It is clear that the digitisers had no intention whatsoever of discarding a single item relating to William of Orange.

It should be stressed that the above-mentioned no-selection or time-/theme-based selection approaches are rather infrequent and that the majority of heritage institutions apply much stricter and narrow criteria when selecting objects eligible for digitisation. Fragility and age are among the most important selection criteria that guide digitisers, especially when they are dealing with special collections. Fragility implies that the physical object cannot be consulted for fear of causing irreparable damage (Hazen *et al.*, 1998: 5), or that the object is deteriorating due to acid-burning or other ink-related chemical damages (Schouten, 2009a: 12-13). As for age, it is all a question of time and, in general, the older the object, the higher its value (Hughes, 2005: 16). This suggests that old age is more likely to imply high historical value and fragility. The equation between age and fragility is certainly true for the Dutch audio and audiovisual heritage, where about half of all films aged more than 60 years [made before 1950] have already been lost forever due to decay, fire or other forms of damages (SNK, 2009: 17). However, the equation does not hold for paper-based heritage, as books from the 15th or 16th centuries are in a relatively better physical state than those published between the mid-19th and mid-20th centuries (Schouten, 2004: 433-434). In the latter period, poor quality paper was produced and used on a mass scale in the book industry. Dennis Schouten, who was involved both in *het Geheugen van Nederland* and *Metamorfoze*, spoke of '*gaten in de geschiedenis*' [lacunas in history], referring to the estimated 20 percent of books produced between mid-19th century and mid-20th century that have been lost forever.

A related criterion that also bridges preservation and access is 'patron use' (Conway, 1994: 43). Then State-Secretary Van der Ploeg (2002b: 23) spoke of the digitisation of 'top objects' [*topstukken*] from collections, which, in one sense, cold refer to the most popular or most frequently visited objects. In another sense, some of the 'top objects' may be so-called because of their historical or intellectual value, a concept that encapsulates many considerations that I shall discuss in the next few paragraphs. Digital preservation, therefore, 'can mean reduced handling of the original', thus ensuring its long-term survival (Bryant *et al.*, 2004: 16; see also Conway, 1994: 43; Hazen *et al.*, 1998: 5). In this respect, virtualisation, which is

87 Author interview with Ineke Huysman, ICT Coordinator in charge of digital resources disclosure at the Huygens Institute of Netherlands History (Amsterdam, 17 November 2009).

closely related to, and almost always linked with, digitisation (see for instance Bolter, 1991: 97-98; Gurian, 2004: 282; Cameron, 2008: 176; Roussou, 2008: 225-241; Van Asseldonk, 2009a: 14-15; Ronchi, 2009: 398), is 'a war against fragility, pain, wear' (Lévy, 1998: 99).

Some heritage institutions digitise on demand, that is, based on requests from their target-users or interested third parties. This demand-based criterion is at the heart of the Eye Film Institute's digitisation within the *Beelden voor de toekomst* project, which primarily targets pupils and teachers, alongside the creative industry and the general public.[88] The Institute selected secondary school teachers who dived into the collection and identified films that matched or illustrated course(s) they were teaching. Once that was done, the often 'lengthy' right-clearance process could begin, prior to initiating the digital conversion of selected films.[89] The Netherlands Institute for Sound and Vision [NIBG], another *Beelden voor de toekomst* partner, adhered to a similar, teacher-centred selection policy. Teachers from 30 participating secondary schools spent about one year designing and testing 'hundreds' of lesson modules that were put online in June 2010.[90]

Conway (1994: 43) added one more criterion: the potential for theft. It could be argued that every preserved cultural heritage material, ranging from a map in an incunabulum to a Rembrandt or a Christiaan Huygens' telescope is a good target for thieves, since preserving it is recognition of the fact that it is actually of some value. Once again, this is a bridge-forming criterion relating to preservation-access, in the sense that an object classified as a potential target for thieves is more likely to require increased protection, including restricted access. Digitising something thus leads to the removal of restrictions without exposing it to the risk of theft.

A few paragraphs earlier I mentioned historical and/or intellectual value as an encapsulating criterion for digitisation. This umbrella criterion implies that there is a need to communicate an object's value to a large audience. Although the October 2003 Charter on the

88 Emjay Rechsteiner [Eye Film Institute digitisation manager] and Frank Cardello, 'Bringing assets online in public-private partnership' (FIAT World Conference paper, Beijing, 22–26 October, 2009. Theme: 'A New World – A New Deal for Archives').

89 Author interview with Hanneke Vroegindeweij, project manager at the Eye Film Institute (Amsterdam, 02 November 2009).

90 LES 2.0, 'Home-LES 2.0'. http://www.les20.nl/ (Accessed 2 July 2010). This name, which translates as 'Lesson 2.0', suggests an analogy with Web 2.0, implying that the project aims to be interactive and user-centred, like Web 2.0. However, unlike Web 2.0, where contents are generated, edited, and re-edited by users regardless of their credentials or expertise, LES 2.0's contents undergo selection and packaging by people with the right credentials, namely teachers.

Preservation of Digital Heritage by the United Nations Educational, Scientific and Cultural Organization [UNESCO] does mention this criterion, it does nothing to reduce its vagueness:

> As with all documentary heritage, selection principles may vary between countries, although the main criteria for deciding what digital materials to keep would be their significance and lasting cultural, scientific, evidential or other value (UNESCO, 2003: art 7).

Admitting that selection is a complicated process, the six partners in the *Beelden voor de toekomst* project mainly used three criteria: the importance of the material, its physical condition and patron use (SNK 2009: 18). The importance of material is yet another term relating to value so it does nothing to help reduce the vagueness of the concept either. The Advisory Commission, which was comprised of historians and heritage professionals and was responsible for proposing the selection policy of the National Library's Historical Newspaper Project, also used this umbrella criterion – importance – for the daily newspapers dating from the 19th and 20th centuries. For each of the sub-periods [colonial period; 1813–1869; 1869–1914; 1914–1965; 1965–1995] the selected titles had to be of political, cultural, social, regional, and journalistic significance or importance.[91] Assessing the significance of the *Vlissingse Courant* in the 1813-1869 period, for instance, the Advisory Commission argued:

> The outlet is especially interesting for the period when Frederik van Sorge (1839 -1843) was editor, as well as for the earlier period because of the Belgian revolt which was extensively covered by the newspaper. The *Vlissingse Courant* was therefore added to the selection list for 1831–1843.[92]

A set of sub-criteria falling under this value/importance/significance umbrella-criterion can be distinguished based on the existing research and on digitisation experience. From an educational point of view, it could be interpreted as referring to educational or pedagogical potential. Nonetheless, the educational or pedagogical potential of heritage objects is an extremely relative concept, since 'All recorded information ... has value, even if temporary, or it would

91 Historical Newspaper Project, 'Minutes of the meeting of the Scientific Advisory Commission' (The Hague: The National Library, 13 April 2007). Project's internal document.

92 Historical Newspaper Project, 'Minutes of the meeting of the Scientific Advisory Commission' (The Hague: The National Library, 14 November 2007). Project's internal document.

not have been recorded ...' (Smith, 1999: 3). Heritage digitisation scholars agree that 'even the most marginal materials can support kinds of research' (Hazen *et al.*, 1998: 3), which turns this criterion into an institution-limited assessment.

Uniqueness is one sub-criterion that serves to measure value. Uniqueness is used here within the context of its double meaning, both as 'the only one in existence' (Feldman, 1997) and as 'the sediment of a specific and unique activity or transaction' (Ketelaar, 1997: 334). In the former sense, president Abraham Lincoln's hand-written draft of the 1863 Proclamation of Emancipation in the United States is a unique object,[93] because it is the only one ever to have ever existed. The final, printed version is unique in the other sense – since print implies multiplicity and reproducibility –,[94] because it embodies and is reminiscent of a unique historical event, namely the abolition of slavery in the United States. Along the same vein, Christiaan Huygens' telescope is unique not because it has no duplicate, but because it is the one through which the Dutch scientist was scrutinising the skies when he discovered Saturn's satellite Titan in 1665.[95]

Rarity is another important criterion that has often been cited. Rare objects are those 'rarely seen or special format materials such as maps or recordings' that are physically not easy to handle (Hughes, 2005: 32). The fact that they are rare makes them unique in the sense that they are [one of] the last surviving copy[ies]. This is the case in respect of the 1568-1572 *Biblia Polyglotta*, also known as *Biblia Regia*, which the Antwerp-based *Plantin-Moretus* Museum described as 'the most monumental work ever accomplished by one printer [Christopher Plantin] from the Netherlands'.[96] 1,100 copies of this eight-volume, five-language Bible were printed, which means that it was not the only copy in existence. However, few have survived, which gives this masterpiece the status of rare [unique] object.

In short, the above shows how the digitised cultural heritage objects that the history learners are likely to encounter while surfing the Web are mostly the result of a selection made by heritage institutions. The decision to make a selection is not made without reason,

---

93 Abraham Lincoln's hand-written draft of the Proclamation of Emancipation on the Library of Congress' American Memory website: http://memory.loc.gov/service/rbc/lprbscsm/scsm0231/001r.jpg (Accessed 28 April 2010).

94 Final printed version of the Proclamation of Emancipation: http://memory.loc.gov/service/rbc/lprbscsm/scsm0907/001r.jpg (Accessed 10 May 2010).

95 *Museum Boerhaave*, '*Telescoop van Huygens, 1683, Christiaan Huygens, Den Haag*'. http://www.museumboerhaave.nl/collectie/voorwerpen/telescoopHuygens.html (Accessed 28 April 2010).

96 Note on the showcase (20 April 2006).

but because it would be an insurmountable task both practically and financially to make digital surrogates for all cultural heritage objects. However, a few institutions, either due to the small size of their collections, or for some other practical reasons, employ no-selection policies or select based on wide-open criteria. Many institutions prefer criteria such as uniqueness, rarity, patron use, user-demand, potential for theft, and intellectual or historical value in order to make narrower selections. Each of these criteria represents a potential for history education but, as the next section shows, if that potential is to be translated into reality, certain essential post-digitisation steps will need to be taken.

3.3 Beyond Scanning: Enhancing Objects' Pedagogical Value

> To grasp the meaning of a thing, an event or a situation is to see it in its *relations* to other things: to note how it operates or functions, what consequences follow from it, what causes it, what uses it can be put to ... Since all knowing, including all scientific inquiry, aims at clothing things and events with meaning – at understanding them – it always proceeds by taking the thing inquired into out of its isolation. Search is continued until the thing is discovered to be a related part in some larger whole (Dewey, [1909] 1933: 137-138).

The two previous sections discussed two of the main steps in the digitisation process, namely the motives and policies underlying the process (Section 3.1) and the selection of objects to be digitised (Section 3.2). At this stage a few other steps follow, including the scanning and presentation or display of objects on a website. After these stages, objects begin a new life in cyberspace where, unlike their analogue counterparts, they can be accessed without the intermediation of heritage professionals. If they are to compete with the other contents of cyberspace and earn the attention of the Digital Generation that is surfing the Web in search of historical information, they will have to undergo some pedagogical value enhancement. In this section I want to review post-digitisation practices among mainly Dutch heritage institutions in order to understand if, and how, these organisations have striven to enhance the pedagogical value of digitised material. Using the scholarly and technical literature as well as interviews with heritage professionals and concrete examples, I shall focus on hyperlinking as one of the most important ways to make digitised material profitable for Digital Natives who are learning history. In the first place, I shall discuss hyperlinking as a contextualisation mechanism that is characteristic of the Web.

Then, based on how search engines bring online contents onto users' screens, I shall discuss hyperlinking as a method of optimising the visibility and findability of cultural heritage contents for potential students of history.

To begin with, History itself as a discipline has always been regarded as being link-based. Historians and philosophers of history alike – both classical and more recent ones – have all converged in reaching the same belief: that physical objects, events and processes all have invisible links connecting them to one another, thereby allowing one to make sense of them (Ranke [1821] 1973: 6, 10, 16; Gallie, 1964: 53-54; Nora, 1984: XVL; Lowenthal, 1985: 218). For these thinkers and scholars, 'The past is a vast chain, every link of which must be kept in good repair' (Howard, 1991: 16). In this respect, Caesar's crossing of the Rubicon is interesting only within the context of its relation to Republican law, and the spilling of his blood makes sense only when linked to the constitutional conflict that caused it (Collingwood, [1946] 1994: 213). Similarly, the history of the printing press makes little sense if it is not linked to 'a whole range of basic changes which were taking place at the time', including, for example, 'the invention of gunpowder and portable firearms' and the 'great sea voyages' (Fèbvre & Martin, [1958] 1984: 10). Other thinkers, including sociologist Bruno Latour ([1991] 1993: 79-80), argued that cross-disciplinary linking is essential for a better understanding of events or phenomena. Thus, a physicist interested in the vacuum pump should link it not only to its inventor, Robert Boyle [1627–1691], but also to the history of 17th-century England.

The Web, the backbone of which is hyperlinking (Hindman, 2009: 40), aims at making these links concrete and visible. This feature has prompted new habits and expectations among the users of digital/digitised cultural heritage collections (Van Mensch, 2009: 5), whether they are archival (Cox, 2004: 20; Van Diepen-Oost, 2000: 18), or museum collections (Cameron, 2010: 80). Beside being the backbone of the Web's architecture, hyperlinking, similarly to the linking process described in the previous paragraph, is, or should be, the cornerstone of historical contents in the cyberworld. For example, the British Museum's website presents the *Table Clock by Henry Jones* with an explanatory, three-paragraph, no-link text that begins as follows:

> Following the introduction of the *pendulum* by *Christiaan Huygens* in 1657, table or bracket-mounted, spring-driven clocks became a popular furniture item for those who could afford them [Italicisation is mine].[97]

This sentence establishes the link between two historical inventions – the Table Clock and the Pendulum Clock – though it does not make that link digitally concrete. The Table Clock could have been hyperlinked to the Pendulum Clock page on the Leiden-based *Boerhaave Museum*'s website.[98] In other words, the British Museum's website informs the user that the object has a context, an origin, but does not go on to provide that context or origin. Since understanding is reached when objects are viewed, not in isolation, but in relation to other objects (see epigraph), one can deduce that the meaning and implications of the Table Clock will not be fully grasped, especially not by digital history learners who expect the two inventions to be hyperlinked.[99] The result of this isolation could be considered anti-pedagogical in the digital age, because, as suggested by Cameron (2007: 58), objects need to be connected to their origins, to their past, to a chain of events. In other words, as argued by Rushkoff ([1996] 2006: 115), 'for objects to take on magical significance [for the screenagers] they must be connected to history and lineage'.

While the case mentioned above could be explained by the fact that the two institutions are physically located in different countries and therefore may not be aware of what is published on each other's website, in other cases institutions have failed to establish links within their own digital collections, thereby missing opportunities to enhance the pedagogical value of those collections. The *Comité des Sages* noted that, within the Hague-based pan-European digital cultural heritage portal *Europeana*, 'there should be a clear link between works that go back to the same original' (Lévy *et al.*: 2011: 23). They were referring to 'translations, adaptations or different

97 The British Museum, 'Table clock by Henry Jones'. http://www.britishmuseum.org/explore/highlights/highlight_objects/pe_mla/t/table_clock_by_henry_jones.aspx (Accessed 19 September 2008).

98 *Museum Boerhaave, 'Klok (Haags slingeruurwerk)'.* http://www.museumboerhaave.nl/AAcollection/nederlands/M03V20.html (Accessed 19 September 2008).

99 Considered from the historiographical perspective, the lack of a hyperlink between two closely related objects would be interpreted as half of the task a historian is supposed to complete in his or her investigation. According to 19th-century German historian Leopold von Ranke ([1821] 1973: 7), a historian must not only investigate events in a way that is as exact, impartial and critical as possible, but also connect the events explored: 'To follow only the first path [investigation] is to miss the essence of truth itself; to neglect this path, however, by overemphasizing the second [connecting] one is to risk falsification of truth in its details'.

editions of the same work' (*Ibid.*). The suggestion is that a translation, an adaptation or a new edition – one might even add an improvement or extension – makes more sense when considered alongside – or in comparison with – the original work, which applies perfectly in the case of the *Table Clock* and the *Pendulum Clock*.

In a recent essay Conway (2010: 369-370) explained that beyond preservation, remediation, and access, digitisers must also transcend originals in a way in which analogue media do not permit. In the same vein, new media theorists Jay Bolter and Richard Grusin (2000: 60) contended that each new medium justifies itself by filling a lacuna or repairing a fault in its predecessor. The Web does this by means of its 'intelligent tools and agents' which make it possible and easy to deliver contents not as raw information, but rather as 'information and knowledge fragments in a structured format' (Rincho, 2009: 398). Bolter and Grusin (2000: 56 & 59) conceptualised remediation – digitisation being remediation *par excellence* – as aiming to 'refashion', 'reform' or improve other media. Due especially to its numerical representation, its modularity, its automation, its variability, and its transcoding, this digital refashioning turns objects into computer data that can complete a variety of operations through various algorithms (Manovich, 2001: 27-48).

Despite being among the top digitisers in the world, Dutch cultural heritage institutions have not done much to appropriate these 'intelligent tools' that permit the presentation not only of objects but also of their contexts. In 2009 a few Dutch cultural heritage scholars and professionals completed a pilot project dubbed *Cultuur in Context* [Culture in Context] in which they wanted to test and subsequently propose a new model for presenting digital cultural heritage.[100] Between 2007 and 2008, nine institutions, including cultural heritage institutions, schools of heritage professionals, and university departments attempted to create an integrated, ontology-driven virtual public entertainment collection (Van Mensch, 2009: 5; Van Asseldonk, 2009a: 12; Brandsma, 2009: 56-57). The resulting database[101] presents, for each object, a web of related information that was obtained from the participating institutions.

A number of initiatives are emerging that are trying to reverse the situation on a large scale. For instance, 27 museums in the province of Gelderland have brought their digital collections together under the name '*Gelderland Collection*'.[102] 40,000 objects can be

100 Nancy van Asseldonk *et al.* (eds.) *Cultuur in Context: Erfgoeddata in nieuwe samenhang* (Amsterdam: *Reinwardt Academie*, 2009).

101 *Cultuur in Context:* http://cultuurcontext.dpc.uba.uva.nl/ (Accessed 29 April 2010).

102 *Collectie Gelderland*: http://www.collectiegelderland.nl/ (Accessed 01 May 2010).

accessed through simple browsing, searching, or via a timeline or map. Timelines and maps function as *contextualisers*, as objects and stories behind them are grouped and connected depending on the periods or places with which they are associated. The result is that objects are not viewed or considered in isolation, but in relation to others. In all probability, this emerging trend is what inspired the March 2010 advisory report of the Council for Culture entitled *Netwerken van betekenis: Netwerktaken in digitale cultuur en media* [Networks of meanings: Networking tasks in digital culture and media]. Intended for the Ministry of Education, Culture and Science, the report estimated that the time was ripe for 'new strategies on the part of both the government and [heritage] institutions' (*Raad voor Cultuur*, 2010 3). More specifically, the Council gave a number of hints about those strategies: 'digitisation makes new forms of relations possible and changes existing links'; 'the digital culture requires reorientation of the actors [including users] in the cultural sense-making chain' (*Ibid.*).

Apart from its contextualising, pedagogical function for historical or heritage contents, hyperlinking fulfils another equally important function in terms of making contents easy to find, especially for Digital Natives. According to theorists, Digital Natives' research begins not with a trip [virtual or physical] to a library or any other heritage institution, but with 'a Google search ... They simply open a browser, punch in a search term, and dive away until they find what they want – what they thought they wanted' (Palfrey & Gasser, 2008: 6). The technical literature on how search engines work suggests that hyperlinks play a much bigger role than traditional metadata systems. Search engine experts Sarah Milstein and Rael Dornfest (2004: 3 & 218), in their book *Google*, claimed that Google ranks Web pages first by looking at links (see also Rushkoff, [1996] 2006: 131; Batelle, 2005: 21; Hindman, 2009: 40 & 42; Van Dijck, 2010: 577), which is also true for Yahoo!, Lycos and other search engines (Introna & Nissenbaum, 2000a: 55-57).

Journalist and author John Batelle (2005: 20-21) – whose book *The Search* extensively details how search engines work – summarised the process that Google's search engines go through in order to index contents as follows: the search engine's crawler or robot 'takes note of any *links* it has found on the page, and queues those *links* in its request file – sending out yet more requests to the newly found *links*, which find more *links* ... and so on, ad infinitum' [italicisation is mine]. Based on the returned and analysed links, Google's PageRank algorithm orders websites and pages in such a way that those deemed more important or popular rise to the top, while less popular ones are pushed down toward the bottom.[103] Therefore, a webpage without a single hyperlink referring to it would be unlikely to be found by search engines,[104] which was the conclusion the *Comité des Sages* reached, as to why it remained difficult to find *Europeana* objects online:

> ... the Comité notes that currently the websites of many cultural institutions which contribute content to Europeana *do not link to the site*. Such a link from the homepage of the website of cultural institutions is a minimum that can be expected. The Comité notes that currently *Europeana search results do not show up in searches in main search engines*. Europeana should continue its talks with the search engines in order to rapidly overcome the barriers that are at the origin of this issue, since accessibility through the search engines will generate considerable supplementary traffic (Lévy *et al.*: 2011: 24-25. Italicisation is mine).

From the perspective of carrying out a Web search, thus, hyperlinks serve as the entrance into a website's database – *i.e.*, without them the site's contents remain 'invisible' or not easy to find (see Introna & Nissenbaum, 2000a: 58) in the cyberworld –, while metadata, which traditionally facilitated search operations, tell Google or any other search engine what the found object is about. The assumption here is that the crawlers first enter the site via hyperlinks before checking what metadata have to say about the objects. One can then deduce that the link between the lack of hyperlinking and the poor search results has been established, and that heritage institutions still have a long way to go if their digital contents are to make it onto the computer screens of Digital Natives.

Thus far, hyperlinking has been presented as a pedagogical tool both in terms of object contextualisation and findability. As such, it appears to be an essential post-digitisation step that could make heritage contents more competitive on the computer screens of Digital Natives. The question worth asking at this stage relates to the rea-

---

103 Named after Larry Page, the co-founder of Google together with Sergey Brin, PageRank takes into account not only 'the number of links into a particular website', but also 'the number of links into each of the linking site' (Batelle, 2005: 75). In other words, a website is deemed 'important' or 'popular' when the sites that link into it are, in their turn, also intensely linked into.

104 In his analysis of political site visibility in the United States, political scientist Matthew Hindman (2009: 55; see also Van Dijck, 2010: 577) introduced the concept of *Googlearchy* to refer to 'the rule of the most heavily linked'. The main principle underlying this rule is that 'the number of links pointing to a site is the *most important* determinant of a site visibility' [Italicisation is mine], which implies that the more the links to a site, the greater its visibility and reversely: non-linked sites require time and skills to discover.

sons why heritage institutions have not embraced hyperlinking. The first reason has to do with the nature of collection-managing activities, which seem to have remained static even after collections went online. The tasks of curators and other heritage professionals have traditionally included selecting and preserving objects, as well as making the preserved objects available. Seen from this perspective, it is clearly up to the exhibition organisers, historians, and any other users or visitors to form their own interpretations and connections in relation to objects that have been made available by heritage professionals.

In the digital era, the above-described vision has consequences for the digitisation budgeting, which does not include hyperlinking in the post-scanning process. Hyperlinking is engaging with contents and interpreting objects, which was not traditionally a task of heritage professionals. For this reason, no budget has been requested or designated for this task, which seems not to have been allocated as anyone's responsibility or field of activity. For example, in the early 2000s, the National Library of the Netherlands, one of the most important digitisers, invested a great deal in making objects available on a large scale but refrained from delving in-depth into the contents of objects (Velthausz & Bruinsma, 2002: 32-33), and thus lacked knowledge as to which parts of the contents needed contextualising or provided a context for other objects. The institution spent 30 percent of the digitisation budget on actual digitisation [scanning, photographing, *etc.*], 25 percent on metadata, 30 percent on making objects available and 15 percent on their management (*Ibid.*: 48). Clearly, the budgeting had not explicitly taken into account the pedagogical organisation of contents, by for instance including cross-linking. Film historian Karel Dibbets maintained that during the digitisation fever, millions of euros were 'blindly spent for the short term', because placing quantities of pictures on the Web did not mean necessarily 'opening up the collection'. To open up collections, digitisers would have to do more than simply provide 'primitive' metadata based on images. They would have to provide contexts based on text.[105]

The second reason relates to the notion of the unique identity of institutions. In one sense, hyperlinking is a form of renouncing to one's identity and uniqueness, since linking to someone else's contents means permitting external stories to become intermingled with the in-house narratives behind individual objects. The case of the 'Gelderland Collection' cited above is a clear instance of how

105 Nancy van Asseldonk, '*Interview met Karel Dibbets over de zoektocht naar ontbrekende kennis*', in Asseldonk, Nancy van *et al.* (eds.) *Cultuur in Context: Erfgoeddata in nieuwe samenhang* (Amsterdam: *Reinwardt Academie*, 2009c: 42-53), p. 46.

hyperlinking means an end to the monopolistic approach to interpretation. According to the Council for Culture, the identity-related policies of institutions needed to be rethought and redefined in order to take into account the now inescapable networking aspect:

> Institutions are being asked to formulate their core tasks in direct relation with their networking tasks, so that meaning-making can take place both 'in-house' and within social cultural networks of which they are a part. For instance, one archive may have no ambition to present itself to a [given] public, but in that case, it should keep its collections open for parties that want to do this with their own collection (*Raad voor Cultuur*, 2010: 4-5).

In the digital era, the identity of an institution forms a substantial obstacle to its full participation in networked environments as advocated by the Council and other voices. Networking means, among other things, that collections and objects would have to be networked, and that will happen only through trans-institutional hyperlinking.[106] Dibbets (2006: 190-191) blamed the lack of collaboration and the fear of cross-fertilisation that would result from it on the 'government's contradictory policy'. On the one hand, institutions were being urged to collaborate and crosslink their collections, while on the other hand, they were being assessed and subsidised on the basis of individually achieved results. Dibbets wondered: 'Why would you invest in collaboration when you are only judged on your own achievements?' The consequence is that institutions' websites strive to get as many visitors as possible and do all they can to keep them inside that restricted environment.

A related question could be: why would one 'chase' visitors away from one's website by showing them the exit, *i.e.*, a hyperlink to another website? This reasoning is part of what Web epistemologist Richard Rogers (2004: 9-14) termed 'front-end information politics', which can be defined as the conscious decisions taken by website owners to prevent certain actions and practices – usually basic ones like adding in- or outlinks – or to orient them in one particular

106 Researching the 'politics of association' implemented by climate change websites in the run-up to the 1997 Kyoto meeting, researchers perceived 'linking as a form of networking' and distinguished five sorts of networking: 1- *social networking*: linking to friends and acquaintances; 2- *reputational networking*: linking to authoritative bodies; 3- *self-referential networking*: linking to their own kind only; 4- *aspirational networking*: linking to potential funders; and 5- *critical networking*: linking to targets (Rogers, 2004: vii). None of these networking sorts has been fully implemented at the level of collections (as opposed to the personal level, via social media [see Section 3.4]) of heritage institutions.

and limited way.[107] Experts in search engines suggest that cyberspace works differently. The more a website links to external websites, the more visibility it gets on search engines and the more visitors it attracts:[108]

> ... provide new links whenever you can. While some Web sites believe that every link provided to other Web sites offers another reason for visitors to leave, in practice the opposite is true. If your site is a rich resource for what's happening on the Web, your readers will come to see you as a trusted friend, putting you on their virtual speed-dial and visiting you more frequently (Milstein & Dornfest, 2004: 227).

These identity-preservation attitudes are much more the result of institutions' management, whose corporate interests reside in striving to remain unique as long as possible. Although heritage professionals at various levels of the leadership or management ladder may have different visions, in the last analysis, it is from top managers, policy-makers, and subsidy-givers at government level that change is to be expected.

The third reason for avoiding hyperlinking is a dilemma, an impasse between on the one hand using new ways of structuring and presenting knowledge and, on the other hand, using tax-payer's money. Cor den Ridder of the educational department of the *Geheugen van Nederland*, said, for instance, that he could not link to relevant sources on third parties' websites, because, by doing so, he would be misusing tax-payers' money to help those parties generate traffic for their website along with all the financial profits [*e.g.*, through advertisement] that this involves.[109] Linking to another site contributes to improving its ranking with Google, which crawling robots determine after checking the number of pages pointing to the site or any of its pages (Milstein & Dornfest, 2004: 226). In this sense, then, hyperlinking is a profit-generating business and it would be wrong to use tax-payers' money in this way. According

107 Richards Rogers (2004: 3-9) further conceptualised 'information politics' from the 'back-end' perspective. 'Back-end information politics' consists of the forces and factors or the 'maneuverings' that come into play on the part of search companies to rank and display some sources as more authoritative and trustworthy than others, without any editorial process.

108 In Part Two, I consider, among other things, the sources pupils use for their history class assignments. Pupils use Web resources *en masse*, though seldom those of cultural memory websites. This may be attributed to, among other things, the no-linking policy, which makes these websites 'invisible' or uninteresting for Google. Those responsible for opening up digitised collections need to understand that traffic on the Web is heavily directed by search engines (Hindman, 2009: 68) and that cultural heritage collections should not form an exception.

109 Author interview with Cor den Ridder, *het Geheugen van Nederland*'s education coordinator (11 November 2009).

to this way of reasoning, it would even be impossible for two government-funded educational projects, with two different [business] plans, to include links to one another. For instance, Den Ridder could not link to LES 2.0, because the latter project has to generate income in order to earn back part of the government's initial investment.[110]

If this kind of multi-directional, cross-institutional linking is not easy among heritage institutions – because of the budgeting and identity issues as well as the tax-money impasse – then it would be even more impossible to envisage large-scale cross-linking with openly commercial sites such as news organisations, which also have relevant context-enriching archives that could be helpful to digital learners of history. News outlets are even more interesting because their role involves reporting news and certain aspects of new discoveries are sometimes related to old objects. Such relationships also often provide a way of reinterpreting and rejuvenating those objects by taking present-day developments into account. For instance, the website of the *Marechaussee* Museum in Buren, which presents pictures and text about its forensic youth laboratory,[111] could have included a link to the 'latest' invention [April 2010] of the museum's partner, the Dutch Forensic Institute, that was reported by a commercial TV channel.[112] The Institute invented the so-called *CSI The Hague*, a sensor-equipped helmet that can digitally scan crime scenes, which, if connected to the *Marechaussee* Museum's laboratory, could trigger new interpretations and a new understanding of preserved objects. It should be pointed out, however, that some heritage institutions have been linking to external resources, including news outlets' websites. For instance, the website of the *Kranenburgh* Museum[113] in Bergen contains links to reports from RTV-NH [North-Holland provincial radio and television channel], while the *Letterkundig* Museum [Literature Museum] in The Hague includes

---

110 Author interview with Paul Vermeulen, Coordinator of *Beelden voor de toekomst*'s educational section [LES 2.0] (Hilversum, 10 November 2009).

111 *Marechaussee* Museum's *Jeugdlaboratorium*: http://www.marechausseemuseum.nl/?show=page&id=15 (Accessed 29 April 2010).

112 RTL4, '*Het NFI presenteert: CSI The Hague*' (4 April 2010). http://www.rtl.nl/%28/actueel/rtlnieuws/binnenland/%29/components/actueel/rtlnieuws/2010/04_april/19/binnenland/NFI_presenteert_CSI_The_Hague.xml (Accessed 29 April 2010).

113 Museum *Kranenburgh*, '*Educatie*'. http://www.museumkranenburgh.nl/kranenburgh-educatie.html (Accessed 22 May 2010).

a link to the VPRO [public broadcaster] on its page on early 20th-century poet Gerrit Achterberg.[114]

Hyperlinking emerges from this section as a pedagogical tool that neither the heritage sector nor its educational counterpart could have dreamed of in the pre-Web era. It is thanks to hyperlinking that linking of historical figures, events, and processes, which used to take place verbally via only narrative, now takes place [or should take place] both verbally and digitally. This way of presenting heritage objects and their contexts simultaneously regardless of their location on the globe has huge implications for digital learners of history. On the one hand, they are empowered to find out for themselves, without any intermediary, the meaning of the various heritage objects and, on the other hand, they have an opportunity to encounter valuable heritage objects on the Web easily, since hyperlinking increases visibility in cyberspace. However, it seems that Digital Natives are being denied the chance of enjoying digitised cultural objects to the full while learning history. In the first place, it is not easy to find these objects because poor hyperlinking renders them invisible in search engines: and even if objects are found, they are isolated from their contexts. All this has largely been attributed to budgeting policies, to the policies of institutions and what they define as core corporate interests, but also to the much more complex issue of public money and its use in a networked knowledge society.

3.4 Taking Digital Heritage Into Web 2.0

> We've all had teachers who made a difference in our lives. But when teachers do great work and give wonderful lessons, they are only helping their 20 or 30 students. In the future, teachers will share their work with other schools across the country and around the world (Gates, [1995] 2008: 24).

The digitisation of cultural heritage collections in the Netherlands has witnessed two major phases in terms of intensity: the digitisation fever that started in the late-1990s and a phase that might be referred to as the 'What next?' phase which started around 2009. The decade of digitisation fever focused on getting digital surrogates for as many objects as possible, often to the detriment of quality and the efficient internal organisation of digitised objects (Dibbets, 2006: 197). Halfway through that decade, the Web entered a new era in its history, the Web 2.0 era, by integrating advanced interactive features

114 *Letterkundig* Museum, 'Gerrit Achterberg'. http://www.letterkundigmuseum.nl/tabid/92/BiographyID/12/BiographyName/GerritAchterberg/Mode/BiographyDetails/Default.aspx (Accessed 22 May 2010).

that, among other things, made it possible for previously passive users to create and share online contents. Since the Digital Generation has been described as wanting to have more choices and more control over contents, it has proven worthwhile to look into the ways in which cultural heritage institutions have created room for direct interaction with digitised materials. Informed mainly by the Web 2.0 and digital heritage literature, as well as interviews and institutions' documents and communications, this section focuses on what I call the 'What next?' period, first by considering the gradual integration of social networking media into the digital heritage environments. It is important to understand this, because this is the place where Digital Natives, who are important users of these media, are likely to come across digitised heritage objects or information about them. I shall then look into attempts that have been made to empower users – mainly teachers and pupils – to become content-generators by using digitised heritage objects as raw materials. At the end, I review the fears and uncertainties that mark this period.

Towards the end of the first decade of the 21st century, Social Media [SM] had already proven to be an efficient means of communication for getting large numbers of people together online and forming communities. Heritage institutions gradually joined the process not only by communicating via that channel, but also by making parts of their collections available there. The National Archives, for instance, has an account on the Yahoo!-owned photo-sharing website *Flickr*, where over a thousand pictures had been posted by May 2010.[115] A similar number of pictures from the same institution could be found on Wikimedia Commons,[116] a volunteer-steered website serving as 'a media file repository making available public domain and freely-licensed educational media content (images, sound, and video clips) to everyone', and using 'the same wiki-technology as Wikipedia'.[117] According to the National Archives' director, Martin Berendse, putting as many pictures as possible on *Flickr* [and similar sites] is a way of promoting the institution and its collection.[118] Between October 2008 and October 2010, the [then] 1,300 National Archives' pictures on *Flickr* attracted 3 million visi-

115 *Nationaal Archief*'s Flickr account: http://www.flickr.com/photos/nationaalarchief/ (Accessed 4 May 2010).

116 Wikimedia Commons, 'Images from *Nationaal Archief*'. http://commons.wikimedia.org/w/index.php?title=Category:Images_from_Nationaal_Archief&oldid=43585619 (Accessed 16 September 2010).

117 Wikimedia Commons, 'What is Wikimedia Commons?' http://commons.wikimedia.org/wiki/Commons:Welcome (Accessed 16 September 2010).

118 Author conversation with Martin Berendse, director of the Netherlands' National Archives (The Hague, 31 August 2010).

tors and, partly as a result of that, the National Archives' website recorded a considerable increase in traffic.[119]

Other institutions, such as the *Nederlands Vestingmuseum* in Naarden, or the *Openluchtmuseum* in Arnhem,[120] have accounts on Twitter – a short-messaging or micro-blogging SM – where they communicate with users about the collections and activities around them. Yet others, like the Museum for Communication in The Hague or the *Natuurmuseum Fryslân* in Leeuwarden, have YouTube accounts to show moving images of, or about, their collections and to trigger reactions from users.[121] Many others have accounts on Facebook, LinkedIn, Hyves, Ning or other networking websites. The table below provides a picture of SM use among museums and archives:[122]

Table 3.2: Uses of Social Media by museums and archives in May 2010.

MUSEUMS				ARCHIVES			
Have website	Have SM account(s)	Link to SM	No SM account(s)	Have website	Have SM account(s)	Link to SM	No SM account(s)
553 (out of 569)	58	14	481	103 (out of 265)	11	2	90
97.1%	10.4%	2.5%	86.7%	38.8%	10.6%	1.9%	87.3%

In Table 3.2, the 'Have SM account(s)' columns list those institutions that have their own accounts or channels on one or more of the Social Media platforms, while the 'Link to SM' columns list institutions that do not have an account of their own but imbed, or provide links to, materials from Social Media platforms.[123] The

119 The National Archives' Tim de Haan announced this during the 12 November 2010 'MuseumFuture! Connect' conference in Zeist, the Netherlands. He clarified the relationship between the *Flickr* venture and the traffic on the website in a short talk we had after a workshop hosted by the National Archives.

120 *Nederlands Vestingmuseum*'s Twitter account: http://twitter.com/Vestingmuseum ; *Openluchtmuseum*'s Twitter account: http://twitter.com/Openluchtmuseum (Both accessed 4 May 2010).

121 Museum for Communication's YouTube account: YouTube: http://www.youtube.com/museumcommunicatie ; *Natuurmuseum Fryslân*'s YouTube account: http://www.youtube.com/user/NatuurmuseumFryslan (Both accessed 4 May 2010).

122 These figures are based on surveys I conducted in April–May 2010 on the websites of museums and archives listed by the *Stichting de Museumserver*, http://www.museumserver.nl and ArchievenWO2, http://www.archievenwo2.nl, respectively.

123 For instance, *Historisch Archief Westland*'s website – http://www.historischarchiefwestland.nl/Smartsite.shtml?id=105151 – links to YouTube channels of users called '*kunstgebouw*' [http://www.youtube.com/user/kunstgebouw], '*maanmist*' [http://www.youtube.com/user/maanmist], '*jeansmovies*' [http://www.youtube.com/watch?v=Qjbz8O1NTiQ&feature=player_embedded] , among others (All websites accessed 27 September 2010).

advantage of this new communication approach between heritage institutions and their audiences is revealing in at least four respects. Firstly, these institutions have understood that their mission has undergone a shift: they are moving from their previous position of passive object-keepers who patiently wait for equally passive users, to a more offensive position that takes them to the most popular venues in cyberspace.

Secondly, they have understood that the user is no longer a passive viewer of objects, but a partner in assigning meanings to objects. This happens on photo-sharing sites like *Flickr*, on video-sharing sites like YouTube and Vimeo, whose tagging or key word-assigning systems are open to any logged-in user. On its *Flickr* account, for instance, the National Archives, which takes current events into account when updating its homepage,[124] invites users in a text below each picture, to become active in the meaning-assigning process:

> You can help us enrich the knowledge about photo collections by adding your tags and comments. If you recognise people or locations or if you have a special story to tell about one of the pictures, please write a comment [if you are logged in onto Flickr] or send us an e-mail: flickrthecommons@nationaalarchief.nl.[125]

This approach has at least two immediate implications: [1] By adding tags, users help create automatic links between all related pictures with the same tag, both within the same collection and within the *Flickr* database. As a result, one particular picture will call up a related one, regardless of its origin (see Bruns, 2009: 178; Shirky, 2008: 32-33; O'Reilly, 2005). In other words, calling upon users to tag and comment on pictures is gaining recourse to the Web 2.0 phenomenon known as 'distributed intelligence' (Anderson, 2006: 108), as crowds act as taggers. Users are therefore engaged in what

---

124 For instance, prior to the 4th and 5th May [2010] celebrations – tribute to the World War II dead and Liberation Day – the homepage showed the pictures relating to the Liberation 65 years ago, including people celebrating in the streets, soldiers triumphantly returning home, Allied war planes, *etc.*

125 E.*g*.: '*Aankomst van Sinterklaas in Amsterdam / Saint Nicholas arrives in Amsterdam*' http://www.flickr.com/photos/nationaalarchief/5220482243/in/set-72157625499989868/ (Accessed 4 May 2010).

new media scholar Axel Bruns (2009: 173) called 'produsage',[126] as they both *use* objects and *produce* new 'knowledge structures' by, for example, assigning them with descriptive key words or tags. [2] Users are likely to form *photo communities*, as often happens with pictures on *Flickr* (*e.g.*: Shirky, 2008: 36; see also Van Dijck, 2009: 45). The Council for Culture commented that this way of producing meaning through user-participation adds considerable value to collections (*Raad voor Cultuur*, 2010: 11). In the end, then, the task is shared between users and heritage professionals and the absolute distinction between the two ceases to exist (Lévy, 2010:109; see also Anderson, 2006: 78; Buckingham, 2007: 170; Deuze, 2007: 77; *Raad voor Cultuur*, 2010: 4).

The above could also be viewed from the perspective of what author and journalist Jeff Howe (2009) has termed *crowdsourcing*. Originating from the open-source movement, crowdsourcing is usually used by commercial companies that take advantage of Web 2.0 technologies by inviting the public 'to perform tasks, usually for little or no money, that were once the sole province of employees' (Howe, 2009: 8). The central idea behind the concept is two-fold: on the one hand, it is believed that 'the crowd will almost always outperform any number of employees', if given the right conditions (*Ibid.:* 11); on the other hand, collaboration, rather than financial incentive, becomes 'its own reward' (*Ibid.*: 15). Since indexing and writing object-related accounts, which were previously the sole province of heritage professionals, are now gradually being done by the crowd, one could even conclude that heritage institutions are actually integrating crowdsourcing by placing objects on SM sites.

Thirdly, institutions are increasing the chance of being 'discovered' by the Digital Generation – who highly figure as users of SM sites (Harwood & Asal, 2007: 162-163; Keen, 2007: 157; boyd, 2008; Palfrey & Gasser, 2008: 21-23) –, as these SM sites are generally better ranked by Google and other search engines [used by pupils] than the institutions' websites. Fourthly, through social media, institutions are fostering polysemy, multiple/hyper-narrativism and multi-layering around their objects. On the Twitter page of

---

126 José van Dijck (2009: 46-47) has criticised theories on 'produsage' and other hybrid terms such us 'co-creation' and 'prosumption', for only stressing the opposition between consumption and production of media contents and failing to take into account the powerful market forces [advertising for instance] underlying the process. Van Dijck argued that before a user can make any contribution [tagging, ranking, commenting, forwarding via social networking sites, *etc.*], he or she has first to open an account whereby a profile with many private details, including consumption habits, are provided to platform owners. The latter (can) use these details for niche or targeted marketing or advertisement. Therefore, Van Dijck (2009: 49) concluded, 'the user's role as data provider is infinitely more important than his role as content provider'.

Figure 3.2: Exchange on Tresoar's Twitter page (Screenshot: 22 April 2010).

the Leeuwarden-based *Tresoar* – the Frisian Historical and Literary Centre – for instance,[127] three postings dated 22 April 2010 came in during a 7-minute interval in relation to a single news event, namely the handing over of a 200-year-old manuscript of *Voyage pittoresque dans la Frise* (1837) by P.J. Gauthier-Stirum [1784–1851], a French civil servant in Friesland [1810–1813] during the French annexation of the Low Countries (see Figure 3.2).

One posting came from user '@GPTVfriesland' [TV station] who announced in English: 'I uploaded a YouTube video' on the manuscript with a YouTube link to the video.[128] It was a report showing the handing-over ceremony, with excerpts from speeches, shots of the manuscript itself and an interview with the museum director announcing the speedy digitisation of the manuscript, all accompanied by some background information. The second user, '@ omrop_fryslan' [TV-radio station], offered a link to a short article in the Frisian language[129] which linked back to the museum.[130] The third, '@wijdenzijd', [a local weekly], provided a link to a longer article[131] that focused much more on the contents of the manuscript

127 *Tresoar*'s Twitter account: http://twitter.com/TRESOARfryslan (Accessed 5 May 2010).
128 YouTube, '*GPTV: Pronkstuk voor Tresoar*'. http://www.youtube.com/watch?v=HMroRJXArGs&feature=youtu.be&a (Accessed 12 May 2010).
129 Omrop Fryslan, '*Aldste tekening aaisiker*' , 21 April 2010. http://www1.omropfryslan.nl/Mear_Nijs_68855.aspx?R=A148529 (Accessed 12 May 2010).
130 This is a good illustration of cross-sectorial hyperlinking.
131 *Wijd & Zijd*, '*200 jaar oud handschrift Sneker ambtenaar naar Tresoar*', 20 April 2010. http://www.wijd-en-zijd.nl/profile/redactie/article165154.ece/leeuwarden_%E2%80%93_200_jaar_oud_handschrift_sneker_ambtenaar_naar_tresoar (Accessed 12 May 2010).

than on the ceremony. The journalist pointed out that the manuscript contains ten drawings that were left out in the published version and informed readers that the text is not a travelogue but rather a work on popular culture of Friesland, its clothing habits, its mores and so on.

Each user – in this case, each journalist – came in with a different narrative, constructed from a different perspective, with different sources and interviews. It could be said that in this case, Tresoar's Twitter account served as a meeting point for the heritage institution and TV stations and Web-based newspapers, each providing inputs and new layers to the cultural heritage object in question. Digital Natives who come across this exchange – provided that there is a link to the digitised object's page – will have access to the multiple choices and perspectives towards which they are claimed to be inclined: they could choose to quote from the news articles, or to imbed the YouTube clip, or to download and edit it, or to use it in a remix, to name a few of the many possibilities. This trend is likely to increase as it involves no substantial financial investment and costs little effort, while it generates more visibility and publicity for collections and favours new ways of approaching cultural heritage objects (see Bakker & Bakker, 2011: 19).

Beside messaging, photo-sharing and video-sharing SM, some heritage institutions have devised others ways to integrate users' narratives. While the Hermitage Museum in Amsterdam was still [by April 2010] inviting users to send in their own stories by e-mail,[132] the Historical Museum in Ede was offering a reaction field under the picture of each object, where users could write their story, send pictures and suggest links to other resources.[133] The heritage professional's account and those of users find themselves side by side in a database and form what Manovich (2010: 69-70; see also Cameron & Robinson, 2007: 168) has termed 'hyper-narratives', which implies that 'a number of database records [are] linked together so that more than one trajectory is possible'. In this perspective, this implies that since heritage institutions – through their websites – have become computer databases (Manovich, 2001: 214), the heritage professional's narrative on the website of the Historical Museum in Ede is one record in the database, linked to the users' narratives – which form other fully-fledged database records on their own. Once again,

132 Hermitage Amsterdam, '*Uw verhaal*'. http://www.hermitage.nl/nl/vertel_uw_verhaal.htm (Accessed 30 April 2010).

133 See for instance this page on the website of the Historical Museum Ede: http://www.historischmuseumede.nl/?q=comment/reply/147#comment-form (Accessed 30 April 2010).

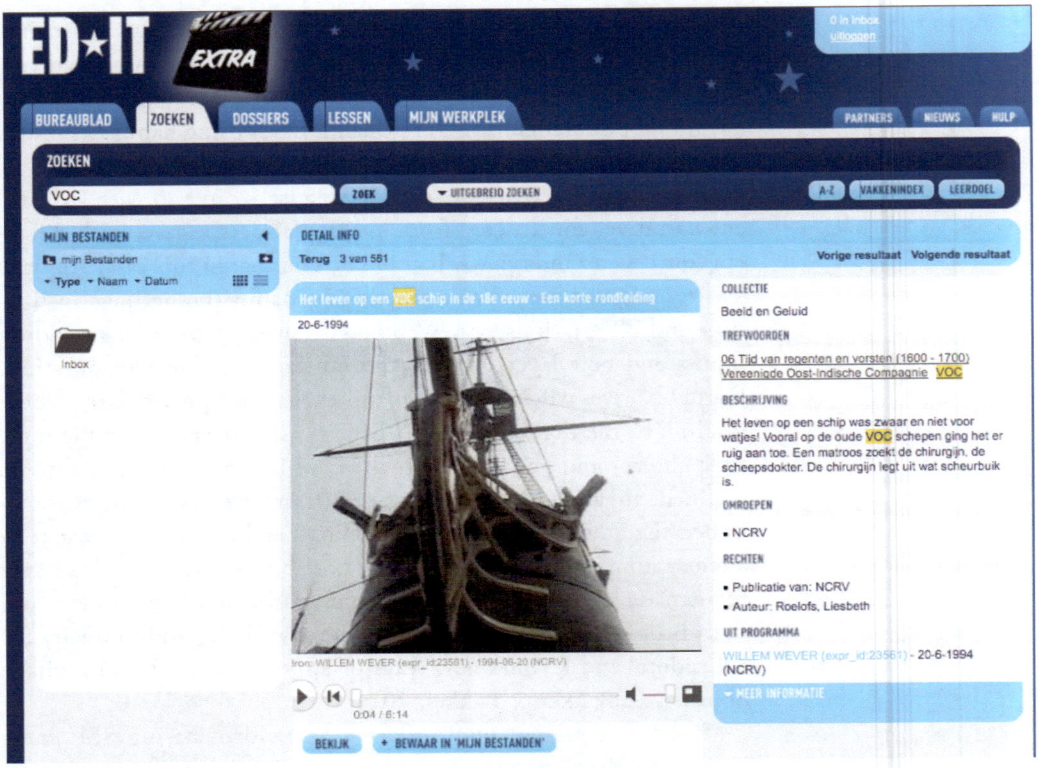

*Figure 3.3: Example of TV archive material that is available in ED*IT and is editable/remixable at will (Screenshot: 19 October 2010).*

the multiple-choice Digital Native is being offered a chance to explore more than one narrative.

Web 2.0 has also prompted a few heritage institutions to get users more involved in content-generation based on digitised materials and in sharing them online. In 2009 the *Geheugen van Nederland*, which in the early 2000s had unsuccessfully developed more than 30 educational modules that later proved to be disconnected from the curricular key targets,[134] came up with a Web-lesson-making tool that could be used by interested teachers and other education professionals to produce more flexible, editable educational modules.[135] A similar but much larger undertaking started in 2009 within the framework of the above-mentioned *Beelden voor de toekomst* project. The project described itself as a 'monster operation' (SNK, 2009:

134 Author interview with Cor den Ridder, *het Geheugen van Nederland*'s Education Coordinator (The Hague, 10 March 2009).

135 *Het Geheugen van Nederland*, '*Weblessen*'. http://weblessentool.geheugenvannederland.nl/index.php/home/ (Accessed 3 May 2010). 30 lessons were accessible at the time the page was last accessed.

14) because of the 'dizzying numbers' of materials it had to produce between 2007 and 2014 (*Ibid.*: 11). As mentioned above, six institutions entered into a partnership in order to achieve this.

Under the working name of LES 2.0 [Lesson 2.0] – a name that suggests an analogy with Web 2.0 and the user-centred, interactive features that go with it – the educational part of the project had two aims: firstly, to recruit and train 50 teachers, 15 of whom would be history teachers, whose task would then be to select relevant audio/visual materials, and arrange them, once they have been digitised, into curriculum-tailored Web-lessons. Launched in the summer 2009, the educational project started piloting completed modules in schools later that year.[136]

Secondly, unlike the *Geheugen van Nederland* project, which provided only a Web-lesson-making tool, LES 2.0 presents an entire environment or platform that serves to retrieve, edit, remix, and display materials. Known as ED*IT (see Figure 3.3), this environment also provides access to the collections of other institutions outside the six above-mentioned partners,[137] and make it possible for users to import materials from photo-sharing and video-sharing sites and any other websites. The resulting lesson packages or personal works are saved within the ED*IT environment, which has been made accessible to all schools since September 2009, though schools are first required to subscribe (SNK, 2009: 25-26).

While this approach undoubtedly greatly empowers both teachers and pupils and encourages them to be creative, the platform itself presents one major disadvantage: Nothing is possible with a computer that is not connected to the Web, or outside the ED*IT environment. All works, in progress or finished, can only be saved on LES 2.0 servers, not on a hard drive, nor on any other portable devices. The everyday experience of teachers reveals that they become very frustrated whenever the Internet connection fails during lesson.[138] Moreover, pupils are unable to display their finished works on their own websites or share them on their SM profile pages. In other words, though the project enables pupils to be 'cultural pro-

136 Author interview with Paul Vermeulen, Coordinator of *Beelden voor de toekomst's* educational section [LES 2.0] (Hilversum, 10 November 2009).

137 The project's April 2011 newsletter announced, for instance, that about 55,000 sources from the Amsterdam Museum, formerly called the Amsterdam Historical Museum, were going to be accessible within the ED*IT environment, beside those from the institutions partner to the Image for the Future project.

138 History teacher Antheun Janse [*Baarnsch Lyceum* in Baarn] frequently used video material from the Canon of the Netherlands, but was often interrupted by disruptions due to poor connections during classes. While observing his class [January–June 2010], he once asked me which software he could use to download and save streaming media from the Web. He wanted to be able to play those clips offline [More in Chapter 5].

ducers', it prevents them from being 'communicators' (Buckingham, 2007: 178).

Another user-centred educational project kicked off in mid-December 2009 under the name of *Wikiwijs* [wikiwise].[139] Funded by the Ministry of Education, Culture and Science, *Wikiwijs* is described as a sort of Wikipedia 'primarily of, for and by the teachers' (Mulder, 2009: 26). According to the project-planners, *Wikiwijs* aims to be a platform of teacher-generated, open-source educational contents, to generate overviews of individual item compilations, to create links between those compilations, and even between the latter and collections external to the project, whether open, closed, or commercial. As such, the project aims to be not only a 'repository', but also a 'referatory' (*Ibid.*: 25). The website is a self-publishing, open environment, which, like all other wiki-driven sites, requires no special tools or technical knowledge. Although *Wikiwijs* has the ambition to be an open platform for open materials (*Ibid.*: 2 & 21), it is not clear how the project intends to handle copyright issues. The intention is even to combine this 'open' and 'free' material with other material, for example, from within ED*IT and from publishers (*Ibid.*: 25), which, by definition are almost always copyrighted.

Unlike many other sites, *Wikiwijs* offers unequalled cross-institutional, cross-sectorial hyperlinking freedom, which is likely to result in a platform with a rich variety of contextualised information. This openness, this freedom, however, is also likely to raise the issue of 'misuse' of tax-payers' money, based on the argument that a government-funded project is offering commercial publishers and other private parties an undreamed of opportunity to 'divert' a maximum number of users to their own sites and [educational] products which, as discussed in the previous section, has considerable commercial implications.[140]

While all the above seems promising and innovative, there is a constant cloud of anxiety hovering over all these undertakings that could hamper their embracement by teachers and pupils. No one can be certain how long these projects will last and whether the material they contain will be accessible in the future. In a newsletter dated February 2009, *Teleblik*, the pilot version and predecessor of LES 2.0 and ED*IT, expressed relief about its future as follows: *Goed nieuws! Teleblik <u>blijft</u> bestaan* [underlining is mine], [transla-

---

139 *Wikiwijs*: http://www.wikiwijs.nl (Accessed 31 March 2010).

140 On the following page for instance, Malmberg BV, a leading educational publisher, 'advertises' its history textbook by means of scans of pages and hyperlinks to the publisher's website. http://www.leermiddelenplein.nl/php/detail.php?id=192474 (Accessed 12 May 2010).

tion: 'Good news! Teleblik is to remain in the ether'].[141] Another article from that same issue added: *Teleblik blijft gratis* [underlining is mine], [*i.e.*, 'Teleblik still free of charge']. The April 2009 issue informed its readers that *Teleblik blijft (groeien)* [underlining is mine], [*i.e.*, 'Teleblik keeps on (growing)']. These words provoke more worries than reassurance regarding the future in the minds of teachers and pupils – the targeted audience: How long will the situation *remain* so? Teachers traditionally rely on previous years' preparations and notes for their current and future classes. Where there is any doubt created about future access to digitised material, teachers will be more likely to revert to more lasting and stable sources, which textbooks have so far proven to be.

Furthermore, the words 'Teleblik still free of charge' suggest that the future might bring surprises. Indeed, the successor of Teleblik, ED*IT, is meant to be a paid-service, because the government's funding was tied to the condition that it must eventually generate income for its own continuity and that this must be the case before the *Beeld voor de toekomst* project ends in 2014.[142] Nobody knows what might happen if the project fails to generate enough money to pay back part of the initial investment. The same uncertainty surrounds the *Geheugen van Nederland* and its lesson packages, as the project is not certain of its future after 2010. There is no way of knowing whether the resources already integrated into individual teachers' lessons will remain accessible at the same Universal Resources Locators [URLs]. The same applies to *Wikiwijs*, whose funding will last until 2015. The hope is that by that time the project will have gathered substantial quantities of educational materials (Mulder, 2009: 31).

The aim of this section was to explore the implementation of Web 2.0 features by heritage institutions. It seems that in the second half of the last decade, an increasing number of institutions were embracing Social Media as a way of reaching out to a wider public, not only for communication purposes but also for object-exhibition. The latter aspect had another important function, namely, getting users involved in the task of meaning-assignation. This practice, which corresponds to one of the most important new media habits of the Digital Generation, is likely to bring heritage objects closer to that generation, especially within the framework of history education. Beside SM, the end of the last decade witnessed the emergence of user-centred projects designed specifically with educa-

141 *Teleblik* Newsletter, February 2009 entitled: '*Goed nieuws! Teleblik blijft bestaan*': http://www.teleblik.nl/nieuwsbrief/0209 (Accessed 23 March 2009, now off the ether).

142 Author interview with Paul Vermeulen, LES 2.0 Coordinator (Hilversum, 10 November 2009).

tion in mind. All these projects not only put digitised objects at the disposal of the Digital Generation and teachers, but also empowered them to engage with them in creative ways for learning or teaching purposes. However, this trend is still only being observed on a very small scale and it does not have the air of long-term certainty.

3.5 Summary

In this chapter I pointed out how multiple motivations triggered the digitisation of cultural heritage collections. Preservation was an initial factor, one on which access and all other subsequent uses depend. Once access is provided to preserved materials, other uses emerge, mainly of an educational and ideological nature. Digitisation has often been cited not only as a means of providing sources for pupils and teachers, but also as providing identity-shaping and citizenship-fostering material. Another motive was the desire to bring formerly united collections back together and to unite objects that are related to the same theme. This [re-]unification has the advantage of forming new collections that transcend geographical distances and boundaries. I indicated how each motive has a potential to present income-generating possibilities.

This chapter also discussed the different methods and levels of selection within digitisation projects, ranging from non-selection and time-based or theme-based projects to projects involving stricter selection criteria. There are financial and practical reasons why selection is an essential stage prior to digitisation, though in some cases, selection itself can become an expensive and time-consuming task. In other cases, collections are too small to necessitate selection. In yet other cases, decisions are made to select a theme or a period within which no further selection is made. As I mentioned, however, in most cases, stricter selections are made. The most frequently used selection criteria are the fragility and old age of objects, their uniqueness, their rarity, and their historical or intellectual significance. I pointed out that this latter criterion is extremely broad, as the importance of objects depends on who is considering them and with what purpose in mind.

While discussing the post-digitisation organisation of contents and the enhancement of their pedagogical value, this chapter presented hyperlinking as an effective way of placing objects within their historical context. I drew a parallel between hyperlinking and the links that historians make between related historical events and processes in order to understand them. This chapter has shown that most heritage institutions have underused hyperlinks, thereby limiting the pedagogical use of heritage objects in at least two ways: Firstly, Digital Natives, who assume and expect related objects to be interconnected, probably think that the objects with which they are presented have no history or context, as none is provided; secondly, the same Digital Natives whose research almost always begins with online search operations, will rarely encounter the poorly indexed and ranked heritage sites. The reason for this poor indexing and ranking is related to the lack of hyperlinking, because the more hyperlinks to and from a site, the better its ranking and the more visible and findable the site will be. I have identified three reasons to explain this poor hyperlinking, namely the rather conservative vision of heritage professionals – in selecting, preserving, and making collections available, while never concerning themselves with the interpretation and organisation of contents – and related fund allocation policies; institutions' policies regarding the preservation of their identity and their corporate interests; and the impasse surrounding the use of public funds in a networked knowledge landscape, where there has been a proliferation in the most unpredictable ways of making money.

Finally, this chapter reviewed the trends among heritage institutions following the coming of Web 2.0. I have signalled the increasing presence of these institutions on Social Media sites, where they both communicate with audiences and present parts of their collections. This practice has brought digitised objects closer to the users who, in the process, have taken up some tasks that were previously entrusted to heritage professionals. One of these is assigning meanings to objects. In addition, Social Media allow institutions to collect exchanges made about their objects, which eventually results in multiple narratives about objects. I also reviewed a few educational projects centred on contents generated by users – mostly teachers and pupils – based on digitised heritage objects. These projects increase the control of teachers and pupils over contents, while facilitating their creativity. This chapter has shown, however, that these projects have an air of uncertainty with regard to their future, due in particular to funding issues.

What the reviews presented so far have shown is that history education (Chapter 1), the Web and the Internet Generation (Chapter 2), and the digitisation of the cultural heritage (Chapter 3), are all enmeshed together within a web, where they are exposed to influences from various actors and factors. As time has passed, the most important influence seems to have come from politicians and policy-makers who determine the direction history education must follow, who lay down ICT plans for schools and provide orientations and directives for the digitisation of this country's cultural heritage. These reviews have considered the main themes separately, while most of the actors and stakes involved in history education are also involved in digitising the cultural heritage and the uses of the Web. The aim of the second part of this book is to go beyond these reviews and empirically explore, in a more integrated fashion, how some of the various points reviewed in part one intermingle in real-life history classes. The next part of this book presents empirical findings on two history classes (Chapter 5 & Chapter 6) and their analysis (Chapter 7). However, before embarking on this presentation and analysis, I shall first explain my methodological approach (Chapter 4).

Chapter 4

Methodological Introduction to Field Research

Since the coming of the Web and its gradual integration into the educational system, particularly during the first decade of the 21st century, many surveys have been conducted into the use of digital media in schools. Some were conducted on a yearly basis,[143] while others were conducted on demand,[144] or occasionally within universities or research institutes.[145] Most of these studies and surveys were essentially quantitative, in the sense that they mostly aimed at mapping the extent to which digital media are used in educational settings. The second part of my research is an attempt to provide an ethnographic account of the uses of digital media and resources in the history class, an account that could serve as a follow-up to the above-mentioned quantitative and performance-oriented studies. The target group is constituted of 13- to 14-year-old secondary school pupils attending two selected classes. Being aware of the fact that the presentation of the results of field qualitative or ethnographic research is closely linked to the methodology and methods used at each phase of the research (Hutjes & Van Buuren, [1992] 1996: 102; Wester & Hijmans, 2003: 7), I shall first explain my methodological approaches. I made use ethnographic research and case study research, but before discussing how I did this, I shall first introduce the research questions and assumptions that I was exploring. I shall then focus briefly on the two techniques that I used most, namely, participant observation and interviews. Finally, I shall explain the context in which I used content analysis to study pupils' written class assignments and the reason for choosing it, and then end the chapter with a description of the recording techniques I used.

---

143 Example: *Vier in Balans Monitor* by *Kennisnet* Foundation.

144 Example: *Internet, een populair medium voor het zoeken van informatie bij schoolopdrachten: Een onderzoek onder scholieren van 12-17 jaar*, (18 April 2006), by Motivaction.

145 Examples: Joke van Velzen's *Instruction and Self-Regulated Learning: Promoting Students' (self-) Reflective Thinking* (PhD dissertation, Leiden University, 2002); and Jannet van Drie's *Learning about the past with new technologies* (PhD dissertation, Utrecht University, 2005).

4.1 Research Questions

> We know well enough that experiment is always influenced by the hypothesis which occasioned it, but I have for the time being confined myself strictly to the discussion of facts. Moreover, for teachers and all those whose work calls for an exact knowledge of the child's mind, facts take precedence over theory. I am convinced that the mark of theoretical fertility in a science is its capacity for practical application (Piaget, [1926] 1959: xix).

In the previous two chapters, a number of assumptions were mentioned regarding the import of the Web and digital media in general in history classes. The same assumptions also appear in the abundant literature on the use of digital media in the classroom. Research methodology literature has suggested not only that researchers are connected to the subject of their enquiry (Davies, [1998] 2008: 3-4), but also that the implication of that connection is that researchers enter the field with a number of philosophical and theoretical assumptions. It has been suggested that 'Good research requires making these assumptions, paradigms, and frameworks explicit ... and, at a minimum, to be aware that they influence the conduct of inquiry' (Creswell, 2007: 15). My own assumptions emerged from my graduate research[146] as well as from my extensive reading of expert and scholarly literature on the subject.[147] In this section, I want to introduce the central question I explored: *how* do pupils interact with digital media and resources during their history classes? I explored it by dividing it into a number of sub-questions related to three of the most frequently recurring assumptions. These assumptions served as the axes around which my observations revolved.

The first assumption was that *digital media and resources have made the history class more attractive and livelier* (*Onderwijsraad*, 1998: 9-10; Wilschut *et al.*, 2004: 200-212; *Kennisnet*, 2009: 63). My aim in considering this assumption was not to check whether or not it was founded, but rather, based on my observations, to describe what happened when one medium was used in one way, and what changed when a medium was used in a different way. Some of the sub-questions that the next two chapters will answer are: what happened when the teacher used Web-based resources to illustrate a particular point? What happened when a pupil shifted from the

146 This was the subject of my MA thesis entitled 'The Memory of the Netherlands: Introducing Cultural Heritage into the New Teaching-Learning Environment' (University of Leiden, the Netherlands: 2006).

147 That literature includes: Wilschut *et al.*, 2004; Haydn & Counsell (eds.), 2003; Harwood & Asal, 2007; Washington, 2008; Oomen, 2003; Roegiers & Truyen, 2008; Ten Brummelhuis, 2006; among others.

textbook to a Web page or *vice versa* in order to check a point in which he or she was interested? How did pupils respond when the teacher played a video clip during the lesson?

The second assumption was that *digital media and resources foster historical thinking* (Wilschut *et al.*, 2004: 210; Van Drie, 2005: 63-87; among others). Historical thinking is defined here from the perspective of cognitive and development psychology rather than from that of professional or academic history.[148] I shall use this concept within the framework of children's thinking, which psychologists Robert Siegler and Martha Wagner Alibali ([1986] 2005: 2) defined as involving 'the higher mental processes: problem-solving, reasoning, creating, conceptualizing, remembering, classifying, symbolizing, planning, and so on'. The adjective 'historical' adds the fact that the object of problem-solving, reasoning, creating and other mental processes is [in] the past. Thus, historical thinking in this sense includes, or is interchangeable with, other concepts used to describe this type of mental activity such as historical reasoning, historical literacy, historical consciousness, among others (Van Drie & Van Boxtel, 2008: 88; see also Lee, 2007: 50-51). These concepts imply that the learner goes beyond 'names and dates', to engage with, and question, historical texts [in the larger sense] in search of sub-texts (Wineburg, 2001: 76, 78, 80 & 82). Thinking or reasoning historically consists of reading historical texts not with a 'receptive spirit' but 'with a question in [his] mind' (Collingwood, [1946] 1994: 269-270; see also Watts, 1972: 20; Van Drie & Van Boxtel, 2008: 90-91), whereby the thinker often has recourse to, among others, associational, analogical, comparative, deductive, inductive, and creative thinking (Watts, 1972: 38; Van Drie & Van Boxtel, 2008: 89; Kuhn, 2009: 159-160 & 162-163).

I also used the concept of historical thinking in the sense of cultural historian Johan Huizinga's (1948: 566) notion of 'historical sensation'. When one experiences historical sensation, he suggested,

148 At this stage it is crucial to remember the distinction psychologists have made between children's or adolescent thinking and expert thinking. While expert historians employ heuristics such as corroboration, contextualisation and author identification to understand not only what the documents say but also what they mean (Wineburg, 1991: 77; Wolfe & Goldman, 2005: 470-471), adolescents often do not discuss the relationship between evidence and opinion but rely mostly on their own judgment of plausibility (Wolfe & Goldman, 2005: 472; see also Torney-Purta, 1994: 104). Despite this distinction, adolescents often show some features of expert thinking, such as contextualisation (Torney-Purta, 1994: 108) and establishing connections between information across multiple texts (Wolfe and Goldman, 2005: 496). The difference is, then, that 'children execute this process ... less skillfully than professional scientists ...' (Kuhn, 2009: 168-169). Similar observations have been made with regard to scientific thinking (Lawson, 1995: 42-67).

one has 'contact with the past' and gets 'an (please resist the urge to laugh) ecstatic sensation of no longer being myself, of flowing in the world outside myself' [parenthesis in original]. This experience is an instance of children's thinking applied to a past event and is thus a form of historical thinking. According to constructivism theorists, digital media foster that process, especially critical thinking, argumentation, concept mapping, and the personal construction of knowledge (Kanselaar *et al.*, 2000: 72). Others suggest that the main goal of education has ceased to be the assimilation of teacher-transmitted facts and has become, among other things, 'learning to think', which includes such skills as 'analogical reasoning', 'critical thinking', and 'logical thinking' (Simons *et al.*, 2000: 13-14). Some of the sub-questions relating to this aspect are dealt with in the next two chapters: How did pupils engage with, and question, Web-based historical texts? How creative were they while dealing with Web-based texts either during the lesson or when doing their assignments? How did the different forms [text, still or moving images] of digital media inspire their discussions and argumentations?

The last assumption was that *digital media and resources provided pupils [and teachers] with an unlimited variety of sources* (Steyaert & De Haan, 2001: 70; Oomen, 2003: 12; *Onderwijsraad*, 2003a: 12-13; Wilschut *et al.*, 2004: 200-212; Cornu, 2004: 40; Barton & Levstik, 2004: 2; among others). Until recently, the main history class sources are said to have been textbooks, on the basis of which other sources were sought, *e.g.*, documentaries, excursions and class guests. As the 21st century dawned, the voices of scholars were heard calling for a system in which a dwindling amount of time would be devoted to teacher–pupil interaction. They suggested a system in which an increasing amount of time would be dedicated to pupils' independent study 'supported by a *rich variety of information sources*' (Steyaert & De Haan, 2001: 70. Italicisation is mine). This change would mark a shift 'from classical lessons to the *studiehuis* [study house]', from 'knowledge to skills, or learning to learn' (*Ibid.*; see also Van Diepen-Oost, 2000: 40; Wilhelm, 2001: 13; Van Velzen, 2002: 6 & 44; Leek & Slot, 2006: 157). Thus, the next two chapters will attempt to answer these as well as other sub-questions: Which sources did pupils use and what were the reasons for their choices? Why did they use those sources rather than others?

4.2 The Case Study Approach

> Working hypotheses are being confronted with masses of details, and as a result are discarded, revised, or quickened. You strive to compel the material facts of the world to reveal their nature, you watch and record their behaviour, and truth is the accurate statement of the facts observed (Baldwin, [1925] 1937: 89).

To explore the above-mentioned assumptions, I conducted field research in the form of case studies. I observed one class at the *Baarnsch Lyceum* in Baarn between January and May 2010 and another class at *Helen Parkhurst Dalton School* in Almere from March to May and from September to October 2010. I explain how the two schools were chosen at the beginning of the chapters [5 and 6] relating to each of the case studies. For the time being I would like to discuss the case study as a research approach, guided as it is by, among others, the principle that the fewer cases one studies, the larger the amount of detailed information one collects: 'usually, "case study" refers to research that investigates a few cases, often just one, in considerable depth' (Hammersley & Gomm, 2000: 3).

Although the results of my two case studies make no pretension to being a reflection of the general situation in Dutch secondary schools, they could provide some insightful indications. As indicated by methodologist Jan Hutjes (2000: 78), case studies do not always aim to produce *generalisable* results. For his colleagues Yvonna Lincoln and Egon Cuba (2000: 27), generalisation is even out of question when one is dealing with case studies: 'The only generalization is: there is no generalization'. In my case, the results are limited to the two classes I observed and to the specific period of my field research. In other words, by opting for the case study approach, my aim was to reach an 'understanding or explanation of a phenomenon [uses of digital media and resources] in its unique context [history class, not in all imaginable contexts]' (Hutjes & Van Buuren, [1992] 1996: 25). The point being made here is that the case study, though limited in time and space, can provide an insight that may be useful for further, broader research. I selected two cases and went deep, 'by placing the complex relationships in which the case[s] function[s] at the heart of the research' (Wester, 2000: 20; see also Creswell, 2007: 73 & 74; see also Hutjes & Van Buuren, [1992] 1996: 21 & 24). In addition to this depth, Jan Hutjes and Hans van Buuren ([1992] 1996: 15) highlighted the 'intensive study of a phenomenon in its natural situation' and 'from different perspectives' (*Ibid.*: 77). In such a study, they added, data are collected using such methods as participant observation, interviews, document analysis, with or without a quantitative and/or qualitative approach (*Ibid.*: 79-93). The next five sections discuss the data collection approaches and methods I used.

4.3 Ethnographic Perspective on the History Class

> … as soon as age permitted me to emerge from the control of my tutors, I entirely quitted the study of letters. And, resolving to seek no other science than that which could be found in myself, or at least in the great book of the world, I employed the rest of my youth in travel, in seeing courts and armies, in intercourse with men of diverse temperaments and conditions, in collecting varied experiences … For it seemed to me that I might meet with much more truth in the reasoning that each man makes on the matters that specially concern him … I learned to believe nothing too certainly of which I have only been convinced by example and custom (Descartes, [1637] 1996: 8).

For my field research, I made use of ethnographic methods for the two case studies. In this section, I want to highlight the features and aspects of ethnography that I found most relevant to the specific purpose of my field research. Originating from anthropology, ethnography or qualitative research is essentially fieldwork-based (Creswell, 2007: 37), and it aims primarily at describing and understanding a culture from the native point of view (Spradley, 1980: 3; see also Atkinson & Hammersley, 1994: 251; Wester & Hijmans, 2003: 9). Three key criteria need to be taken into account: first, the research has to place the 'inner world' of the subjects being studied at the centre; second, the relationships between the concepts and data to be collected must be – and remain – open; and third, the researcher must establish the broadest and most direct possible contact with the reality of the world under consideration (Wester & Hijmans, 2003: 11-12; see also Creswell, 2007: 39). Suggesting more specific ways in which ethnography could be used in observing classrooms, education scholar Edward Wragg ([1994] 1999: 54) noted that it offers numerous approaches 'to probe beneath the surface of events, to elicit the meanings, sometimes deeply buried, the interpretations and explanations, significance and impact of classroom life.'

For the purpose of my research, I opted to embrace ethnography as my main methodological approach to the use of digital media and resources in the history class. To paraphrase Wragg, I wanted to probe beneath the yearly statistics-based reports on digital media uses, to elicit the meaning, the interpretations, and the explanations of certain uses of digital media and resources, rather than merely the extent to which they were used. Although essentially qualitative and descriptive, my approach did not systematically exclude quantitative data where these were deemed necessary (see below Section 4.6). Following Wester (1984: 4; see also Hutjes & Van Buuren, [1992] 1996: 9 & 77; Hardy & Bryman, 2004: 1 and 4; Creswell, 2007: 131), my qualitative approach took some advantage of the quantitative data collected in the two classes, for instance, by using them to illustrate hypotheses.[149]

Since the aim of my field research was, in the words of Agar ([1980] 1996: 30), to 'seek the here and now' in terms of pupils' attitudes and behaviour *vis-à-vis* digital media and resources, I needed to see the pupils as often as possible and for a certain period of time. I should therefore mention the fact that my field research consisted of weekly, sometimes bi-weekly, attendance at the history class in both schools, where I would sit among the pupils, adapt myself to the prevailing code of conduct and avoid making my presence too intrusive (Wragg, [1994] 1999: 16). I would then observe pupils (see next section), talk to them whenever the occasion presented itself and have informal conversations with teachers (see Section 4.5).

4.4 Observing while Attending

> In front of my window is a mound on which the children of the neighbourhood gather to play. Although a bit far from me, I can perfectly distinguish all they say, and I often draw good illustrations [from that experience] for this account (Rousseau, [1768]1966: 83).

In this section I want to focus on the technique – participant observation – that I used most in order to collect data. Of all the qualitative research methods, participant observation has often been preferred as it increases the chance of understanding other cultures (Silverman, 1993: 8-9). However, it needs other methods in order to clarify the phenomena observed – for instance interviewing (see next section) –, to analyse media contents (see Section 4.6), and to record data (see Section 4.7), among others. I chose participant observation as the primary method because, in my opinion, it was

149 Melissa Hardy and Alan Bryman co-edited *Handbook of Data Analysis* (2004), a volume that includes both quantitative and qualitative techniques. Their aim, so they wrote, was to contribute to bringing the two approaches closer together because 'We believe that reinforcing this division is a mistake' (Hardy & Bryman, 2004: 1). They further argued that both approaches have much to gain from one another, as they both 'attempt to "tell a story" from the data' (*Ibid.*).

best suited to my goal of 'understanding the [pupils'] routine [with regard to digital media]' (Silverman, 1993: 30). Participant observation has been defined as

> a method in which a researcher takes part in the daily activities, rituals, interactions, and events of a group of people as one of the means of learning the explicit and tacit aspects of their life routines and their culture ... (DeWalt & DeWalt, 2002: 1).

Depending on the extent of involvement in daily routines, many degrees of participant observation have been distinguished, namely *non-participation*: the observer is not involved in the activities of the subjects studied; *passive participation*: the researcher does not get him- or herself involved to a great extent but acts as a 'bystander'; *moderate participation*: 'the ethnographer seeks to maintain a balance between being an insider and an outsider'; *active participation*: the ethnographer does what everybody else does; and *complete participation*: the highest level of participation on the part of the researcher (Spradley, 1980: 58-61). I opted for observation based on moderate participation, limiting my participation to chatting with pupils before classes started or during group discussions. I joined group discussions not to contribute but to follow and take notes. I would ask questions about points raised during discussions, or about a website the pupil was browsing. My principal role as observer consisted of sitting among the pupils and taking notes of what I saw and heard. This method has been described as being used most frequently for classroom observation, whereby researchers are 'principally [as] observers, not [as] participants' (DeWalt & DeWalt, 2002: 20).

To make this moderate participation possible would require me to build a relationship based on trust with the pupils, whose full cooperation I would need in order to conduct my research successfully (see Fine & Sandstrom, 1988: 16). Winning their trust would transform me into an insider, a phenomenon referred to as 'resocialisation' (Wester, 1984: 56), an essential aspect of participant observation. Resocialisation means that 'One has to go through a learning process that is similar to the process each new member goes through before being fully accepted as a member' (*Ibid.*). Thus, my trust-building efforts started with my introduction on day one, when I had to explain to the pupils who I was and why I had decided to come and sit among them. At the *Baarnsch Lyceum*, this process even continued during breaks when I had to explain the difference between myself and teacher-trainees, to whom they were accustomed.

The pupils tested my knowledge of their world, in what appeared to be some form of admission test. They tested my knowledge of local Dutch football championships, and the UEFA [Union of European Football Association] Champions League, asking about my favourite clubs and asking me for prognoses for upcoming matches. I later received 'condolences' when *Internazionale* of Milan eliminated FC Barcelona, my 'favourite' for the 2010 Champions League tournament. I had the impression that I had passed their test and that some degree of trust had been established. Throughout my research, I would make comments on football before introducing my research-related questions, as football – and to some extent political news[150] – appeared to be a topic of great importance to them. It served as a door into their world. Observation has taught that the first few weeks of child observation are crucial to the success of the research, because this is the period in which children test the researcher (Fine & Sandstrom, 1988: 29). To pass the test, one needs to develop certain behavioural and social skills as well as a flexible approach to new social situations (DeWalt & DeWalt, 2002: 17). In my case, I was already well informed both about football and about political news, which made that task much easier.

Though I achieved the status of 'trustworthy fellow', it was not possible to be a loyal fellow under all circumstances. At the *Baarnsch Lyceum*, pupils would sometimes offer me a chewing gum during the lesson and I felt obliged to decline the offer. Others would urge me to glance at a Web page to which they had browsed on their iPhones while they were supposed to be listening to the teacher, and I would silently reject the invitation.[151] This limitation highlighted the difference between the status of 'trustworthy fellow', which I had, and that of 'peer', which the pupils thought I had. It was a matter of exploring their world, while establishing a balance between involvement and distance (Wester & Hijmans, 2003: 13-14).

I should add that I was fully aware that a number of aspects would prevent, or at least hinder, my full integration into the group. In the first place, I was an adult among minors; secondly, with my swarthy complexion, having come from a different continent – Africa – and speaking not-quite-perfect Dutch with an accent, I was attending classes that were predominantly white; thirdly, I had

150 Several political events occurred during the time I spent observing the *Baarnsch Lyceum* class [January–May 2010]: in February 2010 the government resigned after a profound disagreement among coalition parties. Pupils would comment on the numerous televised political debates. In the same period, polls prior to the March 2010 municipal elections were predicting victory for the recently established extreme-right *Partij voor Vrijheid* [Party for Freedom, PVV]. Pupils seemed excited about this.

151 In her 2007 article entitled 'Friend or Foe? Self-Expansion, Stigmatized Groups, and the Researcher-Participant Relationship', public policy scholar Jocelyn Crowley cited many instances in which the status of 'trustworthy fellow' reached its limits. She managed to collect private information from the studied subjects but systematically refrained from providing private information about herself.

landed in the second year of secondary school, though my world was that of academia. Neither at the *Baarnsch Lyceum* nor at the *Helen Parkhurst Dalton School* did these differences seem to play any noticeable role. However, questions about the languages I spoke [implying my origin and background] or the kind of book I would be writing [academia], showed that the pupils were, nevertheless, aware of these differences. The most decisive step toward compensating for these differences was by getting as close to their worldviews as possible.

4.5 Interviews

> To judge children's logic, it is often enough to chat with them ... (Piaget, 1938: vii).

The ethnographic or qualitative research interview has been defined as a technique that 'employs questions designed to discover the cultural meanings people have learned' (Spradley, 1980: 123; see also Kvale, 1996: 1). The technique differs from everyday conversation in that it has a purpose and 'goes beyond the spontaneous exchange of views ... and becomes a careful questioning and listening approach with the purpose of obtaining thoroughly tested knowledge' (Kvale, 1996: 6; see also Oppenheim, [1966] 1992: 66). Not all interviews have the same structure. Three major sorts of interview have been distinguished: the *unstructured interview*, during which the researcher 'presents topics in an open-ended way and exerts as little control over the interaction as possible'; the *semi-structured interview*, during which the researcher uses an interview guide to ensure that all topics are covered; and the *structured interview*, during which the researcher uses scripted questions (DeWalt & DeWalt, 2002: 122). Whatever type of interview one chooses to use, interviewing remains one of the most important tools for field researchers. Agar ([1980] 1996: 95) maintained that 'For the ethnographer, question asking is vital' in order to learn from a group and to check things that you think you understand. His conclusion is that '[E]thnography without questions would be impossible'.

During my field research I conducted dozens of unstructured interviews with the pupils. In all cases, my questions were inspired mainly by my observations, hence the unstructured, spontaneous nature of the interviews. Agar ([1980] 1996: 158) further suggested that observation and interview interact 'either simultaneously or sequentially, in the course of doing ethnography'. During the field research, some of my interviews were simultaneous with ongoing activities, since questions were about something that was happening; others were sequential, as they were conducted after the situation had passed [after the lesson for instance].[152] At one school, the *Helen Parkhurst Dalton School*, where moving around from one place to another – inside and outside the classroom – was part of the learning style and did not violate any code of conduct (see Chapter 6, Section 6.1), I would sometimes join an individual pupil who was consulting a particular Web page and ask how he or she had come to that source, and how he or she intended to use the information found there. At the other school, the *Baarnsch Lyceum*, where the learning style was very different and did not permit free movement during lessons, I would generally put my questions to pupils either at the end of the lesson or in advance when a teacher was getting ready to start a lesson. For instance, when a teacher made a remark to a pupil, saying he or she had not made joint use of book and Web sources as he had requested, I would ask the pupil why he or she had not complied with the request.

Interviewing teachers was a different matter, and thus, required a different interview technique. I would write down questions that came to my mind in relation to the lesson being given. Asking questions as they rose [unstructured interview] would have been too disruptive for the teacher. I would organise my questions into a semi-structured interview to be conducted after the lesson, or one week later, before the following lesson began. I call these interviews semi-structured because I determined the topics upon which I wanted the teachers to elaborate prior to the interview. Eventually, the answers teachers gave would prompt other questions, hence the semi-structured character. In the next few paragraphs I briefly introduce my approach to content analysis, another method I used at a later stage of my field research.

4.6 Content Analysis

> One never writes for nothing. Any written document announces and denounces the writer … (Gusdorf, 1991: 98).

The literature on content analysis suggests that choosing the variables on which an analysis should be based is an essential starting point for content analysis (see for instance Neuendorf, 2002: 4 & 95; Bryman & Cramer, 2004: 17). It has been suggested that any content analysis 'is a selective reading of [media] material from the perspective of a specific research question' (Wester, 2006: 16; see also Pleijter, 2006: 13). The media texts in which I was interested

152 In this respect, Piaget (1938: xiv) also suggested that observations complement one another: 'There is, in fact, no *a priori* reason why one should not question the children about the points which pure observation leaves unclear'.

were the written assignments done by the pupils in the two classes I had observed. I would like to explain briefly how I approached those texts using content analysis, which, unlike observation and interviews, involves no 'intrusion' of the researcher in the process through which media contents come into being (Wester, 2006: 11-12).

Content analysis has been briefly defined as an organised and empirical study of media materials or messages (Neuendorf, 2002: 1; Pleijter, 2006: 7) that has been often, though not exclusively, used in analysing mass media texts.[153] Media texts in this sense are to be understood as media contents, including radio and television programmes.[154] Content analysis is also used for other kinds of contents outside the realm of mass media. Neuendorf' (2002: 17) indicated that 'so long as other pertinent characteristics apply ... the study of *any type of message pool* may be deemed a content analysis' [Italicisation is mine]. From this point of view, notes, meeting reports, court judgements, ego documents [*e.g.*, diaries], hospital or school archival documents, to name a few, are all eligible for content analysis (Wester, 2006: 11 & 31). In my case, the classes' written assignments formed the object of my content analysis. These assignments were carried out during the period of my field research. I should add that I did not exercise any influence whatsoever in designing the assignments. The teachers were even not aware of the specific assumptions [relating to historical thinking and variety of sources] I was exploring on the basis of the written assignments. The material in which I was interested came into being without any involvement on my part: 'thus', as Wester (2006: 17) suggested, I waited to 'see whether or how the aspects to be studied [would] appear in the document'.

I should also mention that I used two content analysis approaches, one to explore the variety of sources used by the pupils and another to study their historical thinking. In the former case, I used the 'quantitative, descriptive type of content analysis' (Wester, 2006: 20), which aims primarily at obtaining figures and statistics on how a given aspect appears in media contents. Since my research was on a small-scale, I did not need the coding schemes or agents that are usually used for large-scale research. This approach appeared to be

153 Critics Edward Herman and Noam Chomsky's *Manufacturing Consent: The Political Economy of the Mass Media* (1988), and political communication scholar Piers Robinson's *The CNN Effect* (2002), are illustrations of content analysis as applied to mass media texts.

154 Sociologist and methodologist Ellen Hijmans (2006: 121-138) for instance carried out a content analysis of the Oprah Winfrey Show, to explore its 'spirituality'. Her colleagues Fred Wester and Addy Weijers (2006: 161-189) conducted a similar analysis of TV shows to make an inventory of 'life lessons'.

the most appropriate since the notion of variety of sources refers to the *number* of sources used. If one pupil used ten different sources, while another used only two, the former is said to have used *more varied* sources, based on the *number* of sources he or she actually used. I also provided an account of the use of sources, their categories and the relationships between them and the use of, for instance, long quotations, summaries, and paraphrasing. In this regard, sociologist Melissa Hardy (2004: 35) suggested that '[W]hen we work with a data set, our goal is to tell its story – or one of its stories', while her colleague Roberto Franzosi (2004: 556-557) argued that 'By themselves, of course, numbers mean nothing', as they 'need to be analysed ... [and] converted back into words to make them intelligible'. The ultimate goal, he wrote, is 'to discover patterns in the data' (*Ibid.*: 562).

To study historical thinking, I used the 'qualitative, interpretive type of content analysis', which is characterised by 'intensive study of documents' by the researcher him/herself, without any use of coding schemes or coding agents (Wester, 2006: 26-27). Its aim is to explore or describe a central concept [historical thinking], taking into account the background and the context in which the document came into being (*Ibid.*: 32). As historical thinking is an abstract notion involving more than just one aspect (see Section 4.1), I attempted to study the assignments carefully to detect whether – and if so, how – digital media or resources interfered with the thinking processes that led to the arguments presented in the assignments.[155]

Thus, unlike the quantitative, descriptive approach used to study sources, the qualitative, interpretive counterpart focuses on the *how* rather than the *how many*. Sociologist and methodologist Ellen Hijmans (2006: 121-138) used this content analysis approach to explore 'spirituality' in the Oprah Winfrey Show. The aim of her research was 'to show *how* the rather considerable theoretical relationship between the talk show and spirituality receives empirical stature in the Oprah talk show' (*Ibid.*: 123. Italicisation is mine). Fred Wester and Addy Weijers (2006: 161-189) conducted a fairly similar analysis of TV shows in order to make an inventory of 'life lessons'. The point was to use narrative analysis to 'dissect television stories' in search of their 'cultural message', and how this manifested itself both verbally and through gestures. The stress was more on *how* the cultural message manifested itself than on *how many* times

155 Communication scholar Alexander Pleijter (2006: 16-19) sketched the trends in qualitative content analysis, highlighting the influence of hermeneutics, semiotics, narrative and discourse analysis, as well as the study of religious texts, among others. These influences make it possible to have recourse to different kinds of interpretive approaches.

it appeared in a given TV show. To reuse the same terms used by Wester and Weijers (*Ibid.*: 162), I used this qualitative, interpretive approach to 'dissect' the written assignment in order to see *how* historical thinking manifested itself as a result of using the Web.

4.7 Data Recording

> An ethnographic record consists of fieldnotes, tape recordings, pictures, artifacts, and anything else that documents the social situation under study … The major part of any ethnographic record consists of written fieldnotes (Spradley, 1980: 63-64).

To record data, I mainly took notes and made recordings, both video and audio, as well as taking hundreds of pictures. I should stress here that at the *Baarnsch Lyceum*, I was faced with a particular challenge relating to the use of recording devices. As Chapter 5 will show, the class was a conventional one, where on the one hand the teacher strove to maintain silence in the class, while on the other hand, the adolescents never missed an opportunity to take out their digital devices during the lesson. In this environment, to have taken out my own recording devices would have provided the pupils with yet another pretext to wreak 'havoc' in the classroom. As I wanted to avoid diverting pupils' attention from the teacher to my recording devices, I decided not to openly use any recording tool, resorting instead to field notes [to be certain of having *verbatim* messages and exchanges]. I was nevertheless able to take some pictures and make a few videos, though only from the back of the classroom, from where I was generally able to operate unnoticed, and thus without disturbing the class.

The situation at *Helen Parkhurst Dalton School* was entirely different. As Chapter 6 (Section 6.1) will show, the class was saturated with digital technologies: all pupils had their own notebook [laptop computer] and they were free to use their private devices [iPod with earphones, iPhones, *etc.*] during lessons. Making use of my recording technologies was a natural thing to do. No one seemed to have even noticed them. Thus, I used my own laptop [like everyone else in the class] to record 'everything' that was said in class. I also had a pocket sound recorder which I used for informal talks with pupils inside the classroom, or with the teachers outside the classroom. My video camera was permanently switched on, recording 'everything' that happened in the classroom. I also used my photo camera to take a number of pictures.

Ethnography methodologists agree that note-taking is the most typical data recording method (Davies, [1998] 2008: 233; see also Spradley, 1980: 63-64; Kvale, 1996: 160-161). It has even been suggested that the success of qualitative research based on participant observation – as in my case – depends entirely on the quality of the researcher's notes (Wester, 1984: 58). Anthropologists Kathleen DeWalt and Billie DeWalt (2002: 122) added that besides taking on-the-spot field notes, the researcher should try 'to remember verbatim passages of conversations, and record[s] those in field notes'. Thus, note-taking was my primary and most important recording technique.

I also took digital pictures and made video recordings. The aim was to capture certain attitudes and interactions of pupils, ones that would otherwise have been difficult, if not impossible, to describe in words. However, photography as a data-collecting method has been criticised, mainly because 'a camera does not record what the ethnographer sees and hears, but a mechanically limited selection of it', excluding all that is not in front of its lenses (Davies, [1998] 2008: 133-134). Moreover, there is the risk of manipulation through staging (*Ibid.*). Despite these grounded criticisms, I found photography an invaluable method for capturing pupils' interactions with digital media, the ways they engaged in digital-media-driven multitasking and such things. The pictures, together with the written descriptive account, provide a much richer image of the use of digital media in the history class. At the *Baarnsch Lyceum* in particular, video recording helped to capture the attitudes and behaviour both before and during the projection of Web-based videos. Educational psychology and qualitative research theorist Steiner Kvale (1996: 160-161; see also Clayman & Gill, 2004: 592) postulated that video recording is unique in capturing not only interpersonal interaction, but also 'facial expressions and bodily posture'.

In short, I recorded data mostly by taking field notes [observations, discussions, interviews with children and teachers] as well as [only occasionally for the *Baarnsch Lyceum* case study] by taking still and moving images, and recording interviews. Lastly, I should add that I am aware of the foreseeable criticism of my data recording at the *Baarnsch Lyceum*, where I purposely decided to use neither audio nor video [the latter only occasionally and in a few cases] recording devices. The reason was that the research milieu was 'hostile' to their use. The use of recording devices would have hindered my smooth integration into the group.

4.8 Summary

The aim of this short methodological chapter was twofold: to frame the central research question – how do pupils interact with digital media during their history class? – which I decided to explore based on three assumptions or hypotheses raised in existing literature on the subject. I have explained that I opted for an ethnographic approach, applying it to two case studies. My interest was much more in understanding, describing, and subsequently interpreting the uses of digital media and resources by the selected secondary school pupils. Within this approach, I decided to be a moderate participant observer, by sitting among the pupils and following their exchanges, their interactions with teachers and digital media, and conducting unstructured interviews with them. The latter technique proved efficient in the sense that it kept the exchanges natural. My interaction with teachers mainly took the form of semi-structured interviews. I mentioned how I strove to win the pupils' trust while at the same time refraining from becoming their peer. I discussed the context within which I used content analysis to explore two variables – historical thinking and variety of sources – in pupils' written assignments. Finally, I briefly introduced the field data collecting techniques I used, namely note-taking, sound and video recording, and photography. In the next three chapters I first discuss Case Study One (Chapter 5) and Case Study Two (Chapter 6) and then I provide my analysis of the findings of the two case studies (Chapter 7).

Chapter 5

Case Study One: the *Baarnsch Lyceum*

In early April 2009 I met history teacher Antheun Janse at the 26th edition of the *Nationale Onderwijstentoonstelling* [National Education Exhibition, NOT] in Utrecht. To be precise, we met during a workshop hosted by *Noordhoff Uitgevers*, one of the leading Dutch educational publishing houses. The latter was introducing its new product under the name of *Geschiedenis i-Werkplaats* [History i-exercise book]. This i-exercise book was Web- and CD ROM-based, with exactly the same design as the printed version. The difference was that the i-exercise book was *interactive* – hence the *i* – as teachers and pupils could hyperlink to or from any part of the book, import pictures and do many other operations. Each of the participants introduced him- or herself, and it was then that I realised that Janse was a history teacher, interested in using new technologies and media in the history class. There was a degree of convergence in our interests. Mine was in knowing how he and his colleagues integrate the latest technologies in their classrooms, while his was in knowing what the latest technologies had to offer.

It was one of Janse's classes at the *Baarnsch Lyceum* in Baarn that I observed one year later, from January to May 2010. I attended the class once, sometimes twice a week. In this chapter, I shall present the results of that field research. In the first place, I shall briefly place the class in its context, that is, situate it within the Dutch educational system, and describe the class and its pupils; then I shall present the results proper of my field research, organising them around the three points mentioned previously (see Chapter 4, Section 4.1), namely the attractiveness of the history class subsequent to the use of digital media and resources, how the latter fosters historical thinking, and the variety of sources that result from the use of digital media. The findings are analysed in Chapter 7.

Figure 5.1: History teacher starting his lesson at the Baarnsch Lyceum (Photo: O.N., 14 April 2010).

5.1 The System, the Place, and the People

> Every social situation can be identified by three primary elements: *a place, actors,* and *activities.* In doing participant observation you will locate yourself in some place; you will watch actors of one sort or another and become involved with them; you will observe and participate in activities. These primary elements do not exhaust the social and cultural meaning of social situations, but they do serve as a springboard into understanding them. Most important by focusing on a single situation you will greatly simplify the task of beginning your ethnographic research (Spradley, 1980: 39-40).

As suggested by Spradley (see epigraph), I shall briefly introduce my research environment via the *place-actors-activities* triangle. I shall start with the broader framework – the school – by placing it within the Dutch education system, before coming to the actors and finally to the activities in the last three sections. The class I observed had a name: B2D. The B stands for *brugklas*, literally 'bridge class', and stands for the intermediary cycle between primary school and the upper cycle of secondary school; the 2 represents the *second* year of that lower cycle; and the D distinguishes that particular class from other parallel B2 classes. The school offers two sorts of education: *hoger algemeen voortgezet onderwijs* [general secondary education, HAVO]; and *voorbereidend wetenschappelijk onderwijs* [pre-university education, VWO], whereby the latter is subdivided into two types – the *gymnasium* offering Latin, Greek and Classical Arts; and the *atheneum,* which does not offer these classical courses. Thus, the pupils I observed were heading either toward a HAVO or a VWO upper cycle, both of which open the doors to higher education, either at a vocational college [in the case of HAVO] or at a university [in the case of VWO].

The pupils I observed were having history for a second consecutive year, with two 50-minute lessons a week. History is a compulsory discipline in the entire three-year lower cycle of HAVO/VWO schools. The law that provides for the organisation of the lower cycle, the *Wet op het voortgezet onderwijs* [Secondary Education Act, WVO],[156] lists twelve goals that the *Mens en Maatschappij* [Mankind and Society] course – under which the history class [together with Civics, Geography, and Social Studies] falls – should strive to achieve. These goals can be divided into four categories: goals for social studies, for history, for civics and for geography. The goals of history classes are that pupils learn: [1] how to place events, people, and major developments within the framework of the ten historical eras (see Chapter 1), and to establish connections between past events and developments in the twentieth century; [2] how to identify the implications of the image [they have] of their locality, the Netherlands, Europe, and the world *vis-à-vis* their own environment; [3] how to use historical sources; [4] how to view current tensions and conflicts against their historical background. A few other goals, though meant for civics or Social Studies, are also relevant to the history classes. These include for instance the goal stipulating that [5] 'pupils learn how to ask meaningful questions about social issues' and how to take a critical stand about them. Another states that [6] pupils learn how to conduct a simple enquiry into current social issues. The remaining six goals relate to Geography and Civics.

In connection with the class I observed, I should first mention the fact that the *Baarnsch Lyceum* had an entire block reserved for history classes [at the time of my observation]. The very décor of

---

156 Piet Hein Donner [then minister of justice], *Wet op het voortgezet onderwijs (WVO), Besluit Kerndoelen onderbouw VO* (The Hague, 11 July 2006). http://www.st-ab.nl/wettennr06/0728-010_Besluit_kerndoelen_onderbouw_VO.htm (Accessed 10 September 2010).

the block announced that these classes were exclusively dedicated to history: the outer facet of the main window of one of the classrooms in which B2D attended their history class was entirely covered with historical or cultural heritage posters. One poster of the *Hollandsche Schouwburg*, the Amsterdam-based theatre [1892–1942] that served as a deportation centre [1942–1943] during World War II and subsequently became a national monument in memory of the deportees, showed a black-and-white picture of the World War II deportees with the title: '*Theater 1892–1942 – deportatieplaats 1942–1943 … Monument tentoonstelling*'. Next to it, another poster of the *Mauritshuis* – a Hague-based arts museum – announced a *Droom Uit Italië* [Dreams from Italy] exhibition to be held between 11 March and 25 June 2006. Beside it was the poster of the Canon of the Netherlands, followed by two of the Allard Pierson Museum announcing, in both Dutch and English: 'Objects for Eternity. Ancient Egyptian Treasures'; and 'Crete, Cradle of Europe'. Though these four were imposing, they still left room for smaller posters. A similar impression was generated inside of the classroom: the same window was covered with historical maps showing not only local Dutch places, but also other parts of Europe and the world. The rest of the window was almost entirely covered with Canon of the Netherlands' window posters, that is, posters for individual windows as well as other smaller posters. In the corner was a TV set and a showcase containing books, DVDs and a variety of old objects.

Having briefly described the physical environment in which I conducted my research, and having placed it within the educational system, I would now like to move to the second point in Spradley's triangle: the *actors*. The B2D pupils were aged between 13 and 14 years, that is, the early years of adolescence (Steinberg, 1985: 6-7; Fine and Sandstrom, 1988: 11). The class had a total of 24 pupils: 13 girls and 11 boys. Pupils sat in pairs behind a single desk, girls next to girls and boys next to boys. The chairs and desks were arranged in three columns and four rows. The pupils, who all sat facing the blackboard, generally did not change their seats. The next three sections deal with the last aspect of the Spradley triangle: *activities*.

Figure 5.2: B2D pupils watching a Web-based video from the Canon of the Netherlands (Photo: O.N., 14 April 2010).

5.2 Attractiveness

> … a particular medium can be described in terms of its capability to present certain representations and perform certain operations in interaction with learners who are similarly engaged in internally constructing representations and operating on these (Kozma, 1994: 10).

In this section, I shall focus on ways in which the Web appeared to make history lessons more lively and attractive for the pupils. The notion of 'attractiveness' as I use it refers to a state in which learners find themselves subsequent to certain external factors, and whereby they are inclined to undertake a certain action or behave in a certain way that shows interest and engagement. Such external factors are said to be attractive if they create pleasure, interest, concern, and engagement.[157] Attractiveness is first considered in situations whereby the teacher used the Web during class time, mostly as a source of Web-based historical videos. I shall also discuss pupils' inclination to use their mobile phones during class time, especially when the teacher shifted from the Web to a textbook.

The lesson was about to start. Pupils were taking pens and text/note books out of their bags while chatting together about the latest sports or political news. Janse, the teacher, had already switched on the projector and his laptop computer. From a Microsoft Word document with his course plan showing '*Rond de Gouden Eeuw*' [Around the Golden Century (1600–1700)], he clicked on a hyperlink to open a Canon of the Netherlands page dedicated to '*Eise Eisinga 1744–1828. De Verlichting in Nederland*'[158] [Eise Eisinga 1744–1828. The Enlightenment in the Netherlands]. On the right side of the window, he clicked on a thumbnail showing: '*Canonclip voortgezet onderwijs*'[159] [Canon clip for secondary education]. A new page opened, by which time the pupils were ready, although some noisy discussions were still going on, prompting the teacher to ask for silence every now and then. The noise finally stopped when Janse announced the film and asked the pupils to watch and take notes, drawing their attention to the concept of the Enlightenment, the age of Eise Eisinga, and on the latter's achievements.

The video began, full-screen. A male voice began telling the story of Eise Eisinga. Pupils watched and took notes. 'Since the Middle Ages, scientists had relied on the Bible and on the Church Fathers, but as of the 18th century, rationalism was emerging with the idea of enquiring into everything'. This is how the clip began. It went on: 'The Friesland-born Eise Eisinga is a child of the Enlightenment'. The commentator then introduced and commented on the early works and achievements of Eisinga, including a book on arithmetic at the age of 15 and a planetarium showing the solar system hanging from the ceiling of his living room. He also commented on think-

157 John Dewey ([1916]1926: 148-149) conceptualised the notion of interest, which is close to attractiveness as I use it, in terms of absorption by the tasks in which one is engaged: 'To be interested is to be absorbed in, wrapped up in, carried away by, some object. To take an interest is to be on the alert, to care about, to be attentive. We say of an interested person both that he has lost himself in some affair and that he has found himself in it. Both terms express the engrossment of the self in an object'.

158 The Canon of the Netherlands, '*Eise Eisinga 1744-1828. De Verlichting in Nederland*'. http://www.entoen.nu/eiseeisinga (Accessed 6 July 2010).
Eise Eisinga was 'an amateur astronomer who built a planetarium in his own home in Franeker (Friesland). Today this planetarium is recognised as the oldest in the world' (*Ibid.*).

159 The Canon of the Netherlands, '*Canonclip: Eise Eisinga (voortgezet onderwijs)*'. http://entoen.nu/eiseeisinga/beeld-en-geluid/canonclip-eise-eisinga-%28voortgezet-onderwijs%29#beeld (Accessed 6 July 2010).

ers of the age of Enlightenment, Rousseau and Voltaire, while their pictures were shown. Towards the end of the clip, a black screen appeared with a question both in text and audio: 'Science is rational while faith is emotional. Is the society in which we currently live rational or emotional?'[160] 'EMOTIONAL!' the pupils called out loud in unison. The question was not being put to the pupils directly, but to two young girls and one boy who were being interviewed in the clip. They all said the society they lived in was more rational than emotional and explained why. These answers triggered discussions among the pupils, some of whom agreed, while others disagreed. Then there was another black screen and another text with a voice asking: 'Are you [yourself] rational or emotional?'[161] This time, the class was divided. Some said 'RATIONAL!' and others maintained 'EMOTIONAL!'. The teacher asked why the answer was now 'rational' for some while everyone had answered 'emotional' in reply to the first question. When this led to further discussions among the pupils with clearly conflicting views, the teacher asked each to write down their arguments on paper and submit their essays during the next session.

Janse asked the pupils for silence again as he wanted to replay the clip. Unlike the first time, he now pressed the pause button from time to time in order to make comments. When the commentator announced Eise Eisinga's age, he paused and commented. He did it again when the clip reached the planetarium and the arithmetic book. He then paused on the pictures of Rousseau and Voltaire and commented on Liberty-Equality-Fraternity. All in all, the clip and related explanations lasted about 30 minutes. The teacher then moved to the next point. The laptop and the projector remained on, reflecting the Eise Eisinga page, but he made no further use of them.

'Any questions about the assignment [from last time]?' Janse asked. He was referring to the subjects he had handed out the previous week. The pupils were to deal with them in groups of two and submit their written assignments by the end of the period [in about six weeks' time]. Topics related to the Golden Century (see Section 5.4). Pupils who had questions raised their hand and the teacher went to each of them. Noisy discussions erupted between pupils, some of which were close to arguments. Some pupils took out their iPhones and started browsing the Web or SMS-ing. A fight, or what nearly became a fight, broke out in one corner, as a result of which the teacher sent one boy out. Two of the boy's classmates wanted to

---

160 Original Dutch text: '*Wetenschap is rationeel en geloof emotioneel. Leven wij nu in een rationele of emotionele samenleving?*'

161 Original Dutch text: '*Ben jij rationeel of emotioneel?*'

follow him, but the teacher ordered them to stay. Even from outside, the boy kept up a disturbance on the other side of the door. Five minutes later Janse called the boy in, though the class was still as noisy and chaotic as it had been when he was sent out. A few minutes before the end of the lesson, the teacher returned to the front of the classroom and moved on to the last point on his agenda: how to write a good historical article. He showed the class a few examples that he considered to be exemplary. Almost all had titles that had most likely been edited with Microsoft Word Art, some in colours, and all contained more than one picture. The class was more or less silent again and all pupils' eyes were directed at the screen and the teacher standing in front of it. He explained the function of the title, the introduction, the body, the conclusion, and footnotes, as well as how to cite sources and bibliographic references.

The above is a representative sketch of the 50-minute B2D history class during the period of my research. The large screen in front of the class and the moving or still images and texts it showed, as well as the sounds it emitted in combination with those images and texts, all supported by explanations and comments from the teacher, seemed to have the power to keep the pupils calm and – more importantly – attentive. The few minutes during which the teacher stopped using the screen culminated in chaos and a complete lack of concentration and interest on the part of the adolescents. There seemed to be a direct link between on the one hand, quietness, attention and concentration when digital media were used, and on the other hand, noisy discussions, quarrels and lack of attention when digital media were not used. For instance, on one occasion, when Janse shifted from the screen and Web-supported resources to the textbook, two pupils sitting beside me made a shift of their own. Their attention shifted from the large screen and the teacher to the small screen of their iPhones. The first, Rick,[162] browsed to the Ajax football club website, while the other, Mike, browsed to Google.nl, probably to carry out a search. Their talk, though not noisy, went as follows:

> -*Rick*: Ajax won yesterday
>
> -*Mike*: I know.
>
> -*Rick*: They will be champions
>
> -*Mike*: No. I don't think so.
>
> [Then another pupil, Kaj, sitting at the desk in front of them, turned around to face the other two, wanting to glance at the screen on Rick's iPhone]

162 None of the names attributed to pupils are their actual names.

-*Rick*: Where is your iPhone?

-*Kaj*: My mother took it away.

-*Mike*: Wow! What did you did?

-*Kaj*: Nothing bad. I had a bad mark.

The teacher interrupted this talk when he saw Kaj with his back turned toward him. The two phones did not go further than under the covers of the textbooks Rick and Mike were pretending to read. I could see that other pupils were also busy with their phones either covertly or overtly, browsing the Web or something similar, with textbooks lying open on the table. In the meantime, other pupils, at the request of the teacher, were reading aloud from the textbook, paragraph for paragraph. Thus, two categories of activities were going on simultaneously: on the one hand textbook reading and related explanations, and, on the other hand, private activities, most of which centred around the iPhone, *e.g.*, Web browsing, gaming, *etc.* This schedule of digital media and resources, textbook reading followed by teacher's explanation and group or individual assignment, was the one used most frequently during the period of my field research. The order in which the activities took place varied. However, two other schedules were noted: one with no digital media being used at all, and one – rare – comprising nothing but the use of digital media.

On some occasions, thus, Janse used no digital media at all, the whole lesson long. Generally, such lessons were far from quiet. It was no easy task getting the pupils to stop their discussions after they had entered the classroom, as they seemed oblivious of the teacher's injunctions. When the pupils became quiet, it would not take long before their attention shifted away from the blackboard or textbook to their iPhones, either for messaging or Web-browsing. On one such occasion, on 3 March 2010, the teacher announced right from the start that he would not be using a projector or computer. He announced: 'Today, we're going to deal with current affairs [*actualiteit*]'. Municipal elections were taking place on that day. Indeed, even as they entered the classroom, the pupils were commenting on the previous night's TV-debate between political leaders that had been held at the Erasmus University in Rotterdam. The teacher somehow managed to pick up on their discussions. According to the agenda, however, the lesson was supposed to be about 'Louis XIV, an absolute monarch'. Janse explained to the quieter pupils that 'elections are all about power … who has or wants to have power'. He then asked: Who currently has power [in the Netherlands]? The question was not fortuitous, as Prime Minister Jan-Peter Balkenende and his coalition cabinet had resigned in February. 'Is it Balkenende?' he asked. Some said 'yes' while others said 'no'. One girl, who belonged to the former group, argued that the prime ministry as an institution has power. A boy from the latter group counter-argued that the lower chamber of the parliament [the House of Representatives] had power. Yet another said that the Queen had the most power.

After 30 minutes spent discussing this 'news', the teacher asked the pupils to open their textbooks on the page about Louis XIV, explaining that 'Elections such as those we have today have a history', even in the reign of Louis XIV, a history that was marked by internal fights between Prime Minister Mazarin and the knights. Then the paragraph-for-paragraph reading began, interrupted by comments and explanations. However, one boy beside me preferred to take out his iPhone and browse to the website of *de Volkskrant*, a daily newspaper, which had regular postings of updates and pictures of the election.[163] This lesson, which ended with an assignment on 'who has power?', 'the Queen's powers', and 'the relationship between citizens and leaders from a historical perspective', was generally quiet, as pupils seemed to be engaged, though some did shift to their digital gadgets towards the end of the lesson. This concentration and attention could be explained by the fact that the teacher's approach was based on a 'hot', highly mediatised subject, one that the pupils had clearly followed with keen interest.

On another occasion, Janse started his lesson by handing out previously written assignments that he had marked. After a few comments on them, he asked the pupils to choose between a historical film on the Golden Century and group-work on an assignment using laptops. 18 pupils raised their hands in favour of the laptops, while 2 wanted to watch the film. 4 abstained. In the meantime, questions arose. One was: 'Can we do both?' [film and assignments on laptops]. Another was: 'Can we work with iPhones [instead of laptops] Sir?' The teacher rejected both suggestions and went out to fetch the laptops. When the laptops had been distributed, one laptop per two pupils, the pupils started attempting to get them connected to the school's wireless network. All their attempts failed. A message on the screen persistently asked them to be patient but they could not wait longer than five minutes. 'Do you have internet?' one pupil at the front asked. 'No!' replied another. Yet another said: 'Yes, I have it, but on my iPhone'. Pupils' reactions to this technical failure were of three sorts. Some, especially the girls, gave up trying

163 The pupil was on this page: http://www.volkskrant.nl/binnenland/article1354944.ece/Lokale_thémas_ondergesneeuwd

to connect to the network and opened Microsoft Word to work on their assignments, though they could not check their Web-based resources. One pair had a USB stick containing their work. Others, especially the boys, persisted in their efforts to get connected. While some – two pairs – took their laptops out into the corridor, nearer to the network antenna, others started working on the network settings in an effort to get connected. Both attempts did not deliver any results. The last response was simply to shift from the laptop to the iPhone, for which connecting to the network was not an issue, as the iPhone did not depend on the school's inefficient network. I should say that, in the end, most pupils spent their time either attempting to connect to the Internet or using iPhones to navigate the Web on subjects not necessarily related to their assignments. Only a few had taken advantage of the limited off-line advantages offered by the laptop computers. As all them were involved in an activity they seemed to enjoy, the class was quiet.

Similarly to other schools in the country, the *Baarnsch Lyceum*'s computer room got connected to the Internet in the early 2000s, but the connection was not extended to reach the classrooms until 2007. In that same year the school received laptop computers and projectors. However, Internet connectivity remained poor in the block reserved for history classes. Unlike that block, the computer room had a faster connection, but this room was always overbooked.[164] Janse's three colleagues with whom I spoke had renounced using Web-based resources, all blaming their decision on the Internet connectivity issue. [65] As for Janse, he said that, unlike other historical websites, the one of the Canon of the Netherlands website loaded faster, especially videos, which explains his preference for the Canon clips.

164 Author interview with Antheun Janse, history teacher at the *Baarnsch Lyceum* (Baarn, 28 January 2010).

165 Andrea Koomen, who taught a HAVO class of 15- to 16-year olds, told me on 8 March 2010 that she never used the computer during her lesson for a number of reasons, including uncertain Internet connectivity.

Figure 5.3: B2D pupil reacting to a statement made in a Web-based video from the Canon (Video recording: ON., 14 April 2010

5.3 Historical Thinking

> … Finally, at about eleven to twelve years of age, there begins a fourth and final period of which the plateau of equilibrium coincides with adolescence. This period is characterized in general by the conquest of a new mode of reasoning, one that is no longer limited exclusively to dealing with objects or directly representable realities, but also employs 'hypotheses', in other words, propositions from which it is possible to draw logical conclusions without it being necessary to make decisions about their truth or falsity before examining the result of their implications (Piaget, [1969] 1971: 30-33).

In this section, I describe the way in which the historical thinking of B2D pupils manifested itself both through class interactions [among pupils, with the teacher or with digital media] and through their written assignments. As briefly explained in Chapter 4 (Section 4.1), the notion of historical thinking I use relates more to adolescent thinking than to expert thinking. In this respect, any sign indicating that a pupil has gone beyond the surface message to make some relevant associations, comparisons, inductions or deductions, is interpreted as a manifestation of some form of historical thinking. In what follows, I shall first consider 'live' situations, that is, those that happened while a lesson was in progress. They include answers to the teacher's questions and spontaneous, Web-prompted verbal and gestural reactions. I will then look at forms of historical thinking as reflected through written assignments.

One day in January the pupils were entering the classroom while their history teacher, Janse, was preparing the large screen and the laptop computer. When both the pupils and he were ready to start the lesson, he asked a question: 'What does water have to do with the Golden Century?' While the pupils were still *thinking*, he went on to say: 'before answering, let's watch a clip from the Canon'. He asked them to take notes, taking into account five aspects that their final written assignments must also take into account: economic, political, scientific, social, and cultural aspects.

The Canon clip on the *Beemster*[166] then started. A male voice spoke while pictures, including animations, were showing on the screen. Against a backdrop of old maps, the voice announced: 'Four centuries ago the *Beemster* Lake was drained using windmills. [More] Land was needed for food supplies for Amsterdam'.[167] Most pupils were already writing in their notebooks. At this precise moment, Dirk, the pupil beside me, wrote the following: '*Economie: boeren gaan voedsel verkopen*' [Economy: farmers will sell foodstuffs]. Next to him, Stan wrote: '*politieke beslissing droogmaken*' [draining the lake was a political decision]. The clip went on, giving the details of the 1612 project: 38 km-long dike to hold the water, 43 windmills to drain the lake, *etc.*. At a certain moment, the commentator said that 'the *Beemster* project was conducted following a mathematical schema'.[168] This time too, almost all the pupils wrote something down. Dirk and Stan wrote respectively: '*wetenschappen*' [sciences] and '*Wiskunde = wetenschap*' [Mathematics = science]. While the video depicted ancient Greek vases, the commentator suggested that the resulting geometrical forms were similar to those on the Greek vases. He further indicated that the draining of the *Beemster* had a

166 The Canon of the Netherlands, '*Canonclip. De Beemster (voortgezet onderwijs)*'. http://entoen.nu/beemster/beeld-en-geluid/canonclip-de-beemster-%28voortgezet-onderwijs%29#beeld (Accessed 8 July 2010).

167 Original Dutch text: '*Vier eeuwen geleden werd de Beemster meer leeggemalen. Er was land nodig voor de voedsel voorziening van Amsterdam*'.

168 Original Dutch text: '*De Beemster is volgens een wiskundig patroon aangelegd*'.

big impact both inside and outside Europe. This time, a few pupils, including my two neighbours, jotted something down in their notebooks. Dirk wrote: 'VOC???',[169] while Stan wrote: '*handel–economie*' [commerce–economy]. The clip mentioned that the *Beemster* is on the UNESCO World Heritage list and ended with questions and responses regarding the preservation of cultural heritage sites.

At the end of the film the teacher repeated his initial question about the role of water during the Golden Century, narrowing it down to each of the five aspects. 'Who noted something about the economy?' he asked. Five pupils raised their hands. 'The land obtained after draining led to an increase in agricultural production and thus to a growth in the economy', said Jennie. The teacher acquiesced. A few desks away from her, Tess added: 'I *think* that the draining meant the end of a fishing-based economy in the area'. The teacher approved, smiling. The teacher then remarked: 'But there is still one other important economic aspect'. As he did not receive a quick answer, he said: 'The draining led to greater specialisation in agriculture and cattle-rearing. This specialisation resulted in a higher productivity and ultimately in exporting the surplus in products'. Dirk promptly and excitedly said: 'Yes! I noted it! The VOC!' The teacher acquiesced and moved to the scientific aspect. Braham, sitting at the front, said: 'The drainage took place according to a mathematical plan'. Niels added: 'To make windmills powerful enough to drain a lake also involved scientific knowledge'. The teacher acquiesced in response to both answers.

During the 30 minutes that the clip and related exercises lasted, it was easy to notice how the pupils made quick associations between the clip and other prior knowledge they had, and how these associations were guided by the teacher's initial remarks. The teacher's emphasis on the five aspects was a way of telling the pupils that they should go beyond the clip and place it in a broader context. The ideas that the statements and images in the clip brought to the mind of each pupil were different, depending on which perception was prompted by the *thinking* process. For instance, the statement 'Four centuries ago the *Beemster* Lake was drained using windmills. [More] Land was needed for food supplies for Amsterdam' drew the pupils' attention in at least four different ways: Jennie perceived *economy* in it, as farmers would have more land and produce more food items which they could *sell* in Amsterdam; Stan perceived *politics* in it, as such an important, nature-transforming decision could but emanate from *political* authorities; Dirk, Stan and Niels per-

169 VOC stands for *Verenigde Oost-Indische Compagnie,* the Dutch East India Company that was founded in 1602 and was involved in commercial activities between the Netherlands and Asia until around 1800.

ceived *science* in it, as envisaging such a complex project required *technical* and *scientific* knowledge both in *making windmills* and in placing them in strategic places to get the best out of them. As for Tess, she looked at it from the *social* perspective, since draining the lake implied changes in the social status of fishermen and their communities.

On another occasion in April, the teacher spent almost half of the lesson time [about 25 minutes] playing a clip on the 'Patriots' [1780–1795][170] from the school-tv database and which has been integrated into the Canon page on the Patriots (See the vignette at the beginning of the book's introduction). A female voice briefly sketched how the Republic was governed and how State Holder William V emerged as an authoritarian leader. Though the clip started playing while the pupils were still talking noisily, after 10 to 15 seconds they had settled down and were listening silently. At one point, the commentator mentioned the citizens' complaints about their leader: 'Moreover, the State Holder acts as if he were a king'.[171] At this moment, Braham, sitting two desks in front of me, said [to himself]: 'Guillotine'. Then, the commentator mentioned the pamphlets that angry citizens, the Patriots, were distributing to express their opposition to William V. Quoting one of them written by Joan Derk van der Capellen [1741–1784], the commentator said: 'The State Holder controls the army, that is why the citizens have no power. They cannot undertake anything against William V. *He can do whatever he wants'* [Italicisation is mine].[172]

As soon as the italicised passage was pronounced, Braham spontaneously said [to himself again]: '*Echt niet!*' [No way!, meaning, 'that is impossible, unacceptable!']. He completed his response with a revealing gesture: with his right hand, he turned his fingers into a pistol – the index and middle finger forming the barrel and the ring finger and pink the grip – and 'shot' himself in the side of his head (see Figure 5.3). This verbal and gestural reaction shows that Braham had processed the information conveyed by the clip, weighed it against his prior knowledge about the French Revolution [where the *Guillotine* was first used] and, in a fraction of a second, had come to a conclusion: William V – who behaved like the *Ancien Régime* aristocracy – deserved, like that aristocracy, the Guillotine or, at least, a shot in the head.

170 The Canon of the Netherlands, '*Schooltv Beeldbankclip: De Patriotten*'. http://entoen.nu/patriotten/beeld-en-geluid/schooltv-beeldbankclip-de-patriotten#beeld (Accessed 10 September 2010).

171 Dutch original text: '*Bovendien doet de Stadhouder als hij de koning is*'.

172 Original Dutch Text: '*De stadhouder heeft de leiding over het leger, daarom heben de burgers geen macht. Ze kunnen niets beginnen tegen Willem V. Hij kan doen wat hij wil*'.

This association, together with those mentioned in previous examples, resulted from a *thinking* process in which at least four factors came into play: a medium that kept the learner engaged (see previous section), proper guidance from the teacher [on which aspects notes should be taken] and prior knowledge from which learners make associations. It seems that the first factor – a medium that kept the learner engaged – played the most decisive role, since learning and thinking begin when the learner's attention is captured (see Chapter 7).

Similar implications could be detected from the written assignments, though use was made of various media, particularly the Web and books. This fact made it difficult to assess which analogue or digital resources led to which thinking process. In other cases, both book and Web sources were mentioned, which made it difficult to distinguish the role of the Web in the entire thinking process. As I was solely concerned with Web resources, I considered only instances in which it clearly appeared that pupils' historical thinking was backed with, or based on, Web resources. Before considering these texts, I should first mention how they came into being. At the start of the lesson period in January 2010, the teacher made a list of broad topics relating to the Golden Century [1600–1700] and revolving around the five above-mentioned aspects. Each pupil downloaded from the school's intranet [internal network] a two-page document of instructions. The document was entitled:

> Assignment to write an article about one development in 'The Netherlands during the 17th century', the period also known as 'The Golden Century'. The informative character of the article should be enriched with relevant illustrations and suitable captions.[173]

The teacher's instructions also indicated that the pupils must form pairs according to their own affinities. They were also told that it was *mandatory* [*verplicht*] to use at least four sorts of books and at least five sorts of websites as sources (see next section). The document also explained, among other things, how pupils should cite their sources. In the following text analysis, I consider only the passages in which Web sources were clearly used to back the pupils' historical thinking.

173 Original Dutch text: '*Opdracht tot het schrijven van een artikel over een ontwikkeling uit 'De Nederlanden in de 17e eeuw', welke periode ook bekend staat als 'De Gouden Eeuw'. Het informatieve karakter van het artikel dient te worden vergroot aan de hand van enkele relevante illustraties met passend bijschrift*'.

One pair decided to explore the *scientific aspect* by working on '*"Gouden" wetenschap*' ["Golden" science], focusing on mathematician and astronomer Christiaan Huygens [1629–1695], philosopher Benedictus Spinoza [1632–1677] and self-taught astronomer Eise Eisinga [1744–1828]. Their first page, which focused on Huygens mentioned two sources: the Canon's page on Huygens,[174] and the Dutch Wikipedia page on the same scientist which they mistook for the Canon page (see Figure 5.4 below).[175] In other words, no other reference or source was used on this page apart from the above-mentioned Web-pages. The page has 40 lines, with a picture of Huygens without a caption but probably taken from the Wikipedia page on Huygens where the same picture can be found. The first 9 lines contain a general introduction to the assignment, followed by a short introduction to the section on Huygens. Then follows a 9-line quotation from Wikipedia [mistakenly referenced as a Canon page]. The next 12 lines discuss Huygens' education and how his

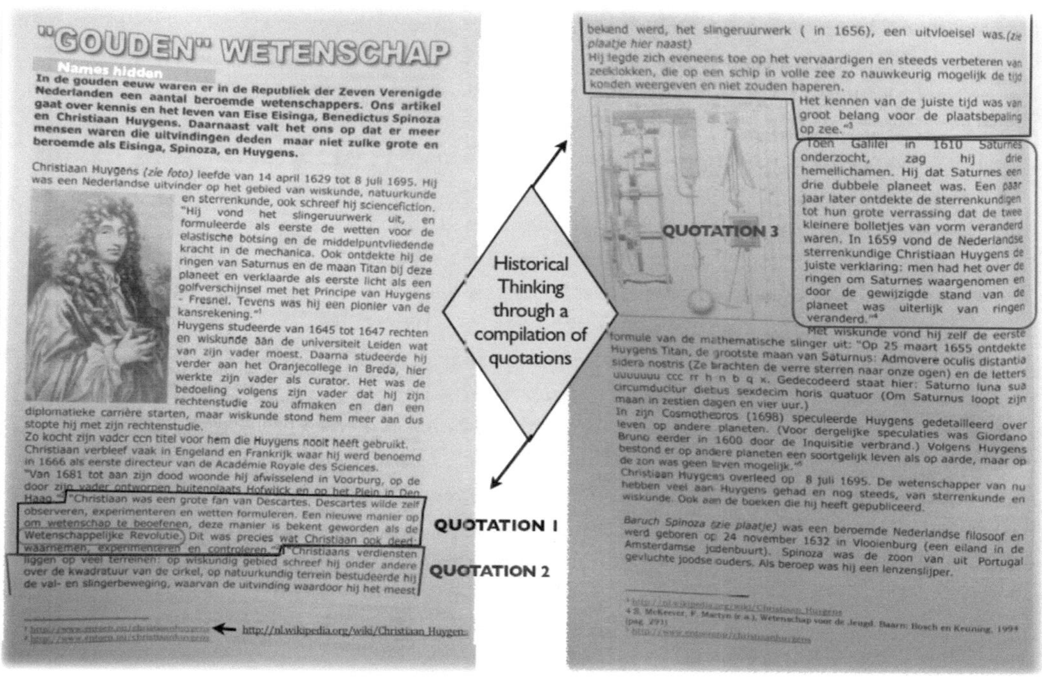

Figure 5.4: Extract from a written class assignment on sciences in the Golden Century.

174 The Canon of the Netherlands, '*Christiaan Huygens 1629–1695. Wetenschap in de Gouden Eeuw*'. http://entoen.nu/christiaanhuygens (Accessed 10 July 2010).

175 Wikipedia, 'Christiaan Huygens'. http://nl.wikipedia.org/wiki/Christiaan_Huygens (Accessed 10 July 2010).

ambitions conflicted with his father's plans. The last 10 lines of this page contain two short quotations from – and a short paraphrasing of – the Canon page, all of which relate to Huygens' admiration of René Descartes, and about his own discoveries in mathematics, physics, and clock making.

On this all-Web inspired page, the first instance of *historical thinking* manifests itself in the following reasoning: the pair *explained* Huygens' work and discoveries by placing them in the broader *historical concept* of the Scientific Revolution, of which Descartes was a part. Like him, they wrote, quoting the Canon, 'he constantly observed, experimented, and monitored'. Half of the second page contains some quotations about Huygens' Pendulum Clock [Wikipedia] and another [from a book[176]] on Galileo's astronomical discoveries, and how these served as the basis for Huygens' subsequent discoveries. Providing the basis on which Huygens' built his own work might be called another instance of *historical thinking*. In other words, of all scientific discoveries made prior to Huygens', the pair *chose* those by Galileo as the most influential on Huygens' own work. However, this historical thinking appears mostly to consist of collecting quotations from Web resources. It is the reasoning behind the choice of often lengthy quotations and the order in which they are placed that show that the pair made an attempt to think historically. Their efforts consisted not in commenting on the associations they highlighted, but in juxtaposing them by using three successive quotations from the above-mentioned sources.

Another pair explored the *cultural aspect* as reflected by '*Rembrandt, de Atlas Major van Blaeu, de Statenbijbel*' [Rembrandt, Blaeu's Atlas Major, the Authorised Dutch version of the Bible]. The two pages on Rembrandt contain 33 lines of text (first page), including an embedded picture of the *Night Watch* [1639–1642]; and, on the second page, five self-portraits, the *Anatomy Lesson of Dr. Nicolaes Tulp* [1632] and *The Jewish Bride* [1664]. The pair cited three Web-pages used for the text: one from *infonu.nl*[177] and two from *scholieren.com.*[178] In this all-Web referenced text, not a single instance of historical thinking could be detected: the first 11 lines discuss Rembrandt's birth and family life; the following 8 lines are a quotation from *infonu.nl*; the last 14 lines describe the *Night Watch*

---

176 Book reference as presented by the pair: S. McKeever, F. Martyn (e.a), *Wetenschap voor de jeugd.*Baarn: Bosch en Keuning, 1994 (pag.291).

177 *InfoNu.nl, 'De vrouwen van Rembrandt'.* http://kunst-en-cultuur.infonu.nl/biografie/3909-de-vrouwen-van-rembrandt.html (Accessed 10 July 2010).

178 *Schoolieren.com, 'Biografie Geschiedenis. Rembrandt van Rijn'.* http://www.scholieren.com/werkstukken/5972; and '*Schilderijverslag CKV. De Nachtwacht*' http://www.scholieren.com/werkstukken/7439 (Both accessed 10 July 2010).

as the most famous of Rembrandt's work [4 lines] and end with a 10-line quotation from *scholieren.com*. All in all, the text does not contain a single *historical*, or *cultural* concept. The pair stuck to the Web resources that they consulted and from which they quoted at length.

The section on Blaeu's *Atlas Major* (see Figure 5.5) follows the same model to some extent: embedded picture of the *Atlas*; an entire page with five pictures of the *Atlas*; and lengthy quotations from Web-pages. The pair added a page with a cartoon. The text is 35 lines long. The introduction is a 7-line quotation from *historische-*

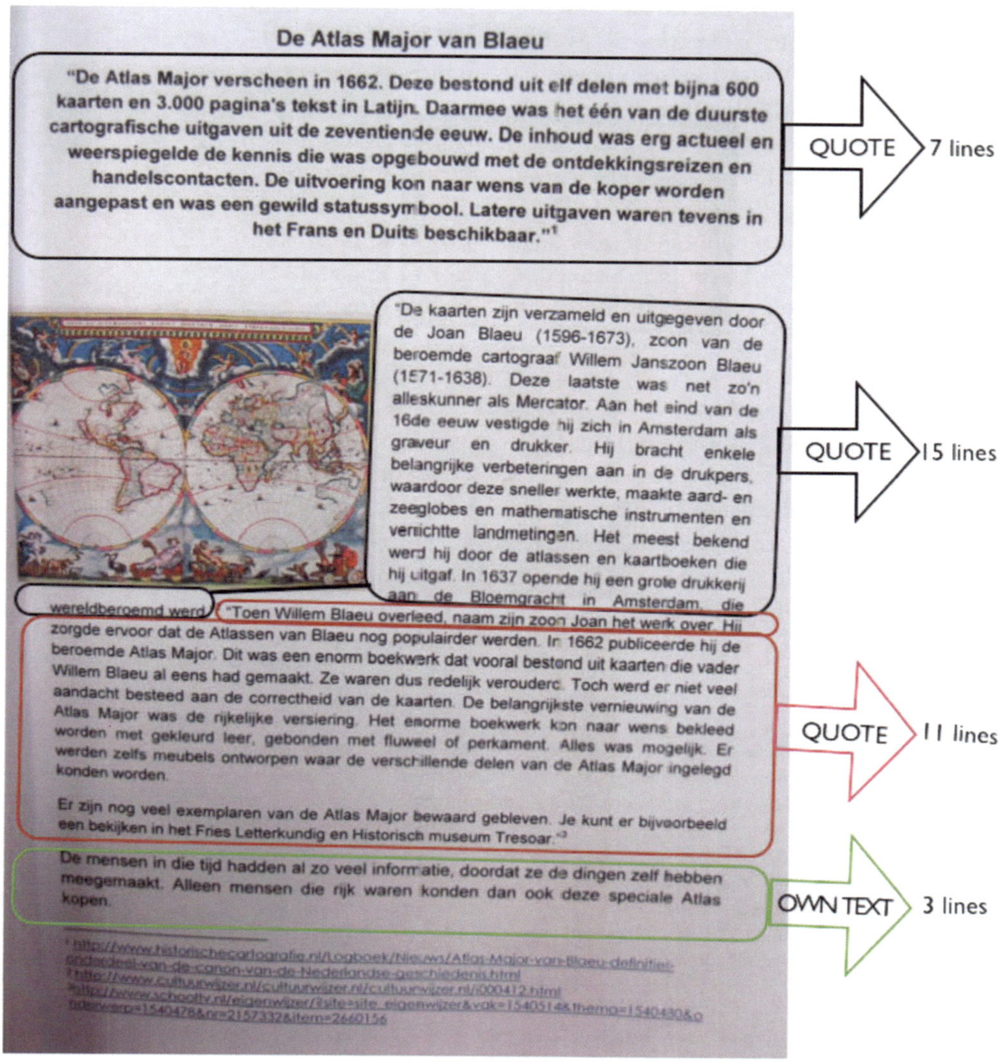

De Atlas Major van Blaeu

"De Atlas Major verscheen in 1662. Deze bestond uit elf delen met bijna 600 kaarten en 3.000 pagina's tekst in Latijn. Daarmee was het één van de duurste cartografische uitgaven uit de zeventiende eeuw. De inhoud was erg actueel en weerspiegelde de kennis die was opgebouwd met de ontdekkingsreizen en handelscontacten. De uitvoering kon naar wens van de koper worden aangepast en was een gewild statussymbool. Latere uitgaven waren tevens in het Frans en Duits beschikbaar."[1]

"De kaarten zijn verzameld en uitgegeven door de Joan Blaeu (1596-1673), zoon van de beroemde cartograaf Willem Janszoon Blaeu (1571-1638). Deze laatste was net zo'n alleskunner als Mercator. Aan het eind van de 16de eeuw vestigde hij zich in Amsterdam als graveur en drukker. Hij bracht enkele belangrijke verbeteringen aan in de drukpers, waardoor deze sneller werkte, maakte aard- en zeeglobes en mathematische instrumenten en verrichtte landmetingen. Het meest bekend werd hij door de atlassen en kaartboeken die hij uitgaf. In 1637 opende hij een grote drukkerij aan de Bloemgracht in Amsterdam, die wereldberoemd werd." "Toen Willem Blaeu overleed, naam zijn zoon Joan het werk over. Hij zorgde ervoor dat de Atlassen van Blaeu nog populairder werden. In 1662 publiceerde hij de beroemde Atlas Major. Dit was een enorm boekwerk dat vooral bestond uit kaarten die vader Willem Blaeu al eens had gemaakt. Ze waren dus redelijk verouderd. Toch werd er niet veel aandacht besteed aan de correctheid van de kaarten. De belangrijkste vernieuwing van de Atlas Major was de rijkelijke versiering. Het enorme boekwerk kon naar wens bekleed worden met gekleurd leer, gebonden met fluweel of perkament. Alles was mogelijk. Er werden zelfs meubels ontworpen waar de verschillende delen van de Atlas Major ingelegd konden worden.

Er zijn nog veel exemplaren van de Atlas Major bewaard gebleven. Je kunt er bijvoorbeeld een bekijken in het Fries Letterkundig en Historisch museum Tresoar."[3]

De mensen in die tijd hadden al zo veel informatie, doordat ze de dingen zelf hebben meegemaakt. Alleen mensen die rijk waren konden dan ook deze speciale Atlas kopen.

[1] http://www.historischecartografie.nl/Logboek/Nieuws/Atlas-Major-van-Blaeu-definitief-onderdeel-van-de-canon-van-de-Nederlandse-geschiedenis.html
[2] http://www.cultuurwijzer.nl/cultuurwijzer.nl/cultuurwijzer.nl/i000412.html
[3] http://www.schooltv.nl/eigenwijzer/?site=site_eigenwijzer&vak=1540514&thema=1540430&onderwerp=1540478&nr=2157332&item=2660156

Figure 5.5: Extract from a written class assignment on culture in the Golden Century.

cartografie.nl;[179] just after this, there is another 15-line quotation from *cultuurwijzer.nl*;[180] this is followed, without any transition, by yet another 11-line quotation from *schooltv.nl*;[181] the 3-line conclusion, the only text that is not [presented as] a quotation and which thus presumably emanated directly from the pair, informs one that: 'People in those days had a lot of information, as they had actually experienced the situations themselves. Only wealthy people could actually afford this special Atlas'. This could be called an instance of historical thinking, as the pupils attempted [rightly] to link the *concept* of access to knowledge to people's *social* and *economic* status.

The same subject was handled by another pair. The difference between the two is the number of quotations used and their length. This pair used four references, all Web-based, for the section on the *Statenbijbel.* These sources included the digitised *Statenbijbel* on the website of the *Nederlands Bijbelgenootschap* [the Dutch Bible Society][182] and the website of the *Statenvertaling* [Dutch Authorised Version].[183] Their three-page, non-illustrated document presents at least two clear instances of historical thinking: at one point, the pair drew an *analogy* between developments in the Republic of the Seven United Netherlands and those taking place in England. The pair pointed out that the 1618 Dordrecht Synod wanted to have an equivalent of the King James Version [1611] of the Bible. At another point, the pair assessed the significance of the *Statenbijbel* for the Dutch language and politics. They suggested that the linguistic rigour that marked the translation paved the way for the Standard Dutch that had emerged since the 17th century. They also mentioned the emergence of new expressions and the integration into Standard Dutch of certain grammatical structures originating from regional dialects. In this respect, historical thinking manifests itself in the way the pair began with a Dutch historical event and *highlighted analogies* with developments in a foreign country as well

179 *Studiekring Historische Cartografie, 'Atlas Major van Blaeu in canon'.* http://www.historischecartografie.nl/Logboek/Nieuws/Atlas-Major-van-Blaeu-definitief-onderdeel-van-de-canon-van-de-Nederlandse-geschiedenis.html (Accessed 10 July 2010).

180 *Cultuurwijzer.nl, 'De drukkerij van de familie Blaeu'.* http://www.cultuurwijzer.nl/cultuurwijzer.nl/cultuurwijzer.nl/i000412.html (Accessed 10 July 2010).

181 *Schooltv.nl, 'De Atlas Major. Grote Wereldatlas van Joan Blaeu'.* http://www.schooltv.nl/eigenwijzer/?site=site_eigenwijzer&vak=1540514&thema=1540480&onderwerp=1540478&nr=2157332&item=2660156 (Accessed 10 July 2010).

182 *Bijbelsdigitaal.nl,* http://www.bijbelsdigitaal.nl/view.php?bible=sv1637&page=50&layout=1 (Accessed 11 July 2010).

183 *Statenvertaling.net, 'De Statenvertaling'.* http://www.statenvertaling.net/info.html (Accessed 11 July 2010).

as *establishing a cause-and-effect* relationship between that event and subsequent linguistic developments.

Dealing with the same subject – the *Statenbijbel* – in a 46-line text that made use of Web sources only [four], another pair relied on a lengthy quotation from *Nederlands Online*[184] [Dutch Online], a website of the *Institut für Deutsche und Niederländische Philologie* [Institute for German and Dutch Philology] of the *Freie Universität Berlin*. The 16-line quotation shows the pair's intention to consider the relationship between the *Statenbijbel* and the Dutch language from a different perspective than that used by the previous pair. The selected quotation draws attention to the view of the general public *vis-à-vis* their language: among other things, it was old-fashioned, with complicated sentence construction.

Yet another pair chose to study *economic* and *political* aspects and they framed their subjects as follows: '*De Gouden Eeuw: economie en politiek*' [The Golden Century: the Economy and Politics]. They focused on the Dutch East India Company [VOC], the Hanseatic League [1356–ca 1450] and Slavery. The section on the VOC starts, on the title page, with a picture of a ship in the middle of a storm. The next three pages, two of which each contain a single picture, are extensively hyperlinked, which suggests two things: firstly, that the pair mostly used Web resources; secondly, that their use could have consisted of copying and pasting chunks of text from the Web-pages they consulted and then modifying them.[185]

In one 8-line paragraph, they discussed competition [*concurreren*], which they hyperlinked, and the 1602 [political] decision of 'the States General, the government of that time' to found the VOC, which is also hyperlinked (see Figure 5.6). In this all-Web inspired paragraph, the pair *linked* the foundation of the VOC to a prevailing *phenomenon* – competition between individual Dutch traders and small-scale companies, and *explained* that the States General's decision was a consequence of that fruitless competition. To arrive at this *cause-and-effect reasoning*, the pair used resources from *scholi-*

184 *Nederlands Online, 'Structuur en geschiedenis van het Nederlands: Een inleiding tot de taalkunde van het Nederlands'.* http://neon.niederlandistik.fu-berlin.de/nl/nedling/taalgeschiedenis/statenbijbel (Accessed 12 July 2010).

185 Most of the hyperlinked words are also hyperlinked on the Wikipedia page they cited: http://nl.wikipedia.org/wiki/Vereenigde_Oostindische_Compagnie (Accessed 10 July 2010).

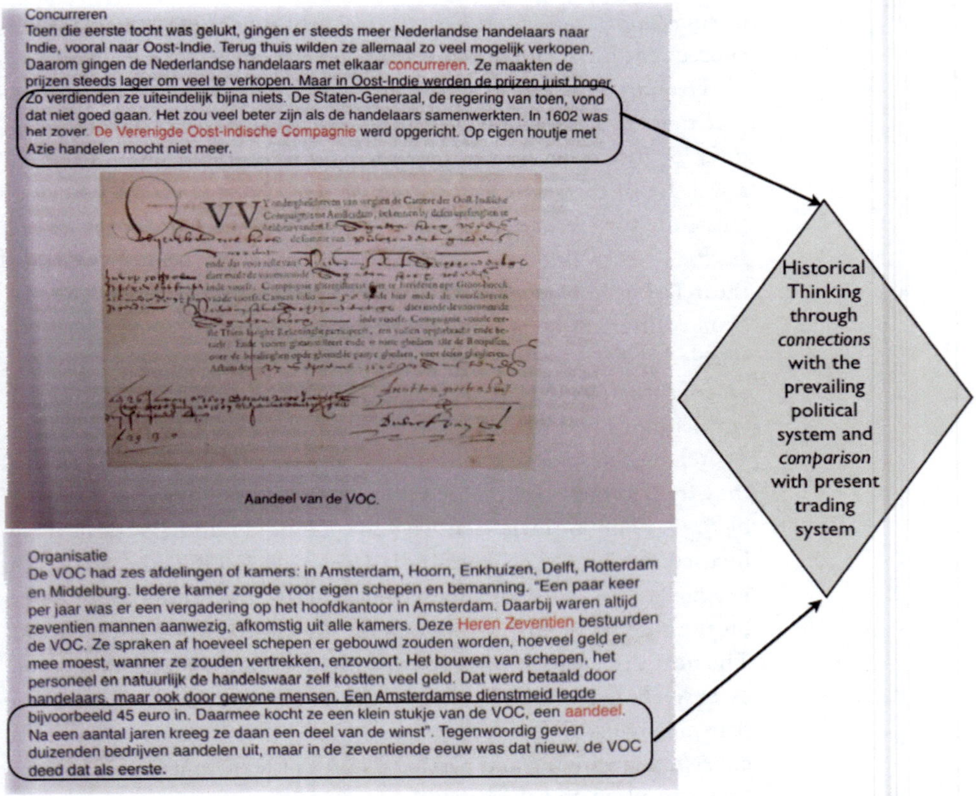

Figure 5.6: Extract from a written class assignment on economy and politics in the Golden Century.

eren.com,[186] the Canon[187] and Wikipedia.[188] In another paragraph on the organisation of the VOC, the pair discussed the birth of *share-holding*, a practice introduced by the VOC in order to raise funds to build new ships and meet other obligations. They drew a *comparison* between then and now: 'Nowadays thousands of companies sell shares, but in the 17th century that phenomenon was new, the VOC was the first to do that'. These two paragraphs show that one of the ways in which the pair made their points, mainly based on *concepts* such as *competition* and *share-holding*, was by placing them in their *contexts*. The use of many hyperlinks and of three Web sources sug-

---

186 *Scholieren.com, 'Spreekbeurt Geschiedenis. De VOC'.* http://www.scholieren.com/werkstukken/16720 (Accessed 10 July 2010).

187 The Canon of the Netherlands, '*De VOC 1602–1799. Nederland breidt uit over zee*'. http://entoen.nu/voc/vo (Accessed 10 July 2010).

188 Wikipedia, '*Vereenigde Oostindische Compagnie*'. http://nl.wikipedia.org/wiki/Vereenigde_Oostindische_Compagnie (Accessed 10 July 2010).

gests that the thinking processes of the pupils were greatly influenced by Web resources.

My aim in this section was to show the different manifestations of historical thinking both during the lesson and via written class assignments. In the first place, it appears that attention-capturing Web resources, especially those that combine audio and visual features, accompanied by some guidance by the teacher, helped to trigger historical thinking. In the second place, the few examples I discussed, which are representative of the 13 assignments, could be summarised as follows: firstly, in more than 50 percent [8 out of 13] of the assignments, attempts at historical thinking consisted of selecting and compiling lengthy quotations deemed relevant to the topic, with very little input from the pair; secondly, attempts at historical thinking resided in the input of pairs, most likely inspired by, and certainly backed up with, relatively short quotations from the Web [3 assignments, one of which contained some paraphrasing]; thirdly, no attempt at historical thinking was made despite the use of Web resources [1 assignment was a perfect pasted copy of Webpages]. The next section discusses the sources pupils used for their written assignments.

Figure 5.7: B2D pupils working on their assignment on the Golden Century (Photo: O.N., 2 February 2010).

5.4 Sources

> ... and in any case it is a necessary part of education that one should acquire the ability to supplement the narrowness of his immediately personal experiences by utilizing the experiences of others. Excessive reliance upon others for data (whether got from reading or listening) is to be depreciated. Most objectionable of all is the probability that others, the book or the teacher, will supply solutions ready-made, instead of giving material that the student has to adapt and apply to the question in hand for himself (Dewey, [1916] 1926: 185).

The document containing instructions on the 'Assignment to write an article about one development in "The Netherlands in the 17th century"...' was very clear on sources the pupils were to use. It was mandatory to use at least four sorts of books, and at least five sorts of websites. Within the category 'books', pupils must use [1] a *textbook* to check 'aspects', 'major lines' and some 'details'; [2] a *general Dutch history book;* [3] an *encyclopaedia* for specific concepts, figures, and situations; and [4] a *specific book on 'your main subject'*. In the 'Web' category, they must use [1] *specific [Canon] 'windows'* and similar windows from [2] *other 'canon sites'*, including *regional canon websites*; [3] a website of choice with an overview of *Dutch history*; [4] *Wikipedia* for specific concepts, figures, and situations; and [5] *online exercises/educational websites*, for instance, www.scholieren.com [*werkstukken* = projects]. In addition to this document, the teacher frequently returned to sources and discussed how to assess them. On one occasion he provided the pupils with – and commented on – a four-point checklist: 1. Is the source *usable* or *relevant* for my research? 2. Is it *representative*? 3. Is it *reliable*? 4. Does it reflect *facts* or is it an *interpretation*? In this section I shall scrutinise the Web-based sources used by the B2D pupils for their written assignments. I shall describe the main types and their uses.

The previous section revealed, among other things, the frequency with which lengthy quotes were used. For instance, one piece of text on the *Statenbijbel,* 46 lines long, contains a 4-line introduction as well as four lengthy quotations [respectively 11, 9, 5, and 16 lines long], all of which were obtained from Web-pages. This 100 percent Web-sourced assignment resulted in a text consisting for about 91 percent of quotation saturation. Another piece of text on '*Politiek in de Gouden Eeuw*' [Politics in the Golden Century], 41 lines long, included a 6-line introduction followed by three lengthy, uninterrupted [*i.e.*: with no transition or comment] quotations, two of which were from websites [18 and 10 lines respectively], the other one [7 lines] having been taken from a print-based encyclopaedia. In other words, this pair had used about 67 percent Web sources and about 33 percent print sources, which resulted in a text comprised for about 15 percent of non-quotation text, 68 percent of Web-sourced quotations and 17 percent of print-sourced quotations. In at least 8 of the 13 cases, the pupils had used Web sources mainly to obtain lengthy quotations for their assignments.

A phenomenon closely related to the use of lengthy quotations is what I shall call 'ripping', which is usually used to refer to copying images or sound files from one electronic carrier [generally streaming media on DVD or the Web] to a computer drive. It involves copying an entire file, which is not the case for copy-pasting. The latter – copy-pasting – was used to refer to the above-mentioned quotations and this does not imply that entire Web-pages were copied. Of the 13 group assignments, one was a case of perfect *ripping* from five Web-pages – 3 from the Canon, 1 from Wikipedia and 1 from *scholieren.com*. In this case, the pair had used 100 percent Web sources and the result was 100 percent transferral of text from the Web onto paper.

The second most important use of the Web for the subjects of the written class assignments consisted of copying images, including pictures, charts and maps. All pairs except one (Pair 13 in Table 5.1) used images. Though all [twelve] of the remaining pairs used

Figure 5.8: Title page of one written class assignment [left] and extract from another [right].

images from the Web, two pairs added scanned images from print documents [books and newspapers] and used them alongside Web-sourced images. I should also add that the twelve pairs had different ways of using images. While some used them soberly, others used as many as they could. For example, one pair used only 3 Web-sourced images for a 5-page document, while another pair used 37 images [32 from the Web and 5 scans] for a final document that was 24 pages long. On the title page alone, 17 images were used to cover the entire page. Yet another pair produced a 12-page document containing 14 Web-sourced images.

Pupils also used Web sources to structure and frame their assignments, often paraphrasing contents they had found on Web-pages. One pair working on the VOC used four Web sources – *voc-kenniscentrum.nl* [a website that is a project of the Royal Netherlands Institute of Southeast Asian and Caribbean Studies], *scholieren.com*, *scholieren.samevattingen.com*, and the *vocsite.nl* – and one book.[189] The text on the two first pages is structured as follows: the title – *De VOC* and three sub-titles – *Oprichting* [Foundation], *Octrooi* [Patent], and *De organisatiestructuur van de VOC* [VOC Organisational structure]. One of the websites cited[190] shows a text with the following structure: the title, *Oprichting, Organisatie en Ondergang van de VOC* [Foundation, Organisation and Fall of the VOC], followed by three paragraphs on the background that led to the *foundation* of the VOC, one paragraph on the *organisation of the VOC* and a final paragraph on the VOC's *Patent*. Though the similarity between the two structures is very striking, this does not imply that this pair had ripped or copy-pasted from that site. Instead, the pair had paraphrased from other websites. For instance, citing – though not quoting from – two sources,[191] the pair used their own words to discuss the VOC's patent and thus formed a new, original text that had been inspired by the two Web-pages.

This kind of paraphrasing of texts could be seen in five assignments. Four of them had one important feature in common: the relatively large number of books used. The first pair cited 6 Web-pages and 3 books and wrote a document that contained almost no quotations. The second cited 5 Web-pages and 3 books and contained a

189 The pair referenced the book as follows: D*e kleurrijke wereld van de VOC, National Jubileumboek VOC 1602-2002.* Leo Akveld en Els M. Jacobs. THOTH, 2002, Bussum, (Blz. 14+14).

190 *VOC Kenniscentrum, 'Oprichting, Organisatie en Ondergang van de VOC'.* http://voc-kenniscentrum.nl/vocbegin.html (Accessed 13 July 2010).

191 *VOCsite.nl, 'Voorcompagnieën'.* http://vocsite.nl/geschiedenis/index.html and *Scholieren.samenvattingen.com, 'Gevolgen van 400 jaar VOC voor de Indiers'* http://scholieren.samenvattingen.com/documenten/show/1469484/ (Both accessed 13 July 2010).

mixture of long quotations, all Web-sourced, and some paraphrasing. The third cited 1 website – in their document of 32 pages, all of which referred to the *Geheugen van Nederland*'s image files – and 8 books (see Pair 3 in Table 5.1). Their text did not contain a single quotation. The fourth pair cited 3 Web-pages and 6 books and contained a few short quotations and many instances of paraphrasing. In these four cases, the greater the number of books used, the greater the extent to which paraphrasing was used and, thus, the fewer quotations there were and the shorter their length. The last case is one pair's assignment in which 22 Web-pages and 1 book were cited. It contained more instances of paraphrasing than those that contained long quotations. The table below gives an overview of the uses of Web and print sources, as well as indicating instances of using long and short quotations and the predominance of paraphrasing and ripping:

Table 5.1: Uses of Web and print sources for class written assignments

	Web Sources						Printed Sources					
	No. of Sources	Quotation predominance		Ripping	Paraphr. Pred.	Images	No. of Sources		Quotation Predominance		Paraphr. Pred.	scans
		Long quot.	Short quot.				Books	News-papers	Long quot.	Short quot.		
Pair 1	20		*		*	20	1				*	
Pair 2	3				*	3	6			*	*	
Pair 3	1					32	8	1			*	5
Pair 4	5	*				7	3					
Pair 5	6				*	4	3	1			*	
Pair 6	24	*				14	6			*		
Pair 7	10	*				20	7	3				3
Pair 8	6	*				5	4					
Pair 9	12	*				8	4					
Pair 10	8	*				4	2					
Pair 11	10	*				23	5					
Pair 12	5	*				4	4			*		
Pair 13	6			*		0	0					

Note: Pair 3 mentioned the *Geheugen van Nederland* as the source of 32 images they used.

The predominance of [long or short] quotations or of paraphrasing, as reflected in Table 5.1, does not refer to their exclusiveness. However, combinations show that paraphrasing predominates where long quotations are absent and *vice versa*, while ripping [Pair 13] excludes every other possibility. Three major points emerge from this table: in the first place, images taken from the Web appear to be omnipresent in all assignments but one, while scans that originated from print media are scarce. This might be explained by the fact that obtaining a scan from the page of a book is a complex, multi-step process, including locating the book, borrowing it [if it is available for loan and if it has not already been loaned out], identifying the relevant page(s), finding a scanner and finally making the scan. The process needs to be repeated for every print-based source. Secondly, many cells in the Print Sources column are empty, which leaves the question about the use of print sources unanswered. Though this falls beyond the scope of this research, I feel that this is due to the ambiguity surrounding the ways in which pupils cited their print-based sources. In many cases, book references were given at the end of the text, but no in-text references were provided to indicate how the source had been used, or where. In most cases involving the use of Web sources, references were presented either in footnotes or endnotes, making it easier to detect where and how they had been used.

Thirdly, there are clearly more long quotations and cases of ripping in the Web Sources column than in the Printed Sources column, where not a single long quotation is noted. This could be explained by the fact that it is easy to search a Web-page and to copy-paste words, sentences, paragraphs, or entire pages into an assignment, while from a printed source this would entail not only physically finding the text in the book, but also retyping it into the assignment. Once, following a remark the teacher made to one pair about the fact that they had neglected to use other sources than websites, I asked one of these two pupils about the reason why they had restricted themselves to using only the Canon and Wikipedia. Her answer was: 'I find it irritating to have to go to the library when I can find everything on the Internet'. She added: 'But since it is compulsory, I shall do it'. Her assignment classmate intervened to add: 'Look! All of us are working on [similar subjects from] the Middle Ages and you cannot be sure of finding the book you are looking for [because other classmates need that same book too]'. Another pupil was busy browsing in a bulky book entitled *De chroniek van de mensheid* [The Chronicles of Humanity]. I asked him how he was enjoying the book and his response was: 'I found information about the three scientists [Huygens, Eisinga, and Spinoza], but it was stupid information [*domme informatie*]. I have forgotten everything [that I've read]'. This pupil formed half of Pair 13 from Table 5.1. That pair had not used a single book and simply ripped the Canon and Wikipedia pages for information on the three scientists. The 'stupidity' of the information in the book might then be interpreted as its refusal to submit itself to the pupil's will. In other words, in all probability the information was regarded as 'stupid' because the pupil could not easily copy or rip it into his assignment.

The next point I want to discuss is the types of Web sources pupils used for their written assignments. In general the Web sources used by the pupils of class B2D can be divided into eleven categories: 1. *Canons*: both the Canon of the Netherlands and the regional canons; 2. *Wikipedia*; 3. *Educational sites*; 4. *Heritage sites* including both those of heritage institutions and those of other non-heritage organisations; 5. *Commercial sites*; 6. *Personal* or *family sites*; 7. *Blogs*; 8. *General information sites*; 9. *Religious sites*; 10. *Academic sites, i.e.*, those maintained by academic research institutes and which contain contents emanating from those institutes; and 11. *Newspaper sites*. Of all these categories, Wikipedia and the Canon appear *ex aequo* to have been used with the greatest frequency, as 11 of 13 pairs cited them or used material from both of them on at least one occasion.

As shown in Table 5.2, Pair 6 cited Wikipedia 9 times and the Canon 4 times. Pair 9 cited the Canon 5 times and Wikipedia twice. The regional canons were cited only five times by four pairs. Pair 9 cited the *Grachtengordel* [the canal ring area of Amsterdam] page of *canon.amsterdam.nl*, while Pair 7 cited the *Utrechtse canons* [Canons of Utrecht], in particular its sub-regional component – the *Canon van Eemland* [Canon of Eemland].[192] Sources relating to the remain-

Table 5.2: Types of Web sources used for class written assignments

Types of websites		Pair 1	Pair 2	Pair 3	Pair 4	Pair 5	Pair 6	Pair 7	Pair 8	Pair 9	Pair 10	Pair 11	Pair 12	Pair 13
Canons	Canon of the NL	2	1		2		4	2	3	5	3	1	2	3
	Reg. Canons						1	1		2				1
Wikipedia		4	1		2	2	9	4	3	2	4		2	1
Educational		8	1		1							4		1
Heritage	Heritage Inst.			1			1	1		1	1	2		
	Others	2				1	4	1		1		1		
Personal /family		3				2	2	1					1	
Commercial						1				1				
Blogs							1							
General Info.		1										1		
Religious							1							
Academic												1		
Newspaper							1							

192 *Regiocanons.nl, 'Utrechtse Canons – Canon van Eemland'*. http://www.regiocanons.nl/Utrecht/eemland (Accessed 15 July 2010).

ing nine categories were not used as frequently. For instance, only six pairs cited sources from educational websites. These include websites such as *schooltv.nl*, *scholieren.com*, *scholieren.samenvatting.com*, which clearly state that pupils are their target audience. Next come the websites of heritage institutions [museums, archives, *etc.*] that were cited on a single occasion by five pairs. In this respect, Pair 11 quoted from a text found on the *Statenbijbel* page[193] of *hetutrechtsarchief.nl* [the Utrecht Archives], which, apart from containing the archives of the city and the province of Utrecht, also serves as 'the national centre for *ecclesiastical archives* and the Dutch Railways' [Italicisation is mine]. There were also six pairs that used resources from other heritage sites, *i.e.*, those maintained by non-heritage institutions. The latter sub-category includes, for instance, *voc-kenniscentrum.nl*, a project initiated [and maintained] by the Royal Netherlands Institute of Southeast Asian and Caribbean Studies [KITLV] in 2002 on the occasion of the 400-year jubilee of the VOC foundation. This sub-category also includes *Bijbelsdigitaal.nl*, a digitisation project of the Dutch Bible Society, and *historische-cartografie.nl*, a website owned and maintained by the *Studiekring Historische Cartografie* [Historical Cartography Study Group].

The next category of cited Web sources consists of personal or family websites. Five pairs had recourse to these for their assignments. For instance, Pair 1 cited *vocsite.nl* and *bertsgeschiedenissite.nl*, owned and maintained by respectively Jaap van Overbeek and someone else who introduces himself simply as Bert.[194] Two other pairs [5 and 7] whose assignments were about, among other things, the *Statenbijbel*, used resources from *statenvertaling.net*, a personal initiative of Ronald Klip.[195] Similarly, for their section on Amsterdam's *Grachtengordel*, Pair 9 cited *klaasschoof.com*, a photo site owned and maintained by a man named Klaas Schoof.[196] In their assignments on politics in the Golden Century, Pair 12 even cited *Engelfriet.net*, a genealogical family site,[197] specifically the section on lawyer

---

193 *Hetutrechtsarchief.nl, 'De Statenbijbel (1637)'*. http://www.hetutrechtsarchief.nl/werkstukken/onderwerpen/statenbijbel (Accessed 15 July 2010).

194 *Vocsite.nl, 'Informatie'*, http://vocsite.nl/contact.html and *bertsgeschiedenissite.nl, 'Over de maker van de Berts Geschiedenissite'*, http://www.bertsgeschiedenissite.nl/maker.htm (Both accessed 14 July 2010).

195 In an e-mail exchange with the author, Ronald Klip – the initiator and owner of the site – wrote: 'The website is my personal initiative. I realised in 1999 that the text [of the *Statenbijbel*] should be available online because of its importance to the Dutch cultural history. Shortly after this, art works were added: [with the aim of] providing information about the paintings and, where possible, establishing a [hyper-]link with the corresponding passage in the [*Statenbijbel*] text' (16 July 2010).

196 *Klaasschoof.com, 'Amsterdam – architectuur in beeld'*. http://www.klaasschoof.com/ (Accessed 14 July 2010).

197 *Engelfriet* site: http://engelfriet.net/ (Accessed 14 July 2010).

Hugo de Groot [1583–1645]. Closely related to personal sites are blogs, a category cited once by Pair 6, who used a picture that came from *1.bp.blogspot.com*. Commercial and general information websites were mentioned by two pairs. Pair 9 cited *vvv.nl*, a tourism and recreation website, for their section on the *Beemster*, while Pair 5, for their section on the *Statenbijbel* and its impact on the Dutch language, cited *gatim.nl*, the website of a company known as *Global Affiliation of Translators & Interpreters & Multilingual Manpower* [GATIM].[198] Pair 11 consulted the art and culture page of *infonu.nl* [which claims to be a library of information from A to Z] for their section on Rembrandt. Finally there are the religious and academic websites and those of newspapers, each being cited by one pair. Pair 6, for their section on the Republic of the Seven United Netherlands, referred to *hervormdonstwedde.nl*, the website of the Reformed Community in Onstwedde; for their section on sailor and marine officer Michiel Adriaenz de Ruyter, the same pair cited *refdag.nl*, the website of the *Reformatorisch Dagblad*, a Dutch daily newspaper; lastly, Pair 11 extensively quoted from *neon.niederlandistik.fu-berlin.de*, the website of the Institute for German and Dutch Philology of the *Freie Universität Berlin*.

Table 5.2 shows that all but one pair [No. 3] used at least two different types of Web sources. Pair 6 used Web sources from all categories and sub-categories [9 in total] except for educational, commercial, general information, and academic sites. As noted above, Pair 3 used no other website apart from the *Geheugen van Nederland*, a website containing material obtained from *heritage institutions* and this was exclusively for the 32 images they used.[199] I should emphasise that many more Web sources were actually used, particularly for images. As can be seen from Table 5.1, Pair 7 used 20 images from the Web but cited only 10 Web sources. Similarly, Pair 11 used 23 images from the Web, while only 10 Web sources are mentioned. Thus, the data in Table 5.2 are based only on the cited and duly referenced Web sources.

5.5 Summary

In this chapter I introduced the class with which I was involved during my research, placing it within the context of the broader educational system. I indicated that the second-year, bridge-class was part of the HAVO/VWO trajectory of secondary education. I also described the 13- to 14-year-old pupils, highlighting not only

198 GATIM, '*Over ons*'. http://gatim.nl/overons.html (Accessed 14 July 2010).

199 As already pointed out in Chapter 1, Section 1.1, one must remember that the *Geheugen van Nederland* was, right from the beginning, an image-based site, and thus text-unfriendly (Schouten, 2009: 11).

their attentive attitude when digital audio-visual media were used, but also their lack of attention when these media were not used. I also discussed the connection between use of the Web and the pupils' historical thinking: in some cases, the attractiveness of the Web-based audiovisual resources triggered not only pupils' attention, but also their engagement in the thinking process. In other cases, the ease with which pupils interacted with Web-based texts and still-images [copy-pasting, ripping, downloading images], prompted some of them to extract long quotations from the Web, though this practice did still leave room for some forms of historical thinking. These consisted mostly of identifying the source and the relevant fragments, and converting them into a new coherent narrative. In yet other cases, a few pupils found another way of making use of Web-based texts, a method that implies some degree of historical thinking: paraphrasing. Finally, I examined the Web sources that the pupils used and realised that most of them had used a variety of sources, including, among others, personal, heritage, religious, news, academic, and educational websites. The next chapter examines the second case study, which took place in a different class and school.

Chapter 6

Case Study Two: The Helen Parkhurst Dalton School

I met David le Clercq in February 2010. Le Clercq is a history teacher at the *Helen Parkhurst Dalton School* [HPDS] in Almere. To be more precise, I came across him after a Twitter exchange with an acquaintance of mine who was working on an education digital media project and had drawn my attention to a project underway at the HPDS under Le Clercq's coordination. I started exchanging e-mails with Le Clercq. In one e-mail he sent me some information about the project with a link to a YouTube clip.[200] In that 3-minute clip Le Clercq announces that teachers have put textbooks aside, and that each pupil has received a portable computer or notebook both for schoolwork and homework.[201] He then went on to claim:

> By dropping textbooks, teachers and students are provided with much more freedom of choice. Students have more topics and assignments from which to choose. It fits in better with their perceptions, and teachers can offer a lot more.

This claim, by itself, summarises to a great extent two of the three claims into which I am enquiring. The suggestion that 'Students have more topics and assignments from which to choose', is claiming that online resources offer *more and varied sources*; the suggestion that 'It fits in better with their perceptions', is claiming that pupils like computer-mediated learning and thus find it *attractive*. I took on the role of observer at one of Le Clercq's history classes once a week from April to June 2010, and again from September to November 2010, at which time it had been taken over by his colleague, Lisanne Beekman. In this chapter, I shall first briefly sketch the background to the Dalton Plan which underlies the teaching

---

200 David le Clercq, history teacher at Helen Parkhurst Dalton School in Almere: '*Een indruk van onze school en de ontwikkelingen die hier gaande zijn*': http://www.youtube.com/watch?v=odJYIPxNgP4 (Accessed 19 January 2011).

201 Le Clercq explained that, for didactic materials, the school received a 300-euro subsidy per child from the government. To purchase the laptops, which cost about 300 euros each, the school funded half the amount, the other half being paid by the pupils [their parents] over a period of two years. The pupils practically owned the computers from the beginning – they took them home everyday – though theoretically, they would only become fully-fledged owners in the third year, that is, after having paid 150 euros [75 euros per year] (Author interview [9 March 2010] and e-mail correspondence [10 March 2011] with David le Clercq, Almere).

and learning processes at the HPDS. I shall then describe the interactions between pupils and digital media to check how [if at all] attractive they are, how [if at all] they foster pupils' historical thinking, and how [if at all] varied the sources are that they offer. I shall analyse the findings in the next chapter.

Figure 6.1: Teacher providing a personalised explanation while other pupils are busy doing their assignments, often pausing to select a new tune on their iPods (Photo: O.N., 27 April 2010).

6.1 The Dalton Approach

> It is enough to look at one and the same child at home, in the street, or at school: now you see a vivacious, curious child, with a smile in his eyes and on his lips, seeking instruction in everything, as he would seek pleasure, clearly and frequently strongly expressing his thoughts in his own words; now again you see a worn-out, retiring being, with an expression of fatigue, terror, and ennui, repeating with the lips only strange words in a strange language, – a being whose soul has, like a snail, retreated into its house. It is enough to look at these two

conditions in order to decide which of the two is more advantageous for the child's development (Tolstoy, [1862] 1967: 16-17).

The pupils of the class I observed were aged 13-14 years and attended the lower cycle that would lead them either to *hoger algemeen voortgezet onderwijs* [general secondary education, HAVO] or *voorbereidend wetenschappelijk onderwijs* [pre-university education, VWO] (see Chapter 5, Section 5.1). Although they attended history classes in both their first and second years, history was not a stand-alone discipline, as it alternated with social studies, geography and civics, which together make up the course in *Mens en Maatschappij* [Mankind and Society]. History, like each of the other sub-disciplines, was taught for a period of six weeks, returning to it again after the other sub-disciplines had been taught, which explains why I was not able to conduct my field research in one go. In order to understand my account of the atmosphere and events that took place in the history class I observed, it is indispensable to first understand the so-called Dalton Plan, implemented by the school. The school is known as a Dalton school, having been named after the plan's initiator, Helen Parkhurst. In this section, thus, I shall trace the origins of that plan and discuss its key principles, while simultaneously describing how these were being applied in the history class during the period of my observation.

The idea had been germinating in the mind of American reformist Parkhurst [1886–1973] since her own school time around 1900 (Van der Ploeg, 2010: 10-11). Her school experience had not been a positive one, as she, like so many other pupils, would sit and either listen to the teacher or repeat what he or she had ordered them to memorise. The school atmosphere was repressive and far from stimulating. According to Parkhurst's contemporary and education scholar S.C. Bokhorst (1924b:19), the same was true in nineteenth-century Netherlands, where the educational system allowed 'a series of mistakes' to develop, one of them being 'the tendency of the system to shift child-development activities from the child to the teacher'. The system stressed the transmission of 'encyclopaedic knowledge' and neglected the 'child's independent thinking capacity [*zelf-denk-capaciteit*]', and 'self-confidence [*vertrouwen in het eigen kunnen*]' (*Ibid.*: 19-20; see also *Ibid.*: 23). It was however in the early 1910s that Parkhurst, then a primary school teacher, started experiments that would later result in the Dalton Laboratory Plan:[202]

202 The concept of 'laboratory' was not new in the discourse on educational reform. Comenius ([1657] 1953: 61) used it in his *Didactica Magna* to describe what the new education system should look like. To truly achieve its goal, he maintained, the school should be 'a true laboratory of men'.

> From its inception the laboratory plan, as I continued to call it even after perfecting it in 1913, aimed at the entire reorganization of school life. My idea was to substitute for the top-heavy machinery actually in use a simple reconstruction of school procedure under which the pupils would enjoy more freedom as well as an environment better adapted to the different sections of their studies in which each instructor should be a specialist. Above all, I wanted to equalize the pupils' individual difficulties and to provide the same opportunity for advancement to the slow as to the bright child (Parkhurst, [1922] 1924: 10-11).

The aim, as the initiator explained, was 'to make school as attractive and as educative as play, and ultimately, to create those fearless human beings' (*Ibid.*: 22). The initial idea was to rethink the school structure, the prevailing approach based on the one hand on the authority of teachers, and on the other hand on the passivity of learners, and to create more room for self-regulated, self-initiated, and self-directed actions of learners. Instead of a classroom with a teacher as instructor and pupils as receivers, she wanted to create educational laboratories, where teachers helped pupils do their work (Van der Ploeg, 2010: 15-16). The way to do that was to organise learning activities around assignments, which the pupils would do independently and at their own speed (*Ibid.*: 16; see also Bokhorst, 1924b: 33).

As this approach was being explored in the mid-1910s, the similar but already established Montessori Method was being applied in Italy and other European countries. Parkhurst ([1922] 1924: 11-12) admitted having refined her own approach during her stay in Italy in 1914, where she served as Maria Montessori's assistant, and during the teacher-training she organised back in the United States on Montessori's behalf. As earlier experiments with crippled children in primary schools were showing positive results, other educationalists, including those involved in secondary education, became increasingly excited and interested in this approach. Boys and girls attending a High School in Dalton, a town in the State of Massachusetts, were the first be part of an experiment in secondary education that started in February 1920 (*Ibid.*: 13). The plan became associated with Dalton High School because news of the new plan spread from there to other parts of the world: 'I then decided to call my plan Dalton Laboratory Plan, by which it has since been known ' (*Ibid.*). The first European country to conduct experiments – from 1920 onwards – was England, under the auspices of educationalist Belle Rennie, who was to become the secretary of England's Dalton Association (*Ibid.*; see also Bokhorst, 1924a: 4). From there, it spread to other parts of Europe and the world.

The Netherlands was among early adopters in the 1920s and quickly emerged as the country with the most robust and popular Dalton tradition in the world (Van der Ploeg, 2010: 7). A commission, set up in early 1924 and which included education scholars, travelled to England to visit primary schools that had been implementing the Dalton Plan. Accompanying the commission, Bokhorst visited secondary schools, including the County Secondary School for Girls in Streatham, London, the first secondary school to implement the Plan in Europe under principal Rosa Bassett (Bokhorst, 1924a: 3). In the early 1950s, when the Netherlands' Dalton Association wanted to start an international training institute, Parkhurst herself wanted to come over and work as a teacher-trainer. In a letter to the Association, she wrote: 'I sincerely believe Holland to be the best place in size and culture and sincerity ... Through Holland the world' (quoted in Van der Ploeg, 2008). In the end, she did not actually come to the Netherlands due to an as yet unexplained misunderstanding with the Dalton Association leaders (*Ibid.*). Her interest proved that the seeds of the Dalton Plan had fallen onto fertile soil in the Netherlands: by the summer of 2010, the country had about 400 Dalton schools, about 350 of which were primary schools (Van der Ploeg, 2010: 7).

The Dalton Plan, as initially conceived, is based on a number of principles, the most important of which are pupils' *freedom, self-regulation*, and *cooperation* (Van der Ploeg, 2010: 124-132). The concept of freedom is based on the assumption that a child naturally 'prefers independent action with simple tools, being more like primitive man in his creative outlook' (Parkhurst, 1951: xvii). If freedom and independent action are part of a child's nature, then it follows that freedom will generate interest and interest, learning. Parkhurst ([1922] 1924: 16) conceptualised this notion of freedom as

> the first principle of the Dalton Laboratory Plan. From the academic, or cultural, point of view, the pupil must be made free to continue without interruption his work upon any subject in which he is absorbed, because when interested he is mentally keener, more alert, and more capable of mastering any difficulty that may arise in the course of his study ... Unless a pupil is permitted to absorb knowledge at his own rate or speed he will never learn anything thoroughly. Freedom is taking one's own time. To take someone else's time is slavery.

Apart from the freedom to organise one's own learning style and rate, freedom also involves freedom of movement, freedom to talk with classmates without disturbing the class, freedom to ask for the teacher's help, *etc.* Thus conceptualised, various forms of freedom were evident in the class I observed. For the sake of this chapter, and in keeping with the media-focused approach of my research, I shall describe only those freedoms that are related to media. For example, one day of April [2010], the teacher was discussing monks and knights in the Middle Ages, and he told the pupils that everything he was telling them could be found on the Web and in the textbook. When he asked who was interested in searching for more information using the Web, about two-thirds of the pupils raised their hands. Among those who preferred books, one boy said he was uncomfortable with the Web 'because everything is in English'. For him 'it is easier to find information in a book'. Even as he spoke, he reached out for the textbook, which suggests that he was referring to the textbook. The teacher said that everyone was *free* to use sources and materials with which they felt comfortable. The last section discusses in more detail the types of sources pupils used for their assignments.

Pupils' freedom *vis-à-vis* media use was also evident from the access point of view. The pupils' laptop computers had no firewall or other control software to prevent them from accessing 'unsuitable' websites. Le Clercq explained that it was a conscious choice because 'anyway, they would always find a way to overcome any hindrance so placing them would be a waste of time'.[203] The logic behind this is that when pupils feel and realise that nothing is being hidden, they do not [always or often] 'waste' much time on what adults deem 'unsuitable' for their age and education.

In addition to using media as information carriers or as tools allowing access to that information, the pupils were free to choose the medium in which they would hand in their class assignments. The majority of them, approximately the same two-thirds, preferred to use their laptop computers to type their assignments and upload them to the school's electronic platform as Microsoft Word files. The rest, who almost corresponded to the one-third who felt more comfortable with books – and by extension with analogue media –, preferred to use analogue means until the very last stage of handing in the assignment. Mendie[204] seldom took her laptop out of her bag and almost never used it to type: 'It's uncomfortable'. On one occasion, when she had completed an assignment, without saying a word, she and another girl with whom she shared a desk, stood up and walked out, both of them holding their handwritten assignments. I followed them and realised that they had gone to the central hall where the photocopier – which also served as a scanner – was located. While they were scanning and saving their work on a USB stick, I asked them why they preferred that method:

203 Author interview with David le Clercq (Almere, 9 March 2010).

204 None of the names attributed to pupils are their actual names.

Figure 6.2: Pupils working with media technologies of their choice (Photo: O.N. 14 September 2010).

Figure 6.3: Pupils scanning their handwritten assignments (Photo: O.N. 20 April 2010).

> -*Q*: Why do you prefer to write by hand and scan your work?
>
> -*Mendie*: It's easier
>
> -*Q*: But you have a laptop!
>
> -*Mendie*: Yes, but for History and French, I prefer to write on paper. I am scanning it because the teacher said that we should upload the assignments.

Susan, another girl, explained to me that the reason why she preferred to write her assignment manually on paper was that the misspelling detection tool of the text-editing software [MS Word] was user-unfriendly:

> ... in the end I have red underlining instead of text. Each word with a capital letter is underlined and I can't do anything to change it. I sometimes type with a computer, but pen and paper are far better.

From Susan's response, it seemed likely that the red reminded her of the teacher's underlining and crossing-out with a red pen that she knew from primary school. She could at least do something to avoid or prevent further underlining with a red pen – *e.g.*, by asking why and where she had gone wrong –, but she couldn't do anything about the software-prompted underlining that underscored her text in red, which to her mind, meant that she had made errors. This could be the reason why she chose the pen-and-paper option for her assignment.

Self-regulation is another key principle of the Dalton Plan. It is closely related to the previous principle in the sense that pupils are free to set their own aims, and to devise their own plan to achieve them. A.J. Lynch, who was headmaster at West Green School, Tottenham in England and one of the early experimenters using the Dalton Plan in the 1920s, conceptualised self-regulation as empowering learners to be masters of their own learning process:

> Have not the pupils, in the past, regarded the teachers, and not themselves, as responsible for their education? Is there any valid reason why the pupils in the schools of the future should not be encouraged to work 'on their own', silently consulting books, and making experiments? Their progress may be slow, but it will be real and solid, and, what is most important, it will be the result of their own doing, experience, and learning. They will develop initiative, versatility, and become responsible in a great measure for their own progress (Lynch, 1924: 15).

Three phrases summarise this concept of self-regulation: 'to work "on their *own*"', 'their *own* doing' and 'for their *own* progress'. The stress on 'own' suggests a certain degree of individuality and independence in the process and excludes 'mere imposition of work by the teacher' (*Ibid.*: 26). Parkhurst ([1922] 1924: 15) herself described the process as 'the pursuit and organization of his *own* studies in his *own* way' [Italicisation is mine]; as absorbing knowledge 'at his *own* rate or speed' and 'taking one's *own* time' (*Ibid.*: 16. Italicisation is mine).

The history class I observed offered many instances of self-regulated learning. The most important one was the structure of the lesson itself. A lesson lasted 70 minutes and consisted of two main parts: the first part lasted 10–15 minutes [25–30 for Beekman] during which time textbook-based, teacher-led instructions were given. One after another, pupils would read paragraphs aloud from the textbook. The teacher would provide some explanations, as well as asking or answering questions. One girl once told me that 10–15 minutes of lecturing or textbook-reading was too long. She said: 'Today was better [the lecture part had lasted 7 minutes]. Other times we have to read from the textbook and I find it boring'. The second part would start with a 10-minute period of absolute silence. Neither the pupils nor the teacher were allowed to move around or speak. Pupils were supposed to concentrate and work on whatever they wanted to work on.[205] This part would end with 40–45 minutes [30–35 for Beekman] dedicated to 'independent work'.[206] The teacher would either sit behind his or her desk waiting for pupils who needed help, or walk around. Pupils were also expected to do their *own* work, based on their *own* plan.[207] In this respect, at the beginning of the six-week period, each pupil had to write down his or

205 Lisanne Beekman explained that all types of pupils can be found in each class: some learn better in a hectic environment, others concentrate better in absolute silence, yet others prefer to isolate themselves from the rest of the class by putting on their earphones and listening to music. She said that the ten minutes were specially meant for the learners who required absolute silence, as they would otherwise have no opportunity to concentrate. When I asked her whether a ten-minute period was not too short, she agreed but suggested that children could not remain silent while sitting in one place for more than ten minutes (Author interview with Lisanne Beekman, Almere, 14 September 2010).

206 'Independent work' time is also referred to as 'free-study' time (Bokhorst, 1924b: 33).

207 This 'independent work' time is the direct result of Parkhurst's ([1922] 1924: 20) view that 'The Dalton Laboratory Plan permits pupils to budget their time and to spend it according to their need'. Writing in the early years of the implementation of the Plan, S.C. Bokhorst (1924a:14; Bokhorst, 1924b:29) suggested that the best system would be a good compromise between the old, classical educational system and the new Dalton working method. Class structures comprised of both the traditional teacher-led instruction and the learner-controlled part could be perceived as a compromise between the old system and the new.

Figure 6.4: The teacher walks around during the 'independent work' time. One pupil [left] is surfing a site on medieval cities[208] *and another [right] is checking her planning. Yet another [behind the teacher] is walking back to her seat (Photo: O.N. 13 April 2010).*

her plan. A plan consisted on the one hand of setting goals that the pupils wanted to achieve and, on the other hand, of setting a time frame in which each goal would be achieved. This means that there were as many personal plans as there were pupils.

The pupils devised their plans based on a course overview and description the teacher had posted on the school's electronic platform prior to the six-week period of history classes. The MS Word document indicated that the course would be about 'Monks and Knights, Cities and States' in the Middle Ages, and it would focus on, among others, the following key concepts: feudalism, Christianity, Islam, and the Crusades. The general goals were that the pupils should be able to define the 'Monk and Knights' and 'Cities and States' periods and provide examples of characteristic events relating thereto

208 J. Strijbos, '*Middeleeuwse stad*'. This personal site was offline at the time of writing, and could not be accessed from its original URL: home.wanadoo.nl/j.strijbos/Middeleeuwen/Hoofdstuk1.htm. However, it could be accessed via Web. Archive.org at this URL: http://web.archive.org/web/20080512170345/home.wanadoo.nl/j.strijbos/Middeleeuwen/Hoofdstuk1.htm (Accessed 19 January 2011).

(see discussion on the 10 historical eras in Chapter 1, Section 1.2); to recognise the difference between – and apply the concepts of – continuity and change with regard to historical developments; and to explain historical developments through cause-and-effect reasoning. Evaluation of the pupils would take into account their personal summaries of each of the course components, two free-choice assignments, and a final test.

Based on this general overview, each pupil had to choose a film or a book on which they would report and, as the course progressed, they were to make summaries of the texts in the textbook. In this respect, on April 6 Carol planned to work on her book and film reports – two free-choice assignments; on April 13, she planned to carry on working on the film report and make two summaries. The progress column beside each activity has four checkboxes: 'Work done'; 'Finish during Dalton Hour';[209] 'Finish next week'; and 'Homework'. Unlike Carol, Tom dedicated the whole of 6 April to summaries. The first entry for April 13 was a telegraph-style entry that clearly showed how he intended to proceed: 'Hand over the summaries, begin report own topic'.[210] Unlike these two pupils, Bert checked the 'Work done' box for summaries 5–14, planned for 6 April. On 13 April, he planned to finish summaries 15–18 and to 'begin with own topic'.

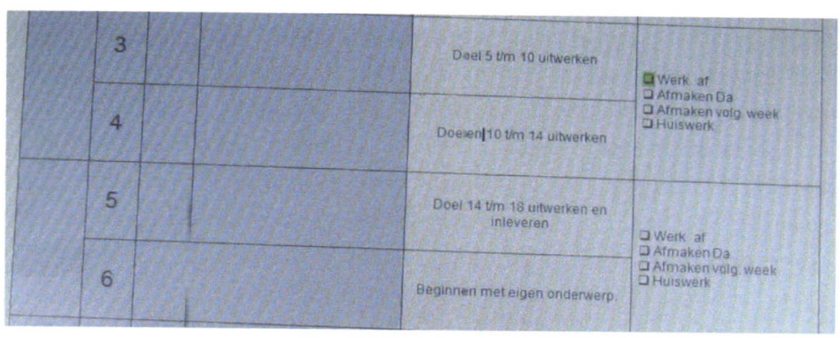

Figure 6.5: Pupil's planning (Photo: ON. 13 April 2011).

209 The Dalton Hour was planned every day except on Tuesday. Pupils chose a course on which they wanted to focus outside the usual class time. Pupils made their plans in advance and indicated the course or assignment on which they would concentrate during the 70 minutes known as the Dalton Hour. Teachers would be present in the various rooms, ready to help where and when needed. Beekman described it as 'a sort of homework time during which pupils receive more attention for a specific course'. This leads to the deduction that a pupil who planned to finish his or her assignment during the Dalton Hour was in need of more explanation or help with the assignment (Author Interview with Lisanne Beekman, Almere, 14 September 2010).

210 The original Dutch text read as follows: '*Inleveren doelen beginnen verslag eigen onderwerp*'. In the teacher's course overview the term *doelen*, which normally means 'goals', was presented as meaning the same thing as *samenvattingen*, 'summaries'. To avoid confusion, I translated it with 'summaries' rather than with 'goals'.

The last key principle of the Dalton Plan is cooperation. The idea behind this concept is that the school should 'function like a community – a community whose essential condition is freedom for the individual to develop himself' (Parkhurst, [1922] 1924: 15). In comparison with other key principles, Parkhurst did not extensively elaborate on cooperation. Its conceptualisation could even be criticised as self-contradictory: the stress is put on the individual, whose *own* work, *own* time management, *own* learning style, *etc.*, should result in his or her *own* development. Nevertheless, this should be an essential condition for a school that is to function like a community. That is most likely the reason why, when referring to 'co-operation', Parkhurst preferred 'to call it, the interaction or group life' (*Ibid.*: 16). Interaction in this sense implies an awareness of the actions of other individuals that inspire, influence, and integrate, *etc.*, the group, without necessarily involving any form of cooperation among individuals. Analysing the key characteristics of the Dalton Plan in its early years, Bokhorst (1924a: 13) mentioned first 'individualisation and differentiation of education', before self-regulation and cooperation. The order in which these characteristics are presented could be interpreted as reflecting the order of their importance.

During my field research, *cooperation* as *interaction* manifested itself in a very limited number of forms. The most common form of cooperation, the joint assignment, was very scarce. Also, during interviews with the pupils, not a single instance of collaborative work was mentioned. Instead, some, like Mark, would inform their classmates about their progress and share completed assignments. After completing his world map of the VOC [Dutch East India Company] and WIC [Dutch West Indies Company] shipping routes, Mark proudly showed it to his rather amazed classmates, Peter and Al (Figures 6.6 and 6.7). The conversation went as follows:

> -*Al*: How did you manage to make it brownish?
>
> -*Mark*: I used coffee to … I just rubbed it with coffee. The coffee [powder] was wet.
>
> -*Peter*: Coffee?
>
> -*Mark*: Yes, coffee [laugh]
>
> -*Peter*: Why did you do that?
>
> -*Mark*: To give it an aged look.
>
> -*Al*: What made you think of that?

-*Mark*: My sister once had a similar assignment and at the time she used tea bags. This time [when I was working on this assignment] I thought: 'I will use coffee instead'.

-*Peter*: And what did you do to make the edges like this?

-*Mark*: I burnt them with fire ... you have to be careful...

Figure 6.6: Pupil showing classmates his VOC and WIC route map shown on Figure 6.7 (Photo: ON. 6 October 2010).

Figure 6.7: VOC and WIC route map shown to classmates (Photo: ON. 6 October 2010).

This exchange could not be called cooperation in the sense of 'working together', but rather in the sense of 'interacting'. Mark shared his artistic exploits with his classmates, who would later be able to build on his experience, as he had done himself *vis-à-vis* his sister. In the end, then, this form of interaction would lead to some form of experience-based learning that the Dalton Plan strives to achieve.

To conclude this section, I should mention that none of these principles were new at the time they were put together to form the Dalton Plan in the 1910s. They can be traced back to 17th-century Czech theologian and education reformer Jan Amos Komenský [1592–1670], commonly known as Comenius, and to other subsequent reformers. In his *Didactica Magna*, for instance, Comenius ([1657] 1953: 110) had advocated, among other things, *less teacher-led instruction* and more pupil's *independent work time*, and a *freedom*-based teaching approach. Like him, Jean-Jacques Rousseau ([1768] 1966: 79) also suggested that pupils should enjoy much more *freedom* and be subjected to *much less authority*; that the teacher should be as a *companion* to pupils and win their trust through sharing their amusement (*Ibid.*: 55; see also Comenius, [1657] 1953: 105); that pupils should learn much more from *their own experience* than from textbooks (*Ibid.*: 328); that a self-directed process would yield far better results than a teacher-directed one (*Ibid.*: 90-91); *etc.* Similarly, the 19th-century Russian thinker and reformer Leo Tolstoy ([1862] 1967: 12; see also Comenius, [1657] 1953: 62) criticised schools as being institutions where children were tortured, where 'they are deprived of their chief pleasure and youthful needs, of free motion'. One cannot help linking these ideas with attitudes I observed in the class, especially in view of the omnipresence of iPods and earphones, and the music that is constantly on, as these are some of the chief pleasures of the Internet Generation. The notion of free movement in the classroom is also perceptible.

The closest thinkers whose philosophy of education greatly inspired Parkhurst's laboratory plan were Ralph Waldo Emerson, whom she regarded as her mentor (Van der Ploeg, 2010: 31) and John Dewey, who had previously conceptualised the idea of self-regulation. For him, 'It is as absurd for the latter [the teachers] to set up their "own" aims as the proper objects of the growth of the children' (Dewey, [1916] 1926: 125). If the teacher has to determine an aim at a certain level, as was the case in the class I observed, it is valued by the pupils only in as 'far as it assists observation, *choice*, and *planning* ... if it gets in the way of the individual's own common sense ... it does harm' (*Ibid.* Italicisation is mine). It has been suggested that the Dalton Plan contributes not only to a more efficient learning process, but also to the education of citizens who understand the ideals of democracy. This is because, according to education scholar Piet van der Ploeg (2007), who published 'Citizenship education is in good hands with the Dalton Plan', the Dalton Plan inculcates democratic principles such as participation, engagement and responsibility, together with necessary cognitive, reflexive, and communicative skills. The next three sections focus more specifically on the three claims that I had set out to explore, namely that digital media make the history class more attractive as well as fostering historical thinking and offering a variety of sources.

Figure 6.8: Pupils concentrating on their class work while absorbed by digital media (Photo: O.N., 13 April 2010).

6.2 Attractiveness

> ... To be interested is to be absorbed in, wrapped up in, carried away by, some object. To take an interest is to be on the alert, to care about, to be attentive. We say of an interested person both that he has lost himself in some affair and that he has found himself in it. Both terms express the engrossment of the self in an object ... (Dewey, [1916] 1926: 148-149).

During the period of my observation, the interactions between the pupils and media were ubiquitous and almost permanent. As I already mentioned, each pupil had received a laptop computer for both schoolwork and homework. This fact of using the same computer both at home and at school, together with the sentiment of ownership, created a strong intimate relationship between the pupils and their computer. Furthermore, they were aware that almost anything was allowed with those computers, including for instance downloading and playing music, and downloading and using whatever software they wanted. Not only had all of them administrator rights, but also there were no firewalls to restrict their Web-surfing activities. All these elements had created a feeling of confidence in the computer during lessons. Though other portable devices were also used to play music or such like, these fall outside the scope of this section. I would rather describe the patterns in which the different Web-related attitudes can be placed, and by doing so, check whether and how they made the history class more attractive.

To begin with, I should stress that the two main parts of the class structure led to two types of attitudes towards using of the Web. During the teacher-led lecture part, pupils would often engage in multitasking – *e.g.*, reading the textbook or listening to the teacher while searching the Web –, whereas during the time spent on 'independent work' they would engage in more sophisticated multitasking, which would now include listening to music, text-editing, e-mailing, Web-surfing, *etc.* For the sake of clarity, I shall deal with these two patterns separately.

In late September, history teacher Beekman was teaching the pupils about 'Regents and Monarchs'. One day in particular she was discussing 'Kings and Parliaments', getting pupils to read one paragraph each from the textbook, pausing now and again to explain. At a given moment the pupils laughed when they came to a page with an illustration showing Louis XIV in high-heeled shoes. While the teacher was explaining that that was fashion for wealthy people during Louis XIV's time, many pupils were listening while their eyes were focused on their laptops' screens and their fingers were typing. Sitting one desk in front of me, Bas was already on the Dutch Google Images site, typing in 'Lodewijk xiv'.[211] He obtained 926,000 results, which he quickly scanned before clicking on the fourth picture on the second row. That picture showed Louis XIV with his high-heeled shoes. He zoomed in, focusing on the 'curious' shoes. All this happened very quickly.

By the time Beekman mentioned how Louis XIV had built the Palace of Versailles not only to live there but also to bring top-ranking officials, including his rivals, closer to him for better and more permanent control, Lianne, a girl sitting at the desk next to Bas, was already on Bing.com, the Microsoft search engine. She typed

211 '*Lodewijk*' is the Dutch for 'Louis'

in 'Versaille' [*sic!*] and, she too, clicked on 'Images'. Of the eight images on the first page, she opened one and zoomed in on it for better inspection (see Figure 6.9). The URL bar showed that it came from www.world-travel-photos.com, a French tourist information

Figure 6.9: Pupil searching for information over the Palace of Versailles while the teacher was discussing that same palace (Photo: O.N., 28 September 2010).

Figure 6.10: Pupil showing a picture of the Palace of Versailles to a classmate during the lesson (Photo: O.N., 28 September 2010).

website. Lianne was so impressed by the palace that she lifted her computer and turned it to show the picture to a classmate sitting in front of her (see Figure 6.10).

As Figure 6.10 shows, the pupil was engaged in at least four activities and her facial expression suggests that she enjoyed them: she was [1] reading the textbook under her elbow, [2] listening to the teacher, and based on what the textbook showed and what the teacher indicated, she [3] surfed the Web for more information, mostly in the form of pictures, and lastly she [4] shared her findings with a nearby classmate.[212] Bas and Lianne did not disrupt the lesson. In fact they used the Web to supplement the information provided by the textbook and the teacher. Each pupil used a different search engine, driven by their desire to find a visual representation that allowed a closer inspection, for instance by zooming in. Given that all these steps took place in a very short time span, the same cycle was continually repeated as more information came in, either from the book or from the teacher.

The consequence of this triangular – textbook-teacher-Web – interaction was a livelier, less boring and calm history lesson. There are two major reasons that can be cited: on the one hand, the atmosphere favoured multitasking, which enabled the pupils to diversify their intellectual activities. When pupils felt that the teacher's talk was getting boring – as some pupils claimed–, the Web offered other possibilities for learning without disrupting the class and without getting bored. On the other hand, the Web contributed to what I would call the *dis-abstraction* of the history class (see Chapter 7, Section 7.1). A piece of information as abstract as the fashion of wealthy people during Louis XIV's time was immediately supplemented by a visual representation, which neither the textbook, nor the teacher had space or time to provide. The Palace of Versailles, which the teacher introduced as being the home to hundreds if not thousands of nobles, remained abstract until the pupils were amazed to discover how sumptuous it actually is. However detailed the teachers' explanations, they could not create a concrete image that would enable the pupils to proceed with the narrative knowing exactly how large and prestigious the palace was. The explanations that followed made more sense because they built on this *disabstracted* information. Having discovered the styles, fashion, and prestige of those old days, the pupils actually wanted to hear more. When they heard more, they immediately wanted to get concrete visual representations of the things about which they had heard, which resulted in a never-ending cycle of hearing, reading, and surfing the Web.

212 This is another form of 'cooperation' in the sense of 'interaction' discussed in the previous section.

Unlike the teacher-led instruction time, the time spent on 'independent work' was pupil-controlled. Pupils would follow their own plans and the teacher would be available for any questions and requests for help. During that time, the Web played a central role, not only as a source of information for class assignments, but also

Figure 6.11: Pupil reading a book for his book report assignment (Photo: O.N., 20 April 2010).

Figure 6.12: Pupil playing an online game to 'relax' between two book-reading sessions (Photo: O.N., 20 April 2010).

as a means of relaxation. Most pupils combined both features, for instance by surfing the Web while listening to Web-based music. Nina, for example, while working on her film report assignment on *Kruistocht in spijkerbroek*,[213] would surf the Web in search of relevant information and images, but she would also go to YouTube to select music clips. She was playing 17-year-old R&B singer Justin Bieber's *Favorite Girl* via YouTube,[214] with her earphones plugged in, when I asked her if she was not distracted by the music. After removing an earplug, she replied that she concentrated better when music was playing. Most pupils whose ears were almost always plugged cited this same reason relating to concentration. The teachers made no problem about pupils doing their schoolwork with plugged ears. As far as they were concerned, if music meant pupils could concentrate better, then they should be allowed to listen to it, provided it was not so loud that it disturbed their classmates.

Other pupils, like Tim, would pause a few minutes to play online games. Tim was playing *Bubble Trouble* when I asked him if that was compatible with classwork (Figure 6.12). He explained that he planned to work on his book report assignment on Anne MacCaffrey's *Zwarte paarden voor de koning* (1997). He had read a few pages (see Figure 6.11) but needed a rest before going on: 'A few minutes of gaming help you relax a bit', he said, while playing at the same time.

As the cases of Nina and Tim show, the Web played the two most important roles that made the history class attractive for pupils. Although their assignments were about other media – films and books – the Web appeared inescapable as a source not only of information, but also of pleasure. According to the pupils, the pleasure or relaxation they gained via music or playing games helped them either to better digest the information they sought and used, or to recover from their intense intellectual efforts. All the reasons that pupils brought forward as to why they played games or why their ears were constantly plugged, converged in one direction: all these

213 The title means 'Crusade in Jeans'. It is a 2006 film directed by Ben Sombogaart and which is based on a book with the same title by Thea Beckman (See the trailer on YouTube: http://www.youtube.com/watch?v=wxjED16qQRg , [Accessed 23 January 2011]).

214 Justin Bieber, 'Favorite Girl'. http://www.youtube.com/watch?v=1djPTCLYnGI (Accessed 23 January 2011).

pleasure-generating activities contributed to their schoolwork.[215] In other words, their *raison d'être* was to increase the efficiency with which schoolwork was done. The teachers felt that preventing pupils from using or accessing their sources of pleasure and relaxation would hinder their productivity. Perceiving and mapping what happens inside the minds of pupils who play games or listen to music via earphones remains a difficult task, one that led some scholars to use the 'swimming duck' metaphor (Van Velzen, 2002: 6; see next section) to describe the situation. However, as the next section shows, the pupils do actually engage in historical thinking while dealing with information found on the Web.

6.3 Historical Thinking

> ... we can distinguish the process of research from the process of reflecting historically upon it. In practice, the two processes take place together: a historian is already reflecting on his material when he chooses a subject and identifies his sources. But they are nevertheless different processes, and an interest in the skilled activities of production should not obscure the fact that the key to the whole activity is in the reflection (Watts, 1972: 46-47).

Unlike the obvious attractiveness of digital media, many and various forms of which could be seen in the class, historical thinking was not as easy to perceive, as it takes place hidden from view. While working on their assignment during the time spent on 'independent work', pupils would mostly keep quiet, surf the Web, often isolated from the rest of their classmates by the incessant music via earphones (see Figures 6.1 and 6.8). This is to make it clear that most of the thinking that took place was internal and internalised, and thus not easily perceptible. In her research into self-regulated learning and reflective thinking, education scholar Joke van Velzen (2002: 6) metaphorically described learners in this situation as swimming ducks. Indeed, though one can see that ducks are moving, their underwater paddling remains invisible. This description might be applied to Figure 6.8 which shows pupils intensely engaged with at least three

215 These findings contradict part of the findings of a recent report by the National Academy for Media and Society [NAMM], an initiative of two foundations, the *Stichting Media Rakkers* and the *Stichting De Kinderconsument*. Conducted from January–May 2011 in 42 primary schools and 78 secondary schools, the research concluded that surfing the Web for, *e.g.*, music or games, which two-thirds of the pupils do during class time, affects pupils' attention and concentration (NAMM, 2011). In my research, music and games appeared to be part of the learning process and, according to the pupils and their teachers, helped them concentrate better.

Figure 6.13: One page of a pupil's 'own report' on religion in the Middle Ages. It shows Adriaan Soeterbroek's cartoon of far-right Party for Freedom leader Geert Wilders in white clothes and a veiled Muslim woman (Photo: O.N., 11 May 2011).

different media forms – the computer [Web or text-editing], the textbook, and music [either from the computer of other portable devices] – though it is not always perceptible exactly what impact these media have on their thinking. However, there were some occasions on which external signs betrayed their inner thinking process. In this section, I want to describe some of the most representative cases of historical thinking that resulted from, or were facilitated by, using the Web.

In late April the pupils were busy working on their assignments. The teacher had in the meantime provided them with more details about the assignments. The pupils had three open-ended options from which to choose: a book report, *i.e.*, reading a book about the Middle Ages and analytically summarising it; a film report, *i.e.*, watching a self-chosen film or the one provided by the teacher about the Middle Ages, and analytically summarising it; and own-topic assignments. In the latter category, Ben decided to write his assignment about faith in the Middle Ages. The work-in-progress had no title yet, but the file was named 'Own Report'. It contained a picture that reflected the kind of historical thinking in which Ben had been engaged. The picture (Figure 6.13) showed far-right Party for Freedom leader Geert Wilders in white clothes beside a veiled Muslim woman. The previous pages contained a summary of the history of the Crusades and the picture was placed in continuation of that history. In other words, it represented the present-day Crusade, as Ben explained to me:

> -*Q*: How did you find this picture?
>
> -*Ben*: On Google
>
> -*Q*: Which website exactly?
>
> -*Ben*: Google Images
>
> -*Q*: What topic are you working on?
>
> -*Ben*: Christianity
>
> -*Q*: How do you intend to use this picture?
>
> -*Ben*: It shows Christianity and Islam … and intolerance, which were also there during the Crusades

The cartoon is the work of Adriaan Soeterbroek, a cartoonist of great renown whose work features politicians and social issues, among others. On his website,[216] the 'Wilders-vs-Islam' cartoon appears in a gallery alongside other political cartoons.[217] Although Ben ignored the exact source of his cartoon, he nonetheless made a choice from Google Images, where there were an abundance of other images showing Wilders together with veiled Muslim women. A search with 'geert wilders islam' on the Dutch Google Images site returned [on 21 January 2011] 'about 120,000 results' and the 'Wilders-vs-Islam' cartoon was third on the second page or thirty-third counting from the first page. Thus, Ben must have gone through a number of images before deciding which one to use in his assignment. It is possible that aesthetic considerations played a role; perhaps the double black-and-white contrast both with regard to clothing and to background were what prompted him to select it; or maybe his choice was prompted by the way the two eyeless persons are looking into one another's eyes. What was clear in his mind was that the cartoon symbolised 'Christianity and Islam … and intolerance' and that these could be traced back to the Crusades.

---

216 Adriaan Soeterbroek has a website with galleries of his artistic works: http://www.adriaan.nu/ (Accessed 21 January 2011).

217 Adriaan Soeterbroek, '*Nieuw werk vanaf 2010 Gallery 1*'. http://www.adriaan.nu/index.php/1 (Accessed 21 January 2011).

The process behind the choice of this cartoon and the interpretation it was given are an instance of historical thinking. A present-day social and political issue was explained and linked to what the pupil regarded as one of its historical origins. The process that led to the choice may have followed this line of thought: Ben was looking for a picture that could reflect both Christianity and Islam as well as reflecting the intolerance he thought evident in both. Knowing that Wilders had been preaching for an Islam-free, Christian Netherlands, he associated him with Christianity. Knowing also that the *Niqaab* – the veil that covers all but the eyes and which is worn by women in some Muslim cultures – was at the centre of political debates in this country, he associated it with Islam. This reasoning, based on associations, is essential for historical thinking. It also seems that the Web and Google Images in particular played a crucial role. In fact, the entire reasoning process is hard to imagine without the display of many pictures from different sources, all at the same time. The thumbnail display feature allows one to scroll up and down, compare pictures, preview or open pictures that one wants to examine closely, zoom in for more details, *etc*. In a matter of minutes or even seconds, a reasoning process takes place, similar to the one I have just described and results in integrating pictures loaded with meaning into the assignment.

I should also mention that other factors may have played a role in this process, for instance, factors that influenced pupils' ideas about 'hot' political issues. At the time that I was conducting the first part of my field research – that is from April-June 2010 – the city of Almere, where the class I observed is located, had emerged as a Geert Wilders' bastion. His party had won the municipal election held in March, though it was unable to govern the city because the remaining parties formed an alliance against Wilders. One electoral promise that had been made by Wilders' party was to either ban the *Niqaab* or instigate a *Niqaab* tax. This then could explain the associations Ben had made and which he thought were reflected by the 'Wilders-vs-Islam' cartoon. Moreover, as Figure 6.13 shows, at the moment Ben was sitting opposite a Socialist Party campaign poster[218] reading: *Steun Afghanistan. Stop de oorlog* [Support Afghanistan. Stop the War]. As Afghanistan is often associated with Islam and the *Niqaab*, it is also possible that the poster played a role in his thinking process. Thus, though all these factors came in from different directions, they all converged on one point: the Web. They created,

---

218 Many political parties, including the Christian Democrats (CDA), the Liberal Party (VVD), the Labour Party (PVDA) and the Party for the Animals, had posters hanging on the walls. Curiously, Wilders' Party for Freedom (PVV) had no poster in that classroom.

or at least, influenced a certain view on the issue and based on this view, search terms were chosen and entered onto the Google Images site. Of all the images available there, the 'Wilders-vs-Islam' cartoon corresponded best to the point Ben wanted to make.[219]

Later in October, when the class had been taken over by Beekman, the pupils were working on other assignments. Like the previous ones, these too were based on pupils' choices. The options were as follows: a world map showing the routes followed by the VOC and WIC ships; a WebQuest,[220] *i.e.*, a Web-based assignment about a specific topic with specific guidelines and instructions on steps to be followed; and a fictional story on a freely chosen topic relating to a child of the same age as the pupil during the Golden Century [17th century]. Everyone was expected to make an assignment based on a combination of two of the three options. While the WebQuest demonstrated many instances of Web-fostered historical thinking, the map-drawing, and to a greater extent, the story-writing assignments, though abound with cases of historical thinking, gave almost no clue as to the role played by the Web. For instance, one pupil wrote a story with the title: 'A new beginning: the story of Koen'. Koen lived in Spain with his father, a blacksmith, and his mother, a health worker. When his mother died, Koen, who survived by stealing, left Spain to go to the Republic [the Netherlands] together with his father. He found a job in a shop selling 'foreign products', while his father was employed as a blacksmith. They became rich, bought a house and 'had everything [they wanted]'. Having reached adulthood, Koen fell in love with a girl, with whom he later got married. The story ends by showing Johannes Vermeer's *Girl with a pearl earring*, whereby Koen's 'wife' was presented as the girl in the painting.

Although fictional, this 556-word narrative contains a number of cases of historical thinking: the use of the term 'Republic' instead of 'the Netherlands', and its portrayal as a better place to which one might run in order to begin a new prosperous life, shows that the

---

219 History education scholars Keith Barton and Linda Levstik (2004: 17 and 18) argued that 'we will be able to make sense of how students have developed their ideas only if we understand the settings in which they have encountered the past'. Cognitive psychologists Robert Siegle and Martha Wagner Alibali ([1986] 2005: 108) added that 'the social world has a profound effect on what children do, on what they think about, and on how they think.' It is clear that the encounter with religions in the Middle Ages took place in a social environment dominated by anti-*Niqaab* politics in Almere and by debates on Afghanistan, which [debates on Afghanistan] ultimately resulted in the fall of the then cabinet.

220 All WebQuests were taken from *Histoforum*, a website for 'ICT and History' run by history teacher Albert van der Kaap. Van der Kaap was among the early adopters of the Internet in the history class (See Chapter 2, Section 2.4). http://histoforum.digischool.nl/ (Accessed 21 January 2011).

pupil could locate her story in a specific historical period and context; the description of professions and such details as 'foreign products' – which is a reference to the VOC and WIC – are indirect connections with the Golden Century. The question one needs to pose is how the Web intervened in the thinking process behind this story. One thing that is certain is that it did intervene in some ways, as this is clear from the use of the *Girl with a pearl earring*, which was most likely downloaded from the website of the *Mauritshuis*, a historical arts museum in The Hague.[221] The historical reasoning that may have led to incorporating this painting could be the following: portrait painting is generally associated with prestige and wealth, which brings one back to the pupils remark that Koen and his father 'had everything', including wealth and prestige. Understood from this perspective, the 'foreign products' that made Koen wealthy form a hidden reference to the VOC and WIC which were responsible for importing them from abroad. Choosing the painting was then a way of reflecting the status Koen had acquired. It could be said then, that through a fictional narrative and with some help of the Web, the pupil engaged in historical thinking by indirectly associating different but related aspects of the Golden Century.

Drawing the map with VOC and WIC routes was less challenging than the story-writing assignment. Almost all those who chose it said they had used the Web to determine the routes the ships used to follow. Mark – the boy who created the antique effect by using wet coffee powder (Figures 6.6 and 6.7) – explained to Peter and Al how he had used the Web:

> -*Peter*: Where did you get [the information on] these pieces of paper [glued here and there on the map]?
>
> -*Mark*: I just searched on the Internet and re-wrote what I found in my own words. I also gave the map a brownish colour [with coffee].
>
> -*Al*: Which site?
>
> -*Mark*: Ehhhh mostly Wikipedia ... I found so much information there.

Unlike Mark, who had completed his assignment at home – thus offering no chance to see him at work – Peter had planned to complete his own assignment during the 'independent work' time at school. He spent a few minutes surfing the Web and at a given mo-

221 *Mauritshuis*, 'Johannes Vermeer - Girl with a pearl earring'. http://www.mauritshuis.nl/index.aspx?chapterid=2342&contentID=18308&ViewPage=68&SchilderijSsOtName=titel&SchilderijSsOv=%25%25 (Accessed 21 January 2011).

ment he stopped to take out his pencil. He had already coloured the different continents and was busy drawing lines across the oceans (Figure 6:14). He would look at the screen and then draw a line. Every now and again he would take hold of the mouse and scroll up and down. He looked to the left of the screen, then to the right and

Figure 6.14: Pupil drawing a VOC route map based on online images shown in Figure 6.15 (Photo: O.N., 6 October 2010).

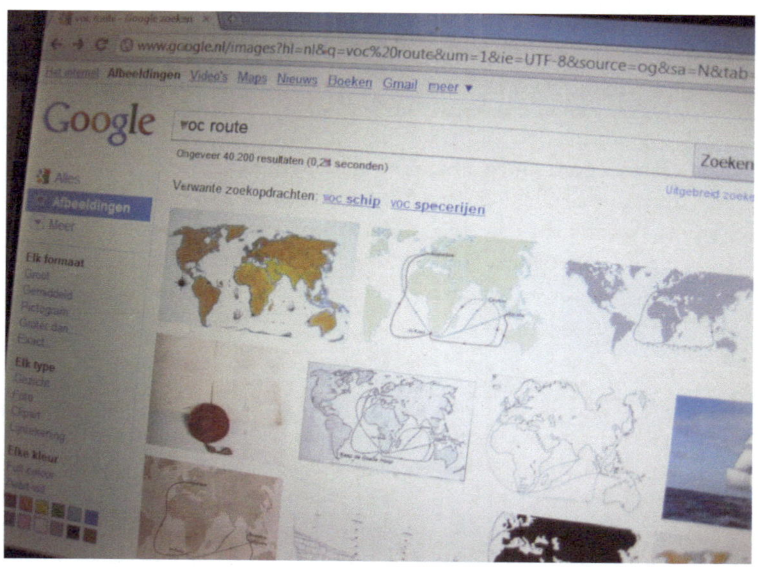

Figure 6.15: Screenshot of images resulting from a search by a pupil for his map-drawing assignment (Photo: O.N., 6 October 2010).

then he would draw another line. Peter was on the Dutch Google Images site (Figure 6:15) where he had searched using the words 'voc route'. The search had returned 'About 40,200 results'. After scrolling up and down, he decided to focus on the second image (see Figure 6:15, second picture on the first row). This image came from the National Library of Australia [NLA] and showed the route the VOC ships took from Amsterdam to Jakarta [called Batavia at that time], in present-day Indonesia and Ceylon [now Sri Lanka, formerly part of India] via the Cape of Good Hope in South Africa, and along either the eastern coast of Africa or the western coast of Australia. It also showed the route back to Amsterdam, which was slightly different.

Peter explained why that particular map was interesting for his assignment:

> -*Q*: I saw you looking at the screen and then drawing lines on your map. What are you doing actually?
>
> -*Peter*: There is an image [on the screen] and when I saw it, I thought immediately: I am going to use that.
>
> -*Q*: On which website is it?
>
> -*Peter*: This one [showing the Google images on Figure 6.15, pointing his pencil towards the NLA image.]
>
> -*Q*: [Placing the cursor on the NLA image] Ah, I see it: nla.gov.au …
>
> -*Peter*: No, no. I don't know. I just searched on Google Images
>
> -*Q*: Why choose this particular map?
>
> -*Peter*: I don't know. Because … all the routes are visible. Also the names [of the seaports]. Here [showing two maps below and one on the right (Figure 6.15)] you can see the routes but there are no names. Here [showing the NLA map] you can see which ship it was. Here [showing two maps below and one on the right] you can't.
>
> -*Q*: Did you use any other websites?
>
> -*Peter*: I simply chose from the overview … I think that for this [VOC] route I shall use only this one [NLA map]. I shall search for another for the WIC.

The judgments that Peter made in choosing his source constitute a form of historical thinking. Peter knew what he was looking for: the 'voc route', as the search terms show. From the Google Images 'overview', one particular map drew his attention and for one reason: it showed not only routes but also names, which other maps in the 'overview' failed to offer. In his mind, the lines crossing the oceans became routes when they connected two or more places with names. The comparisons with neighbouring maps externalised the thinking process that was going on in his mind. Similarly to the case of the 'Wilders-vs-Islam' cartoon, one sees Peter engaged in the compare-and-eliminate process, which ends in the selection of one media object – cartoon or map – that is deemed to be the best.

The last form of assignment was the WebQuest. The various WebQuests had two parts: the *pre-research* part, and the *research-proper* part.[222] In the pre-research part, the pupils were asked to indicate their sources, their relevance to the assignment, and the level of their reliability, which I shall discuss in the last section dedicated to sources. I should mention here that all these sources were necessarily Web-based. In their research-proper, the pupils had to write a piece of text with some illustrations.

In general, the WebQuests, which were either on seventeenth-century painters or on the VOC, appeared to be summaries of information that can be found on different websites. Following the instructions for their research-proper, the pupils had to 'collect data for each aspect about the painter' and, since they could 'only use a few data' to produce a poster, they should 'make a good selection, so that the person viewing your poster will have as precise an image of the painter as possible'. All 8 WebQuests that were returned, including two that were the joint efforts of two pupils, were short summaries on the various aspects – early and later lives, paintings, or the inception of the VOC, its aims, its history, *etc.*, and none of them contained quotations. Generally speaking, summarising more than one text into a coherent narrative about a painter or the VOC involves different levels of historical thinking. The important elements involved in this process include identifying sources (see next section), paraphrasing, and harmonising data taken from different sources. Unfortunately, the pupils did not provide in-text references or footnotes/endnotes which would have allowed me to study the kind of mixture that took place. They simply indicated at the end of their work: 'For my own research I used the following sites' and 'for the pictures I used the following sites'.

One pupil chose the WebQuest on the VOC. In 59 words and with one portrait of Johan van Oldenbarneveld [the VOC head upon its establishment], he answered the question 'What was

222 See the example of *Schilders uit de Gouden Eeuw* [Painters of the Golden Century]. http://histoforum.digischool.nl/lesmateriaal/internetgids5.htm (Accessed 21 January 2011).

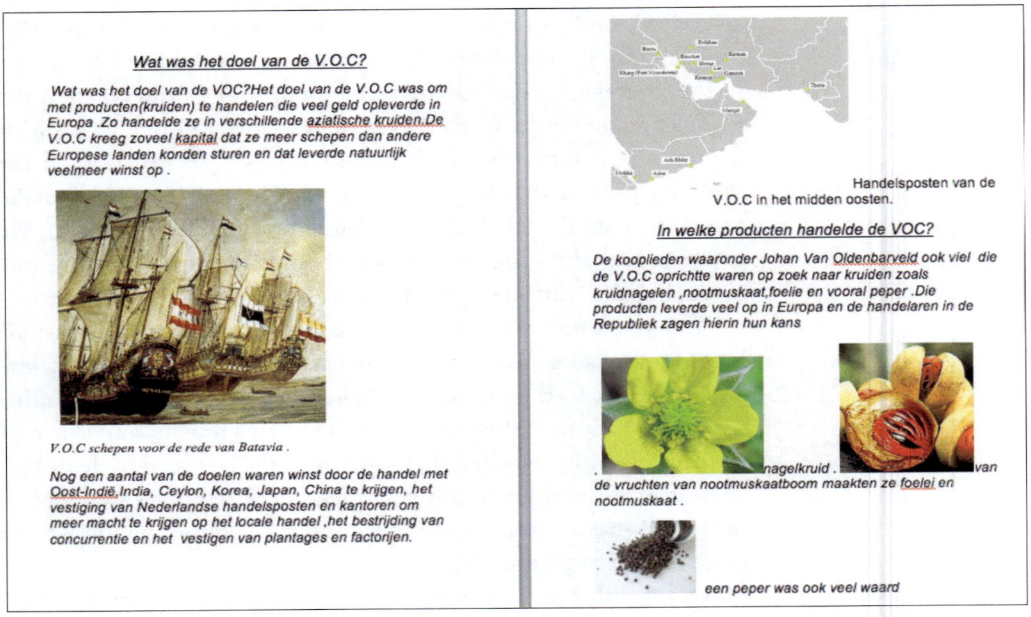

Wat was het doel van de V.O.C?

Wat was het doel van de VOC?Het doel van de V.O.C was om met producten(kruiden) te handelen die veel geld opleverde in Europa .Zo handelde ze in verschillende aziatische kruiden.De V.O.C kreeg zoveel kapital dat ze meer schepen dan andere Europese landen konden sturen en dat leverde natuurlijk veelmeer winst op .

V.O.C schepen voor de rede van Batavia .

Nog een aantal van de doelen waren winst door de handel met Oost-Indië,India, Ceylon, Korea, Japan, China te krijgen, het vestiging van Nederlandse handelsposten en kantoren om meer macht te krijgen op het locale handel ,het bestrijding van concurrentie en het vestigen van plantages en factorijen.

Handelsposten van de V.O.C in het midden oosten.

In welke producten handelde de VOC?

De kooplieden waaronder Johan Van Oldenbarveld ook viel die de V.O.C oprichtte waren op zoek naar kruiden zoals kruidnagelen ,nootmuskaat,foelie en vooral peper .Die producten leverde veel op in Europa en de handelaren in de Republiek zagen hierin hun kans

. nagelkruid . van de vruchten van nootmuskaatboom maakten ze foelei en nootmuskaat .

een peper was ook veel waard

Figure 6.16: Two pages from a WebQuest assignment on the VOC. They show short summaries made from different Web-based sources and the use of Web-sourced illustrations.

the VOC?', which was also the first sub-title of his work. Then, in 98 words illustrated with a painting of the 'VOC ships before the Batavia roadstead' and a map showing the 'VOC trading posts in the Middle East', he answered another question: 'What was the aim of the VOC?' After this, in 40 words, illustrated with two pictures of nutmeg and one of pepper, he discussed products traded the VOC. Finally, in 81 words, accompanied by a map showing the WIC routes – the Triangular Trade – he spoke of VOC successes in Asia and the birth of the WIC in 1622, concluding that 'The WIC would not have the same political influence as the VOC'. Almost all the WebQuests followed this model of short, no-quote, summaries with illustrations.

One aspect that was apparent in these summaries was the use of comparison. The WIC was compared to the VOC and, based on the various sources the pupil consulted, he was able to conclude that the VOC was more influent. This judgment of his is a form of historical thinking: not only did he connect economic, commercial power with the political power, but he also compared two commercial powers. A similar comparison was apparent in one girl's WebQuest on Johannes Vermeer. The 430-word research-proper text contained 3 of Vermeer's paintings, including the *Girl with a pearl earring*. The girl introduced the assignment, explaining why she had chosen that painter:

> I chose to work on this painter because I was not familiar with him. I enquired about him and I was impressed by his painting, the *Girl with a pearl earring*. In my opinion, many people do not know about him. In contrast, Rembrand [*sic*!], for example, is very famous and I know a great deal about him. This is why I chose Johannes Vermeer.

She then provided a short biography [205 words] of Vermeer, a summary of his work [56 words] and ended by concluding [in 70 words] that

> … I have learned so much about him and it was interesting to enquire about a different painter whom I had previously ignored. I found it unfortunate that there is not so much to say about his life. But now I know much more and I think he's great!

This pupil made a very short summary from six websites and started with the expectation that she was going to discover another Rembrandt. This expectation, on its own, shows that the pupil was thinking historically, because she wanted to discover and understand the work of Vermeer by comparing him with another contemporary painter whom she knew better. The comparison failed in part because, as she wrote in her conclusion, none of the websites she visited offered information on Vermeer that was extensive enough to allow such a comparison.[223] This claim implies that she had been looking for some specific details, similar to the ones she had on Rembrandt, but she had been unable to find enough. Another strong indication that an attempt at historical thinking had taken place is the pupil's judgment that the sites told little about Vermeer, although they did help her achieve part of the goals she had set: she was happy that she 'know[s] much more' that led her to believe that he was 'great', but 'unfortunate[ly] there is not much to say about his life'. In other words, some knowledge of Vermeer had been acquired, but much more could have been achieved, if more information had been available on the Websites she consulted. The next section discusses those websites and the variety of the information they offer.

---

223 While the Wikipedia site entry on Johannes Vermeer was extensive – 2,374 words, excluding notes and references [see: http://nl.wikipedia.org/wiki/Johannes_Vermeer (accessed 22 January 2011)] –, the *Rijksmuseum*'s website, which she listed as second source after Wikipedia, contained two very short texts about the painter: one contained 296 words and the other 178, which is indeed relatively short [see: http://www.rijksmuseum.nl/aria/aria_artists/00017083?page=0&lang=nl&context_space=&context_id= (Accessed 22 January 2011)].

Figure 6.17. Wikipedia being used as a source for a class assignment (Photo: O.N., 13 April 2010).

6.4 Sources

> When I wish to write on any topic, 'tis of no consequence what kind of book or man gives me a hint or a motion, nor how far off that is from my topic (Emerson [1876] 2010: 151).

The situations described in the two previous sections suggest that the Web was used very often both during the teacher-led lecture time and the 'independent work' time. The few cases mentioned as an illustration of how the Web has made the history class more attractive while also fostering historical thinking are also evidence of the fact that pupils made comparisons and selections from the objects they found via various sources. While the previous sections did pay some attention to sources, mostly as used in 'live' situations – *e.g.*, searching for supplementary information while the teacher was still explaining – this section discusses sources as referenced by pupils themselves in their assignments. As the pupils were free to choose from a number of options and, within those options, to make other choices and then combine those choices, any attempt to make a systematic study of the sources used during all those assignments would at the very least be challenging. Moreover, in many cases the pupils were not explicitly asked to mention their sources.

Although my observations made it obvious that most pupils would surf the Web for their book or film reports, their own-topic stories, or their VOC and WIC route maps, there was no way of tracing which sources had been used. For this reason, I decided to focus on the WebQuest assignments for which pupils were explicitly asked to use Web sources. The following is, therefore, a discussion of the kind of Websites pupils used, the ways in which they were used and the descriptions of the sites as provided by the pupils.

As already mentioned, the WebQuest comprised of the *pre-research* part, dedicated to sources and their descriptions, and the *research-proper* part, in which the pupils presented summaries of the relevant information and pictures found on the websites they visited. The instructions for the pre-research part of the assignment on painters were as follows: the pupils had to choose a painter from among Johannes Vermeer, Jan Steen, Frans Hals, Jacob Isaacksz. van Ruisdael, and Rembrandt van Rijn. Then they must 'choose and describe a total of 6 websites that offered the most usable (and reliable) information about one or more aspects of the painter'. Each selected site had to be described in a table comprising fields for the URL, language, type of information found there, owner of the site, a description of his or her background, and a rating.[224] Similar instructions were given to those who would preferred the WebQuest on the VOC, except that they could use up to eight websites.[225] In total, 8 WebQuests were returned. 6 of them were done by individuals while 2 were each jointly done by 2 pupils. Thus, 10 pupils out of 28 chose the WebQuest, which they combined either with the VOC-WIC route map or with their own-topic story about a same-age child in the Middle Ages. In this section I shall refer to the joint WebQuests pairs as Pair 1 and Pair 2, while individual pupils will be referred to as Pupil 1, Pupil 2, *etc.*

It should come as no surprise that all pupils used Web sources, although Pupil 4 failed to mention and comment on her sources. However, considering the fact that she included Rembrandt's paintings – 2 self-portraits, *The Night Watch*, and *The Anatomy Lesson* – it is certain that she used Web-sources. The same goes for the 'Summaries' column where I was unable to check her text against her sources. Similarly, in accordance with the instructions and tips provided for the pre-research part, 8 out of 10 pupils used images to illustrate their assignments. Generally, the images corresponded with the nearby text. The picture of *The Anatomy Lesson* appeared fairly near to the paragraph commenting on it. However, since sum-

224 *Histoforum, 'Schilders uit de Gouden Eeuw'* http://histoforum.digischool.nl/lesmateriaal/internetgids4.htm (Accessed 24 January 2011).

225 *Histoforum, 'De VOC'.* http://histoforum.digischool.nl/lesmateriaal/internetgids4.htm (Accessed 24 January 2011).

maries were very short, pictures sometimes had to be condensed one after the other.

Table 6.1: Overview of websites and images used in WebQuest assignments together with the use of online materials for summary purposes.

	Number of Websites	Number of Images	Summaries
Pupil 1	6	0	*
Pupil 2	7	0	*
Pupil 3	6	8	*
Pupil 4	No source mentioned	4	?
Pupil 5	6	5	*
Pupil 6	6	5	Comments on sources
Pair 1	4	5	*
Pair 2	6	11	*

Apart from serving as a source for images, the Web also and most importantly served as a source for raw materials for the textual part of the assignment. All pupils, with the exception of Pupil 6, provided very short, multiple-source, summaries. Pupil 6's assignment ended with the pre-research part, as the pupil only mentioned and commented on her sources. Unlike her, the remaining nine pupils used the textual information they found on the Web, re-writing it in their own words. The aim of the WebQuest, as described in the instructions, was to select the most relevant information from the

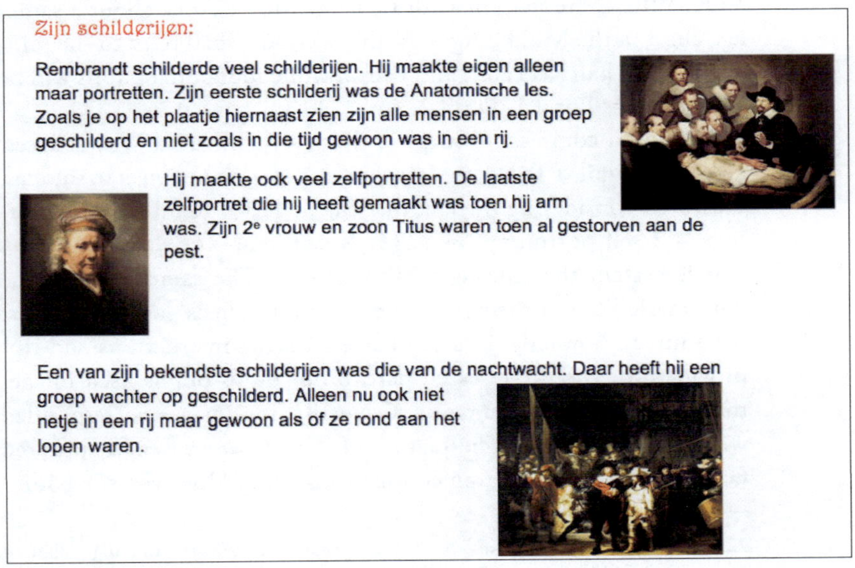

Figure 6.18: Excerpt from a WebQuest assignment on Rembrandt.

various sources and to produce a poster that would convey the image of the painter or the VOC most accurately. Pair 1, for example, provided a very short biography of Rembrandt using four Web pages – including both the Dutch and the English Wikipedia pages – that were all dedicated to that painter. The comparison below shows how the pupils' summaries originated, in one way or another, from the texts they found on the Web. The column on the left shows the first four sentences of the biographic texts from the four Web pages, while the column on the right shows the pair's summary that resulted from them:

Table 6.2: Example of the use of the Web as a source of raw material [left column] for pupils' multiple-source summaries [right column].

Wikipedia.nl: 'Rembrandt van Rijn was born on 15 July 1606 in Leiden on the Weddesteeg, as the ninth child of a miller, Herman [*sic*!] Gerritsz and Neeltje van Zuytbrouck, a daughter of a well-established baker. Rembrandt attended the Latin school and was about 14 years when his parents registered him at the University of Leiden. Obviously the venture stopped there because Rembrandt had indicated that he wanted rather to become a painter. By 1619 he was already an apprentice of the Leiden-based history-painter Jacob van Swanenburgh'.[226]	
People.zeelandnet.nl/acoomens: 'The Dutch most famous artist was born in 1606 in Leiden to Hermen [*sic!*] Gerritsz van Rijn, a well-established miller. After a few short experiences as student in Leiden and Amsterdam, he settled in 1625 in Leiden as an independent painter. In 1632 he moved to Amsterdam, where he stayed at arts trader Hendrik van Uylenburgh's. One year later Rembrandt got married to Saskia, his host's niece'.[228]	Rembrandt van Rijn was born in Leiden [*sic!*], he was the son of a miller Harmen[227] Gerritsz van Rijn. Rembrandt had a few school experiences in Amsterdam and Leiden, and at the time he went to settle in Leiden in 1625. There he became a painter. In 1632, he moved to Amsterdam, and lived a long time at arts trader Hendrik's.
Wikipedia.org: 'Rembrandt Harmenszoon van Rijn was born on July 15, 1606 in Leiden, in the Dutch Republic, nowadays the Netherlands. He was the ninth child born to Harmen Gerritszoon van Rijn and Neeltgen Willemsdochter van Zuytbrouck. His family was quite well-to-do; his father was a miller and his mother was a baker's daughter. As a boy he attended Latin school and was enrolled at the University of Leiden, although according to a contemporary he had a greater inclination towards painting; he was soon apprenticed to a Leiden history painter, Jacob van Swanenburgh, with whom he spent three years'.[229]	
Spreekbeurt.info: 'Rembrandt was born on 15 July 1606 in Leiden, Rembrandt his father [*sic*!] was owner of a mill. This mill was not suitable as a residence. Their house was near the mill, on the Weddesteeg. Rembrandt his parents [*sic*!] were not rich but also not poor'.[230]	

---

226 Wikipedia, 'Rembrandt van Rijn'. http://nl.wikipedia.org/wiki/Rembrandt_van_Rijn (Accessed 24 January 2011).

227 It is worthwhile mentioning that the pupils chose the right spelling of this name – Harmen – while two of the sources got it wrong – Herman and Hermen, which implies that some checks may have been carried out.

228 Toon Oomens, 'Rembrandt Harmensz van Rijn (1606–1669)' http://people.zeelandnet.nl/acoomens/rembrand.htm (Accessed 24 January 2011).

229 Wikipedia, 'Rembrandt'. http://en.wikipedia.org/wiki/Rembrandt (Accessed 24 January 2011).

230 Anouk Claassens, 'Rembrandt van Rijn'. http://spreekbeurten.info/rembrandt.html (Accessed 24 January 2011).

A comparison of these 20 sentences shows that each of the sources in the column on the left provided an element that the pair used for the summary in the column on the right. All sources mentioned the date and place of birth, which gave the pair the confidence to repeat the same information, though in less detail. The Dutch and English Wikipedia pages seemed to offer so many details, which the pair preferred to ignore or to shorten. For instance, instead of mentioning that Rembrandt became an independent painter after a three-year period of apprenticeship with Jacob van Swanenburgh, they simply stated that 'he went to settle in Leiden in 1625. There he became a painter'. The wording of the statement about Rembrandt's short school experiences was inspired by the text from People.zeelandnet.nl/acoomens, while the formulation 'There he became a painter' summarised the two Wikipedia texts which suggest that he stopped his studies because he was more inclined to become a painter.[231]

I should stress that close study of the online sources used by the pupils reveals that they were of very different sorts. Table 6.2 contains two of them: an online encyclopaedia [Wikipedia] and the personal websites http://people.zeelandnet.nl/acoomens/index.htm and http://www.spreekbeurt.info [which also happens to be a child-generated content site, hence the few grammatical errors]. Many other sorts of websites were used as sources, including the Historical

Table 6.3: Categories of Web sources used for the WebQuest assignments.

		Pupil 1	Pupil 2	Pupil 3	Pupil 4	Pupil 5	Pupil 6	Pair 1	Pair 2
Wikipedia		1	1	2	?	1	1	2	1
Personal sites		1	1		?			1	2
Heritage sites	Heritage Inst.		1	1	?	1			2
	Others	1	1		?		1		
Commercial sites			1	1	?		1	1	
Educ. sites		1	1		?	1	1		
Official sites					?	2			1
News Media sites				2	?		1		
Canon of the NL		1			?		1		
General Info sites			1		?	1			
Academic sites		1			?				

231 By moving back and forth between various sources of information and selecting details from each source, the pupils were performing what Jenkins and colleagues (2009: 85-85) called 'Transmedia Navigation', which consists of 'The ability to follow the flow of stories and information across multiple modalities'. They were 'hunters and gatherers' encountering 'the same information, the same stories, the same characters and worlds across multiple modes of representation'.

Canon of the Netherlands, educational sites, the sites of heritage institutions, those of news media organisations and others. Table 6.3 provides a complete overview.

Of the ten categories of Web sources used, Wikipedia emerged as the most popular. All pupils used it at least once, except for Pupil 4 [whose sources are uncertain due to the lack of references]. In all cases, the Wikipedia page was always dedicated specifically to the subject, that is, to one of the painters or the VOC. For instance, Pupils 1 and 6 both worked on the VOC and they cited the VOC Wikipedia page[232] as the first and second source, respectively. Pupil 3 worked on the same subject and cited Wikipedia twice, providing the following comment: 'For my own research I used the following sites: www.wikipedia.nl [and] www.geschiedenis.vpro.nl'. He then provided the names of sites from which he had downloaded pictures, which included another Wikipedia page.[233]

Personal Web pages and those of heritage websites were the second most frequently used sources. Personal websites are those which explicitly indicate that they are owned and run by an individual. Two pupils and the two pairs used personal sites as sources for their assignments. Pupil 2 mentioned www.statenvertaling.net, a personal initiative of Ronald Klip, for her assignment on Rembrandt.[234] Pupil 1 consulted www.VOCsite.nl, another private initiative by someone named Jaap van Overbeek, for his assignment on the VOC. The heritage sites can be put into two categories: those owned and run by memory or heritage institutions such as museums and archives, and those owned and run by other organisations [associations, foundations, clubs, *etc.*] but which focus on cultural heritage or cultural memory. Among the institutional sites were those of the *Rijksmuseum*, which Pair 2 used twice for their assignment on Rembrandt.[235] The sites of non-heritage institutions included http://voc-kenniscentrum.nl, a 400-year jubilee project of the Royal Netherlands Institute of Southeast Asian and Caribbean Studies [KITLV].

---

232 Wikipedia, '*Vereenigde Oostindische Compagnie*'. http://nl.wikipedia.org/wiki/Vereenigde_Oostindische_Compagnie (Accessed 25 January 2011).

233 Wikipedia, '*Handelsposten van de VOC in het Midden-Oosten*'. http://nl.wikipedia.org/wiki/Handelsposten_van_de_VOC_in_het_Midden-Oosten (Accessed 25 January 2011).

234 *Statenvertaling*, 'Rembrandt Harmensz. van Rijn'. http://www.statenvertaling.net/kunst/biografie/rembrandt.harmensz.van.rijn.html (Accessed 25 January 2011).

235 *Rijksmuseum,* Rembrandt Harmensz. van Rijn'. http://www.rijksmuseum.nl/ara/aria_artists/00016943?lang=nl ; and indirectly via *cultuurwijs.nl*: 'Rembrandt van Rijn (1606–1969)'. http://www.cultuurwijs.nl/nwc.rijksmuseumamsterdam/cultuurwijs.nl/i000072.html (Both accessed 25 January 2011).

The next most frequently used categories were commercial and educational sites. Commercial sites are sites whose explicit goal is to generate profit either through selling information directly or through advertisement. For example, Pupil 2 used a text on Rembrandt originating from www.kunstkennis.nl for her assignment.[236] This is explicitly a profit-driven site because under each Rembrandt painting is a 'Buy posters at AllPosters.com' link. The homepage indicates that the site is owned by Kunsttrip v.o.f, a company involved in history and culture-related business which specifically targets travellers and tourists in Western Europe. Educational sites are sites that explicitly claim to target pupils and teachers for educational purposes. In this respect, Pupil 5 used www.scholieren.com to obtain information about Johannes Vermeer.[237]

Official sites were also among the sources pupils used. Official sites are those owned and run by an administrative institution, which could be governmental, provincial or municipal. For his assignment on Vermeer, Pupil 5 consulted both www.delft.nl, the official site of the city of Delft[238] and www.ontdeknederland.org [discover the Netherlands], a website run by the Dutch Ministry of Foreign Affairs which specifically calls upon young people to 'become acquainted with the Netherlands'.[239] News media sites are those that are owned and run by established mainstream newspapers, broadcasting companies, *etc.* Pupil 3 not only downloaded the picture of VOC director Johan van Oldebarneveld from the forum page of Amsterdam AT5 TV,[240] but also consulted www.geschiedenis.vpro.nl, the history site of the VPRO TV channel. The general information website www.info.nu was cited twice, as was the Canon of the Netherlands, whose primary education page on the VOC was used.[241] The sole academic source was the page on 'De VOC: Dutch-Asiatic Shipping 1595–

---

236 *Kunskennis.nl*, 'Rembrandt van Rijn'. http://kunstkennis.nl/kunstgeschiedenis/barok/rembrandt.htm (Accessed 25 January 2011).

237 *Scholieren.com, 'Werkstuk Geschiedenis, Johannes Vermeer'.* http://www.scholieren.com/werkstukken/23402 (Accessed 25 January 2011).

238 This website states that the managing and webmastering of the site are 'in the hands of the webmaster of the municipality of Delft' http://www.delft.nl/Configuratie/Footer/Colofon. The page Pupil 5 consulted is: '*Werk van Johannes Vermeer*', http://www.delft.nl/vermeer/2_1.html (Both accessed 25 January 2011).

239 *Ontdeknederland.org, 'Over de site'.* http://www.ontdeknederland.org/algemene_onderdelen/over_de_site . The Pupil used this page: Jeroen van Dommel, 'Johannes Vermeer'. http://www.ontdeknederland.org/werkstuk_maken/top_10!/johannes_vermeer (Both accessed 25 January 2011).

240 *AT5 News, ' Blauw bloed is zwart bloed (1500–1789)'.* http://forum.at5.nl/viewtopic.php?t=17047&sid=09d10b818e27f61ea14e919ba7cbd26 (Accessed 25 January 2011).

241 The Canon of the Netherlands, '*De VOC 1602–1799: Nederland breidt uit over zee*'. http://entoen.nu/voc/po (Accessed 29 January 2011).

1795' from the website of the Huygens Institute of Netherlands History [Huygens ING],[242] which is 'a scholarly institute engaged in stimulating research into the history of the Netherlands'.[243]

The above survey of categories of websites used by the pupils leaves no doubt as to the variety of sources for historical information. The short summaries were the result of a combination of information emanating from various provenances. The last interesting point is to find out what the pupils thought of those provenances and how they justified their choices. Generally speaking, Wikipedia prompted much more enthusiasm among the pupils. Pupil 1 rated Wikipedia's information on VOC with an 8/10 and commented in these terms: '[It provides] A lot of information about its history'. The Historical Canon of the Netherlands, which he also used, also received an 8/10 together with this comment: '[It discusses] How the VOC expanded'. Pair 1, who used both the Dutch and the English Wikipedia pages on Rembrandt, rated both with a 5/5, commenting as follows: The Dutch page provides '[Information] About his life and his paintings' and the English page '[tells you] Everything about Rembrandt van Rijn'. Toon Oomens' personal website[244] received a 4/5, with this comment: '[It tells you] A little bit about his [Rembrandt's] life, but more about his work'. These few comments and ratings, which could be generalised for all the WebQuest assignments, show that the pupils valued Wikipedia highly. Of all the pupils, Pupil 6 – the one who only commented on the sources – was most eloquent in praising Wikipedia:

> As is almost always the case, Wikipedia is the best, [because] there is always a lot of information. It seems as if all the professors have written their information there. The 2nd [best site] was entoen.nu [Canon of the Netherlands], which is also a sort of Wikipedia though it is much less well-known. You can find everything there too. There are other useful sites as well but they are not as elaborate as the 1st and the 2nd. I judged these sites simply by typing 'The VOC, the United East India Company' in Google.

---

242 Huygens ING, '*De VOC: Dutch-Asiatic Shipping 1595–1795*'. http://www.inghist.nl/Onderzoek/Projecten/DAS (Accessed 29 January 2011).

243 Huygens ING, 'About the Huygens ING'. http://www.inghist.nl/Instituut/OverHetIng/en/index_html (Accessed 29 January 2011).

244 Toon Oomens, 'Rembrandt Harmensz van Rijn (1606–1669)'. http://people.zeelandnet.nl/acoomens/rembrand.htm (Accessed 24 January 2011).

This comment implies that Wikipedia is beyond any possible comparison. It also implies that the information is 'almost always' reliable and authoritative, as it seems to emanate from 'professors'. The 'almost always' suggests that the pupil may have some reservations, but that these are overwhelmed by the amount and the authority of the information found on Wikipedia. Unlike Pupil 6 and most of the other pupils, Pupil 2 is both enthusiastic and critical of Wikipedia. For her,

> Wikipedia *is* often clear *but* sometimes a little bit difficult. It *is* mostly reliable *but* everyone can publish something. The site *is* well-structured and you can choose what you want (such as history, arts, biography, etc.) [Italicisation is mine].

The '*is* ... *but* ...' reasoning shows that Pupil 2 knows how Wikipedia works, in particular the fact that everyone, including both credentialed and non-credentialed authors, can publish and edit articles. She appears to be more enthusiastic than critical, however, as her last '*is*' [well-structured and you can choose what you want] was not accompanied by a '*but*'. Her general feeling is that the site is 'mostly reliable'. As Table 6.2 shows, other websites seem to have compensated for these reservations. When the same information kept coming up on various sites, it was deemed reliable and taken into account in the summaries.

6.5 Summary

In this chapter I discussed how the Dalton approach to teaching and learning, in combination with the one-child-one-connected-laptop policy, led to an atmosphere that stimulated the pupils to use the Web frequently during both the teacher-led lecture time and the 'independent work' time. It appears that the freedom that the pupils enjoy in terms of media uses has led to various forms of interactions with digital media in general, and the Web in particular. During the teacher-led lecture time, pupils would search for details about information that was either provided by the teacher or gleaned from the textbook. During the 'independent work' time, the interactions of pupils would be even more varied, ranging from Web-surfing in search of relevant information for assignments to using it as a means of relaxing from their intellectual efforts. In this respect, the Web appeared to be a crucial factor in creating an atmosphere conducive to learning. I also explored the ways in which the Web interfered with the historical thinking process of the pupils.

It seems that Web image display tools made it easier for pupils to compare and then judge visual representations of the concepts about which they were being taught, or on which they were writing assignments. Moreover, the easy access to various websites enabled pupils to make summaries. Through content analysis, content harmonising, and content structuring – all of which involve comparisons, judgments, and selections – they were able to produce short illustrated texts and maps. Finally, I considered the variety of Web sources used for WebQuest assignments. Ten sorts of websites were used, including Wikipedia, the Canon of the Netherlands, heritage sites, but also, among others, personal, educational, commercial, official, and news sites. It was by weighing information contained in each of them that the pupils managed to write their assignments.

Chapter 7

Analytical Understanding of the Findings

The two case studies discussed in Chapters 5 and 6 revealed a number of uses and impacts of the Web in the history class. They shed some light on ways in which digital media in general, and the Web in particular, have made the history class more attractive, while at the same time stimulating forms of historical thinking and offering a wide variety of sources. In this chapter I want to discuss patterns that emerged from the case studies and provide an analysis for their understanding. The discussion will revolve around the three claims I explored during my field research in the two schools, namely that the Web makes the history class more attractive, fosters historical thinking, and offers a wider variety of historical sources to pupils. Unlike the previous two chapters, these claims will not be considered separately and successively, but rather in patterns, that is, in connection with one another. The first pattern I shall discuss centres on the fact that historical thinking was fostered *ipso facto* by the Web, because it made the history class more attractive. The second pattern stems from the observation that by offering access to a variety of sources, the Web was at the same time fostering historical thinking. The last pattern is linked to the previous ones in the sense that, among the sources used, conventional and unconventional sources were used to complement one another. I shall end this chapter by placing my findings in a broader discussion about the implications of the above-mentioned patterns.

7.1 Attractiveness Means Historical Thinking

> Being with someone I love and thinking about something else; that's how I manage to have the best thoughts, to invent the best of what is necessary for my work. The same is true with the text: it provokes the greatest pleasure in me when it manages to let itself be listened to indirectly; when, while reading it, I am often pushed to raise my head, to hear something else (Barthes, 1973: 41-42).

Some popular and, to some extent, expert, and scholarly opinions often decry the attractiveness of digital media technologies as having a bad influence on the learning process in children. The technologies have been presented as, among other things, diverting learners' attention away from serious matters, favouring only the acquisition of artificial and fragmented knowledge and forming an obstacle to concentration. Other voices, however, including those whose claim on the attractiveness of the Web I explored, argue that the attractiveness of the Web can be turned into an asset, which is what appears to have taken place in the two case studies I presented in the previous two chapters. This section discusses the first pattern that emerged from my ethnographic research into the two classes, namely that the very fact that the Web was attractive to 13- to 14-year-old history-learners paved the way for forms of historical thinking. I shall discuss this pattern first with regard to the Web-based historical videos, which appeared to have not only a huge attention-capturing ability but also the power to take learners beyond what they have seen and heard. Second, I shall focus on multitasking-driven thinking which the Web seems to have made central to learning history.

To begin with, in the *Baarnsch Lyceum* [BL] case study (Chapter 5) it was obvious that Web-based videos, mostly originating from the Historical Canon of the Netherlands, were among the media texts that were most successful at captivating pupils' attention. They constituted one important aspect of the 'if it is attractive, then it triggers historical thinking' pattern. In one case, as noted earlier, a pupil who attentively watched a clip[245] about the alleged excesses of State Holder William V [1748–1806], subsequently responded verbally and with revealing gestures. Instead of raising his head [which was already raised and directed towards the screen] as Barthes did to hear something else (see epigraph), this pupil raised his hand to do something else: make an imaginary pistol and shoot. This shooting gesture could be interpreted as a visible indication of the relationship between the attractiveness of a medium and the thinking process it triggered.[246] On some occasions such thinking was creative as with the shooting gesture, while at other times it would exteriorise verbally, for instance, when the pupil said out loud [and to himself] 'Guillotine!' in reaction to the abuses of William V.

245 The Canon of the Netherlands, '*Schooltv Beeldbankclip De Patriotten*'. http://entoen.nu/patriotten/beeld-en-geluid/schooltv-beeldbankclip-de-patriotten#beeld (Accessed 7 March 2011).

246 Cognitive psychologists have suggested that 'to overcome their limited knowledge' which affects their thinking, children 'use the tools provided by the culture in which they live' (Siegler & Alibali [1986] 2005: 66). From this perspective, it could be deduced that the shooting gesture was inspired by the pistols and shooting scenes to which the Internet Generation is constantly exposed either through games, films or the Web.

The video clip facilitated historical thinking not only by capturing and holding the pupil's attention, but also by ensuring speedy and smooth information-processing. The information captured by the sensory memory – through the eyes and ears – was quickly processed in the working memory, in which on the one hand associations were made with information already stored in the long-term memory, namely the story about the Guillotine,[247] and on the other hand connections were established with the prevailing popular culture among pupils – hence the shooting gesture. It could be assumed that a piece of information that goes through such a process is likely to be stored in the long-term memory where it expands the prior knowledge reservoir for future information or events that the sensory memory will encounter.

The verbal and gestural reactions described above are similar to what Jenkins *et al.* (2009: 52-53) termed 'improvisational performance', a major feature of role-playing activities that is also observed in interaction with digital media:

> Performance brings with it capacities to understand problems from multiple viewpoints, to assimilate information, to exert mastery over core cultural materials, and to improvise in response to a changing environment.

In role-playing activities pupils adopt fictive identities and '*think* through scenarios from those characters' perspectives' (*Ibid.*: 53. Italicisation is mine). The 'shooting pupil', who also 'sentenced' William V to the 'Guillotine', had obviously mentally assumed the identity, and was playing the role, of the French revolutionaries. He assumed the identity and role of the Patriots[248] when, like them, he said '*Echt niet!*' [No way!] in rejection of the alleged abuses. This example shows two important aspects of historical thinking, namely 'the moral response stance' and 'the identification stance' (Barton & Levstik, 2004: 45 and 91). Sentencing William V to the 'Guillotine' is a way of condemning him and his deeds as described in the clip. Exclaiming '*Echt niet!*' is identifying with the morally good side.

---

247 *Sensory memory* is the capacity to briefly retain information just encountered, using the five senses; *working memory* is 'where active thinking occurs', combining information that comes from sensory memory with information stored in the long-term memory; *long-term memory*, for its part, is the capacity to store information over a longer period (Stigler & Alibali, [1986] 2005: 68-72).

248 The 'Patriots' was the name given to the citizens who criticized and opposed State Holder William V in the early 1780s. They considered him to be a dictator and blamed him for the decline of the Republic, which was then at war with England. They took up arms and forced William V to flee to the East [Nijmegen] from whence he returned with the military support of Prussian troops. (The Canon of the Netherlands, '*De patriotten 1780–1795: Crisis in de Republiek*'. http://entoen.nu/patriotten [Accessed 17 February 2011]).

Assuming these identities and roles because of a historical detail in the clip is exactly what Huizinga (1948: 566) meant with 'historical sensation', the one that suddenly makes one cease to be oneself [by making one assume another identity and role] and puts one in contact with the past. Unlike ordinary role-playing activities, this one involved interaction between media texts and pupils, or, if one assumes that those texts represented foregone figures and characters, between the latter and the pupils. The suggestion here is that performance is an external sign of understanding, assimilation, and mastery, which all result from historical thinking.

There are also instances in which such thinking could, to repeat the words of Barthes, be about 'hearing something else', or to quote Huizinga (*ibid.*), consist of 'flowing in the world outside [one]self'. This was the case at the moment when the narrator of a Web video announced that the Beemster had been reclaimed in order to obtain arable land. At that particular moment, one pupil heard something else, or flowed into a world different from the one described by the clip, and realised that fishermen were forced by the new situation to convert to other trades. This media text provoked a sort of ecstasy (*Ibid.*) when it managed to let itself be listened to *indirectly*. The narrator never mentioned the fate of fishermen *directly* or explicitly but the pupil heard it *indirectly*, because the Web-based video provoked 'the greatest pleasure' (Barthes, see epigraph) in her and pushed her to listen to the parallel, *indirect*, voice. The Web-based clip, with its maps, paintings, and pictures, triggered conditional reasoning, the sort based on 'if p then q' reasoning (Klaczynski, 2001: 848; see also Kuhn & Franklin, 2008: 523) both before and after the reclamation. In this case the reasoning took a deductive form, since from the premises provided in the clip – that the water was completely pumped out – the pupil drew a logical conclusion (Kuhn, 2009: 159-160; see also Byrnes, 2003: 231), namely that no further fishing activity would be possible. It could be suggested that the presence of water on some maps and images and its absence on others were central to this syllogistic reasoning, but this was only possible mainly because the medium managed to get the pupil engaged and facilitated her deductive thinking beyond the images provided.

It is in this same 'if it is attractive, then it triggers historical thinking' pattern, that I would place the attitudes of pupils in the Helen Parkhurst Dalton School [HPDS] case study. Unlike the teacher at the BL, his colleagues at the HPDS never used the Web during their short instruction time [at least not during the period of my field research]. However, during the 10–35 minutes of teacher-led instruction time, the Web was omnipresent in the one-pupil-one-laptop class. A comment on Louis XIV's high-heeled shoes provoked not only laughter but also, and most importantly, immediate searches on the Web for more details or more images. The teacher's explanation about the Palace of Versailles was provided while pupils simultaneously searched for images of the palace on the Web. I would call this the second type of the 'if it is attractive, then it triggers historical thinking' pattern.

Unlike the first type, which centred on the use of the Web by the teacher, this one consisted of two parallel processes: a no-Web instruction time on the teacher's part and a listen-and-check-it-on-the-Web process on the learners' part. Multitasking was central to this process, as surfing the Web did not mean pupils were not listening to the teacher or not reading from the textbook. Multitasking in educational settings has been explained as consisting of 'scanning for relevant shifts in the information flow while simultaneously taking in multiple stimuli' (Jenkins *et al.*, 2009: 61-62). Unlike popular opinions that by offering a variety of resources at the same time the Web affects learners' attention and their ability to concentrate, multitasking is presented as being complementary to attention, as a way of 'mapping where different information is externally stored within their immediate environment' (*Ibid.*)

In some cases, this particular phenomenon took the form of a triangle: as shown by the arrows in Figure 7.1, the textbook served mostly as a starting point, not only prompting explanations and comments on the part of the teacher, but also often triggering Web searches. The teacher's comments would also trigger Web searches. As the arrow in the middle of the triangle indicates, after searching the Web, the pupils would shift back to the instruction or to the textbook.

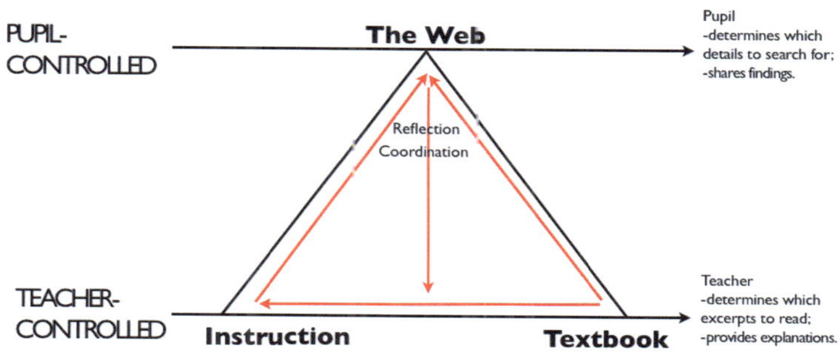

Figure 7.1: Triangular learning process, consisting of a combination of reading from the textbook, listening to the teacher's explanations, and searching for more details on the Web.

It is important to note that no direct arrow links 'The Web' to 'Instruction' or to 'Textbook', because I did not observe a single Web-triggered question to the teacher, or a Web-triggered search in the textbook. In other words, I did not detect any instance whereby the teacher or the textbook provided clarification of a detail found on the Web. I am not suggesting that a Web-to-textbook or Web-to-teacher path is impossible or non-existent, but rather that nothing occurred to substantiate it. The nature of the Web could partly explain why there is no evidence of this path: being a huge reservoir of all sorts of information, the Web does not present its infinite number of resources in an ordered way that forms a coherent narrative. It relies largely on search engines to introduce some order, depending in part on, among other things, the user's search terms and increasingly on search history and behaviour.[249] As such, it serves more as a clarification provider rather than a clarification trigger. Unlike the Web, textbook narratives and the teacher's instructions have a pedagogical structure that consists of tight selections and summaries of resources, in particular due to time constraints on the part of the teacher, who does not have the time to say and show everything. Textbooks for their part have restricted space and cannot, for example, display all relevant pictures or texts and are not even capable of including audiovisual materials. For this reason, the selections and summaries made by the teacher and the textbook are clarification triggers rather than clarification providers.

In Chapter 6 (Section 6.2) I cited two examples of Triangular Learning in connection with a lesson about Louis XIV, his high-heeled shoes and his Palace of Versailles, but there are marked indications leading to the general hypothesis that the Dalton approach to media favours this kind of textbook–teacher–Web interaction. Once again, the fact the pupils were learning like 'swimming ducks' (Van Velzen, 2002: 6) did not always make it possible to detect which detail from the textbook or from a comment made by the teacher triggered which search on the Web. Further research is thus needed to map the connections among the three elements of the triangle and their impact on outcomes, but it is already safe to present this model as a tentative framework for understanding the respective roles of the teacher and the learners. The learning process navigated between the teacher-controlled part, which was when it was initiated, and the pupil-controlled one, which mostly took place on the

249 In recent years, search engines have started offering personalised search results based on the user's demographic data, and his or her browsing and clickstream history. In other words, two people using the same search terms on two different computers will most likely obtain different results (Batelle, 2005: 37; Van Dijck, 2010: 583).

Web. The pupils seem to find the latter appealing as, according to digital media and culture scholars, they 'learn more through direct observation and experimentation than from *reading* about something in a textbook or *listening to a lecture*' (Jenkins *et al.*: 2009: 42. Italicisation is mine).

Although not as openly encouraged as at the HPDS, multitasking also emerged as a major characteristic in the BL case study. Pupils would watch Web-based videos while taking notes and, at the same time, repeatedly turn the video contents over in their minds in order to make notes reflecting the 'something else' they had heard from the video. Writing down that fishermen would convert to other trades, instead of a more to-the-point note on the reclamation of the Beemster, meant that three processes had taken place simultaneously: the pupil [1] watched the video; she [2] reflected on its content and [3] she wrote down the conclusion of her reflections. Reflecting and writing did not mean that she stopped watching completely. Otherwise she would have missed other aspects on politics, culture, and economy. Similarly, the 'shooting pupil' watched, reflected, 'made a gun' and mimed 'shooting'. The last three phases did not prevent him from watching. Indeed, the same process took place on three successive occasions: he made the shooting gesture after the verbal '*Echt niet!*' and 'Guillotine!' exclamations.

One thing that has become increasingly clear up to now is that the computer – more than any other medium – facilitates multitasking among adolescents (Roberts *et al*, 2009: 319). One point that still needs clarification is how this multitasking – based on the attractiveness of the computer and, by extension, the Web – implies some forms of historical thinking among adolescents. Education psychologist David Moshman (1999: 103-104), who suggested that adolescent thinking is best understood from the rational constructivist perspective,[250] maintained that rational constructivism 'highlight[s] reflection, coordination, and peer interaction as key developmental processes'. For the construction of rationality to be possible, he argued, 'individuals [must] have free access to information and ideas and are encouraged to formulate, express, discuss, and justify ideas of their own.' (*Ibid.*: 113). The triangular process reflected in Figure 7.1 shows some ways in which pupils' *reflection* and *coordination* took place. A certain level of reflection is required in order to find the right search term[s], corresponding or relating to either comments made by the teacher or the contents of the

250 According to David Moshman (1999: 103-104) 'Rational constructivism construes the construction of knowledge and reasoning as a rational process that generates justifiable outcomes ... In particular, rational constructivism directs attention to the active role of rational agents in constructing higher levels of understanding and reasoning'.

textbook, that would lead to the clarification they sought. Similarly, searching, digesting the results found, while at the same time keeping an eye on the textbook and an ear open for the teacher's explanations, requires a high level of coordination to keep all those tasks in harmony.

Peer interaction, which developmental and cognitive psychologists have presented as a key characteristic of early adolescence [10–14 years] (Moshman, 1999: 5), was also observed. According to developmental and educational psychologist Judith Torney-Purta (1994: 110), early adolescents are best at organising and processing historical information while interacting with peers, since

> Their understanding of what they experience and their movement toward greater reflectivity are situated within a group of peers grappling with understanding the same material.

Therefore, from the perspective of developmental psychology, searching for a detail on the Web and sharing the results found with peers – for instance by turning the laptop to show it to a classmate – transforms the Web into an attractive, thought-triggering tool that enables pupils on the one hand to move back and forth between the teacher's instruction and the textbook, and on the other hand to engage in peer interaction around historical contents.

In addition to the above, multitasking implies negotiation between continuity and discontinuity in a way that makes both of them complementary. Salvucci and Taatgen (2011: 114-115) called this negotiation 'suspension and resumption', which means that

> When a task is suspended, the task's thread remains active to maintain awareness of the task. Critically, this awareness allows for background processing of the suspended task when needed or desired ... (*Ibid.*: 116).

The various shifts shown in Figure 7.1 involve this kind of suspension and resumption, as the reading or listening task would be briefly paused – that is, the teacher's instruction or the reading task was being processed in the background – and resumed after the Web search. Given the short suspension time between the shifts, this type of multitasking would not be called 'sequential multitasking', which supposes that a task is paused until a later time (*Ibid.*: 115), but rather 'concurrent multitasking', because the interruptions were brief and the switches did not prevent any task from progressing (*Ibid.*: 8-9). Instead, it could be said that the switch to the Web clarified and made the teacher's explanation or the textbook narrative less abstract [*disabstracted*], thereby contributing to the continuity of the reading and listening processes. The *disabstraction* that resulted from this Web-driven multitasking means that the HPDS pupils managed to have an almost concrete experience of Louis XIV's high-heeled shoes and the Palace of Versailles, as they were rendered less abstract to the pupils' through the digital, online accessible representations. In other terms, the pupils went further with the teacher's or textbook narrative with a mental image of what Louis XIV and the Palace of Versailles looked like. This discontinuity in continuity was only possible because the pupils were able to negotiate between suspension and resumption, a process that integrated self-sought, Web-based, concrete objects to elucidate the teacher's and the textbook's accounts.

In sum, the above has presented and explained one important pattern that emerged from the two case studies, namely that the attractiveness of the Web triggers forms of historical thinking. It appears that Web-based videos, where used, not only have the power to get pupils to watch and listen, but also to make them think beyond what the historical clip showed and said. A few thinking processes of pupils and their verbal or gestural manifestations were discussed and presented as indications suggestive of the idea that Web-based moving images stimulate creative and deductive thinking in addition to other forms of thinking. I also discussed the attractiveness of the Web as a triggering factor for a thinking process that integrates more than one task at the same time. The Web appeared to be the motor behind multitasking-driven historical thinking, either in the form of triangular learning or in other forms. I pointed out that navigating between the teacher's instruction, textbook's accounts, and the Web, and eventually sharing information with peers, necessitated a considerable level of reflection and coordination, as well as a sense of harmonisation between continuity and discontinuity. In the next section, I shall discuss another pattern, one that relates to the forms of historical thinking triggered by the variety of Web-based sources.

7.2 Variety of Sources Fosters Historical Thinking

> Each person formulates his questions from a given point of view, determined by the context of his own experience ... The context of the experience of each one of us includes the influence of those with whom we come into contact (Stebbing, [1939] 1952: 28).

In this section I shall elaborate on another pattern revolving around the observation that the pupils' encounter with a multitude of media texts via the Web resulted in a variety of thinking processes. Although not yet fully developed, the seeds of source evaluation, sampling, quoting, image selection, and summarising skills, appear to have fallen on fertile soil when the pupils in the two classes made use of multiple online sources. Quotations are of particular importance because public opinion tends to interpret their relatively excessive use by pupils as early signs of future plagiarism and unoriginal thinking. The case studies, especially the BL one, have shown that considerable historical thinking took place during the quote-compilation process, thereby challenging the popular view that equates quote-compilation with copy-paste thinking or writing. Having discussed the manifestation of historical thinking in connection with attractiveness during instruction time in both the BL and HPDS classes (see previous section), I shall now deal with its various manifestations in class assignments in relation to sources used by the pupils. In the first place I shall deal with the thinking process behind the compilation of quotations, especially their identification from multiple sources. I suggest that this process needs to be understood from the perspective of adolescent thinking, as early adolescents think differently from other age groups. In the second place I shall discuss the thinking process that underlies the summarising of texts which emanate from multiple sources.

The most important form of historical thinking in the BL case study resided in the use of quotations taken from various sources on the Web. I shall to call this the 'Search for it and find a quote' pattern. I have two reasons for refraining from using the words 'Google it ...': first, the teacher had indicated to which sites the pupils should go directly, including the Canon of the Netherlands and regional canons, Wikipedia, and educational sites. Although more websites were used, there was no indication that the pupils arrived at them via Google. Second, unlike the situation at the HPDS, the class structure did not allow me to see the pupils working on their assignments. For that reason, there was no way to see how they arrived at their online sources. Two aspects of this pattern are worth noting: on the one hand the relatively high number of Web sources – on average bout nine online sources per pair compared with four print sources [books and newspapers] – and on the other hand, the excessive use of quotations – 9 out of 13 pairs, 8 of whom made compilations of lengthy quotations. Quotations were excessive in two ways: first, most of the assignments [and in one case, the entire assignment] were comprised of uninterrupted quotations from online sources; second, most quotations were very long, leaving little room for the pupils' own text (see Figures 5.4 and 5.5 in Chapter 5, Section 5.3).

The question that needs to be addressed is how this 'Search for it and find a quote' pattern is connected with historical thinking. One might assume that choices of fragments for use as quotes were motivated by their relevance to the subject, which means that pupils first evaluated the contribution of each quote to their argument. They had a puzzlement that needed resolving, namely to discuss various aspects of the Golden Century, and they *asked* – through search terms – the various recommended or non-recommended websites for help. They then decided which excerpts from the resources they had found provided the answer, or part of it, to the puzzlement. The result was a new narrative, different from each individual online text that was used as a source. Each of these different steps, taken for every website that was consulted, involved some level of historical thinking because, after all, following one particular path, stopping at a particular page, selecting some sentences or paragraphs, or even entire pages, did not happen automatically. These steps only took place after the pupils had answered such questions as: is it relevant to my topic? Does it contradict/confirm/clarify what I have already found? and other similar questions. Selecting which part to quote meant in the first place that the source had been evaluated as trustworthy (Van Drie & Van Boxtel, 2008: 94) and the selected part as worth appropriating.

The example of the written assignment on Huygens, Spinoza, and Eisinga discussed in Chapter 5 (Section 5.3) showed that the pair made a compilation of two quotations from Wikipedia and one from a book. However, the order in which these quotations were placed shows that the choices were not fortuitous: the first quotation placed Huygens' scientific work within the broader context of the Scientific Revolution and stressed the key role played by Descartes; the second focused on Huygens' efforts to make a time-keeping device that would be as precise as possible; the last [from a book] discussed Huygens' astronomical findings and connected them to Galileo's ground-breaking discoveries. In this compilation one perceives a certain reasoning as the pair sought connections between the various historic figures – Huygens, Descartes, and Galileo – and their works. In some ways, the pair had attempted to find a historical background and an explanation for the work of Huygens, even though the words they used to describe it were not their own.[251] The process they engaged in

251 This aspect of the history class is what Barton and Levstik (2004: 69) called 'the analytic stance'. This stance 'involves searching for connections among disparate events to identify some developmental trend, causal pattern, or argumentative structure', which the BL pupils appear to have done with quotations from Web sources.

> involves both *analysis* and *commentary*. *Sampling intelligently* from existing cultural reservoir requires a *close analysis* of the existing structures and uses of this material; *remixing* requires an *appreciation* of emerging structures and latent potential meanings. Remixing involves the *creative juxtaposition* of materials that otherwise occupy very different cultural niches (Jenkins *et al.*, 2009:57-58. Italicisation is mine).

A related question would be to ask whether this form of uninterrupted juxtaposing or stringing of quotations without making any comments, however creative, is precisely what can be expected from 13- to 14-year-old learners. Children of this age are referred to as early adolescents [±11–±14 years], who will subsequently grow to become middle adolescents [±14–±18 years] and eventually late adolescents [±18–±21 years], before entering adulthood (Steinberg, 1985: 6-7; see also Moshman, 1999: 5). Although porous, liminal, and transitional (Elmore, 2009: 195), each of these developmental stages presents specific characteristics with respect to thinking, and research has shown that reasoning competence improves with age (see Byrnes, 2003: 233-234). For instance, 'middle adolescents are more likely to rely on analytic processing than early adolescents' (Klaczynski, 2001: 854); older adolescents are more likely than younger adolescents to understand the difference between the options they have of satisfying either one or multiple goals (Byrnes, 2003: 236); while the processing speed of children is believed to increase from early childhood to mid-adolescence (Kuhn, 2009: 154-155).

Developmental and cognitive psychologists have pointed out that adolescents – in the early stages rather than in the later ones – present a number of distinctive characteristics when it comes to expressing their thoughts in writing or in any other argumentative way. In their research on how 13- to14-year-old adolescents evaluate and generate evidence and explanation in their argumentation, Amnon Glassner and colleagues (2005: 113-114) came to the conclusion that 'when asked to generate either explanation or evidence, participants were far more successful at generating explanation'. In this respect, an explanation refers to elucidating the causal basis of a claim, while evidence refers to the 'indication of the truth of that claim' (*Ibid.*: 107-108). Applied to the BL assignments, explanations could be equated with the lengthy, though coherent quotations, while evidence – in the form of argumentation about the truthfulness of the claims conveyed in the quotations – is lacking.

Psychologists specialised in the field of adolescence and other educational researchers converge in describing adolescents as being unwilling or unable to make arguable claims for many reasons. For example: first, they find it difficult (Kuhn, 2009: 172-173; Graff, 2003: 157); second, they do not see the need to argue about something that they feel is obvious (Kuhn, 2009: 173; Graff, 2003: 44); third, in most cases, they are not explicitly challenged to argue (Graff, 2003: 60). The result of all these factors is that adolescent argumentation consists mostly in 'string[ing] together a series of uncontroversially true statements' (*Ibid.*: 54), ones that '*nobody* is likely to dispute' (*Ibid.*: 53). This, then, might explain why the BL pupils, who were not explicitly asked to argue about any claim made about the Golden Century but rather 'to write an article about one development in "The Netherlands in the 17th century"', came up with compilations of 'true' statements without engaging in controversies.

Another characteristic aspect of adolescent thinking is the lack of connectors, or transitions in the compilation of statements. It has been suggested that this omission is because adolescents believe that the relationships among those propositions and statements are self-evident (Graff, 2003: 44). Indeed, as the example about Huygens, Descartes, and Galileo demonstrates, the lengthy quotations were placed in an order that made their interrelatedness more or less obvious. Thus, as psychologists Michael Wolfe and Susan Goldman (2005: 494) have shown in their research on historical text-processing among 11- to 13-year olds, 'adolescents are indeed capable of processing information about a topic from multiple texts and thinking about relations across the texts'. They do make attempts to establish connections among multiple texts, though they fail to do so in a way that experts would.

The last characteristic of adolescent thinking that I would like to discuss in relation to the 'Search for it and find a quote' pattern is 'inhibition'. Educational psychologist Deanna Kuhn (2009: 155; see also Kuhn & Franklin, 2008: 520-521) has distinguished two types of inhibition: [1] one that is referred to as 'selective attention', which emphasises the ability to ignore irrelevant stimuli that might interfere with information processing; and [2] one that emphasises an ability to refrain from having an already established response when asked to do so. The latter is the case, for instance, when one is instructed to forget a learnt word and inhibit it in subsequent free recall. A third type can be added – the self-decided inhibition – which emphasises the individual's decision about which response to exhibit and which to inhibit (Kuhn, 2009: 155-156; Kuhn & Franklin, 2008: 521). Combined with the adolescents' belief that texts speak for themselves and that relationships between them are obvious, inhibition in adolescent thinking could help explain the self-decided omission of any transitions between the quotations.

For these cognitive and psycho-developmental reasons, the 'Search for it and find a quote' pattern should not be regarded as mere 'potted thinking',[252] or dismissed as 'scissors-and-paste history',[253] or as what Web 2.0 sceptics have called 'intellectual kleptomania', which consists of 'cutting and pasting' from websites (Keen, 2007: 23). It would be more appropriate to study it bearing in mind that 13- to 14-year-old adolescents are not expert thinkers. In this framework, then, quote-compilation should rather be perceived as a form of 'appropriation', a skill consisting of 'the ability to meaningfully sample and remix media content' (Jenkins *et al.*, 2009: 55). The principle underlying appropriation is that 'all cultural expression builds on what has come before' and that 'students learn by taking culture apart and putting it back together' (*Ibid.*; see also Palfrey and Gasser, 2008: 127).

In contrast with the BL pupils, the HPDS ones engaged with online texts in a different way, perhaps because the WebQuest instructions were very specific on the steps to follow. These pupils' thinking took place on at least three levels: choosing the most relevant websites, evaluating those sites, that is, explaining why they were deemed the most relevant, and extracting information from them for short summaries. They had to bear in mind that not only should the poster be the result of a tight selection, but it should also provide a precise image of either the painter being studied or the VOC. The WebQuest approach has been hailed for fostering essential media literacy skills such as 'searching out valuable sources', 'extracting information or images from a series of websites', and compiling them into a final report (*Ibid.*: 93). Apart from broadening pupils' exposure to other, different perspectives and opinions beyond those of the textbook, the WebQuest approach also – and most importantly – 'trains them to synthesize [which I called summarise] their own perspectives' (*Ibid.*: 94).

Unlike the instructions for the BL assignments, thus, no compulsory [*verplicht*] websites were indicated. I shall call the pattern that emerged from this activity, the 'Google it, compare and sum it up' pattern. This time I do use 'Google it …' because my observations and interviews revealed that Google was the default search engine for most pupils, although a few also used *Bing.com*. The WebQuest assignments reflected to a great extent the thinking proc-

252 Philosopher Susan Stebbing ([1939] 1952: 67-68) defined 'potted thinking' as a form of thinking that consists of 'easily fall[ing] into the habit of accepting compressed statements which save us from the trouble of thinking'.

253 Philosopher of history George Collingwood ([1946] 1994: 257-258) explained 'scissors-and-paste history' as 'a kind of history which depends altogether upon the testimony of authority'. It consists in 'determining first what one wants to know about before 'go[ing] in search of statements about it'.

esses that took place and the influence exerted by the instructions. At the source-selection stage, pupils were expected to think in terms of relevance and reliability and to justify their choices. The resulting comments and accompanying ratings were the results of the pupils' own observations and reflection, and formed the first manifestation of historical thinking in relation to the WebQuests. To take one example: Pupil 1 (Table 6.1 in Chapter 6, Section 6.3) used six websites for his assignment on the Dutch East India Company [VOC]: Wikipedia was rated 8/10 and praised for providing 'Much information about its [the VOC's] history';[254] the VOC Knowledge Centre of the Royal Netherlands Institute of Southeast Asian and Caribbean Studies [KITLV] received 7/10, with the comment that it provided 'information about the ships they [the VOC] had and what they looked like';[255] the Huygens Institute of Netherlands History [Huygens ING] was given 8/10, with the comment 'VOC shipping'; [256] *Kennisnet*'s ThinkQuest was rated 7/10 and deemed relevant because it discussed 'The rise of the VOC';[257] the Canon of the Netherlands received an 8/10 for the way it explained 'How the VOC expanded';[258] finally, Jaap van Overbeek's *VOCsite.nl* also, received 8/10 for providing the pupil with information on 'The history of slavery'.[259]

Though the ratings did not add much to my understanding of the thinking processes that lay behind the choices of the various websites, the comments provided a more interesting insight into that process. My initial response was to compare the comments with the titles of each of the cited pages to check if they had not been copy-pasted into the WebQuest. This was not the case for most sources, although some comments did seem exceedingly close to the titles. For instance, Wikipedia's title *Vereenigde Oostindische Compagnie* [United East India Company] bears little resemblance to 'Much information about its history', but Huygens ING's 'De *VOC*: Dutch-Asiatic *Shipping* 1595-1795' [Italicisation is mine] was simply shortened to 'VOC shipping'. In any case, the few words in the comment

254 Wikipedia, '*Vereenigde Oostindische Compagnie*'. http://nl.wikipedia.org/wiki/Vereenigde_Oostindische_Compagnie (Accessed 9 February 2011).

255 KITLV, '*VOC Kenniscentrum.nl*'. http://voc-kenniscentrum.nl/ (Accessed 9 February 2011).

256 Huygens ING '*De VOC: Dutch-Asiatic Shipping 1595–1795*'. http://www.inghist.nl/Onderzoek/Projecten/DAS (Accessed 29 January 2011).

257 *Stichting Kennisnet* [ThinkQuest], '*Het ontstaan van de VOC*'. http://mediatheek.thinkquest.nl/~jra511/ontstaan.html (Accessed 9 February 2011).

258 The Canon of the Netherlands, '*De VOC 1602–1799: Nederland breidt uit over zee*'. http://entoen.nu/voc/po (Accessed 9 February 2011).

259 Jaap van Overbeek, '*Slavernij en slavenhandel bij de VOC*'. http://www.vocsite.nl/geschiedenis/slavernij.html (Accessed 9 February 2011).

fields appeared to be a compressed text reflecting pupils' impressions of the sites' content. Some indications of pupils' engagement with the texts are evident from revealing details contained in phrases such as '*Much* information about …' for Wikipedia, as compared to simply 'Information about …' for KITLV's VOC Knowledge Centre. The latter drew much more attention for its details on what the ships 'looked like'. These phrases betrayed comparisons that pupils had clearly made mentally, but upon which, as noted above, they found it difficult or pointless to explicitly elaborate. By the way, it should be borne in mind that this was in keeping in line with their instructions. Nevertheless, 'Much information' presupposes 'less information', on the other websites, just like '[details about] what they looked like' on one website supposes the absence or lack of such details on other websites.

This source-evaluation brings to light an important aspect, *i.e.*, that early adolescents base their judgment of sources much more on the quantity of information they contain than on the quality of that information. In their research into how early adolescents develop historical understanding based on alternative texts [those not designed for educational purposes, including fictional accounts], either unaided or in conjuction with textbooks, curriculum and instruction scholars Bruce VanSledright and Christine Kelly (1998: 250-252) noted not only that younger learners found alternative texts more informative and enjoyable, but also that they

> frequently used quantity of information as the main criterion to distinguish the value of the different books and accounts they drew from. Students thought that the more information a text contained the better because that meant having to consult fewer books in the long run … (*Ibid.*: 257).

This might explain the frequent use of quantifying expressions such as 'much information' or 'everything about …', even though the ratings did not always follow the same logic. Despite this way of evaluating sources, which differs from the one advanced students and experts would be expected to use, the observation that emerged from the two case studies is that when young learners are dealing with a wide variety of sources they do engage in some forms of historical thinking at the same time. They do so, for example, by weighing, judging, and comparing sources with one another, using criteria that are specific to their developmental stage, identifying specific details in one source and detecting other complementary aspects in another source.

As noted in relation to the 'Wilders-vs-Islam' cartoon and the drawing of the VOC route map based on the National Library of Australia's map on Google Images (see Chapter 6, Section 6.3), very similar processes took place during other sorts of assignments. The key element in all these assignments was first *searching for* information, mostly via Google, *comparing* the results found by *weighing* them up against one another, and *summing up* [*i.e.*, choosing] the one deemed to be more detailed or more illustrative. Although the pupils did not provide in-text or footnote/endnote references, an analysis of their short, generally illustrated texts *vis-à-vis* the Web pages cited revealed that each page had contributed at least one detail. The absence of direct references made it impossible to compare the ratings and comments with the eventual predominance of information obtained from the highly rated and much-praised websites.

In the foregoing, my intention was to show how the use of multiple sources by pupils in the two case studies had certain implications for their thinking about those sources. It seems that even though the use of lengthy quotations caused pupils to desist from explicitly expressing their own ideas and thoughts about the topics of the assignment, the choices and sequence of the quotations reflected a certain degree of historical thinking. On the one hand, the resulting texts, though not entirely original, did show a degree of coherence and generally managed to make causal relationships obvious. On the other hand, this way of reasoning based on multiple texts is typical to early adolescents, who are described as being unwilling or unable to engage directly in controversies and as having a tendency to engage in self-decided inhibiting thinking. I have also shown that summarising involves a number of skills such as identifying sources deemed reliable, weighing them up against one another, and synthesising them into shorter texts. As the next shows, another pattern that was evident from the sources pupils used in the assignments, relates in particular to how they negotiated between conventional sources and their unconventional counterparts.

7.3 Convergence: The Conventional Joins the Unconventional

> One used to start [historical research] from traces (manuscripts, rare objects, *etc.*) in limited numbers, and had to exhaust all their diversity, to unify them into a coherent comprehensive narrative ... The amount of treatable information following those norms has become indefinite with the arrival of the computer. The research front has changed (De Certeau, 1974: 26-27).

The previous section demonstrated, among other things, how the multiplicity and variety of sources managed to foster historical thinking in some important ways. Another aspect that deserves particular attention is the nature and the status of sources. The use of resources from different sorts of websites and pupils' views about them have resulted in making notions such as authoritativeness, conventionality, and the quality of being mainstream even more dynamic and blurrier than ever before. In this section, I shall discuss the shift from the sole and exclusive use of conventional sources of historical information to their combination with unconventional ones as reflected in the assignments of the pupils in the two case studies. The main points will be [1] that the Web, by bringing resources onto the computer screen regardless of their provenance and their authors, has made that shift a reality; and [2] that pupils, by using conventional and unconventional sources side by side and in a complementary way, have confronted teachers, knowledge-brokers, and policy makers with a *fait accompli*.

In the following paragraphs, I shall first outline the interpretation of the terms 'conventional sources' and 'unconventional sources' that I use. In doing so, I shall point out some of the ways in which the Web has blurred the distinction between the two. I shall then discuss the role search engines play in convergence by, among other things, redefining authoritativeness and relevance criteria, and stripping resources of most indications of their provenance. Lastly, I shall focus on Wikipedia, which has not only emerged from the two case studies as the most used source of historical information, but has also been serving as a potential convergence platform for heritage institutions and other more conventional brokers of historical information.

As demonstrated in Chapters 5 and 6, the large number of Web-based sources used for assignments were varied and differed from one another. The BL case study showed that sources could be grouped into 11 categories, namely: [1] *Canons*, including both the Canon of the Netherlands and the regional canons; [2] *Wikipedia*; [3] *Educational sites*; [4] *Heritage sites*, including both those of heritage institutions and those run by other non-heritage organisations; [5] *Commercial sites*; [6] *Personal* or *family sites*; [7] *Blogs*; [8] *General information sites*; [9] *Religious sites*; [10] *Academic sites*; and [11] *Newspaper sites*. A farily similar categorisation emerged from the HPDS case study, where sources could be grouped into 10 categories. All the above-mentioned categories were used, with the exception of religious sites and blogs, while a new category was added to the list, namely, official sites.

The variety of these sources could be further categorised in different ways. They could be classified by taking the following perspectives, among others, into account: authoritative versus non-authoritative sources; conventional versus unconventional sources;

and official versus unofficial sources. In this section, I shall not delve into the authoritative versus non-authoritative debate, as this has been – and continues to be – extensively discussed.[260] Instead, I would like to explore the sources from the perspective of 'conventional versus unconventional'. Conventional sources are those that emanate from traditionally recognised content-providers and brokers such as educational publishers, official organs, cultural heritage institutions, *etc.* Unlike these, unconventional sources are provided by people or organisations with no officially or traditionally established authority to provide educational or pedagogic contents.

In this respect, I classify Wikipedia as unconventional because the principle behind it – everyone can be an author, every one can be an editor, whether credentialed or not – is contrary to the way in which conventional contents come into being. I classify the Canon of the Netherlands as a conventional source for history education because it was set up by the Ministry of Education, Culture and Science, more specifically by scholars and experts who were specially appointed for this educationally oriented project. In the world of film, entertainment and broadcasting, conventional can be taken to mean the same as mainstream, while unconventional is closer to the amateur or creative spirit. As I discuss later in this section, the notion of 'conventionality' is currently so dynamic that it has become difficult to trace any line that divides conventional from unconventional contents. However, for the sake of clarity, I shall adhere to the conventional versus unconventional distinction as described above, while bearing in mind that the distinction is being increasingly challenged by convergence.

A comprehensive study of sources used in the two case studies revealed that 60 percent of sources were conventional, while the remaining 40 percent were unconventional. This is a clear sign that, thanks to the Web, an unprecedented convergence is taking place between conventional and unconventional sources. There are two reasons why the Web and in particular search engines are deemed responsible for this change. In the first place, by making historical sources accessible beyond their physical environments, they [the Web and the search engines] have rendered all marks of authoritativeness, conventionality, and the concept of being mainstream invisible. In other words, they have flattened the hierarchies of information, which Rogers (2004: 22) considers to be a 'highly infopolitical move' due to all the manoeuvres behind that result in sources being ranked by those search engines. Actually going into a museum, an archive, or a library would *ipso facto* tell the pupil

260 See for instance, among others, Kress, 2004: 33 and 34; Bruns, 2009: 200; David, 2007: 179-180; Anderson, 2006: 66-67 and 69; Keen, 2007: 95-96.

that what he or she would finds in those institutions will be conventional, because its reliability will have been checked by some credentialed authorities.

On the Web, however, the pupil could access the same object without seeing the physical museum, archive, or library, which makes the object found there no different from one found via Wikipedia, a weblog or a commercial site. In most cases, when interviewed pupils said that they ignored the source of their texts or simply mentioned that they had found them via Google, which poses a problem concerning their still-to-be- acquired new-media literacy skill of judgment or source-evaluation (see Jenkins *et al.*: 2009: 79). This answer suggests that after two steps – typing in the search terms and scanning the results – most pupils knew which resource they would use.[261] This also appears to have been the case with Google Images' results. What this says is that the provenance of the media object was of very little importance for pupils. Researching how historians [experts] and adolescents [novices] solve historical problems based on documentary and pictorial evidence, historical cognition scholar Samuel Wineburg (1991: 83-84) noted that 'students seemed to view texts as vehicles for conveying information in which the attribution was just the last thing to be read', while historians 'used the attribution to erect elaborate scenarios about authors and the circumstances of document generation', the bits of information 'from which all else emanated'. One conclusion could be that the increased presence of conventional contents on unconventional platforms would be beneficial to young learners, especially those who have yet to acquire source-evaluation or judgment skills (Jenkins *et al.*: 2009: 79 and 83).

In the second place, search engines apply new rules for defining which sources are deemed authoritative and worth visiting. Media studies and Law scholar Siva Vaidhyanathan (2011: 7) noted that Google imposes its own biases in determining what is true, important, and reliable: pieces of information matter depending on how Google's algorithms have ranked them. As discussed in Chapter 3 (Section 3.3), Google's ranking algorithms rely heavily on hyperlinks to other websites. Given that mainstream, conventional sources of information have – for commercial reasons or others relating to corporate interests (see Chapter 3, Section 3.3) – been reluctant [or not authorised] to include hyperlinks not only to one another's websites but also to unconventional sites in whose content they would tra-

261 The 'Digital Natives' have been described as choosing intuitively the materials they want to use (Palfrey & Gasser, 2008: 128). Bearing in mind that in many cases unofficial accounts outplay their official counterparts (Rogers, 2004: 45), in all probability this intuitive choice will take them to unofficial sources.

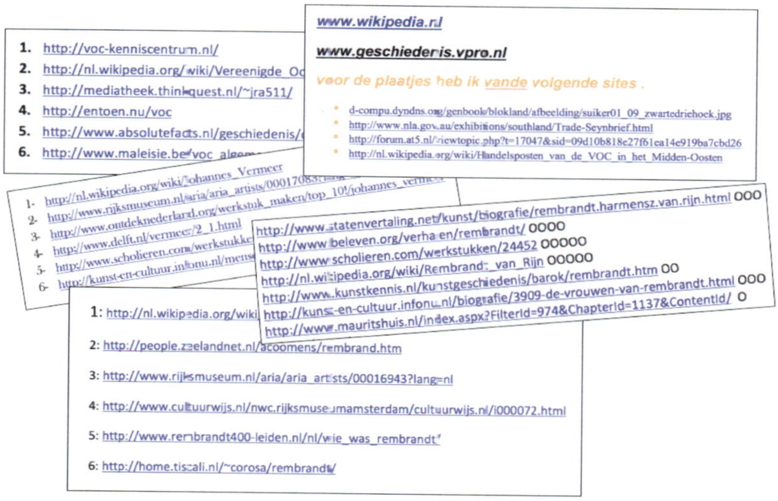

Figure 7.2: Sources used for some of the WebQuest assignments at the HPDS.

ditionally have little confidence (Tsui, 2008: 70), their ranking has always been low. As a consequence, Google and other search engines do not present them as the most relevant, authoritative sources, because unconventional websites, less exigent in their multidirectional hyperlinking practices,[262] meet the new criteria for relevance and authority. Thus, on the Web 'hyperlinks somehow transmit power or credibility', as 'the search engine [Google] sends more traffic to the heavily linked sites, reinforcing that position of authority and leading even to more links' (Halavais, 2008: 49).

The immediate consequence of this situation is the increased presence of unconventional sources among the best-ranked sources and their convergence with conventional sources, both of which pupils used in a complementary way (see Figure 7.2). For instance, Pupil 6 in the HPDS case study (Table 6.1) used two unconventional sources and four conventional ones for her assignment on the VOC. The unconventional ones included Wikipedia, which provided the pupil with 'Everything about the VOC' and earned a 9/10 rating; and the Belgian travel [commercial] site *Maleisie.be*,[263] which elicited the simple comment 'VOC' and received 7.5/10; while the conventional sources included the Canon, which also discussed 'Everything about the VOC' and earned a score of 8/10; KITLV's VOC Knowledge

262 Practices are emerging such as 'Google bombing' – associating a keyword search with a particular Website – and 'Link-whoring' and 'Link-doping', which aim to increase the ranking of a particular weblog on the Web, making it easier to manipulate search engines' algorithms (Halavais, 2008: 49-50).

263 *Maleisie.be*, *'VOC Algemeen'*. http://www.maleisie.be/voc_algemeen.html (Accessed 15 February 2011).

Centre, which the pupil rated with only 7.5/10 even though she felt that it provided 'Much information about the VOC'; the historical news part of *Absolutefacts.nl*,[264] which received 7.5/10 for providing 'Relatively much [information] about the VOC'; and *Kennisnet*'s ThinkQuest,[265] which scored only 7/10 for its information 'About the VOC'. From the comments and ratings, one might deduce that the understandings that Pupil 6 eventually gleaned about the VOC was based primarily on information found on Wikipedia and the Canon – where 'everything' could be found –, complemented with details from *Maleisie.be*, the VOC Knowledge Centre, *Absolutefacts.nl*, and *Kennisnet*'s ThinkQuest. The same can be said of the BL case study (Table 5.1 in Chapter 5, Section 5.3), where Pair 2, for example, used two conventional sources and one unconventional source, for their assignment on 'Travel in the Golden Century: Michiel de Ruyter'. The conventional ones were *Schooltv.nl* [educational] and the Canon, while the unconventional source was Wikipedia.[266]

I should mention that the more or less 60-40 ratio of conventional and unconventional sources was not limited to categories of websites used, but also applied to the frequency with which individual sites were used. In terms of frequency, each website is counted not as a single source, but as a provenance of individual materials (texts, images, *etc.*). An analogy could be drawn with individual books as independent sources and a library as the provenance or mother source. In the BL case study, for instance, Pair 3 cited one website – the Memory of the Netherlands – as source, but used 32 pictures from 32 different pages of that same site (see Table 5.1 in Chapter 5, Section 5.4). Viewed from this perspective, unconventional sources represented about 41 percent [47 out of 116 indi-

264 *Absoltutefacts.nl, 'Verenigde Oost-Indische Compagnie'.* http://www.absolutefacts.nl/geschiedenis/data/voc.htm (Accessed 8 March 2011). This site is classified as conventional or mainstream because its contents are authored and edited by a team of knowledgeable editors specialising in the history of the Royal House and Castles, in automobile and political history, and in the history of the Church, faith and philosophy (see: http://www.absolutefacts.nl/redactie.htm [Accessed 8 March 2011]).

265 *Stichting Kennisnet* [ThinkQuest], '*De Verenigde Oostindische Compagnie*'. http://mediatheek.thinkquest.nl/~jra511/ (Accessed 8 March 2011). This is a conventional source *par excellence* because *Kennisnet* is a government-funded expertise centre for ICT in education.

266 It is worth returning to the discussion about the Canon and its one-sidedness that has been denounced by some history education scholars and experts. This convergence of conventional and unconventional sources suggest that the Canon is one source among many that has to compete with Wikipedia and other sources. Maria Grever (2007: 42-43), who opposes 'a singular canonized perspective', argued that working with competitive or incompatible perspectives 'enhance[s] historical understanding'. It could then be maintained that convergence, which turns competitive sources into complementary sources, greatly contributes to historical understanding.

vidual Web pages cited] in the BL case study (Table 5.2) and about 44 percent [18 out of 41 individual Web pages cited] in the HPDS case study (Table 6.3).

One point requiring particular attention is the predominance of Wikipedia in both case studies. At the BL, for instance, Wikipedia was cited 35 times by all 13 pairs, while the most cited conventional source – the Canon – appeared 28 times (Table 5.2). At the HPDS, the situation was almost the same: Wikipedia – the first unconventional source used – was cited nine times, while heritage institutions' websites – the first conventional sources – were cited five times, as were personal sites. In the same case study, commercial sites [unconventional] and educational sites [conventional] were both cited four times. As shown by HPDS pupils' comments on sources, Wikipedia seems to have relegated conventional sources to second-choice category. The pupils felt that it offered *much information about* .. or *everything about* ..., while most conventional sources offered only *information about* ... or *a bit of this or that aspect* ... In their eyes Wikipedia contained *everything* and if something was not there, that was probably because it did not exist or it was not worth noting. Also the '*Everything about* ...' comment on the Canon seemed to have a different meaning from the '*Everything about* ...' used for Wikipedia, as one pupil's comment shows: '... The second [best site after Wikipedia] was *entoen.nu* [The Canon of the Netherlands], *which is also a sort of Wikipedia*, though it is much less known. You can also find *everything* here' [Italicisation is mine]. This means that Wikipedia is becoming a reference against which conventional sources are judged and evaluated.

Parallel with this increasing popularity of Wikipedia among the wider public[267] in general and among pupils in particular, is the increasing interest cultural heritage institutions are showing in the platform, as it allows them to present [parts of] their collections to a much wider audience. In September 2010, the National Archives offered 1,000 pictures to Wikipedia Commons, the photo database of Wikipedia.[268] This means that the National Archives was granting tens – if not hundreds – of thousands of Wikipedia authors and editors – I should add *Googlers* for whom Wikipedia almost always tops

267 Wikipedia is more widely visited, read and cited by many more people than mainstream, conventional institutions' websites such as *The New York Times*, the Library of Congress and its direct rival *Encyclopaedia Britannica* (Rosenzweig, 2006: 118-119).

268 *Nationaal Archief*, '*Nationaal Archief-foto's op Wikipedia: ex-premier Gulielmus Kok zeer populair*' (The Hague, 28 January 2011). http://www.nationaalarchief.nl/nieuws/nieuws/nationaal-archief-foto-s-op-wikipedia.asp?ComponentID=17607&SourcePageID=16483#1 (Accessed 1 February 2011).

the results list (Rosenzweig, 2006: 137; Bakker & Bakker, 2011: 32) – the authorisation to use them to illustrate their articles, which, as shown by the case studies, is the first place pupils go to when working on assignments. The National Archives reported that

> In a two-month period over half of the [1,000] National Archives photos were linked to Wikipedia articles by the Wikipedia community. The entries illustrated with National Archives pictures were viewed more than 400,000 times in this period, with the most page views coming from the Dutch version of Wikipedia.[269]

This is another clear instance of convergence of conventional and unconventional sources of historical information being facilitated by the Web. Unlike the first form of convergence, which resulted from the fact that search engines display a mixture of categories of sources in the order of their popularity and without any reference to their [un]conventionality, this one is the result of a conscious effort on the part of the keepers of conventional sources. In other words, heritage institutions and similar have taken conventional media texts out of their tightly controlled sanctuaries and placed them in an unconventionally controlled environment. The narratives written about these texts and the contexts in which they are placed are beyond the institutions' traditional, gatekeeping authority and subjected to the gatewatching dynamics of most Web 2.0 platforms.[270]

For example, the Wikipedia entry on former Dutch Prime Minister Wim Kok (see Figure 7.3)[271] is illustrated with a picture from the National Archives. The initial article, which saw the light of the day on 15 October 2001, was written by 'Tsja' and by 1 June 2011 it had been edited on more than 250 occasions. Many of the dozens of users who added, removed, or modified parts of the initial article are identifiable only via the IP [Internet Protocol] addresses of their computers. Despite this *unconventional* form of authorship [with a username rather than a proper name] and means of gener-

---

269 *Ibid.*

270 The concept of gatewatching is described as the new quality-control and value-conferring mechanism on user-content-generated websites. Involving no authority or hierarchy in the traditional sense, 'Gatewatching, instead, relies exactly on that ability of users to decide for themselves what they find interesting and worth noting and sharing with their peers' (Bruns, 2009: 73-74). It consists of continuously and collectively observing 'the output gates of conventional [news] organizations, as well as of the primary sources of [news] information' (*Ibid.*). In this process, the authority previously vested in a few experts [curators, editors, journalists, *etc.*] is now in the hands of 'large numbers of amateur contributors … [who] create a dynamics in which "good" information drives out "bad"' (David, 2007: 179-180).

271 Wikipedia, 'Wim Kok' http://en.wikipedia.org/wiki/Wim_Kok (Accessed on 28 May 2011).

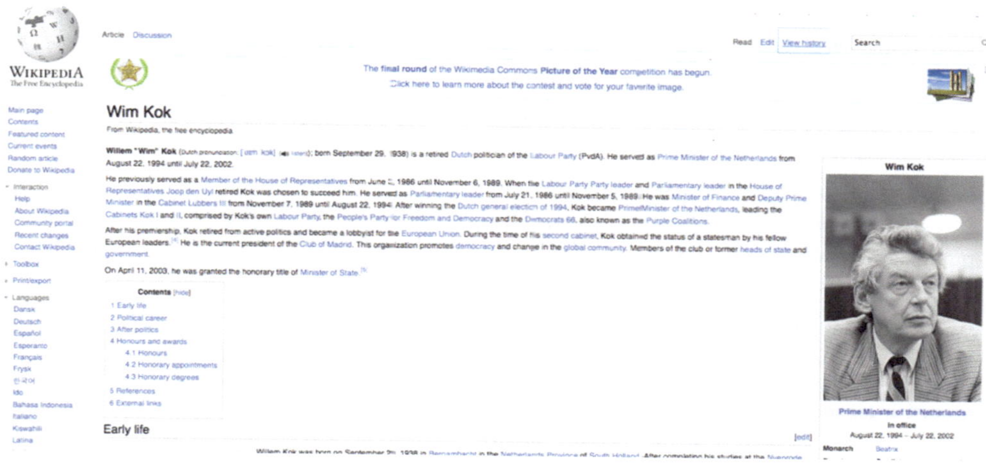

Figure 7.3: Wikipedia entry on former Prime Minister Wim Kok, illustrated with a picture from the National Archives.

ating information [multiple anonymous edits], the picture itself is presented as authentic, with a *conventional* description mentioning the circumstances under which it was taken, the date on which it was taken, the name of the photographer, for which media organisation he worked and the institution responsible for preserving the original together with the photograph ID number.[272]

The Netherlands Institute for Sound and Vision, for its side, simply started sharing its image database with Wikipedia since February 2008. At the moment of writing [14 June 2011], any Wikipedian could access and use 10,430 photographs together with the corresponding [conventional] metadata.[273] This form of convergence differs from the use of social media that was discussed in Chapter 3 (Section 3.4), where the claim was made that the growing presence of cultural heritage institutions on social media networks is helping to increase awareness about heritage objects while providing users with an opportunity to tell their own stories about the objects. This awareness-raising effort is an alternative to encountering the same objects after they have been contextualised [by Wikipedians, for instance] and are ripe for remixing and new appropriations.

---

272 Wikipedia, 'File: *Wim Kok van de PvdA in de Tweede Kamer* - NL-HaNA Anefo 934-4587 WM645.jpg'. http://en.wikipedia.org/wiki/File:Wim_Kok_van_de_PvdA_in_de_Tweede_Kamer_-_NL-HaNA_Anefo_934-4587_WM645.jpg (Accessed 28 May 2011).

273 Author phone interview (14 June 2011) with René Koenders, editor-in-chief of *Beeld en Geluid Wiki* [http://www.beeldengeluidwiki.nl/index.php/Hoofdpagina (Accessed 14 June 2011)], the Wiki website of the Netherlands Institute for Sound and Vision.

Historian Roy Rosenzweig (2006) reflected about the challenges Wikipedia poses for professional historians and tried to answer the question of whether history could be open source. One of the points he made is that Wikipedia, despite some factual errors and style issues due to the multiplicity of authors, is a valuable source of historical information. Rosenzweig (2006: 126-127) noted that in the domain of biographies of historical figures, Wikipedia competed with the classical and commercial rivals and scored better than many of them in terms of coverage. However, the most relevant discussion for the purpose of the conventional-unconventional convergence became evident when Rosenzweig (2006: 136) wondered: 'Why should we care?' His answer was: 'One reason professional historians need to pay attention to Wikipedia is because our students do', which, as the findings of my two case studies show, was certainly the case among these 13- to 14-year old history learners. The same answer also applies to heritage professionals, most of whom, as demonstrated in Chapter 3, count pupils among their key targets. For this reason – and this applies equally to historians and to heritage professionals – Rosenzweig (2006: 140) explicitly advocated the convergence of the conventional with the unconventional:

> Should those who write history for a living join such popular history makers in writing history in *Wikipedia*? My own tentative answer is yes. If *Wikipedia* is becoming the family encyclopedia for the twenty-first century, historians probably have a *professional obligation to make it as good as possible* [Italicisation is mine].

Similar convergences are taking place in many other cultural sectors. For instance, the TV and music industries are experiencing this phenomenon via YouTube, where major mainstream channels appear side by side with amateur contents (Burgess & Green, 2009: 41-42 & 91); the British Broadcasting Corporation [BBC] and Cable News Network [CNN], among others, encourage and have recourse to amateur contents (Gillmor, 2004:104; Atton & Hamilton, 2008: 64-70); and leading newspapers have put in place new redaction processes to integrate user-uploaded leaks into conventional news flows (see Leigh & Harding, 2011; Domscheit-Berg, 2011). Similarly, the film and game industries have already entered an era where do-it-yourself tools enable fan film-makers and game-makers to generate their own media contents by making creative use of original mainstream contents (Jenkins, [2006] 2008: 136-137 & 153-155; see also Deuze, 2007: 75). It would therefore be nothing short of normal if heritage institutions and other keepers of conventional sources of historical information were also to move in that direction in order to reach a wider audience, in particular the Internet Generation.

In the case of history education, which my two case studies explored, the reasoning would be as follows: since sources have converged at the grassroots level, that is, in the history class, where pupils use both conventional and unconventional sources, then it would be reasonable and even advisable to engage fully in the same convergence on a corporate or institutional level, that is, on the content-providers' side (Jenkins, [2006] 2008: 18). It has even been suggested that the future of conventional contents lies in their success at finding their place in that 'digital convergence' (Rheingold, 1993: 75), which has become especially inescapable due to the fact that, in practice, search engines remain the almost exclusive door to historical sources. These engines favour popularity, which is another term for the authority conferred on them by the larger user community,[274] rather than conventionality, which for a long time has been associated with a small group of credentialed experts (Bruns, 2009: 139 & 212).

In his book on *Collective Intelligence*, new media theorist Pierre Lévy (1997: 8) conceptualised cyberspace as mainly symbolised by the Internet. This means that by putting their collections on that medium, cultural heritage institutions have joined cyberspace and cannot escape the rules that govern other objects in that space. Those rules involve a certain *nomadism* and demand rapid change in, among others, scientific, technical, economic, professional, and mental areas (*Ibid.*: 10-11). If they attempted to escape, Lévy (1997: 10-11) maintained, then 'the world would change around us [meaning: they will be disconnected from that world]'. In contrast, by adapting to those changes, they would end the cult of 'fetishised or hypostasised communities' (*Ibid.*: 29) and join the dynamics of cyberspace's collective intelligence, based on the principle that 'intelligence is distributed everywhere, incessantly valued, [and] coordinated in real time, [and which] results in the effective mobilisation of competences' (*Ibid.*). They would move from 'the Cartesian *cogito* to *cogitamus*' (*Ibid.*: 33).

274 This value-assessment mechanism is commonly known as 'collective intelligence', a concept coined by media theorist Pierre Lévy (1997: 29) to mean that everyone knows something, while no one knows everything. This suggests that the more people evaluate a media text, the bigger the chance of having a better result (see for more discussions: Lévy, 2010: 110-111; Jenkins, [2006] 2008: 4; Anderson, 2006: 106-107; Cornu, 2004: 42-43; Keen, 2007: 6; among others). Other related terms were also used to describe this mechanism, including 'distributed intelligence' (Negroponte, 1995: 19-20; Anderson, 2006: 108, among others) 'wisdom of crowds' (Anderson, 2006: 68; Keen, 2007: 95-96).

Private and other unconventional initiatives adapt more rapidly and do indeed have bigger opportunities to garner knowledge and competences from cyberspace's *intelligent collectives*. Projects like Wikipedia are a good illustration of the *cogitamus* approach, as one historical article [or on any other subject] could have hundreds, even thousands of authors thinking together on the same subject (Rosenzweig, 2006: 126 & 135; David, 2007: 179-180). These projects also score better among pupils because they have more time to dedicate to improving the *findability* of their contents and are confronted with fewer legal [copyright, taxpayer's money, *etc.*] constraints. It could then be concluded that if heritage institutions and other keepers of conventional sources were to join *cogitamus* platforms, pupils would have a better chance of finding, for instance, the Rembrandt House Museum – one of the rare references for Rembrandt's etchings, drawings and copper plates[275] – which was mentioned by *none* of the assignments on Rembrandt in the two case studies. Unlike the latter, a number of personal sites, which – though not necessarily collaborative projects – face fewer bureaucratic constraints, [www.vocsite.nl, www.statenvertaling.net, among others], were used by pupils in both case studies, which suggests that these sites were more findable than the Rembrandt House Museum's website.

In short, this section has distinguished between conventional and unconventional sources among the Web-based sources used by pupils in the two case studies. Conventional sources were presented as those originating from traditionally established bodies, while their unconventional counterparts emanate from those vested with no traditional and official authority to produce educational, pedagogic contents. I have stressed how the Web and search engines have greatly contributed to the blurring of this distinction, as they present sources without the traditional marks of conventionality and authoritativeness. Moreover, new criteria for relevance and authoritativeness have emerged that seem to favour unconventional sources. In addition, the common attitude of adolescents in not checking the provenance and authorship of information is actually hastening that convergence. It seems that a similar convergence trend is also emerging among heritage institutions, whose websites are surpassed [though not all conventional websites put together] by unconventional websites in terms of frequency of use. Some major institutions have made their objects available to Wikipedia – the most cited source in the two case studies – thereby heralding an-

275 The Rembrandt House Museum, 'History of the collection'. http://www.rembrandthuis.nl/cms_pages/index_sub.php?url=/2004/geschiedeniscollectie_en.html&path=3,0&nav_lang=en (Accessed 14 February 2011).

other convergence on an institutional level. An analysis of some of the major findings of my case studies revealed a number of patterns, some of which I shall now discuss in relation to certain current scholarly discussions.

7.4 Findings in Broader Discussions

> Any research to be recognized and taken seriously within a discipline must also be relevant to some of the current intellectual concerns of the discipline. Social research thus links ordinary phenomena that may appear puzzling in daily life with the theoretical concerns of the disciplines that take social life as their subject matter (Davies, [1998] 2008: 30-31).

The previous three sections have provided an interpretation, in the form of patterns, of the major findings of my ethnographic research in the two case studies. However, as suggested by social research methodologist Aull Charlotte Davies (this section's epigraph), research findings make more sense when considered within the context of current intellectual debates. In this section, therefore, I plan to demonstrate the relevance of my findings by linking them to current concerns and discussions about history education and the use of the Web and digital resources by pupils. The first issue I shall discuss in the light of the two case studies is the digital divide that has appeared in both the technological infrastructure and the approach to the Web in the two case studies. It is important to evaluate the digital divide more than two decades after the 'Big Project' (see Chapter 2, Section 2.2) which aimed to get all schools connected to the Web. The findings of the two case studies shed some light on certain aspects of the impact the Big Project had on history education. The second point emanates from the previous one, as it examines the concepts of 'New Learning' and 'New Heritage', which are mainly the result of the integration of digital media into education and the digitisation of heritage objects, respectively. The practices described in the previous two chapters and in the first three sections of this one are a part of New Learning, while the heritage websites and their contents constitute the New Heritage. The following first discusses the sense in which the concept of the digital divide is used before going on to explore some of the ways it seems to have impacted on the two classes I observed. I shall then briefly explain the concepts of New Learning and New Heritage, pointing out how they intersected in the two classes.

The concept of a digital divide has often been used to refer to the gap that exists between people with a different economic and social status and, as a result, unequal access to digital technologies.

On one side of the divide are those who are 'technology-rich' and on the other side those who are 'technology-poor' (Downes, 2004: 115-116). This divide can be observed among individuals, groups, regions, countries, *etc.* It is applicable to my two case studies in that the HPDS offered a Web-driven class, with permanent unlimited access to the Web both at school and at home. This class was definitely a 'technology-rich' one, as opposed to the partially 'technology-poor' class at the BL. This 'technology poverty' was incomplete as the teacher did have permanent access to the Web, though the pupils almost never did during school time. Moreover, as shown in Chapter 5, this school's Internet connectivity was also poor, as it was incapable of permitting simultaneous wireless connection for the entire class.

Digital divide has also been used to describe the disparity in the uses of new technologies at home and at school. It has been claimed that pupils' homes often provide not only an environment saturated with new technologies but also more freedom to enter into unhindered interaction with them (Hutchby & Moran-Ellis, 2001: 1; Roberts *et al.*, 2009: 314), while schools tend to be very restrictive (Buckingham, 2007: 76 & 93; Somekh, 2004: 71). This is what educational and technology scholar David Buckingham (2007: 76) termed the 'new digital divide', whereby technology-rich pupils at home become technology-poor at school:

> ... this new 'digital divide' between in-school and out-of-school use could also be seen as symptomatic of a much broader phenomenon – a widening gap between children's everyday 'life worlds' outside school and the emphases of many education systems (*Ibid.*: 96).

The digital divide was not an issue at the HPDS, where, as shown in Chapter 6 (Section 6.1), freedom to choose technologies and media was part of the Dalton approach. In contrast, the BL pupils showed signs and clues leading to the conclusion that the classroom provided a technology-poor environment. The repeated shifts to the iPhone either to SMS or to surf the Web suggest that the pupils' desire to interact with technologies could only be quenched clandestinely. The question at this point might be to find out how this digital divide interfered with, for example, historical thinking. The three previous sections showed how the attractiveness of the Web is related to the variety of sources and how both [Web and sources] are connected with historical thinking in various ways. The triangular learning process described in Section 7.1 (see Figure 7.1) suggests that new technologies in the hands of young learners at school are far more than simply a form of distraction. Where free use of the

Web is permitted, as it was at the HPDS, its use does not provoke distraction but rather enhances the liveliness of a class.[276] Where it is forbidden, as it was in the BL class, it does indeed constitute a distraction.

On one occasion, under the cover of his textbook, a pupil at the BL surfed the Web on his iPhone in order to check the latest news on *De Volkskrant* daily newspaper about the March 2010 municipal elections. The teacher had announced that the lesson that day would be about *actualiteit* [current affairs], which at that moment were dominated by the municipal elections taking place that very day. The teacher used this political *actualiteit* to introduce 'Louis XIV, an absolute monarch' (see Chapter 5, Section 5.2). The pupil's clandestine but legitimate curiosity could have led to the triangular learning process shown in Figure 7.1, with all the multitasking features and learning benefits that go with it. Under these clandestine circumstances, however, one cannot contend that the child was multitasking in terms of continuity imbedded in discontinuity (see Section 7.1), because the fear of being discovered and blamed is incompatible with the rapid and coordinated thinking that is required at each step and shift. Instead of putting listening and reading on

---

276 A recent *New York Times* article entitled 'Speaking Up in Class, Silently, via Social Media' reported about an increase in local initiatives both in secondary school and in higher education in the United States to implement so-called 'backchannels' or 'hot seats'. These consist of integrating the use of social media networks in the classroom to encourage more participation in discussions. Teachers say that this provides pupils and students who refrain from expressing their views in conventional ways – by raising their hand and speaking for instance – with an alternative way to be part of class discussions. However, this phenomenon is still very limited and has many opponents among teachers (Gabriel, 2011).
http://www.nytimes.com/2011/05/13/education/13social.html [Accessed 14 May 2011]).
Greater participation of shy students was also cited in a 9 June 2011 report by CNN which featured a history class at Hollenbeck Middle School in East Los Angeles, where Twitter has been integrated and fully embraced by the students (Simon, 2011.
http://edition.cnn.com/2011/TECH/social.media/06/08/twitter.school/index.html?hpt=hp_bn7 [Accessed 16 June 2011]).

standby, the pupil simply disconnected from them to connect to the Web.[277]

In this way, then, suppressing the use of digital media prevents the dynamics that could create a fertile ground for historical thinking. By the same token, the transition from teacher-led instruction time to 'independent work time' at the HPDS, and the transition from Web-video and related activities to the textbook at the BL, showed that digital technologies can make a big difference in keeping pupils engaged. At the HPDS, the transition was smooth and the shift was clearly marked by earplugs that, according to the pupils, prevented external noises from disrupting their concentration. The rest happened almost internally, as with 'swimming ducks' (see Van Velzen, 2002: 6). At the BL, the end of Web-video and related activities meant disintegration into noisy chaos and the clandestine use of digital devices.

Considered side by side from this 'digital divide' perspective, the technology-rich HPDS and the partially technology-poor BL reveal two different faces in need of deeper reflection. At the HPDS, technology was in the hands of the learners, which gave them an important role in determining what to do with the teacher's instruction and the textbook's contents. The same technologies remained in their hands both during formal learning time [in school] and informal learning time [at home]. At the BL however, technology was in the hands of the teacher rather than the learners, who could only enjoy it when the teacher decided they could. Thus, during formal learning time pupils had no access or control over the most attractive tool that could offer access to sources of historical information. It was assumed that these sources would be accessed during the informal learning time, at home. This digital divide might then help explain [though more research is needed about this aspect] why lengthy quotations predominated in one case study [BL], while in the other [HPDS] the pupils were capable of generating summaries which demanded more analysis, corroboration checks, and oth-

277 The May 2011 report by the National Academy for Media and Society concluded that two-thirds of pupils used mobile phones during class time for non-class-related activities, including digital bullying and blackmailing, playing music and games, sending SMSes or other messages via social networking sites, among others (NAMM, 2011), which is similar to what happened in the BL case study whenever the teacher moved away from the projector and the Web. However, as the example of the pupil secretly surfing to *de Volkskrant* website shows, the mobile phone can be used in ways that contribute to learning. NAMM's spokeswoman, Lisbeth Hop, said in a televised interview with the NOS (2011) that schools' mobile phone policies should include not only ways to prevent negative uses, but also positive ways to turn mobile phones into educational tools (see: NOS, '*Maak gebruik van smartphones in de les*' [30 May 2011] http://nos.nl/video/244513-maak-gebruik-van-smartphones-in-de-les.html [Accessed 30 May 2011]).

er intellectual efforts. One reason could be that in the former case [BL] time and full, unhindered access to the sources [the Web] were problematic, while in the latter the opposite was the case.

Solutions are needed at the level of 'policy and practice' (Buckingham, 2007: 76). At policy level, schools need to think out pedagogical approaches that provide learners with more responsibilities. This shift in responsibilities should include putting technologies – thus historical sources to which pupils are given access – into their hands through 'personal computer *ownership* by all students' (Somekh, 2004: 71. Italicisation is mine). Ownership of computers, together with little or no restriction in terms of access [firewall] and use [administrator rights], is very important because, as demonstrated in Chapter 6, it generates more confidence and intimacy between pupils and their computers, to which they can entrust their thoughts whether they are in the classroom or their bedroom. It also implies an increased sense of freedom that makes it possible for young learners not only to express but also to quench their curiosity, using the tools that are most attractive to people of their age. Educational psychologists even suggest that restricting access to information and ideas [using a firewall for instance] or otherwise applying censorship is harmful to the development of rationality and intellectual freedom among adolescents (Moshman, 1999: 114). It could then be said, along with Jenkins *et al.* (2009: 17), that

> What a person could accomplish with an outdated machine in a public library with mandatory filtering software [firewall] and no opportunity for storage or transmission [administrator rights] pales in comparison to what the same person could accomplish with a home computer with unfettered Internet access, high bandwidth, and continuous connectivity.

Consequently, the digital divide described above urgently needs to be addressed (Buckingham, 2007: 76; Jenkins *et al.*, 2009: 18) if history education is to take full advantage of the Web and other digital media in order to keep up with the rest of society, where new ways of interacting with online media and sources of information are already common currency.[278]

278 These new ways, which are all mainly Web-driven, include permanent *networking* [thus permanent connectivity] (Castells, [1994] 1999: 48; see also Deuze, 2007: 17-18); *flexibility* [ability to work in different locations (school, home, *etc.*)]' (Castells, [1994] 1999: 47) and *flexitime* [ability to work at different times] (Deuze, 2007: 4-5); *adaptability* [ability to adapt to changing environments and conditions] (Castells, [1994] 1999: 47); *self-reliance* [ability to rely on oneself] (Deuze, 2007: 8); and *Multitasking* (see Section 7.1); among others.

Despite the existence of that digital divide, the findings in the two case studies show that learning styles and approaches can largely be subsumed, though to varying degrees, under what educational scholars have called 'New Learning'. Though the concept of 'New Learning' or 'New School' has a long history (see Chapter 6, at the end of Section 6.1) in recent years it has mainly been used to refer to a system or environment in which learners have more autonomy and control a large part of their learning (Simons *et al.*, 2000: 7). Writing about this concept, digital didactics scholar Robert-Jan Simons and colleagues (2000: 13-14) identified the goals of the approach as being: [1] *learning to think*, including skills such as analogical reasoning, critical thinking, and logical thinking; [2] *learning to learn*, including cognitive [comparing, criticising and structuring, overview skills] and metacognitive [*e.g.*, making a time-plan and strategies for learning, for instance]; [3] *learning to collaborate and learning from collaboration*, which involves acquiring 'skills like dividing tasks between group members'; [4] *learning to regulate*, which implies, among other things, 'a gradual increase of independence in learning and thinking'; [5] *gradual increase of independence*; and [6] *process-oriented instruction*.

Writing in the same volume – *New Learning* – educational psychology and technology scholar Gellof Kanselaar and his colleagues (2000: 62) suggested that in this approach emphasis is on 'learning as the *personal construction* of knowledge' and on 'Technology [which] can play an important role ... by providing environments that encourage learners to engage in self-directed constructive learning processes'. It could then be concluded that New Learning is largely dependent on new digital technologies, especially the Web, which, as the two case studies have shown, gives pupils unequalled control over sources and confers upon them the autonomy to weigh them up against one another without relying on the teacher or other intermediaries. The result of this is that they learn to think – albeit not in the same way as experts – about those sources and their relevance. The BL case study has shown how most pupils claimed this autonomy and control by, for example, neglecting the teacher's instruction to include books among their sources. Instead, and contrary to the instructions, they used other categories of sources [blogs, personal sites, newspapers, *etc.*], thereby highlighting the learner-empowering potential of the Web in New Learning.

As indicated in Chapters 2 and 3, at the time when the infrastructure was being put in place that intended to bring about New Learning was being put in place, heritage collections were being put into new, digital formats to transform them into the *New Heritage*. The main aspects of this concept were extensively explored in a volume published in 2008, entitled *New Heritage: New Media and Cultural Heritage* (edited by Yehuda Kalay *et al.*). This title and the volume itself, show that when *new media* and *cultural heritage* intersect they result in *new heritage*. Contributing to the volume, museum studies scholar Fiona Cameron (2008: 172) explored one related concept, namely 'Digital Heritage', which 'can be defined as a selected pool of materials in a digital format deemed worthy of preservation for posterity'. Another contributor, new technologies and museum scholar Maria Roussou (2008: 225), discussed the notion of 'virtual heritage' which she introduced as 'the intersection of Virtual Reality (VR) and cultural heritage ... [that] facilitate[s] the synthesis, conservation, reproduction, representation, digital reprocessing, and display of cultural evidence'.

The findings of the current two case studies show some interesting ways in which New Learning and New Heritage intersected and, together, resulted in some forms of creative historical thinking. It was noted in Chapter 5 that the Web-based videos appeared to be regarded as most attractive during class time at the BL. One possible explanation for their attractiveness could be the virtualisation of the cultural heritage, including through simulations. The Canon's clip on the Beemster,[279] for instance, belongs to 'virtual heritage' because, in addition to the compilation of digitised cultural heritage images [old maps, pictures, scanned books, *etc.*], sophisticated computer animations were used to simulate the water being pumped out (Figure 7.4). In other words, pedagogical value was added through all sorts of editing and voiceovers, but most importantly through animation which, better than any other means, provided pupils with a fairly concrete idea of how the windmills worked.[280] It most likely inspired the pupil's answer that one scientific aspect of draining the Beemster resided in the technique and power [as shown via animation] of windmills. In terms of historical thinking, it could be claimed that thanks to simulation the pupil was able to imagine the state of scientific advancement in that historical period. Roussou (2008: 226) did therefore have a point when she argued that virtual heritage can on the one hand 'fulfill the requirements of a society of mass image consumption' and, on the other hand 'serve as indisputable means to disseminate knowledge and raise public awareness'.

---

279 The Canon of the Netherlands, '*Canonclip: De Beemster (voortgezet onderwijs)*'. http://entoen.nu/beemster/beeld-en-geluid/canonclip-de-beemster-%28voortgezet-onderwijs%29#beeld (Accessed 18 February 2011).

280 French cultural theorist and philosopher Jean Baudrillard (1983: 2) explored the concept of simulation, which he presented as 'hyperreality', *i.e.*, 'the generation by models of a real without origin or reality'. That hyperreality is not opposed to truth (*Ibid.*: 5), even though it starts from a utopia (*Ibid.*: 11). It 'produces "true" symptoms' (*Ibid.*: 5).

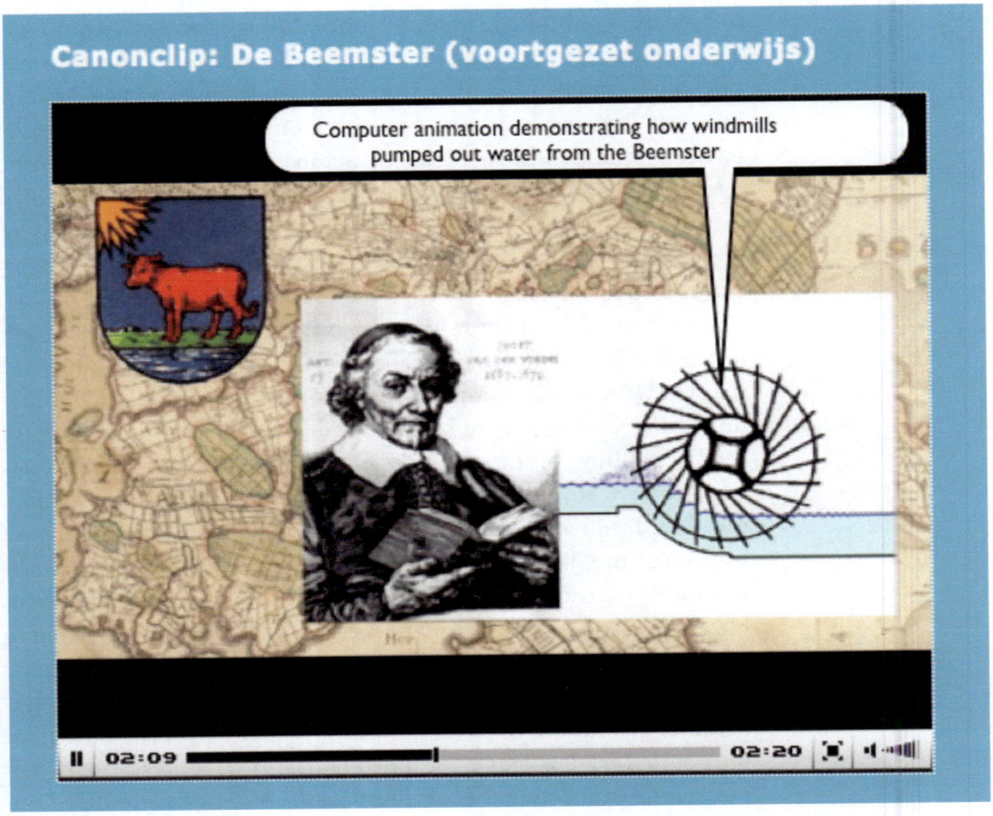

Figure 7.4: Canon clip displaying digitised cultural objects [map and portrait] together with a computer simulation (Screenshot: 3 August 2011).

In many other cases, New Heritage does not need simulations or other types of manipulation to trigger historical understanding in the New Learning environment. For example, the reasoning of the HPDS pupil described in Chapter 6, Section 6.3, who wrote a fictive story of Koen, a boy living in Spain in the Middle Ages, showed that New Learning in the sense of autonomous search for sources of inspiration or information and New Heritage can result in quite unexpected outcomes. She described how Koen escaped a life of poverty in Spain by moving to the Republic [the Netherlands], how he subsequently became rich and married a girl whom she represented as the girl in Johannes Vermeer's *Girl with a pearl earring*. It could be said that her free, autonomous search for information [New Learning] which led her to come across the famous painting online [New Heritage], probably on the website of the *Mauritshuis*

Museum,[281] resulted in the direct association of wealth with portrait-painting [a practice reserved for the rich at the time]. More importantly, the painting dates back to the period [circa 1665] in which the fictive boy – Koen – lived, which suggests that the painting provided her with an opportunity to introduce a plausible, real-life face into her fictive story.

To conclude, this section described the digital divide as evident in the two classes I observed. This digital divide resides in the intensive and almost unlimited use of digital media by pupils in one case study, and its use being limited to the teacher in the other. I remarked that while both schools were connected to the Web, not all pupils were in a position to connect to that medium at will. The free-media-access approach of the HPDS indicated some signs of the development of advanced learning styles such as the ability to summarise from multiple sources and to multitask, while this was not the case at the partially technology-poor BL class. This section also placed the findings of the two case studies within the framework of New Learning and New Heritage, both of which are Web-driven. I pointed out that, despite the digital divide, both classes showed many instances in which New Learning and New Heritage had intermingled. New Heritage objects, either pedagogically enhanced in the form of video, with or without simulations, or presented in their original form, gave rise to new ways of representing and imagining the past, thereby triggering historical thinking among the pupils.

7.5 Summary

My aim in this chapter was to map my findings into patterns so that interconnections between the various uses and impacts of the Web can be understood comprehensively, rather than in isolation. Based on these findings, I suggested that the Web and its properties were attractive for the pupils, and it was that attractiveness that served as a triggering factor for historical thinking. The point underlying this argument is that the Web has proven to have the power to captivate the Internet Generation learners' interest. When thus interested, such learners become mentally disposed to develop their judgment and other thinking skills. The Web-based video in particular demonstrated those captivating features which in many cases prompted pupils to go beyond the surface message and deduct the unsaid from that which was said. The Web also emerged as central to multitasking, serving as a *disabstracting* tool, that is, as a virtual place where

281 *Mauritshuis*, Johannes Vermeer – Girl with a pearl earring'. http://www.mauritshuis.nl/index.aspx?chapterid=2342&contentID=18308&ViewPage=68&SchilderijSsOtName=titel&SchilderijSsOv=%25%25 (Accessed 21 January 2011).

learners can go in search of clarifications about comments made by the teacher or accounts found in the textbook. In one case study this phenomenon which involves suspension and resumption, or discontinuity within continuity, took the form of a triangular process, whereby there were a clear indications that it facilitated the development of historical thinking.

I also pointed out that the wide variety of online sources of historical information demanded recourse to certain source-evaluation skills which, in turn, fostered historical thinking in the sense that pupils had to extract the details deemed the most relevant and integrate them into their assignments in the form of either summaries or quotations. Taking into account recent adolescent cognitive psychology literature which distinguishes adolescent thinking from expert thinking, I regarded the compilation of quotes not as a sign of intellectual weakness that is aggravated by the Web, but rather as a task that involves some degree of historical thinking. It is apparent that the Web does indeed make quote-compilation easier; however, on the other hand, it has also given rise to such skills as finding the relevant Website or page, the right excerpt and, more importantly, the ability to transform the various excerpts into a coherent account. Summarising, which implies more advanced thinking skills and efforts, is another activity that the Web apparently facilitated, through searching for the right sources and relevant corroborative details.

Among the online sources used for assignments, I distinguished conventional and unconventional sources. An analysis of those sources revealed a convergence of sources in assignments, as both categories were used. This convergence is mostly due to the new relevance and authoritativeness criteria brought about by the Web and its search engines, and to the fact that the marks of conventionality of physical objects are not transferable in cyberspace. These factors, among others, have tended to blur the distinction between conventional and unconventional sources. I discussed the growing trend among heritage institutions to make their digitised objects available on unconventional platforms such as Wikipedia – the online source cited most frequently in the assignments. Based on what has been going on in other new-media-driven sectors, I suggested that this shift to Wikipedia and similar sites could have a significant impact on history education and give added visibility to conventional sources, which are disfavoured by the current rules employed by search engines.

Finally, I attempted to connect the findings of my field research to two discussions currently being held in scholarly circles, namely about the digital divide and the New learning–New Heritage twins. This research has shown that where pupils had permanent and unrestricted access to digital media and freedom to surf the Web whenever they pleased, those same pupils engaged in fruitful multitasking and were capable of producing assignments that demand a great deal of effort. In cases where they had no digital technologies at their disposal, nor access to the Web, they would frequently tune out by shifting to their private digital devices in order to surf the Web clandestinely. Assignments made by these pupils tended to be quote-compilations. Another important finding relates to the intersection of New Learning and New Heritage, two phenomena that rely heavily on digital media, especially the Web. While New Learning emphasises autonomy and a more learner-controlled learning process, New Heritage implies not only digitised objects, but also all other related types of virtualisation, including animations and simulations. Some examples have shown that the use of New Heritage objects in the classroom triggers new ways of visualising the past.

Chapter 8

Conclusions

In this research I have attempted to understand how the Internet Generation learns about the past using the Web. In tackling this rather broad topic which involves other areas in addition to education, I first provided literature reviews about the themes in which I was interested (Part One) and then a field-research-based study of those subjects in relation to two real-life history classes (Part Two). The central themes were [1] history education, with a focus on the lower cycle of secondary education; [2] new media technologies, particularly the Web, which have been presented as one of the most decisive factors determining ways in which the Internet Generation interacts with [historical] information; and [3] the digitisation of cultural heritage. In this chapter I would like to provide some final observations that not only offer a broad picture of the major points I discussed, but also highlight the new insights this research has brought to one's understanding of the uses of digital media in history-learning, and the role they seem to play in achieving the official key targets of history education. In what follows, I shall first sketch some of the ways the Internet Generation appears to learn history using the Web, and then make some observations about the extent to which heritage institutions' digitisation strategies and expectations fit in with those Web-driven learning styles. Lastly, I shall consider those learning styles in the light of the key targets of history education in the lower cycle. Concluding each of these points I shall provide a set of recommendations and perspectives for further research.

8.1 What Digital Learners Do with the Web

This research strove to shed light on some of the ways in which the Digital Generation, especially those aged 13–14 years, learn history using the Web. The exploration of three assumptions in two case studies has revealed the emergence of new Web-driven ways of becoming acquainted with the past. It seems that the combination of the availability on the Web of a multitude of historical sources [some conventional, others unconventional] with the psycho-cognitive developmental stage of early adolescents and their corresponding thinking patterns, has given rise to a number of changes in the ways in which history is learnt. In this section, I propose to make some concluding observations about these changes, starting with the ways in which young history learners approach the multitude and variety of sources accessible via the Web. I shall then deal with the ways in which their approaches have resulted in the convergence of sources and given rise to practices such as multiple-source quote-compilation and summarising. Finally, I shall make a number of observations about ways in which the Web appears to be turning young pupils into multitasking-minded learners, while at the same time fostering peer interaction on the subject matter.

One major change the Web has brought about relates to the knowledge and information landscape itself, where, in contrast with the pre-Web era, all kinds of information, official and non-official, conventional and unconventional, authoritative and non-authoritative, *etc.*, appear side by side. The result of this in the history class, as this research has shown, is that digital learners have embraced this multitude of sources including ones that were previously regarded as unusual for class assignments. The sources used by the pupils in the two case studies included the websites of individual people [or blogs], families, newspapers, TV stations, churches, municipalities and other official bodies, academic and research institutions, canons, user-generated-content sites like Wikipedia, travel agencies, heritage institutions, educational projects and many others. In one case study (Chapter 5), although the pupils were given instructions to use specific sources, the end result showed that none of them had used all the mandatory sources, most of which were conventional sources, while most of them made use of non-recommended sources, including many unconventional ones. In the second case study (Chapter 6), the instructions given for a WebQuest assignment were not about the sources to be used, but rather about the procedures to be followed. In terms of source categories used, the results were almost identical for both case studies. This finding might lead one to conclude that, when it comes to using the Web as a source of historical information, pupils tend to take advantage of their sense of freedom to decide for themselves which sources they will use.

On the premise that early adolescents are cognitively speaking less skilful than experts (Chapter 7), and that search engines have introduced new relevance and reliability criteria based on popularity rather than on conventionality (Chapters 3 and 7), this freedom has shed light on several aspects. First, with respect to frequency, as demonstrated in Chapters 5 and 6, unconventional sites – including Wikipedia and personal sites – were used more often than conventional ones. Also noted was the fact that the websites of some institutions, though considered prime references for the topics to be discussed in the assignments, were totally absent. Some scholars have equated unconventional sites with 'bad' or 'less good' information and conventional ones with 'good' information, especially for early adolescents, who find it difficult to check authorship or practice the corroboration heuristics. From the two case studies, however, there is no evidence suggesting that blogs or personal sites contained 'bad' information or that official or heritage institutions' sites contained 'better' information.

What did appear is a mixture of, and a convergence between, the two categories of sources (Chapter 7). One might therefore conclude that the young digital learners' search for historical information on the Web leads to convergence, which takes one back to the debate on approaches to history teaching that was discussed in Chapter 1. One of the main points discussed there was whether pupils should be expected to acquire a certain body of knowledge that fosters identity and citizenship education, or alternatively, acquire some historical awareness, including learning how to negotiate between competing sources. An analysis of Web-driven instruction alongside an analysis of the pupils' assignments reveals that the Web is exceptionally favourable towards the development of historical awareness together with corresponding reasoning and thinking skills. In the case study in which Web-based videos were frequently used (Chapter 5), forms of associative and deductive reasoning [among others] were observed as being connected with some intrinsic features of the Web. In the second case study, in which pupils had more freedom to use digital media (Chapter 6), there was clear evidence that source-evaluation and other skills were being fostered.

This research has also shed some light on two ways in which digital learners deal with the historical information they find on the Web: quotations and summaries. The findings in one case study (Chapter 5) suggest that caution is called for with respect to the widespread belief that lengthy, uninterrupted, non-interpreted quotations are a sign of intellectual weakness that is exacerbated and encouraged by the Web, where the [supposed] right quote can be found after only a few clicks. This research has shown on the one hand that quote-compilation is not as effortless as it has often been presented, and on the other hand that it is in keeping with the thinking patterns of early adolescence. Despite the lack of verbal, written connections – causal, consequential or otherwise – between quotations, it was clear that locating the sources and the relevant fragments, and then ordering them in a certain way that results in a new coherent narrative is a reflection of the pupils' multiple-source-based historical understanding of subject matter. Viewed from the point of view of the contemporary digital culture, quote-compilation has been equated with new forms of artistic creativity based on sampling, remixing, mashing up, and similar practices that are in vogue among the Digital Generation.

Also noted was the fact that quote-compilation was not only the result of the open way in which the assignment and the tasks were designed and described [Write an article about ...], as it was also influenced by the limited time and access to the Web. In the case study in which the assignment and the tasks were designed and described in a more restrictive way [Use Web sources and make a short poster ...], and where access to the Web was not an issue (Chapter 6), summaries emerged as the sole, dominant method of processing and converting multiple-source-based materials into short accounts. An analysis of the summaries revealed that the pupils spent more time and energy weighing sources up against one another and in trying to detect corroborative details. In some cases sources even contained false information [a misspelling for instance], but the pupils still managed to detect the right information.

This research also made it apparent that Wikipedia plays a particularly significant role among digital learners. In the two case studies, Wikipedia emerged as easily the most frequently cited source, meaning that it was dominant as a source not only of quotations, but also of corroborative details for all summaries. In some cases, both the Dutch and the English pages of Wikipedia on the same topic [*e.g.*: Rembrandt] were cited in a single assignment. Pupils' comments and ratings of sources in one case study (Chapter 6) show that Wikipedia has become incomparable and a reference against which other sources, including official ones, are measured. However, as the comments show, Wikipedia is mostly praised for its huge quantity of information and the widespread coverage it offers.

In addition, the Web appears to be the focal point of a learning style that involves some forms of multitasking-driven thinking, consisting of conducting more than one task in a coordinated manner. Contrary to the widespread belief that web- or digital-media-centred multitasking and the thinking process underlying it are distractive, this research showed that the circumstances under which digital media are used determine whether their use is distractive or not. In one of the case studies, where the pupils enjoyed almost unlimited freedom to use digital media wherever and however they pleased for Web-surfing, listening to music and even for gaming (Chapter 6), these same pupils appeared to be more concentrated and, as indicated by some of the signs observed, were engaged mostly in tasks related to the subject they were supposed to be studying. The triangular learning process, which was explained in Chapter 7, is one instance of how the Web has rendered the history class not only attractive but also efficient through what I termed *disabstrac-*

tion, or rendering an abstract object or concept concrete through a visual representation. In the other case study, where the use of the Web was teacher-centred and inaccessible to the pupils, digital media did appear to constitute a distraction (Chapter 5). This distraction does not necessarily mean that the pupils engaged in tasks that were unrelated to the subject they were studying, as observation has demonstrated that some were actually relevant to the topics being discussed. The distraction resided more in the clandestine way in which the pupils engaged with digital media rather than in the media themselves or the information they were seeking.

A related phenomenon that could be thought to constitute, or be misinterpreted as Web-generated distraction, is peer interaction. Here also the digital divide observed between the two classes (Chapter 7) was what made productive peer interactivity possible in one case but distractive in another. While in one case study every pupil owned a portable computer with no content-filtering software that was connected to the Web (Chapter 6), in the other, only the teacher was able to connect to the Web. Moreover, the use of digital devices such as mobile phones was not permitted (Chapter 5). The result of this digital divide was that in the former case study, pupils would share information, thereby prompting instant comments from one another about Web-based historical information in a way that appeared not to disturb the rest of the class. In the latter case study, pupils had little time and few opportunities to share Web-based information, as the use of personal devices – the sole means of having Internet connectivity – was prohibited during class time. As shown in Chapter 6, Web-driven interactivity, even during class time, presents a considerable potential in terms of discussing and understanding self-sought historical information.

The observations I made above about some of the ways digital learners used the Web to acquaint themselves with the past lead to suggest the following recommendations: [1] to provide pupils with portable computers or allow them to bring into the classroom their own private devices, including mobile phones; and having done that, then [2] to grant them the necessary freedom to explore whatever sources they think relevant. Computer-ownership is a crucial and motivating factor as it leads to an intimate trust-based relationship between the learners and their computers. As a consequence, they would probably engage much more with online historical information wherever they are [at home or at school]. What also becomes apparent is that adolescent digital learners are keen on learning how to learn while they are learning. In other words, they seemed to be learning to construct their own knowledge [with self-sought, self-interpreted information, *etc.*] while listening to the teacher and reading from the textbook. They would gain much from this learning style if they were allowed and encouraged to learn to surf the Web even during class time, because if a detail is not checked, clarified, *i.e.*, disabstracted *here and now*, it will most likely be forgotten or pushed into the background by other details during the lesson or during subsequent lessons that day. In other words, waiting until the evening when they can access the family computer is not the best way to enable pupils to *disabstract* the many abstract historical concepts, figures, events, places, *etc.*, they come across during their history lessons.

Further research is needed into a number of subjects to which I alluded, for example, the relationship between media freedom [in all senses] or lack of it and quote-compilation. The assumption made in this research is that when pupils have less time and restricted access [due to the computer room almost always being occupied and the use of fire-walled Web-browsers] to interact with online historical information during formal learning time [at school], they tend to put less effort into making their assignments. In other words, having little time to dig deeply into texts, and then into cross-textual thinking, they would simply locate the appropriate texts and paragraphs and copy-paste them into their assignments. A related assumption that needs further investigation is that in the long run a constant *disabstraction* effort during the course of a lesson, would provide pupils with the opportunity to progressively read multiple texts full of relevant details. Further research is also needed to enquire into Web-driven forms of multitasking, especially the one I described as the Triangular Learning Process. Understanding exactly what kind of sources pupils consult and what kind of details trigger most Web-based *disabstraction* efforts would be important for teachers in classrooms where media freedom is already a reality, and inspire those who envisage to embark on similar or related Web-driven innovations.

8.2 Digitised Heritage in Digital Learners' Eyes

In Chapter 3, which was entirely dedicated to the digitisation of cultural heritage, I discussed how history education, especially history education for the Digital Generation, became a prime target for heritage institutions. In practice one saw that the strategies and approaches used to reach that Generation initially raised questions in particular about the findability and the pedagogical enhancement of objects through contextualising hyperlinking. In short, that chapter was a discussion of what heritage institutions and policy-makers thought digitised heritage would mean for history education. In this section I would like to examine this from the other way round, by drawing some conclusions about the extent to which digitised heritage has managed to actually make it onto the history-learners' computer screens. By doing so, I shall assess the place of heritage institutions among the other historical sources pupils used, weighing it up against some of the expectations that policy-makers and heritage institutions brought forward to justify the initial investments. In the paragraphs below I shall first sum up the ways in which – and the extent to which – digitised heritage sites were used as sources of historical information, before evaluating whether they have, in one way or another, achieved the educational aims with which they were assigned.

The findings of the two case studies are conclusive about the extent to which the pupils used heritage institutions' websites for their class assignments. They were *underused*, especially if one considers that the assignment topics were often historical figures who have institutions dedicated to preserving their heritage but which were not cited. Rembrandt [Rembrandt House Museum] and to some extent Huygens [Museum Boerhaave] are two of the many examples. Furthermore a comparison with personal sites reveals that these were more popular with the pupils than the websites of heritage institutions. In addition to that, it seems that heritage sites were only interesting for their images rather than for their narratives. Many pupils delivered highly illustrated assignments whereby most of the pictures originated from heritage websites. In some cases a single website [*e.g.*, the Memory of the Netherlands] provided dozens of images for one assignment. At the same time, learners' comments from one case study (Chapter 6) indicated criticism of the poor and insufficient textual contents provided by heritage institutions.

Two conclusions can be drawn from this underuse of heritage websites: firstly, as explained in Chapter 3, the no-hyperlinking policy resulted in those websites being difficult to find, to the extent that better-linked personal sites scored far better with the pupils. Secondly, the sites that pupils did occasionally manage to find offered little more than pictures, as almost all quotations and summaries were referenced as mostly having been obtained from Wikipedia, the Canon of the Netherlands, and a few other sites. The result was that pupils were able to view pictures of historical figures, old ships or painters, but without being informed about what they meant, as this would have resulted in such comments as 'Everything/much information about …' those figures, ships or painters.

In a similar vein, this research did not reveal any particular indication that digitised heritage has specifically and explicitly fostered national identity and citizenship. However, there was a number of indirect ways in which some identity-shaping and citizenship education aspects could be observed, especially in the case study in which Web-use was teacher-centred (Chapter 5). In that case study, the Canon clips on land reclamation in the 17th century and on a citizen-led rebellion in the 18th century, both of which include digitised objects, could be interpreted as indirectly conveying some ideological message. Even in this respect, pupils still made some transnational connections, for example, with the French Revolution. The former clip could be understood from the perspective of '*our* scientific heritage', while the latter could be viewed as an attempt to get the generally uninterested young generation to participate in civic activities.

Considered from the pupils' perspective, that is, based on their assignments, it is apparent that the Web made their thinking more global than local. Dutch scientist Huygens, canonised as embodying 'our scientific heritage', was presented as inspired by, and having much admiration for, non-Dutch Descartes and Galileo. The drawing of the map of the Dutch East India Company routes was not necessarily created using a Netherlands-based digitised map, but rather, as in the case of one assignment, a map from the National Library of Australia's website. Even the canonised artists were mostly discussed based on Wikipedia and, to a lesser extent, on personal websites, where people have other motivations and perspectives than those of fostering national identity and citizenship. In none of the assignments were expressions used such as 'our nation', 'our culture', 'our values' or 'our heritage'.

From these observations, it could be concluded that there is one reason why digitised cultural heritage was not completely successful at achieving its identity-shaping and citizenship-fostering aims. As the sites created by heritage institutions for their digitised collections were not at the top of the results list returned by search engines, nor even on its first page, they were as I have already emphasised, hardly in any position to limit inquisitive digital learners to the sole perspective of politicians, policy-makers, and heritage institutions. Interacting constantly with other multiple-perspective sources, mostly Wikipedia, digital learners seem to include the non-Dutch perspective by making associations and via links – ones that have largely failed to materialise within the websites of heritage institutions – to foreign but relevant sources. Although no generalisation can be made on the basis of two case studies, the Web might be credited as being a global-identity and global-citizenship fostering tool, as it counters politicians' efforts to focus on the local and protect it from the influence of the global (Chapter 3).

Given that digitised heritage appears to have been underused by the digital learners in the two classes, and that its national identity-shaping and citizenship-fostering functions seem to be indissociably linked with Web-fostered global identity and citizenship, a few recommendations could be made that might render it more profitable for history education. If heritage institutions are to reverse the tendency to underuse them, they must [1] engage in large-scale, intensive cross-linking, both in-house within collections and to other institutions' collections. Since hyperlinking is the new criterion for visibility, the many valuable sources will never succeed in getting onto digital learners' screens if they are not placed in a hyperlinked environment. This would involve a number of sacrifices – the most important of which is the renouncement of [part of] the institutions' identity – and a redefinition of collection management tasks to include content organisation and contextualisation. The Ministry of Education, Culture and Science could help speed up this process by creating a system for rewarding visibility and contextualisation-oriented efforts among cultural heritage institutions.

However, in addition to hyperlinking, institutions must [2] provide sufficient textual information from which links can be made. This would turn them into sources of textual information, which is what digital learners are generally seeking, rather than image databases. The same Ministry could also [3] help heritage institutions out of the impasse *vis-à-vis* tax-payers' money, as this does not seem to be a major issue for other State-sponsored media sectors. One solution could be to explore sharing traffic-related revenues with third parties engaged in online, traffic-based commercial activities, which could even generate more income for institutions. Since it is evident that Wikipedia is ahead of heritage websites and the overall list of pupils' sources shows a clear convergence of conventional and unconventional sources, heritage institutions would be well-advised to [4] join the convergence trend, for example, through Wikipedia.

As the above does not even begin to exhaust all aspects of digitised heritage and its use in history education, further research is needed to investigate some of the issues that have been raised. For instance, the review in Chapter 3 referred to the existence of educational modules by teachers either within closed or open environments or in the form of Wikis, as well as the emergence of do-it-yourself tools. As none of these were used in either of the classes, there was no reason to enquire about them any further. However, further research would help to check, for instance, whether the same remixing and mashing-up skills observed in other aspects of digital culture are also being used here, and whether – and if so in what ways – they are also fostering pupils' creative thinking based on digitised heritage and their convergence with other sources. This aspect of the use of digitised heritage is still virgin territory in need of explorers. Finally, Chapter 7 also cited a number of heritage institutions that are pioneering with convergence by surrendering [part of] their digitised collections to unconventional, user-generated-content websites. Further investigation is necessary to understand not only the significance of this move for history-learners, but also its implications for digitised collections in terms of online visibility.

8.3 The Web and History Education Targets

As shown at the beginning of Chapter 5, there is a law that defines the goals officially and legally assigned to history education in the lower cycle of secondary education (Donner, 2006). Of the twelve targets of the umbrella discipline known as *Mens en Maatschappij* [Mankind and Society], of which history is a part, four relate specifically to history education, namely [1] learning how to place events, people, and major developments within the framework of the ten historical eras, in order to establish connections between past events and developments in the twentieth century; [2] learning how to identify the implications of pupils' image of their locality, the Netherlands, Europe, and the world for their own environment; [3] learning how to use historical sources; and [4] learning how to view current tensions and conflicts against their historical background. In what follows, I would like to identify some of the findings that could provide some indications about ways in which the Web appeared to help achieve the above-mentioned targets.

I would like to begin with a caveat relating to the methodology used for the field research. As I mentioned in Chapter 4, I did not use any experimental method meant to check the kind and level of understanding the pupils had of any particular subject matter. Instead, as a moderate participant observer, I carefully observed the various ways in which the pupils interacted with online contents and I subsequently analysed those interactions as well as the written assignments that resulted from them. This methodological approach was not intended as a detailed evaluation of achieved and non-achieved targets. Moreover, the targets are described as a process [learning being itself a process] to be achieved during the three years of the lower cycle, one that could not be compressed into the six months I spent observing the two classes. Having posited this caveat, I nevertheless feel I am in a position to say that some of the elements observed could provide some indications of how the Web seemed to help the pupils come closer to achieving those targets.

With regard to the first target, which could be interpreted as acquiring the ability to place past events in the right historical era and connect them to relevant 20th-century developments, the Web could clearly be observed making a contribution to its achievement. A Web-based Canon clip on the 'Patriots' [1780–1795] triggering a reaction that refers back to the 1789 French Revolution could be interpreted as a sign of the pupil's ability to locate an event in its historical era, in this case the Era of Wigs and Revolutions [1700–1800]. In relation to the second target, which could also be extended to mean the ability to identify the global implications and connections of a local place, event, or figure and *vice-versa*, there were a few instances suggesting indications that the Web fosters this ability. For instance, moving from Huygens to Descartes and then to Galileo, thereby presenting their scientific works as being related to one another, is a sign that the pupil was able to understand the local [Dutch] scientist's work in the light of, and in connection with, those of two other European scientists.

Unlike the two previous goals, the third one about learning how to use historical sources was explored in depth in Chapters 5 and 6, and subsequently analysed in Chapter 7. In short, my observations show that the Web, by presenting a variety of sources online, has created a situation in which pupils have to negotiate their way among those sources in order to find the ones they deem relevant. Two main sorts of uses were identified, namely summaries and quotations, to which a third could be added, namely the use of images. I also discussed how at their psycho-developmental stage, namely early adolescence, and due to the new relevance criteria brought about by search engines, the pupils approached sources in a manner that resulted in the convergence of conventional and unconventional sources. Their convergence-minded approach consisted in using both categories of sources in a complementary way.

Finally, the fourth target, which could be interpreted as acquiring the ability to view current tensions against their historical background, it appears that the Web has a potential to facilitate how pupils express their understanding of current major socio-cultural tensions, and how they perceive them as being rooted in the past. In one case (Chapter 6) an assignment on religions in the Middle Ages resulted in an essay on the Crusades being illustrated with the Wilders-vs-Islam cartoon. A peer discussion revealed that the pupil was viewing a current tension, embodied by far-right political leader Geert Wilders' anti-Islamic opinions against a historical background that he regarded as relevant and appropriate.

All the above-mentioned targets could be said to contribute to pupils' understanding of – and their ability to cope with – the present world. As shown in Chapter 1, there are different conceptualisations of this general aim of history education, with on the one hand scholars and history education experts emphasising mostly the acquisition of historical awareness and literacy – that is, understanding how history works as a discipline and how historical narratives come into being – and on the other hand politicians emphasising an understanding revolving around a specific body of core historical knowledge. This research has revealed a number of aspects of the kind of understanding pupils arrive at from their interaction with historical information on the Web.

The most important finding in this respect is that because of the search engines, pupils go first to the most popular sites, the most important of which appeared to be Wikipedia. In the case study in which the pupils were specifically asked to use, among others, the Canon as a mandatory source together with Wikipedia (Chapter 5), the former – a core historical-knowledge site – appeared the same number of times as the latter – an open-source history site. When no mandatory sources were indicated, Wikipedia retained first place, while the Canon was relegated to position eight on a list of ten source categories. The conclusion one might draw from this convergence and the relationships between core historical-knowledge sites and their open-source historical knowledge counterparts is that the Web has rendered any exclusive approach extremely difficult, if not impossible, and this can be regarded as an indication of the enormous import of the Web to history education.

Since three of the four key targets of history education in the lower cycle are about linking – events, people, and developments to historical eras, the local and the national to the international and *vice-versa*, and the present to the past – and since the Web is mainly about hyperlinking, I would like to recommend [1] the full integration of the Web into history teaching plans and strategies in a way that highlights and encourages those links. One way to do that would be by encouraging pupils to check those links, for example, by clicking on Descartes on the Huygens page on Wikipedia, in order to better understand the connections between the two scientists. In other words, they need to be taught to go beyond merely mentioning such links to finding the evidence that justifies the links. Regarding the use of sources, I also recommend that [2] pupils are given the freedom to explore all sorts of historical sources, provided that they are informed about the various sorts of online source categories and about the differences between them.

The above made references to a number of elements that appeared in this research, indicating the Web's potential to contribute to achieving the key targets of history education in the lower cycle. However, no firm conclusions can be drawn based on the few examples provided above. This means there is a need of further research in order to provide a more detailed and systematic picture of the role the Web plays in achieving those targets. One way would be to follow a particular class from the first to the third year of the lower cycle, evaluating the stages reached at each level using experimental methods such as Think-aloud protocols, among others, and correlating these stages with test scores. At the end of the lower cycle, a comparative study of the progress achieved at each stage would be capable of showing more clearly whether or not, and how, the Web as a source of historical information contributes to the achievement of the key targets. What this research has shown in this respect is that the Web does have that potential.

General Summary

How do young secondary school pupils use digital media and resources during their history education? The central question of this research is: to understand not only the ways in which digitally-minded learners engage in and interact with new media technologies, especially the World Wide Web, as sources of historical information, or as aids in their history education, but also the extent to which they learn with those technologies. In order to grasp the contours of the subject, this research first reviewed a number of subjects: the various and often conflicting ways in which scholars, experts, policy-makers, and politicians have conceptualised history education; the history of the Web and its integration into history education, as well as the literature about the Internet Generation; and the digitisation of cultural heritage whose targeted audiences include both history teachers and learners of history. By means of case studies, this research also explored some of the prevailing assumptions in relation to history education, namely that digital media make history education livelier, more multiple-source-driven, as well as favouring and stimulating historical thinking. In what follows, I shall present a chapter-by-chapter summary of the points discussed.

Chapter 1 presents the various ways in which an 'understanding of the world' has been conceptualised as the main goal of history education. I mention how history education has been presented as preparing pupils to make sense of situations, phenomena, and events in the present, while also enabling them to foresee what the future might be like. History education has also been considered as a pipeline that connects learners with 'their roots', thereby imbuing in them an awareness of their identity. I point out that while politicians are generally enthusiastic about this way of 'understanding the world', scholars and history didactics experts are generally opposed to its being a part of history education. Closely linked to this is an understanding of the world through the lenses of citizenship education. Education officials and politicians regard this as a key aim of history education, as it informs pupils about 'our democratic values' and 'our culture'. Opposing this view, history education scholars generally feel that the best way to prepare democratically minded citizens is to allow them to practice the application of democratic values during history lessons.

Two broad categories of approaches to history education can be distinguished: on the one hand politicians, who are generally interested in history education as an identity-fostering and citizenship education framework, prefer that a specific body of knowledge

– with a set of 'must-know' figures and events – is placed at the heart of history education. On the other hand there are the scholars and history didactics experts who generally regard the aim of history education as being to make learners alert, increasing their awareness of how history functions as a discipline by, for instance, getting them to acknowledge the nature of historical accounts with their multiple perspectives and to question the taken-for-grantedness of accounts. However, one trend within this approach presents a limited body of key historical knowledge as *sine qua non*. A related topic in this discussion is the relevance of any given body of knowledge at any given time. Some history education scholars propose a balance that allows learners to know subjects relevant to their era, while understanding how history works in order to be able to interpret for themselves the relevance of historical events and processes in the future.

Lastly, this chapter contains a discussion of the contents presented by the various stakeholders as being suitable for history education. The scholarly literature presents world history – or the international approach to history – as the most suitable form in which history education contents should be delivered. As such, although world history does accommodate local, regional, and national histories, it goes beyond local boundaries to integrate non-national perspectives and contexts. Some advocates of local history have conceptualised local historical figures, events, and processes as laboratory materials that make the study of history more direct while leading to a much broader, transnational, understanding. In the eyes of the politicians, however, national history, protected from the influence of globalisation and the effects of immigration, and aimed at preserving and perpetuating the national identity, is seen as the most suitable form that history contents should take.

The idea behind Chapter 2 is to provide a short but comprehensive background of four of the main aspects relevant to this research, namely, the Web, official policies leading to its integration in education, the Internet Generation, and the early attempts of history teachers to appropriate the Web. On the matter of the Web, I refer to the fact that just after its birth in the early 1990s, activists and hackers made it available to a wider Dutch public and even managed to associate themselves with local official institutions in creating the freely accessible Digital City. Unlike this involvement of local official institutions in digital cities and villages, central government remained in the margins. The main loser in this situation was the educational sector, as its finance generally depends to a large extent on government rather than private investment.

On the subject of government policies aimed at connecting education to the Web, I review the various steps the Ministry of Education, Culture and Science took to bridge the gap between education and the rest of society in terms of connectivity. I discuss the Big Project [*Groot Project*], the multi-million investment plan that ran from 1997 until 2005, highlighting its successive stages. Although the implementation of the plan witnessed many shifts in focus, it ultimately managed to fill the gap. All schools had been equipped with computers connected to the Web by 2005.

The Internet Generation, central to my research, is presented as referring to the cohort of people born around or since 1980, who grew up – or are growing up – with digital technologies. Interactivity is identified as one major feature about which members of the Internet Generation are enthusiastic. They are particularly keen on media objects that offer them the possibility of engaging with them bi-directionally. The desire for control over media contents is another major characteristic of the Internet Generation. In one sense, control refers to the freedom to choose which path to take when examining media objects and their contents. In another sense it implies the possibility of engaging with many of those contents and objects simultaneously, without losing track of any of them. Image-mindedness is also identified as an important characteristic, one that is amplified by the visually inclined nature of the Web itself.

Lastly, this chapter traces the early appropriation of the Web by some history teachers. A number of pioneer initiatives by individual teachers reveals how the Web was seducing history teachers. Some hailed the new ways in which it made providing historical contexts easy; others discovered that it created a favourable environment for collaborative learning that brought to the surface previously undiscovered strengths and weaknesses of certain pupils; yet others found that it was an empowering tool as it enabled pupils to self-publish their own historical accounts.

Chapter 3 is dedicated to the digitisation of cultural heritage collections, a process that is presented as having multiple motivations. Preservation emerges as the initial motivating factor, on which access and all other subsequent uses depend. Once access had been provided to preserved materials, other uses emerged, mainly educational and ideological ones. Digitisation is often cited as a way of providing sources for pupils and teachers, but also as providing identity-shaping and citizenship-fostering materials. Another motive is the desire to bring formerly united collections back together again and also to unite objects that relate to the same theme. An advantage of such [re-]unification is that new collections are formed that transcend geographical distances and boundaries. Attention is drawn to the fact that each motive has the potential for presenting new opportunities for generating income.

This chapter also discusses the different levels of selectiveness among digitisation projects, ranging from non-selective and time-based or theme-based projects to strictly selective ones. Though selection is an essential stage prior to digitisation both for financial and practical reasons, in some cases, the selection process itself became an expensive and time-consuming task. In other cases, collections were too small to necessitate selection. In yet other cases, decisions were made to select a theme or a period within which no further selection was made. However, stricter selections tended to be made in most cases. The most frequently used selection criteria are the fragility and old age of objects, their uniqueness, their rarity, and their historical or intellectual significance. The latter criterion is extremely broad as the importance of objects depends on who is making the consideration and with what purposes in mind.

Discussing the post-digitisation organisation of contents and the enhancement of their pedagogical value, this chapter presents hyperlinking as an effective way of placing objects in their historical contexts. I draw a parallel between hyperlinking and the links that historians make between related historical events and processes in order to make sense of them. This chapter shows that heritage institutions have largely underused hyperlinks, which resulted in the pedagogical uses of heritage objects being limited in at least two ways: firstly, Digital Natives, whose expectations lead them to assume that related objects will be interconnected, probably interpret the lack of links by thinking that the objects being presented have no history or context, as none is provided; secondly, those same Digital Natives, whose research almost always begins with online search operations, will rarely find themselves landing on the poorly indexed and ranked heritage sites. The reason for this poor indexing and ranking is related to poor hyperlinking, because the more hyperlinks to and from a site, the better its ranking and the greater that site's visibility and findability will be. I identify three reasons explaining this poor hyperlinking, namely the more or less conservative vision of heritage professionals in restricting their task to selecting and preserving collections and making them available, without ever concerning themselves with the interpretation and organisation of their contents, which results in fund allocation policies that preclude hyperlinking; institutions' policies regarding the preservation of their identity and their corporate interests; and the impasse surrounding the use of public funds in a networked knowledge landscape that has resulted in a proliferation of the most unpredictable ways of generating profit.

This chapter closes with a review of the trends among heritage institutions since the arrival of Web 2.0. I signal the increasing presence of such institutions on Social Media sites, where they not only communicate with their audiences but also present parts of their collections. This practice has brought digitised objects closer to the users, who, in the process, are taking over some of the tasks previously entrusted to heritage professionals. One such task is assigning meanings to objects. In addition, Social Media provide institutions with an opportunity to gather exchanges made about their objects, which eventually results in multiple narratives about objects. I also review a few educational projects centred on contents generated by users – mostly teachers and pupils – based on digitised heritage objects. These projects increase the control of teachers and pupils over contents, while also facilitating their creativity. Nonetheless, there is little certainty regarding the future of these projects, mainly due to funding issues.

Chapter 4 outlines the methodological approach used for the field research. It begins by framing the central research question – how do pupils interact with digital media during their history class? – which I explored based on three assumptions raised in existing literature on the subject. I opted for an ethnographic approach, applying it to two case studies. My interest was mainly to understand, describe, and then interpret the uses of digital media and resources by the selected secondary school pupils. Within that approach, I opted to play the part of a moderate participant observer by sitting among the pupils and following their exchanges, their interactions with the teachers and digital media, and by conducting unstructured interviews with them. The latter technique proved efficient in that it ensured that exchanges remained natural. My exchanges with teachers were mostly based on semi-structured interviews. Though I strove to win the pupils' trust, I refrained from becoming their peer. I used content analysis, to explore two variables – historical thinking and variety of sources – in the pupils' written assignments. At the end of this chapter I briefly introduce the field data collecting techniques that I used, namely note-taking, sound and video recording, and photography.

Chapter 5 presents the findings of the first case study at the Baarnsch Lyceum in Baarn. It opens with a descriptive introduction of the class involved in my research, placing it within the context of the broader educational system. I indicate that the second-year bridge-class was in the HAVO/VWO trajectory that leads to higher education. I also describe the 13- to 14-year-old pupils, highlighting not only their attentive attitude when digital audiovisual media were used, but also their lack of attention when these media were not used. The connection between use of the Web and the pupils' historical thinking is discussed: in some cases, the attractiveness of the Web-based audiovisual resources appeared to trigger not only pupils' attention, but also their engagement in the thinking process. In other cases, the ease with which pupils interacted with Web-based texts and still-images [copy-pasting, ripping, image-downloading] prompted them to compile long quotations taken from the Web, though this did leave some room for certain forms of historical thinking. These consisted mostly in identifying the sources and the relevant fragments and then converting them into a new coherent narrative. In yet other cases, a few pupils found another way of using Web-based texts that implies some degree of historical thinking: paraphrasing. Finally, I examine the Web sources used by the pupils and reach the conclusion that most of them had used a variety of sources, including, among others, personal, heritage, religious, news, academic, and educational websites.

Chapter 6 is about the second case study at the Helen Parkhurst Dalton School in Almere. It first discusses how the Dalton approach to teaching and learning in combination with the one-child-one-connected-laptop policy created an atmosphere that stimulated the pupils to make frequent use of the Web during both teacher-led lecture time and 'independent work' time. It appeared that the freedom enjoyed by the pupils in terms of media use led to various forms of interactions with digital media in general, and with the Web in particular. During teacher-led lecture time pupils would search for details about information that had either been provided by the teacher or which emanated from the textbook. During 'independent-work' time their interactions would be even more varied, ranging from Web-surfing in search of relevant information for their assignments to using it in other ways in order to relax from their intellectual efforts. In this respect, the Web appeared to be a crucial factor in creating an atmosphere conducive to learning. I also explore ways in which the Web interfered with the historical thinking process of the pupils.

It seems that Web image display tools made it easier for the pupils to compare and then judge visual representations of the concepts about which they were learning, or about which they were writing assignments. Moreover, the easy and unlimited access to various websites enabled pupils to make summaries. Through certain forms of content analysis, content-harmonising, and content-structuring – all of which involve making comparisons, judgments, and selections –, they were also able of producing short illustrated texts and maps. Lastly, I pay attention to the variety of Web sources used for WebQuest assignments. Ten sorts of websites were used including not only Wikipedia, the Canon of the Netherlands, and heritage sites, but also, among others, personal, educational, commercial, official, and news sites. It was by weighing up the information contained in each of them that the pupils managed to write their assignments.

While Chapters 5 and 6 are descriptive in nature, Chapter 7 is more analytical as it maps the findings of the case studies into patterns so that interconnections among the various uses and impacts of the Web might be understood comprehensively rather than in isolation. On the basis of these findings, I suggest that the Web and its properties, attractive as they are for the pupils, served as a triggering factor for historical thinking. The underlying point of this argument is that the Web has proven to have the power to captivate the interest of the Internet Generation learners. When thus interested, they become mentally disposed to develop their judgment and other thinking skills. The Web-based video in particular revealed these captivating features which, in many cases, prompted pupils to go beyond the surface message and deduct the unsaid from that which was said. Furthermore, the Web has emerged as central to multitasking, serving as a *disabstracting* tool, that is, as a virtual place where learners can go in search of clarifications about comments made by the teacher or accounts found in the textbook. Involving suspension and resumption, or discontinuity within continuity, this phenomenon appeared in the form of a triangular learning process in one case study, and showed clear indications that it facilitated the development of historical thinking.

In addition, the wide variety of online sources of historical information demanded recourse to some source-evaluation skills, which in their turn fostered historical thinking in the sense that they required pupils to extract the details deemed the most relevant and integrate them into their assignments, either in the form of summaries or as quotations. Taking into account recent adolescent cognitive psychology literature, which distinguishes adolescent thinking from expert thinking, I regard quote-compilation not merely as an intellectual weakness that has been aggravated by the Web, but rather as involving some amount of historical thinking. Though it is true that the Web has made quote-compilation easier, it has also given rise to such skills as finding the relevant Website or page, then finding the right excerpt and – more importantly – converting the various excerpts into a coherent account. Summarising, which implies more advanced thinking skills and more efforts, is another activity that the Web appears to have facilitated, as it involves searching for the right sources and relevant details that corroborate one another.

Among online sources used for assignments, I distinguish between conventional and unconventional sources. The analysis of those sources shows that there was convergence of sources in the assignments, as both categories were used. This convergence was mostly due to the new relevance and authoritativeness criteria brought about by the Web and its search engines, but also to the fact that the marks of conventionality of physical objects are not transferable to cyberspace. These factors, among others, do tend to blur the distinction between conventional and unconventional sources. I discuss the burgeoning trend among heritage institutions to make their digitised objects available on unconventional platforms such as Wikipedia [the most frequently cited of all online sources in the assignments]. Based on what has been going on in other new-media-driven sectors, I suggest that this collaboration with Wikipedia and similar sites could have a significant impact on history education, and help increase the visibility of conventional sources which are so disfavoured by the new rules employed by search engines.

Finally, I attempt to connect the findings of the two case studies to two discussions currently going on in scholarly circles, namely about the digital divide and the New Learning – New Heritage twins. This research shows that where pupils had permanent and unrestricted access to digital media as well as the freedom to surf the Web whenever they pleased, those same pupils apparently started to engage in fruitful multitasking and produced written pieces of prose that demanded a great deal of effort. In the case study in which the pupils had no digital technologies at their disposal and no access to the Web, they would frequently tune out by shifting to their private digital devices in order to surf the Web clandestinely. These pupils eventually produced assignments that tended to be quote-compilations.

Another important finding concerns the intersection of New Learning and New Heritage, two phenomena that rely heavily on digital media, in particular on the Web. While New Learning emphasises autonomy and a more learner-controlled learning process, New Heritage implies not only digitised objects, but also all other related types of virtualisation, including animations and simulations. Some examples presented in this research show that the use of New Heritage objects in the classroom triggers new ways of envisaging the past.

In conclusion, Chapter 8 contains some observations about what digital learners appear to do with digital media, the apparent place of digitised heritage as a source of historical information, and the contribution digital media appear to make towards achieving the key targets of history education. Digital learners who do have access to the Web appeared to engage in the convergence of conventional and unconventional sources, in multiple-text-based historical thinking and in multitasking. The latter includes the tendency to disabstract *here and now*. I recommend that pupils are provided with connected computers, preferably as owners, or at least that they are allowed to use their own devices, freely – though with guidance – even during class time. The investigation of certain other points, such as the link between the digital divide and quote-compilation and the *disabstraction* phenomenon, are suitable subjects for further research.

This chapter also includes remarks on the fact that digitised cultural heritage was underused in the two case studies, where even personal websites scored better. This is the result of poor hyperlinking which renders heritage sites invisible in search engines. Furthermore, in the eyes of digital learners, heritage sites seemed to have gained a reputation as image databases, as they tend to present images rather than explanatory texts with links. Moreover, no indications were evident to suggest that digitised heritage is fostering national identity and citizenship, as pupils made much more frequent use of other multiple-perspective sources such as Wikipedia. To remedy the underuse of digitised heritage, I recommend that institutions engage in large-scale hyperlinking both in-collection and cross-institutional, as this would provide more textual information relating to images, while a second recommendation is that they should join the convergence trend. Two steps must first be taken if the hyperlinking tactic is to succeed: first, heritage institutions will have to concede some sacrifices in terms of corporate interests and identity, as well as redefining certain collection management tasks in order to realise greater involvement with contents; second, the relevant authorities will have to address the impasse relating to the use of tax-payers' money, which precludes many institutions from generating traffic – and thereby profits – for third-party organisations. Further research is needed to explore the impact and uses of the current trend among heritage institutions that involves providing teachers and learners not only with contents and platforms, but also with do-it-yourself tools.

Finally, the last chapter identifies four key targets of history education in the lower cycle and discusses some of the ways the Web appears to be contributing to their achievement. A few instances have shown that the Web appears to facilitate acquisition of the ability to [1] place events, people, and major developments within the framework of the ten historical eras; to [2] identify the global implications and connections of a local place, event, or figure and *vice–versa*; to [3] know how to use historical sources; and to [4] view current tensions against their historical background. Since three of the four key targets of history education in the lower cycle are about linking – events, people, and developments to historical eras; the local and the national to the international and *vice–versa*; and the present to the past – and since the Web is mainly about hyperlinking, I recommend the full integration of the Web into history teaching plans and strategies in a way that highlights and promotes all these links. Another recommendation is to provide pupils with an opportunity to encounter all sorts of historical sources, while also ensuring that they know how to deal with each of them. Further long-term research is needed to look into the Web's contribution to key targets, in particular research that involves a more experimental approach.

Samenvatting in het Nederlands

Op welke wijze maken middelbare scholieren gebruik van digitale media en middelen bij hun geschiedenislessen? In dit onderzoek was het mijn streven niet alleen de manieren te begrijpen waarop leerlingen zich bezighouden en reageren op nieuwe mediatechnologieën (in het bijzonder het wereldwijde Web) als bronnen van historische informatie of als hulpmiddelen bij het geschiedenisonderwijs, maar ook de mate waarin ze met die technologieën leren. Om de contouren van dit onderwerp neer te zetten, laat het onderzoek eerst een aantal concepten de revue passeren: de verschillende en vaak botsende manieren waarop academici, experts, beleidsmakers en politici tegen het geschiedenisonderwijs aan kijken; de geschiedenis van het Web en zijn integratie binnen het geschiedenisonderwijs; de literatuur over de Internetgeneratie; en het digitaliseren van het culturele erfgoed, de doelgroep waarvan zowel de leraren als de leerlingen in het geschiedenisonderwijs omvat. Dit onderzoek verkende ook, door middel van casestudies, een aantal gangbare aannames over het geschiedenisonderwijs, namelijk dat digitale media de lessen levendiger maken, dat ze door meervoudige bronnen worden gedreven, en dat ze het historische denken ondersteunen en stimuleren. Wat volgt is een samenvatting per hoofdstuk van de bevindingen.

Hoofdstuk 1 beschrijft de verschillende manieren waarop een 'begrip van de wereld' geconceptualiseerd is als het hoofddoel van het geschiedenisonderwijs. Geschiedenisonderwijs wordt voorgesteld als het klaarstomen van leerlingen zodat ze de betekenis kunnen inzien van situaties, fenomenen en gebeurtenissen in het heden, terwijl ze ook in staat worden gesteld om een mogelijke toekomst te kunnen voorspellen. Het geschiedenisonderwijs wordt ook voorgesteld als een soort verbindingslijn die de leerlingen verbindt met 'hun wortels', waardoor ze bewust worden van hun identiteit. Hoewel politici veelal enthousiast zijn over een dergelijk 'begrip van de wereld', zijn academici en experts in de geschiedenisdidactiek in het algemeen gekant tegen dit aspect van het geschiedenisonderwijs. Nauw verbonden hiermee is een begrip van de wereld gezien door de bril van het burgerschapsonderwijs. Onderwijsfunctionarissen en politici beschouwen dit als een hoofddoel van het geschiedenisonderwijs omdat de leerlingen worden geïnformeerd over 'onze democratische waarden' en 'onze cultuur'. Academische experts op het gebied van geschiedenisonderwijs verzetten zich hiertegen. Zij vinden het oefenen met het toepassen van democratische waarden in het geschiedenisonderwijs de beste manier om democratisch burgerschap te bevorderen.

De benadering van het geschiedenisonderwijs kan in twee categorieën worden ingedeeld. Aan de ene kant staan de politici die het geschiedenisonderwijs bij voorkeur in een identiteitskoesterend en burgerschapsonderwijzend kader; zij zien het liefst dat een specifieke hoeveelheid kennis – bestaande uit personages en gebeurtenissen die geleerd moeten worden – een centrale plaats krijgt in het geschiedenisonderwijs. Aan de andere kant staan de academici en deskundigen op het gebied van de geschiedenisdidactiek die het doel van het geschiedenisonderwijs erin gelegen zien dat leerlingen alert worden, dat ze bewuster worden van het functioneren van de geschiedenis als een academische discipline, zodat leerlingen bijvoorbeeld het karakter van historische verhalen – met hun meervoudige perspectieven – erkennen en gaan twijfelen aan de vanzelfsprekendheid ervan. Binnen deze benadering is er echter een tendens die een zekere hoeveelheid historische kennis als *sine qua non* presenteert. Een aanverwant thema in deze discussie is de relevantie van een bepaalde hoeveelheid kennis op een willekeurig moment. Sommige experts op het gebied van geschiedenisonderwijs stellen een balans voor. Hierbij krijgen leerlingen de mogelijkheid om kennis op te doen over onderwerpen relevant voor hun tijdperk, terwijl ze ook leren begrijpen hoe de geschiedenis werkt, zodat ze zelf de relevantie van historische gebeurtenissen en processen in de toekomst zullen kunnen interpreteren.

Als laatste besteedt dit hoofdstuk aandacht aan de inhoud die de verschillende belanghebbenden geschikt achten voor het geschiedenisonderwijs. De wetenschappelijke literatuur presenteert de wereldgeschiedenis – of de internationale benadering van de geschiedenis – als de meest geschikte vorm waarin de inhoud van het nationale geschiedenisonderwijs kan worden ondergebracht. Hoewel ze ook aandacht heeft voor lokale, regionale en nationale geschiedenissen gaat wereldgeschiedenis verder dan de lokale grenzen en integreert ze ook niet-nationale perspectieven en verbanden. Voorstanders van een plaatselijke vorm van geschiedenis conceptualiseren lokale historische personages, gebeurtenissen en processen als grondstoffen die ervoor zorgen dat het leren van de geschiedenis veel directer geschiedt, terwijl het tot een veel breder, supranationaal begrip leidt. In de ogen van de politici echter wordt een nationale geschiedenis, beschermd tegen de invloed van globalisering en de effecten van immigratie, met als doel het conserveren en vastleggen van de nationale identiteit, beschouwd als de meest aangewezen vorm waarin de inhoud van geschiedenis gegoten dient te worden.

Hoofdstuk 2 schetst een beknopte maar veelomvattende achtergrond van vier van de belangrijkste aspecten van dit onderzoek, namelijk het ontstaan van het Web, het ambtelijk beleid dat leidde tot de integratie daarvan in het onderwijs, de Internetgeneratie en de vroege pogingen van geschiedenisleraren om het Web in te zetten in hun werk. Kort na het ontstaan in de vroege jaren negentig van de vorige eeuw, maakten activisten en hackers het Web toegankelijk voor een breder publiek. Bij het opzetten van de vrij toegankelijke Digitale Stad zochten zij zelfs aansluiting bij lokale ambtelijke organisaties. De landelijke overheid was minder sterk betrokken bij de vroege ontwikkeling van het Web. De grootste verliezer van deze situatie was de sector onderwijs, omdat die grotendeels financieel afhankelijk is van de landelijke overheid en niet van de investeringen van particulieren.

Met betrekking tot het beleid van de overheid die moest zorgen voor het aansluiten van het onderwijs op het Web, bespreek ik de stappen die het ministerie van Onderwijs, Cultuur en Wetenschap nam om het gat te dichten tussen het onderwijs en andere delen van de maatschappij. Ik bespreek het Grote Project, het multi-miljoen investeringsplan dat liep van 1997 tot 2005, waarbij ik enig licht werp op de verschillende stadia waaruit dat plan bestond. Hoewel de implementatie van dit plan vele tussentijdse aanpassingen kende, is het uiteindelijk toch gelukt om het gat te dichten. Tegen 2005 waren alle scholen voorzien van computers die aangesloten waren op het internet.

De 'Internetgeneratie' is de benaming van een cohort van jonge mensen geboren rond 1980, die opgroei(d)en omgeven door digitale technologieën. 'Interactiviteit' wordt aangemerkt als iets waarover leden van de Internetgeneratie enthousiast zijn. Het verlangen om controle te hebben over media content is een ander belangrijk kenmerk van de Internetgeneratie. Aan de ene kant doelt controle op de vrijheid om te kiezen hoe media en hun content te doorzoeken. Aan de andere kant is het simultaan omgaan met veel van die content en onderwerpen ('multitasken') kenmerkend. Beeldgerichtheid wordt ook aangemerkt als een belangrijk kenmerk dat door het beeldkarakter van het Web zelf wordt versterkt.

Als laatste gaat dit hoofdstuk in op de vroege toe-eigening van het Web door een aantal geschiedenisleraren. Een aantal pioniersinitiatieven door individuele leraren laat zien hoe leraren geschiedenis door het Web werden aangetrokken. Sommigen verwelkomden de nieuwe manieren om historische contexten te verschaffen; anderen ontdekten dat het Web een stimulerende omgeving bood voor een collaboratieve vorm van leren die ervoor zorgde dat de tot dan toe onzichtbaar sterke en zwakke eigenschappen van bepaalde leerlingen tevoorschijn kwamen; weer anderen zagen het als een stuk gereedschap waarmee leerlingen in staat waren zelf hun geschiedenisverhalen te publiceren.

Hoofdstuk 3 is gewijd aan het digitaliseren van culturele erfgoedcollecties, een proces dat vanuit een veelvoud aan motieven op gang kwam. Het conserveren van erfgoedstukken was de initiële motiverende factor waarop alle daaropvolgende doelen berustten. Nadat geconserveerde materialen digitaal toegankelijk waren gemaakt, traden andere – voornamelijk educatieve of ideologische – vormen van gebruik op de voorgrond. Digitalisering wordt beschouwd als een manier om bronnen beschikbaar te maken aan leerlingen en leraren, maar ook als identiteitsvormend en burgerschapsversterkend materiaal. Een andere beweegreden is het verlangen om collecties die verspreid zijn geraakt te herenigen of om objecten die verband houden met eenzelfde thema te verenigen. Een voordeel van dergelijke [her-]verenigingsacties is dat hierdoor nieuwe collecties worden gevormd die geografische afstanden en grenzen overstijgen. Elke beweegreden heeft het in zich om meerwaarde te bieden.

Dit hoofdstuk gaat ook in op de verschillende niveaus van selectie binnen de digitaliseringsprojecten, variërend van geen selectie en tijd- of thema-gebaseerde projecten tot projecten met strenge selectie. Hoewel selectie voorafgaand aan het digitaliseren essentieel is – om zowel financiële als praktische redenen – is het selectieproces in een aantal gevallen zelf een dure en tijdrovende taak. In andere gevallen zijn de collecties te klein om selectie noodzakelijk te maken. In nog andere gevallen is ertoe besloten een thema of een periode te selecteren waarbinnen geen verdere selectie plaatsvond. In de meeste gevallen vond er wel een strengere selectie plaats. Selectiecriteria die het vaakst werden gebruikt zijn de kwetsbaarheid en leeftijd van de erfgoedobjecten, hun uniciteit, hun zeldzaamheid en hun historische of intellectuele betekenis. Het laatste criterium is zeer breed, daar de significantie van objecten afhangt van degene die deze eraan toekent en de doeleinden die daarbij in gedachten zijn gehouden.

Na een bespreking van de organisatie (post-digitalisering) van content en de versterking van de pedagogische waarde van objecten, wordt in dit hoofdstuk hyperlinking gepresenteerd als een effectieve manier om objecten in hun historische context te plaatsen. Ik trek een parallel tussen hyperlinking en de verbanden die historici leggen tussen verwante historische gebeurtenissen en processen om de betekenis ervan beter te kunnen doorgronden. Het hoofdstuk laat zien dat erfgoedinstellingen relatief weinig gebruik hebben gemaakt van hyperlinking, waardoor de pedagogische doelen waarvoor erfgoedobjecten kunnen worden gebruikt op minstens twee manieren beperkt zijn gebleven. Ten eerste is het waarschijnlijk dat de leden van de Digitale Generatie – die ervan uitgaan en verwachten dat verwante objecten aan elkaar worden gekoppeld – de indruk hebben gekregen dat de objecten die ze via het Web vonden geen geschiedenis of context hebben, omdat er geen context bijgeleverd werd. Ten tweede zullen diezelfde Digitale Nederlanders, wier onderzoek bijna altijd met online zoekacties begint, zelden zijn gestuit op de slecht-geïndiceerde en -gerankte erfgoedsites. De reden voor die povere indicering en ranking is gelegen in een slechte hyperlinking, want hoe meer hyperlinks van en naar een website, hoe beter de 'ranking; van een site wordt en hoe zichtbaarder en vindbaarder die is. Ik noem drie verklaringen voor die povere hyperlinking, namelijk (1) de nadruk die erfgoeddeskundigen hebben gelegd op het selecteren, digitaal conserveren en beschikbaar stellen van collecties ten koste van aandacht voor de interpretatie en het organiseren van de content (2) het beleid van instellingen omtrent het beschermen van hun bedrijfsidentiteit en belangen (het voorkomen van 'wegklikken'); en (3) voorzichtigheid in het gebruik van publieke gelden binnen een genetwerkt kennislandschap waar de meest onwaarschijnlijke manieren om winst te genereren opgeld doen.

Het hoofdstuk eindigt met een overzicht van de tendensen die zich onder erfgoedinstellingen voordoen met de komst van Web 2.0. Ik signaleer een toenemende aanwezigheid van deze instellingen op sociale mediasites, waar ze niet alleen het gesprek aangaan met hun publiek, maar ook (een deel van) hun collectie presenteren. Deze praktijk brengt gedigitaliseerde objecten dichter bij de gebruikers, die sommige taken overnemen die voorheen in handen waren van de deskundigen binnen de erfgoedinstellingen. Een voorbeeld van een dergelijke taak is het toekennen van betekenissen (via trefwoorden, 'tags') aan objecten. Bovendien verschaffen sociale media de instellingen een mogelijkheid om discussies over hun objecten te genereren, wat uiteindelijk leidt tot meervoudige verhalen over die objecten. Ik laat ook een paar onderwijsprojecten de revue passeren die focussen op door gebruikers gegenereerde content – meestal leraren en leerlingen – gebaseerd op gedigitaliseerde erfgoedobjecten. Deze projecten verhogen de betrokkenheid van leraren en leerlingen bij de content, terwijl tegelijkertijd hun creativiteit bevorderd wordt. Desondanks kunnen deze projecten zich op weinig zekerheid betreffende hun toekomst beroepen, voornamelijk door geldkwesties.

Hoofdstuk 4 schetst de methodologische benadering die gebruikt is voor het veldwerk. Eerst wordt de centrale onderzoeksvraag – hoe gaan leerlingen om met digitale media tijdens hun geschiedenisles? – toegelicht die ik baseerde op drie aannames die naar voren kwamen uit de literatuur over het onderwerp. Ik heb gekozen voor een etnografische benadering bij twee casestudies. Mijn belangstelling ging primair uit naar het begrijpen, het beschrijven en daarna het interpreteren van de manieren waarop digitale media en hulpbronnen door de geselecteerde scholieren in het voortgezet onderwijs werden gebruikt. Binnen deze benadering besloot ik mezelf de rol aan te meten van gematigd participerend observator door tussen de leerlingen te zitten, waar ik hun gesprekken, hun interacties met de leraren en met digitale media kon volgen, en niet-voorgestructureerde vraaggesprekken met hen kon houden. De laatste techniek bleek effectief in die zin dat de gesprekken daardoor 'natuurlijk' bleven. Mijn gedachtewisselingen met de leraren waren hoofdzakelijk gebaseerd op semigestructureerde topiclijsten. Hoewel ik ernaar streefde het vertrouwen van de leerlingen te winnen, heb ik niet gepoogd om als hun gelijke te worden beschouwd. Ik heb inhoudsanalyse gebruikt om in de geschreven werkstukken van de leerlingen twee variabelen te onderzoeken: het historische denken en de verscheidenheid aan bronnen. Ter besluit van dit hoofdstuk beschrijf ik in het kort de dataverzamelingstechnieken die ik heb ingezet, namelijk het maken van aantekeningen, geluids- en video-opnames en foto's.

Hoofdstuk 5 presenteert de bevindingen van de eerste casestudy bij het Baarnsch Lyceum in Baarn. Het begint met een beschrijving van de klas die betrokken was bij mijn onderzoek in de context van het bredere onderwijssysteem. De tweedejaars brugklas maakt onderdeel uit van het havo/vwo-traject. Ik beschrijf ook de 13- tot 14-jarige leerlingen, waarbij ik zowel hun aandachtige houding benadruk wanneer audiovisuele media werden gebruikt, als hun gebrek aan aandacht wanneer dit niet het geval was. Het verband tussen het gebruik van het Web en het historische denken van de leerlingen komt ook aan bod. In een aantal gevallen leek de aantrekkelijkheid van Webgebaseerde audiovisuele hulpbronnen niet alleen de aandacht van de leerlingen te triggeren, maar ook hun denkproces. In andere gevallen leidde het gemak waarmee de leerlingen omgingen met Webgebaseerde teksten en beelden [kopiëren-plakken, rippen, het downloaden van beelden] ertoe dat ze lange citaten combineerden die van het Web waren geplukt, hoewel dit wel enige ruimte overliet voor historisch denken. Deze bestonden meestal uit het identificeren van de bron en relevante fragmenten, om ze daarna om te zetten naar een nieuw samenhangend verhaal. In nog andere gevallen gebruikte een aantal leerlingen Webgebaseerde teksten op een manier die een mate van historisch denken impliceert: het parafraseren. Als laatste bekijk ik de door de leerlingen gebruikte Webbronnen en kom ik tot de conclusie dat de meeste leerlingen een verscheidenheid aan bronnen hadden gebruikt, waaronder persoonlijke, erfgoed-, godsdienstige, nieuws-, academische en onderwijskundige websites.

Hoofdstuk 6 gaat over de tweede casestudy bij de Helen Parkhurst Daltonschool in Almere. Eerst bespreek ik hoe de Daltonmethode van lesgeven en leren in combinatie met het één-kind-één-laptop beleid een sfeer creëerde die de leerlingen stimuleerde om het Web vaak te gebruiken, zowel gedurende de door de leraar gecontroleerde lestijd als gedurende de lestijd voor 'zelfstandig werk'. Het bleek dat de vrijheid die de leerlingen genoten in hun mediagebruik leidde tot diverse vormen van interactie met digitale media in het algemeen en met het Web in het bijzonder. Tijdens de door de leraar gecontroleerde lestijd zochten de leerlingen naar details over informatie die van de leraar of uit het schoolboek afkomstig was. Tijdens 'onafhankelijke' werktijd kwam er nog meer variatie in hun interactie met digitale media, variërend van het Websurfen op zoek naar relevante informatie voor hun werkstukken tot het gebruik als een manier om zich te ontspannen na hun intellectuele inspanningen. Wat dit betreft leek het Web een cruciale factor te zijn in het creëren van een sfeer die bevorderlijk is voor het leren. Ik bekijk ook de manieren waarop het Web een struikelblok vormde voor het historische denkproces van de leerlingen.

Het bleek dat de gereedschappen waarmee op het Web beelden worden gerangschikt het voor leerlingen gemakkelijker maakt om de afbeeldingen van concepten – waarover ze hebben geleerd of waarover ze hun werkstukken moeten schrijven – te vergelijken en te beoordelen. Bovendien konden de leerlingen door het gemak en de onbeperkte toegang tot de verschillende websites samenvattingen maken. Via bepaalde vormen van contentanalyse, contentharmonisering en contentstructuur – allemaal onderdeel van het maken van vergelijkingen, beoordelingen en selecties –, lukte het hen om korte geïllustreerde teksten en posters te maken. Tot slot ga ik in op de verscheidenheid aan Webbronnen die gebruikt werden voor WebQuest-werkstukken. Van tien soorten websites werd gebruikgemaakt, waaronder niet alleen Wikipedia, de Canon van Nederland en erfgoedwebsites, maar ook persoonlijke, onderwijskundige, commerciële, officiële en nieuwssites. Door het naast elkaar leggen van de informatie die ze bij elke site vonden, konden de leerlingen hun werkstukken maken.

Terwijl hoofdstukken 5 en 6 een beschrijvend karakter hebben, is hoofdstuk 7 meer analytisch van aard. In dit hoofdstuk breng ik de bevindingen van de casestudies in kaart in de vorm van patronen, waarmee we de verbindingen tussen de verschillende gebruikers en de invloed van het Web in onderlinge samenhang kunnen begrijpen. Op basis van deze bevindingen concludeer ik dat het Web en zijn eigenschappen, doordat ze zo aantrekkelijk zijn voor de leerlingen het historische denken stimuleert. Het onderliggende argument is dat het Web zijn kracht heeft bewezen om de historische interesse van leerlingen uit de Internetgeneratie te wekken. Eenmaal geïnteresseerd, neigen ze ernaar een historisch beoordelingsvermogen en andere denkvermogens te ontwikkelen. Vooral de Webgebaseerde video bleek historische interesse op te wekken, waardoor in veel gevallen de leerlingen dieper gingen graven om datgene wat niet werd gezegd te destilleren uit datgene dat wel gezegd werd. Bovendien speelt het Web een centrale rol bij multitasking, dat ook helpt bij het *disabstraheren*, d.w.z., als een virtuele plaats waar leerlingen op zoek kunnen gaan naar verklaringen voor opmerkingen van de leraar of voor verhalen uit het schoolboek. Dit fenomeen, dat in de ene casestudy in de vorm van een driehoekig leerproces tevoorschijn kwam, en opschorting en hervatting impliceert, of discontinuïteit binnen continuïteit, liet duidelijke tekens zien van een bevorderend rol in de ontwikkeling van het historische denken.

De brede verscheidenheid aan online bronnen van historische informatie vereiste van de leerlingen een aantal bronbeoordelingsvaardigheden die zelf ook het historische denken bevorderen, doordat de leerlingen de voor hun opdracht meest relevante details moesten extraheren en die daarna in hun werkstukken integreren, ofwel in de vorm van samenvattingen, ofwel als citaten. Rekening houdend met de recente literatuur op het gebied van de adolescente cognitieve psychologie, die onderscheid maakt tussen het denken van adolescenten en dat van deskundigen, beschouw ik het compileren van citaten niet als slechts een teken van intellectuele zwakte die door het Web verergerd wordt, maar eerder als iets dat een bepaalde mate van historisch denken vergt. Hoewel het waar is dat het compileren van citaten vergemakkelijkt wordt door het Web, stimuleert het Web ook vaardigheden als het vinden van de relevante Website of pagina, het juiste uittreksel en – nog belangrijker – het converteren van de verschillende uittreksels tot een samenhangend verhaal. Het maken van een samenvatting, iets dat een gevorderd denkvermogen impliceert en meer inspanning vergt, is nog een activiteit die het Web lijkt te bevorderen, vanwege de noodzaak om te zoeken naar de juiste bronnen en relevante details die elkaar versterken.

Binnen het geheel aan online bronnen die werden gebruikt voor werkstukken maak ik een onderscheid tussen conventionele en niet-conventionele bronnen. De analyse laat zien dat convergentie plaatsvond tussen de in de werkstukken gebruikte bronnen uit beide categorieën. Deze convergentie ontstond voornamelijk uit de nieuwe relevantie- en gezagscriteria die het Web en zijn zoekmachines opleggen, maar ook uit het feit dat de conventionaliteit van fysieke objecten niet overdraagbaar is in het virtuele domein. Deze factoren en andere hebben een vervaging van het onderscheid tussen conventionele en niet-conventionele bronnen tot gevolg gehad. Ik bespreek de ontluikende trend dat erfgoedinstellingen hun gedigitaliseerde objecten beschikbaar stellen op niet-conventionele platforms zoals

Wikipedia (in de werkstukken de meest frequent geciteerde van alle online bronnen). Analoog aan wat gaande is in andere door nieuwe media gedreven sectoren, stel ik voor dat de samenwerking met Wikipedia en soortgelijke websites een belangrijke impuls zou kunnen geven aan het geschiedenisonderwijs doordat ze conventionele bronnen zichtbaarder kan maken die zo in ongenade zijn gevallen vanwege de door zoekmachines ingestelde regels.

Tot slot van dit hoofdstuk probeer ik een verband te leggen tussen de bevindingen van de twee casestudies en twee discussies die momenteel gaande zijn in kringen van historici, namelijk over de digitale scheidslijn en de Nieuw Leren–Nieuw Erfgoed tweedeling. Dit onderzoek laat zien dat wanneer leerlingen permanente en onbeperkte toegang hadden tot de digitale media en ook de vrijheid hadden om zo vaak ze wilden op het Web te surfen, zij tot een vruchtbare multitasking kwamen en ze schriftelijke werkstukken produceerden die veel inspanning vergden. In de casestudy waarin de leerlingen tijdens de les geen digitale technologieën tot hun beschikking hadden en geen toegang tot het Web, gebruikten ze stiekem toch hun eigen digitale apparaten om op het Web te surfen. Deze leerlingen kwamen uiteindelijk met werkstukken op de proppen die veel weg hadden van citaatcompilaties.

Een laatste belangrijke bevinding betreft het raakvlak tussen het Nieuw Leren en het Nieuw Erfgoed, twee fenomenen die zeer afhankelijk zijn van digitale media, vooral van het Web. Terwijl het Nieuwe Leren de nadruk legt op autonomie en meer controle voor de leerling over het leerproces, betreft het Nieuwe Erfgoed niet alleen gedigitaliseerde objecten, maar ook andere verwante vormen van virtualisatie, waaronder animaties en simulaties. Een paar voorbeelden in dit onderzoek die de revue passeerden, laten zien dat het gebruik van Nieuw Erfgoed-objecten in het klaslokaal nieuwe manieren creëert om het verleden in beeld te brengen.

Bij wijze van conclusie bevat hoofdstuk 8 een aantal waarnemingen over wat digitale leerlingen lijken te doen met digitale media, de plaats die gedigitaliseerd erfgoed lijkt in te nemen als bron van historische informatie, en de bijdrage die digitale media lijken te leveren aan het bereiken van de hoefddoelen van het geschiedenisonderwijs. Leerlingen die tijdens lesuren wel toegang hebben tot het Web lijken conventionele en niet-conventionele bronnen te combineren, in het op meervoudige tekst gebaseerde historische denken en in multitasking. Het laatstgenoemde houdt in een neiging om te abstraheren van het *hier en nu.* De aanbeveling luidt dat leerlingen computers tot hun beschikking hebben, het liefst in eigendom, of op z'n minst dat hun de vrijheid wordt gegeven hun eigen toestellen te gebruiken – zij het onder begeleiding –in de lestijd. Het onderzoeken van andere onderwerpen, zoals de link tussen de digitale scheidslijn/het compileren van citaten en het *disabstraheer–verschijnsel* zijn onderwerpen voor verder onderzoek.

Dit hoofdstuk signaleert ook dat er in de twee geobserveerde klassen weinig gebruik werd gemaakt van gedigitaliseerde cultureel erfgoed, en persoonlijke websites van amateurhistorici zelfs beter scoorden. Dit komt door slechte hyperlinking waardoor de erfgoedwebsites moeilijk vindbaar zijn door zoekmachines. In de ogen van de leerlingen lijkt het alsof de erfgoedwebsites een reputatie hebben verworven als afbeeldingendatabases, daar ze eerder afbeeldingen presenteren dan verklarende en van links voorziene teksten. Er was bovendien geen enkele indicatie dat gedigitaliseerd erfgoed de nationale identiteit en burgerschap bevorderde, want leerlingen maakten veel meer gebruik van andere bronnen (zoals Wikipedia) met een meervoudig perspectief. Om het gebruik van gedigitaliseerde erfgoed te stimuleren, adviseer ik dat instellingen zich veel sterker gaan toeleggen op hyperlinking, zowel binnen de collecties als tussen de instellingen, om meer tekstuele informatie over de afbeeldingen te verschaffen, en ook dat ze zich bij de convergentietrend voegen, door actief en aanwezig te zijn op populaire onconventionele platformen zoals Wikipedia. Om van de hyperlinkingtactiek een succes te maken dienen erfgoedinstellingen op de eerste plaats een aantal zaken prijs te geven wat betreft bedrijfsidentiteit en belangen, en ook zullen ze bepaalde collectiebeheerstaken opnieuw moeten definiëren om meer integratie met de content te realiseren. Op de tweede plaats moet de impasse betreffende het gebruik van publieke middelen, die vele instellingen weerhoudt van het genereren van verkeer – en daarom winst – voor commerciële partijen, moet door de relevante autoriteiten worden aangepakt. Meer onderzoek is nodig naar de invloed en het nut van de huidige trend onder erfgoedinstellingen waarbij leraren en leerlingen niet alleen worden voorzien van content en platforms, maar ook van doe-het-zelf gereedschap waarmee ze content zelf kunnen creëren.

Als laatste benoemt dit hoofdstuk vier kerndoelen van het geschiedenisonderwijs in de onderbouw en worden een paar manieren besproken waarop het Web een bijdrage lijkt te leveren aan het realiseren daarvan. Een paar voorbeelden lieten zien hoe het Web de verwerving lijkt te faciliteren van het vermogen om: [1] gebeurtenissen, mensen en belangrijke ontwikkelingen te plaatsen binnen het kader van tien historische tijdperken; [2] de globale implicaties en connecties te identificeren van een lokaliteit, gebeurtenis of personage en *vice versa*; [3] te weten hoe historische bronnen moeten worden gebruikt; en [4] huidige spanningen of conflicten tegen hun historische achtergrond te bezien. Aangezien drie van de vier kerndoelen van het geschiedenisonderwijs in de ouderbouwjaren schakels betreffen – tussen gebeurtenissen, mensen, ontwikkelingen en historische tijdperken; tussen het lokale, het nationaal en het internationaal en *vice versa*; en tussen het verleden en het heden – en daar het Web voornamelijk over hyperlinking gaat, adviseer ik de volledige integratie van het Web in plannen en strategieën voor het geschiedenisonderwijs op een manier die al deze schakels benadrukt en bevordert. Een andere aanbeveling is dat leerlingen de mogelijkheid krijgen in aanraking te komen met allerlei historische bronnen, terwijl ze ook de kennis krijgen over hoe ze met iedere bron om moeten gaan. Verder langetermijnonderzoek, vooral onderzoek met een meer experimentele benadering, is nodig om te kijken naar de bijdrage van het Web aan de kerndoelen van het geschiedenisonderwijs.

Bibliographic References

Abbott, Chris (2001) *ICT: Changing Education* (London: RoutledgeFalmer).

Adviescommissie Geschiedenisonderwijs (1998) *Het verleden in de toekomst: Advies van de commissie geschiedenisonderwijs* (The Hague).

Agar, Michael ([1980] 1996) *The Professional Stranger: An Informal Introduction to Ethnography* (San Diego: Academic Press).

Anderson, Chris (2006) *The Long Tail: Why the Future of Business Is Selling Less of More* (New York: Hyperion).

Anderson, Chris (2009) *Free: The Future of a Radical Price* (New York: Hyperion).

Anderson, Chris & Wolf, Michael (2010) 'The Web Is Dead. Long Live the Internet', *Wired*, 17 August. <http://www.wired.com/magazine/2010/08/ff_webrip/all/1>

Asseldonk, Nancy van (2009a) 'Erfgoeddata in nieuwe samenhang' in Asseldonk, Nancy van, Mensch, Peter van & Vliet, Harry van (eds.) *Cultuur in Context: Erfgoeddata in nieuwe samenhang* (Amsterdam: Reinwardt Academie), pp. 9-19.

Asseldonk, Nancy van (2009b) 'Interview met Daan Hertogs over dromen en de weerbarstigheid van de praktijk', in Asseldonk, Nancy van, Mensch, Peter van & Vliet, Harry van (eds.) *Cultuur in Context: Erfgoeddata in nieuwe samenhang* (Amsterdam: Reinwardt Academie), pp. 21-29.

Asseldonk, Nancy van (2009c) 'Interview met Karel Dibbets over de zoektocht naar ontbrekende kennis', in Asseldonk, Nancy van, Mensch, Peter van & Vliet, Harry van (eds.) *Cultuur in Context: Erfgoeddata in nieuwe samenhang* (Amsterdam: Reinwardt Academie), pp. 42-53.

Atkinson, Paul & Hammersley, Martyn (1994) 'Ethnography and participant observation', in Denzin, Norman & Lincoln, Yvonna (eds.) *Handbook of qualitative research* (London: Thousand Oaks), pp. 248-261.

Atton, Chris & Hamilton, James (2008) *Alternative Journalism. Journalism Studies: Key Texts* (London: Sage).

Bakker, Tom & Bakker, Piet (2011) *Handboek Nieuwe Media: Digitale technologieeën begrijpen en gebruiken* (Alphen aan de Rijn: Kluwer).

Baldwin, Stanley ([1925] 1937) 'Truth and Politics' [1925] in Baldwin, Stanley, *On England and Other Addresses* (Harmondsworth: Penguin Books), pp. 33-98.

Bank, Jan & Rooy, Piet de (2004) 'Wat iedereen moet weten van de vaderlandse geschiedenis: Een canon van het Nederlands verleden', NRC Handelsblad, 30 October. <http://vorige.nrc.nl/europa/in_europa/article1623083.ece/De_canon_wat_iedereen_moet_weten_van_de_geschiedenis>

Barlow, Jeffrey (1998) 'Historical Research and Electronic Evidence: Problems and Promises', in Trinkle, D.A., (ed.) *Writing, Teaching, and Researching History in the Electronic Age: Historians and Computers* (New York: M.E. Sharpe), pp. 194-225.

Barthes, Roland (1973) *Le plaisir du texte* (Paris: Editions du Seuil).

Barton, Keith & Levstik, Linda (2004) *Teaching History for the Common Good* (Mahwah: Lawrence Erlbaum Associates).

Batelle, John (2005) *The Search: How Google and Its Rivals Rewrote the Rules of Business and Transformed Our Culture* (New York: Portfolio).

Baudrillard, Jean (1983) *Simulations* (New York: Semiotext[e]).

Beetham, Helen (2007) 'An approach to learning activity design', in Beetham, Helen & Sharpe, Rhona (eds.) *Rethinking pedagogy for a digital age* (London: Routledge), pp. 26-40.

Benjamin, Walter ([1936] 2008) 'The Work of Art in the Age of Its Reproducibility', in Benjamin, Walter, *The Work of Art in the Age of Its Reproducibility, and Other Writings on Media* (Cambridge: Harvard University Press), pp. 19-55.

Blanken, Henk (2003) 'De laatste geschiedenis', in Blanken, Henk & Deuze, Mark (eds.) *De mediarevolutie: 10 jaar www in Nederland* (Amsterdam: Boom), pp. 11-32.

Bloch, David (2007) *Aristotle on Memory and Recollection* (Leiden: Brill).

Boer, Pim den (1998a) 'Geschiedenis op school en aan de universiteit', in Boer, Pim den & Muller, G.W. (eds.) *Geschiedenis op school* (Amsterdam: KNAW), pp. 93-108.

Boer, Pim den (1998b) 'Het slagveld van het geschiedenisonderwijs', *Spiegel Historiael,* 4-33, April, pp. 136-139.

Bokhorst, S.C. (1924a) *Het Dalton Stelsel voor het Middelbaar en M.U.L. onderwijs* (Groningen: J.B. Wolters).

Bokhorst, S.C. (1924b) *Individueel onderwijs en het Dalton-plan* (Rotterdam: Nijgh & Van Ditmar's Uitgevers-Maatschappij).

Bolter, Jay David (1991) *Writing Space: The Computer, Hypertext, and the History of Writing* (Hillsdale: Lawrence Erlbaum Associates).

Bolter, Jay David & Grusin, Richard (1999) *Remediation: Understanding New Media* (Cambridge: MIT Press).

Borghuis, Gerdie (2009) 'Digitale ontsluiting van erfgoedinformatie: basis van denken en doen voor de erfgoedprofessional', in Asseldonk, Nancy van, Mensch, Peter van & Vliet, Harry van (eds.) *Cultuur in Context: Erfgoeddata in nieuwe samenhang* (Amsterdam: Reinwardt Academie), pp. 31-41.

Bossenbroek, M.P. & Berendse, M. (2009) 'Voorwoord', in Patijn, Maria, Doe, Erik van der, Langedoen, Andrea, Schouten, Dennis & Verheul, Ingebord (eds.) *Dertig in een dozijn: Een selectie uit twaalf jaar Metamorfoze Nieuws* (The Hague: KB & Nationaal Archief), pp. 7-8.

Bowker, Geoffrey (2007) 'The Past and the Internet', in Karaganis, Joe (ed.) *Structures of Participation in Digital Culture* (New York: Social Science Research Council), pp. 20-34.

Boxtel, Carla van (2009) *Geschiedenis, erfgoed en didactiek* (Amsterdam: Erfgoed Nederland).

Boxtel, Carla van & Drie, Jannet van (2004) 'Historisch redeneren: Verschillen tussen beginners en experts', *Kleio*, 1, pp. 8-14.

Boxtel, Carla van & Grever, Maria (in press) 'Between disenchantment and high expectations. History education in the Netherlands, ca. 1968–2008'. Book chapter.

Boxtel, Carla van & Oattes, Huub (1997) 'De mediatheek als impuls voor vernieuwingen', *Kleio,* 4, pp. 26-29.

Boxtel, Carla van & Timmer, Meriam (2002) 'De Middeleeuwen in beeld', *Kleio*, 6, pp. 9-16.

Boxtel, Carla van *et al.* (2008) *Brief aan de leden van de Kamer der Staten-Generaal* (Amsterdam: 30 October). Co-signed with 22 historians and history didactics scholars. <http://ivgd.nl/Historici_tegen_Canon.pdf>

boyd, danah (2008) 'Why Youth Heart Social Network Sites: The Role of Networked Publics in Teenage Social Life', in Buckingham, David (ed.) *Youth, Identity, and Digital Media* (Cambridge: The MIT Press), pp. 119–142.

Brandsma, Renze, Bouissaghouane, Mohamed, Brussee, Rogier, Smit, Saskia & Wartena, Christian (2009) 'Virtuele collectie openbare vermakelijkheden', in Asseldonk, Nancy van, Mensch, Peter van & Vliet, Harry van (eds.) *Cultuur in Context: Erfgoeddata in nieuwe samenhang* (Amsterdam: Reinwardt Academie), pp. 55-63.

Broekhuizen, Jolijn & Huysmans, Frank (2002) *Cultuur op het Web* (The Hague: SCP, June).

Brummelhuis, Alfons ten (2006) 'Aansluting onderwijs en digitale generatie', in Haan, Jos de & Hof, Christian van 't (eds.) *Jaarboek ICT en samenleving 2006: De digitale generatie* (Amsterdam: Boom), pp.125-141.

Bruns, Axel (2009) *Blogs, Wikipedia, Second Life, and Beyond: From Production to Produsage* (New York: Peter Lang).

Bryant, Josephine, Dobbie, Allison & Froud, Robert (2004) *Digitizing Cultural Resources: A Practical Guide for Public Libraries* (Gutersloh: Bertelsmann Stiftung).

Bryman, Alan & Cramer, Duncan (2004) 'Constructing Variables', in Hardy, Melissa & Bryman, Alan (eds.) *Handbook of Data Analysis* (London: SAGE), pp. 17-34.

Buckingham, David (2006) 'Is There a Digital Generation?', in Buckingham, David and Willett, Rebekah (eds.) *Digital Generations: Children, Young People, and New Media* (Mahwah: Lawrence Erlbaum Associates, Inc.), pp.1-13.

Buckingham, David (2007) *Beyond Technology: Children's Learning in the Age of Digital Culture* (Cambridge: Polity).

Burgess, Jean & Green, Joshua (2009) *YouTube: Online Video and Participatory Culture* (Cambridge: Polity Press).

Buskop, Herald *et al.* (1998) 'Het kaf en het koren', *Geschiedenis in de klas*, 50, January, pp. 4-20.

Bush, Vannevar (1945) 'As We May Think', *The Atlantic Monthly*, July. <http://www.theatlantic.com/doc/194507/bush>

Buzink, Robert (2009) 'Docenten spieken voortaan op eigen Wikipedia', *De Volkskrant*, 14 December. <http://www.volkskrant.nl/binnenland/article1327172.ece/Docenten_spieken_voortaan_op_eigen_Wikipedia>

Byrnes, James (2003) 'Cognitive Development During Adolescence', in Adams, Gerald and Berzonsky, Michael (eds.) *Blackwell Handbook of Adolescence* (Malden: Blackwell Publishing), pp. 227-246.

Cameron, Fiona (2008) 'The politics of Heritage Authorship: The case of digital heritage collections', in Kalay, Yehuda, Kvan, Thomas & Affleck, Janice (eds.) *New Heritage: New Media and Cultural Heritage* (London: Routledge), pp.170-184.

Cameron, Fiona (2010) 'Museum Collections, Documentation, and Shifting Knowledge Paradigms', in Parry, Ross (ed.) *Museums in a Digital Age* (London: Routledge), pp. 80-95.

Cameron, Fiona & Robinson, Helena (2007) 'Digital Knowledgescapes: Cultural, Theoretical, Practical, and Usage Issues Facing Museum Collection Databases in a Digital Epoch', in Cameron, Fiona, & Kaderdine, Sarah (eds.) *Theorizing Digital Cultural Heritage: A Critical Discourse* (Cambridge: The MIT Press), pp. 165-191.

Castells, Manuel ([1994] 1999) 'Flows, Networks, and Identities: A Critical Theory of the Informational Society', in Castells, Manuel, Flecha, Ramón, Freir, Paulo, Giroux, Henry, Macedo, Donaldo & Willis, Paul (eds.) *Critical Education in the New Information Age* (Lanham: Rowman & Littlefield), pp. 37-64.

Castells, Manuel (2006) 'The Network Society: From Knowledge to Policy', in Castells, Manuel & Cardoso, Gustave (eds.) *The Network Society: From Knowledge to Policy* (Washington D.C.: Center for Transatlantic Relations), pp. 3-21.

Castells, Manuel, Fernández-Ardèvol, Mireia, Qiu, Jack Linchuan & Sey, Araba (2007) *Mobile Communication and Society: A Global Perspective* (Cambridge: The MIT Press).

Certeau, Michel de (1974) 'L' operation historique', in Goff, Jacques le & Nora, Pierre (eds.) *Faire de l'histoire: Nouveaux problèmes* (Paris, Gallimard), pp. 3-41.

Chakrabarti, Soumen (2003) *Mining the Web: Discovering Knowledge from Hypertext Data* (San Francisco: Morgan Kaufmann).

Claparède, Jean-Louis (1931) *L' enseignement de l'histoire et l' esprit international* (Paris: Les Presses Universitaires).

Clayman, Steven & Gill, Virginia (2004) 'Conversation Analysis', in Hardy, Melissa & Bryman, Alan (eds.) *Handbook of Data Analysis* (London: SAGE), pp. 589-606.

Comenius, Jan Amos ([1657] 1953) *La grande didactique: Traité de l' Art universel d' enseigner tout à tous* (Paris: Presses Universitaires de France).

Commissie historische en maatschappilijke vorming (2001) *Verleden, heden en toekomst* (Enschede: SLO).

Commissie Ontwikkeling Nederlandse Canon (2006a) *Entoen.nu: de Canon van Nederland. Rapport van de Commissie Ontwikkeling Nederlandse Canon. Deel A* (The Hague: The Ministry of Education, Culture and Science, October).

Commissie Ontwikkeling Nederlandse Canon (2006b) *Entoen.nu: de Canon van Nederland. Rapport van de Commissie Ontwikkeling Nederlandse Canon. Deel B* (The Hague: The Ministry of Education, Culture and Science, October).

Conway, Paul (1994) 'Digitizing Preservation', *Library Journal*, 1 February, pp. 42-45.

Conway, Paul (2010) 'Rationale for Digitization and Preservation', in Parry, Ross (ed.) *Museums in a Digital Age* (London: Routledge), pp. 365-378.

Collingwood, Robin George ([1946] 1994) *The Idea of History* (Oxford: Oxford University Press). Revised Edition with Lectures 1926-1928.

Cornu, Bernard (2004) 'Networking and collective intelligence for teachers and learners', in Brown, Andrew & Davis, Niki (eds.) *World Yearbook of Education 2004: Digital technology, communities and education* (London: RoutledgeFalmer), pp. 40-45.

Cox, Richard (2004) *No Innocent Deposits: Forming Archives by Rethinking Appraisal* (Oxford: The Scarecrow Press).

Crowley, Jocelyn Elise (2007) 'Friend or Foe? Self-Expansion, Stigmatized Groups, and the Researcher-Participant Relationship', *Journal of Contemporary Ethnography*, vol. 36, nr. 6, December, pp. 603-630.

David, Shay (2007) 'Toward Participatory Expertise', in Karaganis, Joe (ed.), *Structures of Participation in Digital Culture* (New York: Social Science Research Council), pp. 176-196.

Davies, Aull Charlotte ([1998] 2008) *Reflexive Ethnography: A Guide to researching selves and others* (New York: Routledge). Second edition.

Descartes, René ([1637] 1996) *Discourse on the Method* (New Haven: Yale University Press).

Derrida, Jacques & Stiegler, Bernard (2002) *Echographies of Television. Filmed Interviews* (Cambridge: Polity).

Deuze, Mark (2007) *Media Work* (Cambridge: Polity Press).

DeWalt, Kathleen & DeWalt, Billie (2002) *Participant Observation: A Guide for Fieldworkers* (Oxford: AltaMira Press).

Dewey, John ([1909] 1933) *How We Think: A Restatement of the Relation of Reflective Thinking to the Educative Process* (New York: D.C. Heath and Company).

Dewey, John ([1916]1926) *Democracy and Education: An Introduction to the Philosophy of Education* (New York: MacMillan).

Dibbets, Karel (2006) 'Op zoek naar een digitale conservator', in Lauwers, Mieke & Hogekamp, Bert (eds.) *Audiovisueel: Van emancipatie tot professionalisering. Jaarboek 2005* ('s-Gravenhage: Stichting Archiefpublicaties), pp. 189-197.

Diepen-Oost, Frieda van (2000) *Archieven in de Etalage* (The Hague: Ministry of Education, Culture and Science, March).

Dijck, José van (2002) 'Geen beelden zonder woorden: Continuïtiet binnen een multimediale cultuur', in Gierstberg, Frits & Oosterbaan, Warna (eds.) *De plaatjesmaatschappij: Essays over beeldcultuur* (Rotterdam: Nai Uitgevers), pp. 36-46.

Dijck, José van (2007) *Mediated Memories in the Digital Age* (Stanford: Stanford University Press).

Dijck, José van (2009) 'Users like you? Theorizing agency in user-generated content', *Media, Culture & Society, 31-1,* pp. 41-58.

Dijck, José van (2010) 'Search engines and the production of academic knowledge', *International Journal of Cultural Studies*, 13-6, pp. 574–592.

Dijk, Jan van (2005) *The Deepening Divide: Inequality in the Information Society* (London: SAGE).

Domscheit-Berg, Daniel (2011) *Inside WikiLeaks: My Time with Julian Assange at the World's Most Dangerous Website* (New York: Crown Publishers).

Donner, Piet Hein (2006) *Wet op het voortgezet onderwijs (WVO). Besluit Kerndoelen onderbouw VO* (The Hague, 11 July). <http://www.st-ab.nl/wettennr06/0728-010_Besluit_kerndoelen_onderbouw_VO.htm>

Doppert, Monique (2002) *Internetpioniers: De eerste internetgeneratie* (Amsterdam: Otto Cramwinckel Uitgever).

Doppert, Monique (2003) 'De houdbaarheid van internetidealen', in Blanken, Henk & Deuze, Mark (eds.) *De mediarevolutie: 10 jaar www in Nederland* (Amsterdam: Boom), pp. 50-69.

Downes, Toni (2004) 'Playing and learning with digital technologies – at home and at school', in Brown, Andrew & Davis, Niki (eds.) *World Yearbook of Education 2004: Digital technology, communities and education* (London: RoutledgeFalmer), pp. 115-130.

Drie, Jannet van (2005) *Learning about the past with new technologies* (Utrecht: ICO). PhD dissertation.

Drie, Jannet van & Boxtel, Carla van (2008) 'Historical Reasoning: Towards a Framework for Analyzing Students' Reasoning about the Past', *Educational Psychological Review*, 20, pp. 87-110.

Driel, Hans van (1999) *Internet & communicatie* (Rotterdam: Media Business Press).

Driel, Hans van (2003) 'Multimedia en eigenaardige gebruikers', in Blanken, Henk & Deuze, Mark (eds.) *De mediarevolutie: 10 jaar www in Nederland* (Amsterdam: Boom), pp. 129-145.

Driel, Hans van (2004a) 'Inleiding', in Driel, Hans van (ed.) *Beeldcultuur* (Amsterdam: Boom), pp. 11-14.

Driel, Hans van (2004b) 'Beeldcultuur in een geletterde samenleving', in Driel, Hans van (ed.) *Beeldcultuur* (Amsterdam: Boom), pp. 15-40.

Dunk, Herman von der (1998) 'Geschiedenis: wat, waarvoor, voor wie?', in Boer, Pim den & Muller, G.W. (eds.) *Geschiedenis op school* (Amsterdam: KNAW), pp. 11-25.

Dunk, Herman von der (2005) 'Geschidenis als bijsluiter: Historisch besef in de schaduw van de actualiteit', *Spiegel Historiael*, 4/5 – 40, April/May, pp. 214-219.

Durkheim, Emile ([1922] 1966) *Education et Sociologie* (Paris: PUF).

Economou, Maria & Pujol Tost, Laia 'Educational Tool or Expensive Toy? Evaluating VR Evaluation and Its Relevance for Virtual Heritage', in Kalay, Yehuda, Kvan, Thomas & Affleck, Janice (eds.) *New Heritage: New Media and Cultural Heritage* (London: Routledge), pp. 242-260.

Eijk, Dick van (1994) 'Overheid laat te weinig zien op infobaan', *NRC Handelsblad,* 27 December, p.9. <http://archief.nrc.nl/index.php/1994/December/27/Overig/9/Overheid+laat+te+weinig+zien+op+infobaan>

Eijk, Dick van (1995) 'Supersnelle Internettoegang schept virtuele marktplaats; Kabel opent offensief tegen PTT', *NRC Handelsblad,* 05 May, p. 2 <http://archief.nrc.nl/?modus=l&text=Internet&hit=276&set=9>

Egmond, Annelou van, Büdgen, Frits & Koreneef, Leo (2005) *Pionieren met Passie: Directie ICT 1997-2005* (The Hague: Ministry of Education, Culture and Science, August).

Elmore, Richard (2009) 'Schooling Adolescents', in Lerner, Richard & Steinberg, Laurence (eds.) *Handbook of Adolescent Psychology. Volume 2: Contextual Influences on Adolescent Development* (Hoboken: John Wiley), pp. 193-227. Third Edition.

Emerson, Ralph Waldo ([1876] 2010) 'Inspiration', in Emerson, Ralph Waldo, *The Collected Works of Ralph Waldo Emerson. Volume VIII. Letters and Social Aims* (Cambridge: Harvard University Press).

Engelbart, Douglas (2004) 'The Click Heard Round The World', *Wired,* 12 January. <http://www.wired.com/wired/archive/12.01/mouse.html>

Erkens, Gijsbert, Jaspers, Jos & Schijf, Hermina (2000) 'Computerondersteuning bij zelfstandig en coöperatief leren', in Stokking, Karel, Erkens, Gijsbert, Versloot, Bert & Wessum, Loes van (eds.) *Van onderwijs naar leren: Tussen het aanbieden van kennis en het faciliteren van leerprocessen* (Apeldoorn: Garant), pp. 129-142.

Fèbvre, Lucien & Martin, Henri-Jean ([1958] 1984) *The Coming of the Book: The Impact of Printing 1450-1800* (London: Verso).

Feldman, Susan (1997) '"It was here a minute ago!": archiving the Net', *Searcher,* 5(9), October, pp. 52-64. <http://search.ebscohost.com/login.aspx?direct=true&db=rzh&AN=1999014453&loginpage=Login.asp&site=ehost-live>

Fine, Gary Alan & Sandstrom, Kent (1988) *Knowing Children: Participant Observation with Minors. Qualitative Research Methods Series 15* (Newbury Park: SAGE).

Fisher, Peter (2002) *Thinking Through History* (Cambridge: Chris Kington Publishing). With Ian Wilkinson & David Leat.

Flew, Terry ([2002] 2008) *New Media: An Introduction* (Oxford: Oxford University Press). Third edition.

Franzosi, Roberto (2004) 'Content Analysis', in Hardy, Melissa & Bryman, Alan (eds.) *Handbook of Data Analysis* (London: SAGE), pp. 547-565.

Gabriel, Trip (2011) 'Speaking Up in Class, Silently, via Social Media', *New York Times*, 13 May, pp. 1 & 16 . <http://www.nytimes.com/2011/05/13/education/13social.html>

Gal, Roger (1972) *Histoire de l'éducation* (Paris: PUF).

Gallie, Walter Bryce (1964) *Philosophy and the Historical Understanding* (London: Chatto & Windus).

Gates, Bill ([1995] 2008) *The Road Ahead* (Harlow: Pearson Education Limited). With Nathan Myhrvold & Peter Rinearson.

Gerrits, Robin (2009) ' "Wikipedia" voor het onderwijs staat online', *De Volkskrant*, 14 December. <http://www.volkskrant.nl/binnenland/article1327415.ece/Wikipedia_voor_het_onderwijs_staat_online>

Gierstberg, Frits & Oosterbaan, Warna (2002) 'Inleiding: de plaatjesmaatschappij', in Gierstberg, Frits & Oosterbaan, Warna (eds.) *De plaatjesmaatschappij: Essays over beeldcultuur* (Rotterdam: Nai Uitgevers), pp. 7-9.

Giesen, Peter (2003) 'In den beginne was het beeld', in Blanken, Henk & Deuze, Mark (eds.) *De mediarevolutie: 10 jaar www in Nederland* (Amsterdam: Boom), pp. 97-110.

Gillmor, Dan (2004) *We the Media: Grassroots Journalism by the People, for the People* (Sebastopol: O'Reilly Media, Inc.).

Glassner, Amnon, Weinstock, Michael & Neuman, Yair (2005) 'Pupils' evaluation and generation of evidence and explanation in argumentation', *British Journal of Educational Psychology*, 75, pp. 105–118.

Goldin-Meadow, Susan, Alibali, Martha Wagner & Church Breckinridge (1993) 'Transitions in Concept Acquisition: Using the Hand to Read the Mind', *Psychological Review*, 100 - 2, pp. 279-297.

Goodman, Greg (2008) 'Critical Thinking: How Good Questions Affect Classrooms', in Goodman, Greg (ed.) *Educational Psychology: An Application of Critical Constructivism* (New York: Peter Lang), pp. 33-52.

Grever, Maria (1998) 'Opvattingen en misvattingen over het geschiedenisonderwijs', in Boer, Pim den & Muller, G.W. (eds.) *Geschiedenis op school* (Amsterdam: KNAW), pp. 27-48.

Grever, Maria (2005) 'Wat doen we met de canon?', in Wilschut, Arie (ed.) *Zinvol, Leerbaar, Haalbaar: Over geschiedenisonderwijs en de rol van een canon daarin* (Amsterdam: Vossiuspers), pp. 21-29.

Grever, Maria (2006) 'Nationale identiteit en historisch besef: De risico' s van een canon in de postmoderne samenleving' in Grever, Maria, Jonker, Ed, Ribbens, Kees & Stuurman, Siep (eds.) *Controverses rond de canon* (Assen: Van Gorcum), pp. 29-58.

Grever, Maria (2007) 'Plurality, Narrative and the Historical Canon' in Grever, Maria & Stuurman, Siep (eds.) *Beyond the Canon: History for the Twenty-First Century* (New York: Palgrave MacMillan), pp. 31-47.

Grever, Maria, Jonker, Ed, Ribbens, Kees & Stuurman, Siep (2006) 'Het behouden huis: Een commentaar op De canon van Nederland', in Grever, Maria, Jonker, Ed, Ribbens, Kees & Stuurman, Siep (eds.) *Controverses rond de canon* (Assen: Van Gorcum), pp.106-116.

Grossman, Lev (2006) 'Time's Person of the Year: You', *Time,* 13 December. <http://www.time.com/time/printout/0,8816,1569514,00.html>

Grusin, Richard (2010) *Premediation: Affect and Mediality After 9/11* (New York: Palgrave MacMillan).

Gurian, Elaine Heumann (2004) 'What Is the Object of This Exercise? A Meandering Exploration of the Many Meanings of Objects in Museums', in Anderson, Gail (ed.) *Reinventing the Museum: Historical and Contemporary Perspectives on the Paradigm Shift* (Walnut Creek: Altamira Press), pp. 269-283.

Gusdorf, Georges (1991) *Auto-bio-graphie. Lignes de vie 2* (Paris: Editions Odile Jacob).

Haan, Jos de, Huysmans, Frank & Steyaert, Jan (2002) *Van huis uit digitaal* (The Hague: SCP). <http://www.scp.nl/publicaties/boeken/9037700896/Van_huis_uit_digitaal.pdf>

Haan, Jos de & Hof, Christian van 't (2006) 'De digitale generatie', in Haan, Jos de & Hof, Christian van 't (eds.) *Jaarboek ICT en sameleving 2006: De digitale generatie*, (Amsterdam: Boom), pp. 11-23.

Haan, Jos de & Steyaert, Jan (2003) 'ICT en samenleving', in Haan, Jos de & Steyaert, Jan (eds.) *Jaarboek 2003: ICT en samenleving. De Sociale dimensie van technologie* (Amsterdam: Boom), pp. 11-20.

Haan, Jos de, Mast, Renée, Varekamp, Marleen & Janssen, Susanne (2006) *Bezoek onze site: Over de digitalisering van het culturele aanbod* (The Hague: SCP).

Hack-Tic (1989) 'Hackers beginnen Nederlands eerste kritische computerblad', *Hack-Tic,* no. 1.

Hack-Tic (1993) 'Hacking at the End of the Universe: Belevenissen van de organisatie', *Hack-Tic*, no. 22-23.

Haenens, Leen d' (2003) 'ICT in de multiculturele samenleving', in Haan, Jos de & Steyaert, Jan (eds.) *Jaarboek 2003: ICT en samenleving. De Sociale dimensie van technologie* (Amsterdam: Boom), pp. 91-112.

Halavais, Alexander (2008) 'The Hyperlink as organizing Principle', in Turow, Joseph & Tsui, Lokman (eds.) *The Hyperlinked Society: Questioning Connections in the Digital Age* (Ann Arbor: The University of Michigan Press), pp 39-55.

Hammersley, Martyn & Gomm, Roger (2000) 'Introduction', in Gomm, Roger, Hammersley, Martyn & Foster, Peter (eds.) *Case Study Method* (London: SAGE), pp. 1-16.

Hardy, Melissa (2004) 'Summarizing Distributions', in Hardy, Melissa & Bryman, Alan (eds.) *Handbook of Data Analysis* (London: SAGE), pp. 35-64.

Hardy, Melissa & Bryman, Alan (2004) 'Introduction: Common Threads among Techniques of Data Analysis', in Hardy, Melissa & Bryman, Alan (eds.) *Handbook of Data Analysis* (London: SAGE), pp. 1-13.

Harwood, Paul & Asal, Victor (2007) *Educating the First Digital Generation* (Westport: Praeger).

Havekes, Harry, Aardema, Arnoud, Rooijen, Bas van & Vries, Jan de (2005) *Geschiedenis Doordacht. Actief Historische Denken 2* (Boxmeer: Stichting Geschiedenis, Staatsinrichting en Educatie).

Havekes, Harry, Vries, Jan de & Oolbekking, Helma (2009) 'Geschiedenis doordacht: Bevlogen verder met het vak', in Imants, Jeroen & Oolbekkink, Helma (eds.) *Leren denken binnen het schoolvak* (Apeldoorn: Garant), pp. 43-61.

Havekes, Harry, Vries, Jan de & Aardema, Arnoud (2010) 'Active Historical Thinking: Designing Leaning Activities to Stimulate Domain-Specific Thinking', *Teaching History*, 139 (June), pp. 52-59.

Haydn, Terry (2003) ' Computer and History: Rhetoric, reality and the lessons of the past', in Haydn, Terry & Counsell, Christine (eds.) *History, ICT and Learning in the Secondary School* (London: RoutledgeFalmer), pp. 11-37.

Hazen, Dan, Horrell, Jeffrey & Merrill-Oldham, Jan (1998) *Selecting Research Collections for Digitization* (Amsterdam: European Commission on Preservation and Access).

Herman, Edward & Chomsky, Noam (1988) *Manufacturing Consent: The Political Economy of the Mass Media* (New York: Pantheon Books).

Herman, Edward & McChesney, Robert (1997) *The Global Media: The New Missionaries of Corporate Capitalism* (London: Cassell).

Hermans, Loek (2001) *Onderwijs on line: actualisatie* (The Hague, March). <http://www.minocw.nl/documenten/actualisatie.pdf>

Hermes, Joke & Janssen, Skylla (2006) 'De nieuwe contentmakers', in Haan, Jos de & Hof, Christian van 't (eds.) *Jaarboek ICT en sameleving 2006: De digitale generatie* (Amsterdam: Boom), pp. 159-175.

Hijmans, Ellen (2006) 'De rol van sensitizing concepts: Spiritualiteit in de talkshow van Oprah Winfrey', in Wester, Fred (ed.) *Inhoudsanalyse theorie en praktijk* (Place?: Kluwer), pp. 121-138.

Hindman, Matthew (2009) *The Myth of Digital Democracy* (Princeton: Princeton University Press).

Historical Newspaper Project (2007), Minutes of the meeting of the Scientific Advisory Commission (The Hague: The National Library, 13 April). Project's internal document.

Historical Newspaper Project (2007), Minutes of the meeting of the Scientific Advisory Commission (The Hague: The National Library, 14 November). Project's internal document.

Hoeven, Maria van der (2006) 'Taakopdracht voor de commissie Ontwikkeling Nederlandse Canon', in Commissie Ontwikkeling Nederlandse Canon (2006a) *Entoen.nu: de Canon van Nederland. Rapport van de Commissie Ontwikkeling Nederlandse Canon. Deel A* (The Hague: The Ministry of Education, Culture and Science, October), p. 95.

Hoeven, Maria van der & Pechtold, Alexander (2006) 'Letter to the Speaker of the House of Representatives. Object: Centre for history and democracy' (The Hague, 22 June). <http://www.minocw.nl/documenten/1438.pdf>

Howard, Michael (1991) *The Lessons of History* (New Haven: Yale University Press).

Howe, Jeff (2009) *Crowdsourcing: How the Power of the Crowd is Driving the Future of Business* (London: Random House Business Books).

Hutchby, Ian & Moran-Ellis, Jo (2001) 'Introduction: Relating children, technology and culture', in Hutchby, Ian & Moran-Ellis, Jo (eds.) *Children, Technology and Culture The impact of technologies in children's everyday lives* (London: RoutledgeFalmer), pp. 1-10.

Hughes, Lorna (2004) *Digitizing collections: strategic issues for the information manager* (London: Facet).

Huizinga, Johan (1948) 'Het historisch museum', in Huizinga, Johan, *Verzamelde werken II: Nederland* (Haarlem: H.D. Tjeenk Willink & Zoon N.V.), pp. 559-578.

Hutjes, Jan (2000) 'De casestudy als strategie in het toegepast onderzoek', in Wester, Fred, Smaling, Adri & Mulder, Lambert (eds.) *Praktijkgericht kwalitatief onderzoek* (Bussum: Coutinho), pp. 63-84.

Hutjes, Jan & Buuren, Hans van ([1992] 1996) *De gevalstudie: Strategie van kwalitatief onderzoek* (Heerlen: Open universiteit).

Huysmans, Frank & Haan, Jos de (2003) 'De langzame revolutie', in Blanken, Henk & Deuze, Mark (eds.) *De mediarevolutie: 10 jaar www in Nederland* (Amsterdam: Boom), pp.168-192.

Huyssens, Andreas (2003) *Present Pasts: Urban Palimpsests and the Politics of Memory* (Stanford: Stanford University Press).

Iggers, Georg G. (1999) 'The Role of Professional Historical Scholarship in the Creation and Distortion of Memory', in Ollila, Anne (ed.) *Historical Perspectives on Memory* (Helsinki: SHS), pp. 49- 67.

Introna, Lucas & Nissenbaum, Helen (2000a) 'Defining the Web: The Politics of Search Engines', *Computer*, January, pp. 54-62 <http://cs.wellesley.edu/~cs315/Papers/Introna_politics_SE.pdf>

Introna, Lucas & Nissenbaum, Helen (2000b) 'Shaping the Web: Why the Politics of Search Engines Matters', *The Information Society*, 16:3, pp. 169-185

Ito, Mizuko (2007) 'Technologies of the Childhood Imagination: *Yu-Gi-Oh!* Media Mixes, and Everyday Cultural Production', in Karaganis, Joe (ed.) *Structures of Participation in Digital Culture* (New York: Social Science Research Council), pp. 88-110.

Ito, Mizuko, Baumer, Sonja, Bittanti, Matteo, boyd, danah, Cody, Rachel *et al.* (2010) *Hanging Out, Messing Around, and Geeking Out: Kids Living and Learning with New Media* (Cambridge: The MIT Press).

IVGD [Instituut voor Geschiedenisdidaktiek] (2007) *Een beter geschiedenisonderwijs met een canon? De reactie van het IVGD* (Amsterdam).

Jansz, Jeroen (2006) 'De uitdaging van videogames', in Haan, Jos de & Hof, Christian van 't (eds.) *Jaarboek ICT en sameleving 2006: De digitale generatie* (Amsterdam: Boom), pp. 63-79.

Jenkins, Henry ([2006] 2008) *Convergence Culture: Where Old Media and New Media Collide* (New York: New York University Press).

Jenkins, Henri, Clinton, Katie, Purushotma, Ravi, Robison, Alice & Weigel, Margaret (2009) *Confronting the Challenges of Participatory Culture: Media Education for the 21st Century* (Cambridge: The MIT Press).

Jonker, Ed (2006) 'Sotto Voce: Identiteit, burgerschap en de nationale canon', in Grever, Maria, Jonker, Ed, Ribbens, Kees & Stuurman, Siep (eds.) *Controverses rond de canon* (Assen: Van Gorcum), pp. 3-28.

Joyce, Michael (1995) *Of Two Minds: Hypertext Pedagogy and Poetics* (Ann Arbor: University of Michigan Press).

Kalay, Yehuda (2008) 'Introduction: Preserving cultural heritage through digital media', in Kalay, Yehuda, Kvan, Thomas & Affleck, Janice (eds.) *New Heritage: New media and cultural heritage* (London: Routledge), pp. 1-10.

Kanselaar, Gellof & Andriessen, Jerry (2000) 'Ontwikkelingen in leertheoreën en leeromgevingen', in Stokking, Karel, Erkens, Gijsbert, Versloot, Bert & Wessum, Loes van (eds.) *Van onderwijs naar leren: Tussen het aanbieden van kennis en het faciliteren van leerprocessen* (Apeldoorn: Garant), pp. 89-102.

Kanselaar, Gellof, Jong, Ton de, Andriessen, Jerry & Goodyear, Peter (2000) 'New Technologies', in Simons, Robert-Jan, Linden, Jos van der & Duffy, Tom (eds.) *New Learning* (Dordrecht: Kluwer Academic Publishers), pp. 55-81.

KB [*Koninklijke Bibliotheek* – National Library of the Netherlands] (2009) *Annual Report 2009* (The Hague, KB). <http://kb.nl/bst/jaar/kb2009/eng/kbannualreport2009.pdf>

Keen, Andrew (2007) *The Cult of the Amateur: How Today's Internet Is Killing Our Culture* (New York: Doubleday/Currency).

Kennisnet (2009) *Vier in Balans Monitor 2009: ICT in het onderwijs: de stand van zaken* (Zoetermeer, August).

Kennisnet (2010) *Four in Balance Monitor 2010: ICT at Dutch Schools* (Zoetermeer).

Ketelaar, Eric (1997) 'Can We Trust Information?', *The International information & library review*, 29, pp. 333–338.

King, Geoff & Krzywinska, Tanya (2002) 'Introduction: Cinema/ Videogames/ Interfaces', in King, Geoff & Krzywinska, Tanya (eds.) *Screenplay: Cinema/ videogames/ interfaces* (London: Wallflower Press), pp. 1-32.

Klaczynski, Paul (2001) 'Analytic and Heuristic Processing Influences on Adolescent Reasoning and Decision-Making', *Child Development*, Vol. 72, No. 3 (May – June), pp. 844-861.

Kooij, Pim (1996) 'De wereld in een waterdruppel', *Kleio*, 4, pp. 4-11.

Kozma, Robert (1994) 'Will Media Influence Learning? Reframing the Debate', *Educational Technology Research and Development*, 42-2, pp. 7-19.

Kuhn, Deanna (2009) 'Adolescent Thinking', in Lerner, Richard & Steinberg, Laurence (eds.) *Handbook of Adolescent Psychology. Volume 1: Individual Bases of Adolescent Development* (Hoboken: John Wiley), pp. 152-186. Third Edition.

Kuhn, Deanna & Franklin, Sam (2008) 'The Second Decade: What Develops (and Why)?', in Damon, William & Lerner, Richard (eds.) *Child and Adolescent Development: An Advanced Course* (Hoboken: John Wiley & Sons), pp. 517-550.

Kvale, Steiner (1996) *InterViews: An Introduction to qualitative Research Interviewing* (London: SAGE Publications).

Landow, George & Delany, Paul (1991) 'Hypertext, Hypermedia and Literary Studies: The State of the Art', in Delany, Paul & Landow, George (eds.) *Hypermedia and Literary Studies* (Cambridge: The MIT Press), pp. 3-50.

Latour, Bruno ([1991] 1993) *We Have Never Been Modern* (New York: Harvester Wheatsheaf).

Lawson, Anton (1995) *Science Teaching and the Development of Thinking* (Belmont, Wadsworth Publishing Company).

Lee, Peter (1984) 'Why Learn History?', in Dickinson, Alaric Keith, Lee, Peter & Rogers, P. J. (eds.) *Learning History* (London : Heinemann Educational Books), pp. 1-19.

Lee, Peter (2004) 'Understanding History', in Sexias, Peter (ed.) *Theorizing Historical Consciousness* (Toronto: University of Toronto Press), pp. 129-164.

Lee, Peter (2007) 'From National Canon to Historical Literacy' in Grever, Maria & Stuurman, Siep (eds.) *Beyond the Canon: History for the Twenty-First Century* (New York: Palgrave MacMillan), pp. 48-62.

Leek, John & Slot, Pim (2006) 'Audiovisuele bronnen en het nieuwe leren', in Lauwers, Mieke & Hogekamp, Bert (eds.) *Audiovisueel: Van emancipatie tot professionalisering. Jaarboek 2005* ('s-Gravenhage: Stichting Archiefpublicaties), pp. 156-165.

Leeuw-Rood, Joke van der (1997) 'Inleiding', in Bouwman, Will (ed.) *Youth and History in Nederland* ('s-Hertogenbosch: KPC Groep), pp. 3-4.

Leeuw-Rood, Joke van der (1998) 'Geschiedenis op school in Europa', in Boer, Pim den & Muller, G.W. (eds.) *Geschiedenis op school* (Amsterdam: KNAW), pp. 49-62.

Leeuw-Rood, Joke van der (2001) 'The Past is no History! Controversial History Teaching as a Hazardous Challenge for the European History Teacher', in Pellens, Karl, Behre, Goeran, Erdmann, Elisabeth, Meier, Frank & Popp, Susanne (eds.) *Historical Consciousness and History Teaching in a Globalizing Society* (Frankurt am Main: Peter Lang), pp. 71-80.

Leeuw-Rood, Joke van der & Kuiper, Marjon (1997) 'Jongeren en geschiedenis – Is historisch besef te meten?', in Bouwman, Will (ed.) *Youth and History in Nederland* ('s-Hertogenbosch: KPC Groep), pp.13-19.

Leigh, David & Harding, Luke (2011) *WikiLeaks: Inside Julian Assange's War on Secrecy* (New York: Public Affairs).

Lenhart, Amanda, Lewis, Oliver & Rainie, Lee (2001) *Teenager life online* (Washington D.C.: June). <http://www.pewinternet.org/pdfs/PIP_Teens_Report.pdf>

Lévy, Pierre (1997) *L' Intelligence collective: Pour une anthropologie du cyberespace* (Paris: Les Editions La Découverte).

Lévy, Pierre (1998) *Becoming Virtual: Reality in the Digital Age* (New York: Plenum Press).

Lévy, Pierre (2010) 'Building a Universal Digital Memory', in Parry, Ross (ed.) *Museums in a Digital Age* (London: Routledge), pp. 107-115.

Licklider, Joseph Carl (1960) 'Man-Computer Symbiosis in IRE Transactions on Human Factors', *Electronics*, vol. HFE-1, March, pp. 4-11. <http://groups.csail.mit.edu/medg/people/psz/Licklider.html>

Ligtenberg, Lucas (2005) 'De terugkeer van het vaderlansch gevoel', *Spiegel Historiael*, 6 – 40, June, pp. 237-241.

Limburg, Dirk (1993) '"Digitale stad" geeft Amsterdam nieuwe dimensie', *NRC Handelsblad* , 28 December, p. 3. <http://archief.nrc.nl/index.php/1993/December/28/Binnenland/3/%22Digitale+stad%27+geeft+Amsterdam+nieuwe+dimensie>

Limburg, Dirk (1994) 'Amsterdam heeft er een kleine stad bij', *NRC Handelsblad*, 17 January, p. 2. <http://archief.nrc.nl/index.php/1994/Januari/17/Binnenland/2/Amsterdam+heeft+er+een+kleine+stad+bij>

Lincoln, Yvonna & Cuba, Egon (2000) 'The Only Generalization Is: There Is No Generalization', in Gomm, Roger, Hammersley, Martyn & Foster, Peter (eds.) *Case Study Method* (London: SAGE), pp. 27-44.

Linde, Hans van der (1997) 'De eigen omgeving als historische informatiebron', *Kleio*, 5, pp. 2-4.

Linden, Jos van der (2000) 'Leren in samenspraak: Van theorie via onderzoek naar onderwijs- en opleidingspraktijk', in Stokking, Karel, Erkens, Gijsbert, Versloot, Bert & Wessum, Loes van (eds.) *Van onderwijs naar leren: Tussen het aanbieden van kennis en het faciliteren van leerprocessen* (Apeldoorn: Garant), pp. 103-116.

Ling, Rich (2004) *The Mobile Connection: The Cell Phone's Impact on Society* (Amsterdam: Morgan Kaufmann Publishers).

Livingstone, Sonia (2007) 'Interactivity and Participation on the Internet: Young People's Response to the Civic Sphere', in Dahlgren, Peter (ed.) *Young Citizens and New Media: Learning for Democratic Participation* (London: Routledge), pp. 103-124.

Locke, John ([1693] 2000) *Some Thoughts Concerning Education* (Oxford: Clarendon Press).

Lowenthal, David (1985) *The Past is a Foreign Country* (Cambridge: Cambridge University Press).

Luyendijk, Wubby (1998) 'Scholen wachten nog steeds op digitale revolutie', *NRC Handelsblad*, 10 June, p. 2. <http://archief.nrc.nl/index.php/1998/Juni/10/Overig/2/Scholen+wachten+nog+steeds+op+digitale+revolutie>

Lynch, A.J. (1924) *Individual Work and the Dalton Plan* (London: George Philip & Son).

Maarleveld, Reinard (1996) 'Internet in de les', *Kleio*, 6, pp. 26-27.

Manovich, Lev (2001) *The Language of New Media* (Cambridge: MIT Press).

Manovich, Lev (2010) 'Database as Symbolic Form', in Parry, Ross (ed.) *Museums in a Digital Age* (London: Routledge), pp. 64-71.

Marijnissen, Jan (2005) 'Een nationaal, historisch museum: Historisch besef verdient herwaardering', *Kleio*, 2, pp. 2-6.

Marijinissen, Jan & Verhagen, Maxime (2006) 'Huis van de Geschiedenis', *Trouw*, 13 May. <http://www.trouw.nl/achtergrond/Dossiers/article1284940.ece>

Mayes, Terry & Freitas, Sara de (2007) 'Learning and e-learning: The role of theory', in Beetham, Helen & Sharpe, Rhona (eds.) *Rethinking pedagogy for a digital age* (London: Routledge), pp. 13-25.

McClung Lee, Alfred (1970) 'On Context and Relevance', in Jabocs, Glenn (ed.) *The Participant Observer* (New York: Gearge Braziller), pp. 3-16.

Mensch, Peter van (2009) 'Inleiding', in Asseldonk, Nancy van, Mensch, Peter van & Vliet, Harry van (eds.) *Cultuur in Context: Erfgoeddata in nieuwe samenhang* (Amsterdam: Reinwardt Academie), pp. 5-7.

Mijnhardt, Wijnand (2005) 'De zinloosheid van een nationale canon', in Wilschut, Arie (ed.) *Zinvol, Leerbaar, Haalbaar: Over geschiedenisonderwijs en de rol van een canon daarin* (Amsterdam: Vossiuspers UvA), pp. 11-20.

Milstein, Sarah & Dornfest, Rael (2004) *Google: The Missing Manual* (Cambridge: O'Reilly Media).

Ministry of Education, Culture and Science (1997) *Commissie geschiedenisonderwijs ingesteld* (The Hague, 15 September). Press release. <http://www.minocw.nl/actueel/persberichten/11607/Commissie-geschiedenisonderwijs-ingesteld.html>

Ministry of Education, Culture and Science (1999) *Kennisnet krijgt centrale rol bij ICT in het onderwijs: Ministerraad stemt in met hoofdlijnen nieuwe aanpak* (The Hague, 19 February). Press release. <http://www.minocw.nl/persberichten/11609>

Ministry of Education, Culture and Science (2006) *Oude boeken op het net: onderzoek makkelijker* (The Hague, 5 July). Press release. <http://www.minocw.nl/actueel/persberichten/12001/Oudeboeken-op-het-net-onderzoek-makkelijker.html>

Moshman, David (1999) *Adolescent Psychological Development: Rationality, Morality, and Identity* (Mahwah: Lawrence Erlbaum Associates).

Motivaction (2006) *Internet, een populair medium voor het zoeken van informatie bij schoolopdrachten: Een onderzoek onder scholieren van 12-17 jaar* (18 April)

Mulder, Fred (2009) *Programmaplan Wikiwijs 2009 – 2011 – ...*, (July). <http://www.rijksoverheid.nl/bestanden/documenten-en-publicaties/kamerstukken/2009/08/04/bijlage-programmaplan-wikiwijs-2009-2011/146048a.pdf>

Museumvereniging & DEN [Digitaal Erfgoed Nederland] (2008) *ICT-gebruik in musea* (Almere: Reekx Advies, April). <http://www.den.nl/getasset.aspx?id=Website/rapport_ICT-gebruik_in_musea_met_bijlage[1].pdf&assettype=attachments>

NAMM [De Nationale Academie voor Media & Maatschappij] (2011) *Mobieltjesbeleid op scholen ware chaos: Samenvatting onderzoek 'Mobieltjes op school' door de Nationale Academie voor Media & Maatschappij, januari – mei 2011* (Amsterdam, May). <http://www.mediaenmaatschappij.nl/images/stories/pdf/Samenvatting%20onderzoek%20%27Mobieltjesbeleid%20op%20scholen%20ware%20chaos%27,%20mei%202011.pdf>

Nationaal Archief (2011) *Nationaal Archief-foto's op Wikipedia: ex-premier Gulielmus Kok zeer populair* (The Hague, 28 January). <http://www.nationaalarchief.nl/nieuws/nieuws/nationaal-archief-foto-s-op-wikipedia.asp?ComponentID=17607&SourcePageID=16483#1>

Nevaer, Louis (2002) *The Dot-Com Debacle and the Return to Reason* (Westport: Quorum Books).

Netelenbos, Tineke (1998) *Toespraak van mevrouw T. Netelenbos, staatssecretaris van Onderwijs, Cultuur en Wetenschappen bij de aanbieding van het rapport van de Commissie Geschiedenisonderwijs van 16 april 1998 in Nieuwspoort te Den Haag* (The Hague, 16 April). <http://www.minocw.nl/actueel/toespraken/483/toespraak-van-mevrouw-t-netelenbos-staatssecretaris-van-onderwijs-cultuur-en-wetenschappen-bij-de-aanbieding-van-het-rapport-van-de-commissie-geschiedenisonderwijs-van-16-april-1998-in-nieuwspoort-te-den-haag.html>

Negroponte, Nicholas (1995) *Being Digital* (London: Hodder and Stoughton).

Neuendorf, Kimberley (2002) *The Content Analysis Guidebook* (London: SAGE, 2002).

Nietzsche, Friedrich ([1874] 1980) *On the Advantage and Disadvantage of History for Life* (Cambridge: Hackett Publishing Company, Inc.).

Lévy, Maurice, Niggemann, Elisabeth & Decker, Jacques de (2011) *The New Renaissance: Report of the 'Comité des Sages'. Reflection Group on Bringing Europe's Cultural Heritage Online* (Brussels, 10 January). <http://ec.europa.eu/information_society/activities/digital_libraries/doc/refgroup/final_report_cds.pdf>

Nora, Pierre (1984) 'Entre Mémoire et Histoire: La problématique des lieux', in Nora, Pierre (ed.) *Les lieux de mémoire I- La République* (Paris: Editions Gallimard), pp. XV-XLII.

NOS (2011) *Maak gebruik van smartphones in de les*, 30 May. <http://nos.nl/video/244513-maak-gebruik-van-smartphones-in-de-les.html>

NRC Handelsblad (1994) 'Opnieuw subsidie voor digitale stad', *NRC Handelsblad*, 1 July, p. 3. <http://archief.nrc.nl/index.php/1994/Juli/1/Binnenland/3/Opnieuw+subsidie+voor+digitale+stad>

NRC Handelsblad (1995) 'De Digitale Stad verbouwd: meer beeld en interactie', *NRC Handelsblad*, 12 June, p. 3 <http://archief.nrc.nl/index.php/1995/Juni/12/Binnenland/3/De+Digitale+Stad+verbouwd%3A+meer+beeld+en+interactie>

NRC Handelsblad (1996) 'Onderwijs, cultuur en wetenschappen: Meer aandacht voor het leren leren', *NRC Handelsblad*, 17 September, p. 32. <http://archief.nrc.nl/index.php/1996/September/17/Binnenland/32/ONDERWIJS,%20CULTUUR%20EN%20WETENSCHAPPEN;%20Meer%20aandacht%20voor%20het%20leren%20leren>

NRC Handelsblad (1997a) 'Europese ministers: leraren aan computer', *NRC Handelsblad*, 4 March, p. 8. <http://archief.nrc.nl/index.php/1997/Maart/4/Binnenland/8/Europese%20ministers:%20leraren%20aan%20computer>

NRC Handelsblad (1997b) 'Netelenbos: een computer per tien leerlingen', *NRC Handelsblad*, 11 March, p. 10. <http://archief.nrc.nl/index.php/1997/Maart/11/Binnenland/10/Netelenbos%3A+een+computer+per+tien+leerlingen>

NRC Handelsblad (1997c) 'Bijscholing voor leraren: Extra geld voor computers op scholen', *NRC Handelsblad*, 28 April, p. 3. <http://archief.nrc.nl/index.php/1997/April/28/Binnenland/3/Bijscholing+voor+leraren%3B+Extra+geld+voor+computers+op+scholen>

NRC Handelsblad (1998a) 'Leraar heeft thuis PC nodig voor bijscholing', *NRC Handelsblad*, 24 April, p. 6. <http://archief.nrc.nl/index.php/1998/April/24/Overig/6/%27Leraar+heeft+thuis+PC+nodig+voor+bijscholing%27>

NRC Handelsblad (1998b) 'Ritzen "tevreden" over computerplan', *NRC Handelsblad*, 24 June, p. 2. <http://archief.nrc.nl/index.php/1998/Juni/24/Overig/2/Ritzen+%27tevreden%27-over+computerplan>

NRC Handelsblad (1998c) 'Meer investeren in computer op school', *NRC Handelsblad*, 3 December, p. 3. <http://archief.nrc.nl/index.php/1998/December/3/Overig/3/%60Meer+investeren+in+computer+op+school%27>

NRC Handelsblad (1999a) 'Fiscus beloont geven computer', *NRC Handelsblad*, 16 January, p. 3. <http://archief.nrc.nl/index.php/1999/Januari/16/binnenland/3/Fiscus+beloont+geven+computer>

NRC Handelsblad (1999b) 'Plan: school beslist zelf over computers', *NRC Handelsblad*, 20 February, p. 2. <http://archief.nrc.nl/index.php/1999/Februari/20/Binnenland/2/Plan%3A+school+beslist+zelf+over+computers>

Oattes, Huub (1997a) 'Film, Geluid en Nieuwe Media', *Kleio*, 1, pp.17-20.

Oattes, Huub (1997b) 'Internet: de eerste keer', *Kleio*, 2, pp. 40-42.

Oattes, Huub (1998) 'Het Net in de les', *Kleio*, 1, pp. 20-22.

Oattes, Huub (2001) 'Kleiogesprek met geschiedenisdocent/webmaster Albert van der Kaap – Is er een digitale toekomst voor het geschiedenisonderwijs?', *Kleio*, 3, pp. 20-23.

Onderwijsraad (1998) *Informatie- en communicatietechnologie en onderwijs* (The Hague: Onderwijsraad, 18 March).

Onderwijsraad (2000) *Kennisnet: Advies Kennisnet, uitgebracht aan de Minister van Onderwijs, Cultuur en Wetenschappen* (The Hague: Onderwijsraad, May).

Onderwijsraad (2003) *www.web-leren.nl* (The Hague: Onderwijsraad).

Onderwijsraad (2006) *Naar meer evidence based onderwijs* (The Hague: Onderwijsraad).

Oosterbaan, Warna (2002) 'De beelden van de beeldcultuur: pretenties, definities en de werkelijkheid', in Gierstberg, Frits & Oosterbaan, Warna (eds.) *De plaatjesmaatschappij: Essays over beeldcultuur* (Rotterdam: Nai Uitgevers), pp.10-22.

Oppenheim, Bram ([1966] 1992) *Questionnaire Design, Interviewing and Attitude Measurement* (London: Pinter Publishers). New Edition.

O'Reilly, Tim (2005) 'What Is Web 2.0: Design Patterns and Business Models for the Next Generation of Software', (30 September). <http://oreilly.com/lpt/a/6228>

Oudheusden, Jan van (1994) 'Driedimensionaal bronnenmateriaal in de klas: Voelbaar verleden', *Kleio*, 3, pp. 9-13.

Oudheusden, Jan van (1998) 'Het rapport-De Wit: Inhoud en Reacties – Een nieuwe balans', *Kleio*, 4, pp. 2-9.

Oudheusden, Jan van (2004) 'Actief historisch denken', *Kleio*, 6, pp. 10-15.

Pachler, Nobert (2001) 'Connecting schools and pupils: To what end? Issues related to the use of ICT in school-based learning', in Leask, Marilyn (ed.) *Issues in Teaching using ICT* (London: RoutledgeFalmer), pp. 15-30.

Palfrey, John & Gasser, Urs (2008) *Born Digital: Understanding the First Generation of Digital Natives* (New York: Basic Books).

Parkhurst, Helen ([1922] 1924) *Education on the Dalton Plan* (London: G.Bell and Sons).

Parkhurst, Helen (1951) *Exploring the Child's World* (New York: Appleton-Century Crofts).

Parry, Ross (2007) *Recoding the Museum: Digital Heritage and the Technologies of Change* (London: Routledge).

Parry, Ross, Poole, N. & Pratty, J. (2010) 'Semantic Dissonance: do we need (and do we understand) the semantic web?', in Parry, Ross (ed.) *Museums in a Digital Age* (London: Routledge), pp. 96-106.

Perfetti, Charles, Britt, Anne, Rouet, Jean-François, Georgi, Mara & Mason, Robert (1994) 'How Students Use Texts to Learn and Reason About Historical Uncertainty', in Carretero, Mario & Voss, James (eds.) *Cognitive and Instructional Processes in History and the Social Sciences* (Hillsdale: Lawrence Erlbaum Associates), pp. 257-283.

Piaget, Jean ([1926] 1959) *The Language and Thought of the Child* (London: Routledge & Kegan Paul). Third Edition.

Piaget, Jean (1938) *La représentation du monde chez l'enfant* (Paris: Librairie Félix Alcan).

Piaget, Jean ([1969] 1971) *Science of Education and the Psychology of the Child* (London: Longman Group).

Plasterk, Ronald (2007a) 'Letter to the Speaker of the House of Representatives. Object: National Historical Museum' (The Hague, 2 July). <http://www.minocw.nl/documenten/16533.pdf>

Plasterk, Ronald (2007b) 'Letter to the Speaker of the House of Representatives. Object: Canon van Nederland' (The Hague, 3 July). <http://www.minocw.nl/documenten/27731.pdf>

Pleijter, Alexander (2006) *Typen en logica van kwalitatieve inhoudsanalyse in de communicatiewetenschappen* (Ubbergen: Uitgeverij TandemFelix). PhD dissertation.

Ploeg, Rick van der (2002a) 'Letter to the Speaker of the House of Representatives. Object: Digitalisering van het cultureel erfgoed' (Zoetermeer, 27 May).

Ploeg, Rick van der (2002b) *Beleidsbrief eCultuur* (The Hague: OC&W).

Ploeg, Piet van der (2007) *Democratie en Daltonplan: verwante idealen.* <http://www.pietvanderploeg.nl/Democratie%20en%20Daltonplan.pdf>

Ploeg, Piet van der (2008) *Helen Parkhurst wilde in Nederland komen werken, maar ving bot bij NDV* (April). <http://www.pietvanderploeg.nl/Parkhurstwilde.pdf>

Ploeg, Piet van der (2010) *Dalton Plan: Oorsprong en theorie van het daltononderwijs* (Deventer: Saxion Dalton University Press).

Raad voor Cultuur ([2003] 2004) *From ICT to E-Culture: Advisory report on the digitalisation of culture and the implications for cultural policy* (The Hague, August).

Raad voor Cultuur (2010) *Netwerken van betekenis: Netwerktaken in digitale cultuur en media* (The Hague, March).

Ranke, Leopold von ([1821] 1973) 'Wilhelm von Humboldt, "On the Historian Task"', in Ranke, Leopold von, *The Theory and Practice of History* (Indianapolis: The Bobbs-Merrill Company).

Rechsteiner, Emjay & Cardello, Frank (2009) 'Bringing assets online in public-private partnership' (Beijing, 22 - 26 October). FIAT World Conference paper.

Rheingold, Howard (1993) *The Virtual Community: Homesteading on the Electronic Frontier* (New York: Addison-Wesley).

Ribbens, Kees (2006) 'Ruimte voor multiculturaliteit: De vaderlandse canon en de veranderende historische cultuur', in Grever, Maria, Jonker, Ed, Ribbens, Kees & Stuurman, Siep (eds.) *Controverses rond de canon* (Assen: Van Gorcum), pp. 80-105.

Roberts, Donald, Henriksen, Lisa & Foehr, Ulla (2009) 'Adolescence, Adolescents, and Media', in Lerner, Richard & Steinberg, Laurence (eds.) *Handbook of Adolescent Psychology. Volume 2: Contextual Influences on Adolescent Development* (Hoboken: John Wiley), pp. 314-344. Third Edition.

Robinson, Piers (2002) *The CNN Effect: The myth of news, foreign policy and intervention* (New York: Routledge).

Roegiers, Sara & Truyen, Frederik (2008) 'History is 3D : Presenting a framework for meaningful historical representations in digital media', in Kalay, Yehuda, Kvan, Thomas & Affleck, Janice (eds.) *New Heritage: New Media and Cultural Heritage* (London: Routledge), pp. 67-77.

Rogers, Patricia (2000) 'Lays of Navigation for Hypermedia Environments: Designing Instructional Web Sites', in Abbey, Beverly (ed.) *Instructional and Cognitive Impacts of Web-Based Education* (Hershey: Idea Group Publishing), pp. 217-226.

Rogers, Richard (2004) *Information Politics of the Web* (Cambridge: The MIT Press).

Ronchi, Alfredo (2009) *eCulture: Cultural Content in the Digital Age* (New York: Springer).

Rooy, Piet de (2001) 'Geschiedenisonderwijs op de schop: deel twee – En nu de praktijk...', *Kleio*, 1, pp. 2-4.

Rosenzweig, Roy (2006) 'Can History Be Open Source? *Wikipedia* and the Future of the Past', *The Journal of American History*, June, pp. 117-146.

Rousseau, Jean-Jacques ([1768] 1966) *Émile ou de l' éducation* (Paris: Garnier-Flammarion).

Roussou, Maria (2008) 'The Components of Engagement in Virtual Heritage Environments', in Kalay, Yehuda, Kvan, Thomas & Affleck, Janice (eds.) *New Heritage: New Media and Cultural Heritage* (London: Routledge), pp. 225-241.

Roussou, Maria (2010) 'Learning by Doing and Learning Through Play: an exploration of interactivity in virtual environments for children', in Parry, Ross (ed.) *Museums in a Digital Age* (London: Routledge), pp. 247-265.

RTL Nieuws (2009) *Het digitale schoolboek komt er aan*, 14 December. <http://www.rtl.nl/%28/actueel/rtlnieuws/binnenland/%29/components/actueel/rtlnieuws/2009/12_december/14/binnenland/digitaal_schoolboek_komt_eraan.xml>

Rushkoff, Douglas ([1996] 2006) *ScreenAgers: Lessons in Chaos from Digital Kids* (Cresskill: Hampton Press).

Russo, Angelina & Watkins, Jerry (2007) 'Digital Cultural Communication: Audience and Remediation', in Cameron, Fiona & Kaderdine, Sarah (eds.) *Theorizing Digital Cultural Heritage: A Critical Discourse* (Cambridge: The MIT Press), pp. 149-164.

Salvucci, Dario & Taatgen, Niels (2011) *The Multitasking Mind* (New York: Oxford University Press).

Schouten, Dennis (2004) 'Gaten in de geschiedenis', *Spiegel Historiael, 10* – 39, October, pp. 433-438.

Schouten, Dennis (2008) *Metamorfoze: Programmaplan 2009-2012* (The Hague, November).

Schouten, Dennis (2009) 'Inleiding: Van alarmfase rood tot groen licht. Metamorfoze 1997-2008', in Patijn, Maria, Doe, Erik van der, Langedoen, Andrea, Schouten, Dennis & Verheul, Ingebord (eds.) *Dertig in een dozijn: Een selectie uit twaalf jaar Metamorfoze Nieuws* (The Hague: KB & Nationaal Archief), pp. 9-17.

Shirky, Clay (2003) 'Social Software And The Politics Of Groups' (10 March). <http://www.informationweek.com/story/showArticle.jhtml?articleID=7600047>

Shirky, Clay (2008) *Here Comes Everybody: How Change Happens When People Come Together* (London: Penguin Books).

SICTS [Stichting ICT op School] (2001) *Vier in Balans: Verkenning stand van zaken met het oog op effectief en efficiënt gebruik van ICT in het onderwijs* (The Hague, August).

SICTS [Stichting ICT op School] (2004) *Vier in Balans Plus: Verkenning stand van zaken met het oog op effectief en efficiënt gebruik van ICT in het onderwijs* (The Hague, February).

Siegler, Robert & Alibali, Martha Wagner ([1986] 2005) *Children's Thinking* (Upper Saddle River: Prentice Hall). Fourth Edition.

Silverman, David (1993) *Interpreting Qualitative Data: Methods for Analysing Talk, Text and Interaction* (London: SAGE).

Simon, Dan (2011) 'Twitter finds a place in the classroom', *CNN* (9 June) <http://edition.cnn.com/2011/TECH/social.media/06/08/twitter.school/index.html?hpt=hp_bn7>

Simons, Robert-Jan, Linden, Jos van der & Duffy, Tom (2000) 'New Learning: Three ways to Learn in a New Balance', in Simons, Robert-Jan, Linden, Jos van der & Duffy, Tom (eds.) *New Learning* (Dordrecht: Kluwer Academic Publishers), pp. 1-20.

SNK [Stichting Nederland Kennisland] (2009) *Beelden voor de toekomst: de eerste successen* (Amsterdam).

Smith, Abby (1999) *Why Digitize?* (Washington, D.C.: Council on Library and Information Resources, February).

Sniekers, Jan & Wilschut, Arie (2001) *Verleden, heden en toekomst: Een bespreking van reacties of het rapport* <http://www.minocw.nl/document-en/download-doc-verledenhedentoekomst.pdf>

Somekh, Bridget (2004) 'Children's concepts of ICT: Pointers to the impact of ICT on education within and beyond the classroom', in Brown, Andrew & Davis, Niki (eds.) *World Yearbook of Education 2004: Digital technology, communities and education* (London: RoutledgeFalmer), pp. 57-73.

Spradley, James (1980) *Participant Observation* (London: Thomson Learning, 1980).

Raad van State (2009) *Ontwerpbesluit houdende wijziging van het Besluit vernieuwde kerndoelen WPO en het Besluit kerndoelen onderbouw VO in verband met de invoering van de can-*

on in de kerndoelen, met nota van toelichting (The Hague). <http://www.raadvanstate.nl/adviezen/zoeken_in_adviezen/zoekresultaat/?advicepub_id=9022>

Stake, Robert (2000) 'The Case Study Method in Social Inquiry', in Gomm, Roger, Hammersley, Martyn & Foster, Peter (eds.) *Case Study Method* (London: SAGE), pp. 19-26.

Stebbing, Susan ([1939] 1952) *Thinking to Some Purpose* (London: The Whitefriars Press).

Steensel, K.M. van (2000) *Internetgeneratie: De broncode ontcijferd* (The Hague: SMO, November).

Steinberg, Laurence (1985) *Adolescence* (New York: Alfred A. Knopf).

Stephens, Mitchell (1998) *The rise of the image the fall of the word* (New York: Oxford University Press).

Steyaert, Jan & Haan, Jos de (2001) *Geleidelijk digitaal: Een nuchtere kijk op de sociale gevolgen van ICT* (The Hague: SCP & Fontys Hoogeschool sociaal werk, December).

Stielstra Theo (1995) 'Digitale Stad is eerste succesvolle telematica-project in Nederland', *De Volkskrant*, 30 January. <http://www.volkskrant.nl/archief_gratis/article628227.ece/Digitale_Stad_is_eerste_succesvolle_telematica-project_in_Nederland>

Stuurman, Siep (2006) 'Van nationale canon naar wereldgeschiedenis' in Grever, Maria, Jonker, Ed, Ribbens, Kees & Stuurman, Siep (eds.) *Controverses rond de canon* (Assen: Van Gorcum), pp. 59-79.

Stuurman, Siep & Grever, Maria (2007) 'Introduction: Old Canons and New Histories' in Grever, Maria & Stuurman, Siep (eds.) *Beyond the Canon: History for the Twenty-First Century* (New York: Palgrave MacMillan), pp. 1-16.

Tapscott, Don (1998) *Growing Up Digital: The Rise of the Net Generation* (New York: McGraw-Hill).

Thompson, D. (1984) 'Understanding the Past: Procedures and Content', in Dickinson, Alaric Keith, Lee, Peter & Rogers, P. J. (eds.) *Learning History* (London: Heinemann Educational Books), pp. 168-186.

Tolstoy, Leo ([1862] 1967) *On Education* (Chicago: The University of Chicago Press).

Torney-Purta, Judith (1994) 'Dimensions of Adolescents' Reasoning about Political and Historical Issues: Ontological Switches, Developmental Processes, and Situated Learning', in Carretero, Mario & Voss, James (eds.) *Cognitive and Instructional Processes in History and the Social Sciences* (Hillsdale: Lawrence Erlbaum Associates), pp. 103-122.

Tsui, Lokman (2008) 'The Hyperlink in Newspapers and Blogs', in Turow, Joseph & Tsui, Lokman (eds.) *The Hyperlinked Society: Questioning Connections in the Digital Age* (Ann Arbor: The University of Michigan Press), pp 70-84.

UNESCO (2003) *Charter on the Preservation of Digital Heritage* (15 October). <http://portal.unesco.org/en/ev.php-RLID=17721&URL_DO=DO_TOPIC&URL_SECTION=201.html>

Vaidhyanathan, Siva (2011) *The Googlization of Everything (and Why We Should Worry)* (Los Angeles: University of California Press).

Valéry, Paul (1931) *Regards sur le monde actuel* (Paris: Librairie Stock).

VanSledright, Bruce & Kelly, Christine (1998) 'Reading American History: The Influence of Multiple Sources on Six Fifth Graders', *The Elementary School Journal*, Vol. 98, No. 3 (January), pp. 239-265.

Velthausz, Daan & Bruinsma, Eelco (2002) *Inventarisatie Infrastructuur Digitaal Erfgoed: Een onderzoek naar visies, belemmeringen en oplossingen* (Telematica Instituut, October).

Velzen, Joke van (2002) *Instruction and Self-Regulated Learning: Promoting Students' (self-) Reflective Thinking* (Leiden University). PhD dissertation.

Volkskrant, de (1995) 'Gemeente Lopik opent als eerste digitaal dorp', *De Volkskrant*, 26 January. <http://www.volkskrant.nl/archief_gratis/article627748.ece/Gemeente_Lopik_opent_als_eerste_digitaal_dorp>

Volkskrant, de (1995) 'Internet ongeschikt voor diepgravend debatteren', *De Volkskrant*, 18 April. <http://www.volkskrant.nl/archief_gratis/article636849.ece/Internet_ongeschikt_voor_diepgravend_debatteren>

Voss, James & Carretero, Mario (1994) 'Introduction', in Carretero, Mario & Voss, James (eds.) *Cognitive and Instructional Processes in History and the Social Sciences* (Hillsdale: Lawrence Erlbaum Associates), pp. 1-14.

Vree, Frank van (1998a) *De schreven van de geschiedenis: Over crisisverschijnselen in de hedendaagse historische cultuur* (Amsterdam: Vossiuspers AUP).

Vree, Frank van (1998b) 'Media als tijdmachines: Over de visualisering van de historische cultuur', *Boekmancahier*, 35, pp. 7-19.

Vree, Frank van (2002) 'De sensatie van het beeld: Over de visualisering van de historische cultuur', in Gierstberg, Frits & Oosterbaan, Warna (eds.) *De plaatjesmaatschappij: Essays over beeldcultuur* (Rotterdam: Nai Uitgevers), pp. 60-71.

Walsh, Peter (2010) 'The Web and the Unassailable Voice', in Parry, Ross (ed.), *Museums in a Digital Age* (London: Routledge), pp. 229-236.

Washington, Joanne (2008) 'Communication, Culture, and Media Influence in the Classroom', in Goodman, Greg (ed.) *Educational Psychology: An Application of Critical Constructivism* (New York: Peter Lang), pp. 71-94.

Watts, David George (1972) *The Learning of History* (London: Routledge & Kegan Paul).

Wells, Herbert George (1938) *World Brain* (London: Methuen & Co. Ltd).

Wester, Fred (1984) *De gefundeerde theorie-benadering: Een strategie voor kwalitatief onderzoek* (Nijmegen: Sociologisch Insttituut). PhD dissertation.

Wester, Fred (2000) 'Methodische aspecten van kwalitatief onderzoek', in Wester, Fred, Smaling, Adri & Mulder, Lambert (eds.) *Praktijkgericht kwalitatief onderzoek* (Bussum: Coutinho), pp. 15-40.

Wester, Fred (2006) 'Inhoudsanalyse als onderzoeksontwerp', in Wester, Fred (ed.) *Inhoudsanalyse theorie en praktijk* (Place?: Kluwer), pp. 11-44.

Wester, Fred & Hijmans, Ellen (2003) 'Inleiding', in Wester, Fred (ed.) *Rapporteren over kwalitatief onderzoek* (Utrecht: Lemma), pp. 7-17.

Wester, Fred & Weijers, Addy (2006) 'Narratieve analyse en transcriptie: Culturele thema's in de sitcom', in Wester, Fred (ed.) *Inhoudsanalyse theorie en praktijk* (Place?: Kluwer), pp. 161-189.

Wilhelm, Pascal (2001) *Knowledge, Skills and Strategies in Self-Directed Inductive Learning* (Leiden University). PhD dissertation.

Wilschut, Arie (1995) 'Beelden uit het verleden, beelden van het verleden: beeldmateriaal als bron', *Kleio*, 4, pp. 29-35.

Wilschut, Arie (2005) 'Zinvol, leerbaar en haalbaar', in Wilschut, Arie (ed.) *Zinvol, Leerbaar, Haalbaar: Over geschiedenisonderwijs en de rol van een canon daarin* (Amsterdam: Vossiuspers UvA), pp. 31-43.

Wilschut, Arie (2010) 'History at the mercy of politicians and ideologies: Germany, England and the Netherlands in the 19th and 20th centuries', *Journal of Curriculum Studies*, 42 – 5, pp. 693-723.

Wilschut, Arie, Straaten, Dick van & Riessen, Marcel van (2004) *Geschiedenisdidactiek: Handboek voor de vakdocent* (Bussum: Coutinho).

Wineburg, Samuel (1991) 'Historical Problem Solving: A Study of the Cognitive Processes Used in the Evaluation of Documentary and Pictorial Evidence', *Journal of Educational Psychology*, Vol. 83, No. 1, pp. 73-87.

Wineburg, Samuel (2001) *Historical Thinking and Other Unnatural Acts: Charting the Future of Teaching the Past* (Philadephia: Temple University Press).

Wolfe, Michael & Goldman, Susan (2005) 'Relations between Adolescents' Text Processing and Reasoning', *Cognition and Instruction*, Vol. 23, No. 4, pp. 467-502.

Wragg, Edward Conrad ([1994] 1999) *An Introduction to Classroom Observation* (London: Routledge). Second Edition.

WRR [Wetenschappelijke Raad voor het Regeringsbeleid] (2007) *Identificatie met Nederland* (Amsterdam: Amsterdam University Press).

WTR [De Wetenschappelijk Technische Raad van SURF] (1998) *Alles uit de kast* (Utrecht: July). <http://www.surffoundation.nl/SFDocuments/WTR_de_kast.pdf>